RESEARCH
PATHWAYS

Writing Professional Papers, Theses, and
Dissertations in Workforce Education

Edited by
Edgar I. Farmer
Jay W. Rojewski

University Press of America,® Inc.
Lanham · New York · Oxford

Copyright © 2001 by
University Press of America,® Inc.
4720 Boston Way
Lanham, Maryland 20706

12 Hid's Copse Rd.
Cumnor Hill, Oxford OX2 9JJ

Library of Congress Cataloging-in-Publication Data

Research pathways : writing professional papers, theses,
and dissertations in workforce education /
edited by Edgar I. Farmer, Jay W. Rojewski.
p.   cm
Includes bibliographical references and index.
1. Occupational training—Research—Methodology.
2. Employees—Training of—Research—Methodology.
3. Report writing. 4. Dissertations, Academic.
I. Farmer, Edgar I. II. Rojewski, Jay W., 1959-

HD5715 .R457 2001   808'.0666583124—dc21   2001027754 CIP

ISBN: 978-0-7618-2059-8

Dedications

To our graduate students and colleagues in pursuit of excellence on research issues in career and technical education. Your commitment to the Academy is a source of inspiration for all of us. — The Editors

To my wife, Barbara, and children, Edgar Jr., Eric, and Becky for their love, encouragement, and optimism. You are the wind beneath my wings. — Edgar I. Farmer

To my parents for nurturing in me a love of learning and their enduring support; and to my wife, Jacy, and daughters, Emily and baby Claire, for their love and for providing me with the richness and meaning in my life. — Jay W. Rojewski

Contents

Foreword

Edwin L. Herr

This first edition of *Research Pathways: Writing Professional Papers, Theses, and Dissertations in Workforce Education* is a welcome addition to the available literature directed to graduate students learning to conduct and report research and to faculty members who supervise them. Professors Edgar I. Farmer and Jay W. Rojewski, the editors of this excellent book, have assembled an outstanding group of contributors who apply their unique research expertise to one of the categories of research conceptualization, design and analysis into which the book is divided. The latter include such important emphases as finding a researchable topic, different qualitative and quantitative research paradigms, considerations in dissertation development, data analysis, and such fundamental concerns as proofreading and editing one's work.

The excellence and insightfulness of each of the chapters of this book are framed by the assumptions and experience of the Editors as teachers of research courses. Their knowledge of student needs and anxieties related to the development of research skills give the book cohesion, substance, and relevance.

While, by definition and purpose, a foreword is limited in space and content, there are several unique contributions of this book that deserve identification. One is that while the book's content is suitable for graduate students in any discipline, there is a special utility here for teacher-educators, practitioners and graduate students in workforce education and development programs. The examples and language used throughout the book illustrate the importance of workforce education and development and the continuing need for comprehensive research in this field so vital to national economic goals.

A second contribution of this book is the accessibility to students of its contents. The authors have given special attention to including in the individual chapters information that is practical, straightforward, and designed to serve as a guide for students to all aspects of the research process. This focus is intended to reduce the anxiety and frustration many students experience as they anticipate or begin writing theses, dissertations, and other types of professional papers. Much of the design of the book has evolved from the Editors' interactions with graduate students in their research methodology classes and for whom they have served as dissertation advisors.

A third contribution of the book is its emphasis on presenting one's findings. Many books on research emphasize how to conduct particular types of research. Fewer talk in pragmatic terms about how to prepare your findings for publication, how to use professional style guides, how to write the summary and conclusions, how to edit and revise your scholarly writing. These emphases in the book are an antidote to premature termination of the research process by students and practitioners who can apply research methodology but do not have the confidence or the knowledge to convert their research findings into an acceptable scholarly document.

A final contribution of the book to be noted here is the range of research approaches addressed. Not only does the book address quantitative and qualitative research as different ways of knowing, but it presents approaches within these classes of methodology that are omitted from many books. Examples of particular relevance to workforce education and development are focus group and case study research, use of secondary data sources, alternatives to statistical significance testing and multiple research designs. Each of these chapter emphases and others dealing with research designs are discussed in terms of their advantages and disadvantages.

This is a book for beginning graduate students and for experienced researchers. Its contents are important to workforce education and development students, professors, and practitioners as well as to professionals in other disciplines and settings. I learned much from this book; I am sure that my colleagues in workforce education and development, and in other educational specialties will learn from and value this book as well.

Preface

Edgar I. Farmer and Jay W. Rojewski

"Who's there?" Act I of Shakespeare's famous tragedy, *Hamlet*, opens with these words as Barnardo, an officer in the court of Claudius, King of Denmark, confronts the sentinel Francisco. What does Shakespeare have to do with this book? Well, if truth be told not much. But the question Barnardo posed to Francisco has held a central focus for us throughout our planning, development, and completion of this volume. In answering the question, *"Who's there?"* we anticipate that you will join a diverse mix of interested readers including inquisitive (or maybe desperate?) graduate students, teachers, school administrators, researchers, and other scholars who want to know more about research methods, design, data collection and analysis, and related inquires in order to conceptualize, and conduct better research projects, and write better research papers, journal articles, Master's theses, and doctoral dissertations in workforce education.

"Who's there?" Regardless of your professional position or depth of knowledge about educational research, we think you will be able to find information in this book that can help you become a better scholar. *Research Pathways* can be a useful guide for developing research competencies and writing skills that are essential for publishing professional papers in scholarly journals. Although this book is not a panacea for every research woe, we do consider it the *"real deal."* Our authors have tried hard to de-mystify a process that is often perceived as obscure and remote or reserved for a chosen few. Graduate students and novice researchers, in particular, will benefit from the wealth of information contained in this text. Almost two dozen different authors have contributed to this volume, each a noted scholar in their respective

fields of study. We're glad you decided to give this book a try. We think you'll be pleased with the results. And if you'd like, drop us a line and let us know *"Who's there?"*

Pamela Bettis and James Gregson (Chapter 1) start us out by exploring the philosophical origins and principles of quantitative and qualitative research approaches. They overview the various purpose(s) of research, roles of investigators, methods of data collection, styles of data reporting, and methods of ensuring research credibility. Chapter 2 presents our thinking about finding a researchable topic. Strategies and issues to consider when identifying potential research topics are presented. While we can't give you a research topic—that would take all the fun out of it, wouldn't it?—the suggestions we offer may provide you a jump-start on topic selection.

After a research topic has been identified, a thorough review of all related literature must be conducted. Carol Wright's chapter provides a thorough treatment of how to conduct a review of the literature. Wright discusses the purpose of the extant literature and its importance in guiding and interpreting qualitative and quantitative studies. She also describes how to use technological resources and other specific techniques available for searching the literature.

Chapter 4, authored by Saundra Wall Williams and James Burrow, describes the elements to consider in developing an introduction chapter or section from both qualitative and quantitative perspectives. The authors stress the importance of clearly presenting a purpose statement, delineating research questions or hypotheses, and situating your study in terms of its significance to theory and practice.

Research on workforce development–related topics has often been criticized for a lack of theoretical grounding. There are a number of reasons for this situation. We suspect, however, that a prominent one is the difficulty many novice researchers experience when trying to identify and then apply existing theories or conceptual frameworks to their topics of interest. In Chapter 5, Gregory Petty examines the use of theory for topic development, construct and variable identification, and data interpretation.

When weighing specific research approaches or design options, check out Chapter 6 where Fadia Nasser describes the criteria to consider when selecting an appropriate research design. Used in conjunction with Chapter 1, Nasser's chapter provides a useful framework for conceptualizing and constructing a research project. In Chapter 7 Ernest Brewer takes up the challenge of designing mixed methods research designs. He talks about the issues that can surface when adopting this increasingly common approach to data collection. In the next two chapters, Lee Jones and Barbara Farmer, and Derek Mulenga describe strategies and techniques employed with several prominent qualitative research designs; case study (Chapter 8) and focus group (Chapter 9), respectively.

A complementary look at quantitative research designs is provided in Chapters 10, 11, and 12. First, Theodore Lewis overviews quantitative design alternatives including experimental, quasi-experimental, survey, causal-comparative, and factorial designs. Then, Roger Hill provides a detailed look at one of the most common educational designs, survey research. Specifically, Hill outlines issues connecting with developing and using survey instruments. In Chapter 12 Gene Gloeckner, Jeffrey A. Gliner, Suzanne M. Tochterman, and George A. Morgan continue the look at data collection methods with a comprehensive treatment of instrument validity and reliability, as well as the process of field testing and pilot testing data collection instruments prior to actual use in empirical studies.

Chapters 13–18 address commonly encountered quantitative and qualitative data analysis issues. For example, Paul Krueger (Chapter 13) discusses a major issue in quantitative data analysis, that is, how to determine appropriate sample size. Krueger systematically describes a process to ensure that any given sample adequately represents the population of interest. Li-Shyung Hwang, Zhicheng Zhang, and Jeffrey Chen, authors of Chapter 14, argue that educational researchers should consider using a variety of available data sources. Interested readers will learn more about accessing available or secondary data, how to classify and locate secondary data sources, and analyzing secondary data. Hwang and her colleagues also list a number of exemplary databases in postsecondary education and their sources.

The topic of Chapter 15 is the analysis of categorical data using chi-square and log-linear models. Chapter 16 examines analysis of variance (ANOVA), a statistical test used to determine whether observed differences in the mean scores of a dependent variable for two or more groups are statistically significant. Stephen J. Olejnik and Brian Hess describe, in very practical terms, the primary reasons for and approaches used with ANOVA. They argue that the use of ANOVA should be informed, intentional, and focused. Then, Carl J Huberty and Mohamed Hussein (Chapter 17) provide a state-of-the-art approach to conceptualizing and analyzing data in multiple correlation and multiple regression studies. In Chapter 18, Rojewski discusses how scholars should use and interpret statistical testing and statistical significance. He argues that investigators must carefully consider whether the results of a quantitative investigation are of practical importance rather than only relying on the results of statistical analysis.

The last two chapters of this text focus on aspects of research preparation and dissemination that are sometimes overlooked. Chapter 19, by Curtis Finch, briefly highlights several ideas about the preparation of the Summary, Conclusions, and Recommendations sections research papers or dissertations. Sherilee Carpenter (Chapter 20) offers valuable tips on proofreading and editing your work using APA and other style guides. Carpenter also provides insight for putting the finishing touch on your thesis or dissertation. Finally, if you have followed this text from start to finish, you are ready to submit your work to a committee or journal review panel—Go for it!

And so we end as we began by asking, *"Who's there?"* We want to know if you are using *Research Pathways* in your academic or career and technical education programs; for example, seminars, design and methods courses, and so forth. Your feedback is not only welcome, but important to us as we seek to improve the quality of this work. Please contact us and let us know your thoughts about the usefulness of this text. We await your response and look forward to finding out *"Who's there?"*

Chapter 1

The *Why* of Research: Paradigmatic and Pragmatic Considerations

Pamela J. Bettis and James A. Gregson

These are exciting, confusing and intriguing times in which to contemplate and conduct research. The concept of research itself has been troubled by the postmodern/poststructural turn so that even the definition is contested. Traditionally, research has been conceptualized as the systematic, objective, valid, reliable collection and analysis of empirical data to solve a problem (applied research), or as a means to build theory and add to the existing knowledge base (basic research). However, these characteristics of what constitutes research have been scrutinized, critiqued, and sometimes eliminated from the traditional definition. The importance assigned to empiricism and the form in which data are traditionally presented are being contested with research being constructed as fiction (Tierney, 1997), poetry (Glesne, 1997; Richardson, 1994), and readers' theatre (Adams et al., 1998). Further, objectivity, once considered central to "rigorous" research, has been deconstructed and questioned so often that acknowledging a researcher's subjectivities, values, or "bias" in a qualitative project is common practice. The meaning of validity and reliability has also been the focus of critique and reconceptualization (Collins, 1991; Harding, 1991; Lather, 1991; 1993; Lincoln & Guba, 1985) with validity characterized as "obsession"(Lather, 1993). Finally, the broad goal of some social science research, to improve the quality of life for human beings, is being critiqued as part of a naive belief in "redemptive social theory" (Britzman, 1997; Cary, 1999; Popkewitz, 1998).

What do these critiques and reconfigurations of traditional research mean for workforce education graduate students? In this changing research world order how do workforce education graduate students make sense of their thesis or dissertation work? We think that discussions of what constitutes research have engendered healthy (albeit sometimes vitriolic) debates and conversations in the field. The scholarly context in which theses and dissertations are now being conceptualized, developed, and defended no longer reflects the unified view of research that previously existed in workforce education. Where once only quantitative research designs dominated, qualitative forms of inquiry now flourish and a multitude of theoretical positions abound (Gregson, 1998). However, with the proliferation of ways to conceptualize and conduct research in workforce education there comes a greater responsibility to be knowledgeable about the philosophical issues embedded in research and their pragmatic implications. Students must make thoughtful research decisions and defend their positions to advisors and committee members within this broader context of what it means to·do research. The purpose of this chapter is to enable students to begin thinking about these issues.

To accomplish our goals for this chapter we first explore the philosophical origins and, thus, the underlying assumptions of a positivistic research paradigm (typically quantitative research), post-positivistic (typically quantitative and some qualitative research) and alternative paradigms (typically, qualitative research). We then examine three workforce education studies and point out the relationships among paradigms, theoretical or conceptual orientations, and research methods. We maintain that these facets of research are all interconnected. Thus, the paradigm you use to situate your study will inform the theoretical or conceptual stance applicable to your study, as well as the methodology and methods you use (Crotty, 1998). However, we acknowledge that researchers do not always operate with a unified conceptual understanding of their project. Further, we agree with Lincoln and Guba (2000) who argue that the current status of research exemplifies a blurring of paradigms and provides the opportunity "for interweaving of viewpoints, for the incorporation of multiple perspectives, and for borrowing or bricolage, where borrowing seems useful, richness enhancing, or theoretically heuristic" (p. 167).

We hope that after reading and reflecting on this chapter you can explain why research should not be considered merely a set of techniques or methods. Whether conducting a quantitative or qualitative study thoughtful researchers should be able to articulate how their philosophical stance or paradigm informs their use of theory, their methodology and their selection of methods. We hope that this chapter will prepare students for that discussion. We begin by introducing you to the world of paradigms.

Paradigms of Inquiry

The word *paradigm* is very much in use today. However, it is not an easy term to define and has been used in a plethora of ways (Kuhn, 1970). In this chapter we use *paradigm* in its most common or generic sense, a basic set of beliefs that guides action in inquiry or research (Crotty, 1998; Guba & Lincoln, 1994; Lincoln & Guba, 2000). In a sense, a scientific paradigm can be thought of as an all-encompassing way of thinking that organizes scientific endeavors; it is a pair of glasses in which we "see" the world. Obviously, operating from an agreed upon worldview is helpful in facilitating action. However, at the same time, an all-encompassing way of thinking may constrain the investigator when imagining different visions of what science could be and do. The paradigm that has guided workforce education for many years, positivism, is now being contested in the wider research arena as well as in our field. In other words, there is no longer an agreed upon set of assumptions and procedures, an all-encompassing world view, for conducting research in workforce education. There has been, and is on going, a paradigm(s) shift, or some would say there is a paradigm proliferation.

Paradigms, those past and those currently emerging, are often characterized by the way their proponents respond to ontological, epistemological, and methodological questions (Guba, 1990; Guba & Lincoln, 1994) and to a series of research issues such as inquiry aim, researcher values, voice, representation, and goodness or quality criteria (Lincoln & Guba, 2000). For many scholars, the three types of questions we mentioned earlier are at the heart of the research act itself.

Ontological questions focus on discerning the nature of reality, asking, What is reality? Is it "out there," existing independently of human thought systems? Or, is it a product of human construction resulting in multiple realities all dependent on the various worldviews of humans? Is it fixed and static or ever changing and dynamic? For example, if you maintain that reality is fixed, "real," independent of human understanding, and knowable (a positivist stance), you can more easily advocate for the generalizabilty of your research findings to comparable populations. This would be a common assumption that

4 → 95

4 *Research Pathways*

those who practice quantitative forms of research would hold. However, if you believe that reality is only somewhat apprehendible (a postpositivist paradigm stance) or that it is always in flux and only known through the various understandings that humans hold (constructivist stance), then generalizing your findings and replicating your study would be considered problematic since people and their understandings of the world are always changing. Finally, some postmodern/poststructural researchers trouble the notion of reality by asking Gertrude Stein's question, "Is there a there?"

Epistemological questions explore the nature of knowledge and the relationship between researchers and the people or phenomena under study. If you maintain that reality is governed by universal laws and facts, then, with appropriate methods, we should be able to ascertain those facts and predict natural and social behaviors. For example, if a researcher positions herself behind a one-way mirror to control for researcher intervention and bias, she is exhibiting a belief in the positivist stance of objective knowledge. If a researcher immerses herself in the culture and lives of those studied, she is exhibiting a belief in the postpositivist or alternative paradigm stance of the social construction of knowledge. Further, if a researcher aids those studied or works in conjunction with them in solving a local injustice, then she may be operating from one of several alternative paradigms, such as feminist or critical. Working with research participants in solving a local problem is a very different researcher position than one who stands behind a one-way mirror, observing without being seen. The goals of these two researchers, prediction versus emancipation, would be very different as well and would impact every facet of the research process.

Finally, methodological questions focus on the methodology used to collect and analyze data. In this discussion, methodology refers not only to techniques of data collection but also to such issues as voice, ethics, values, and rigor of an investigation (Guba & Lincoln, 1994; Lincoln & Guba, 2000). So, for example, if you operate from a positivist paradigm a survey that ascertains individuals' views on select topics is a very appropriate method. Maintaining distance from your research participants and analyzing their survey responses statistically both lead to more "objective" research. If you operate from a postpositivist or a critical, feminist, or poststructural paradigm, surveys would appear to be inhibiting for a number of reasons (i.e., ontological and epistemological reasons along with issues of voice and ethics perhaps).

In today's introductory paradigm discussions most authors focus on positivism and postpositivism and then mention a variety of other paradigms that have recently emerged. However, there is no agreed upon delineation of this multitude of new paradigms as various scholars label and categorize them in a variety of ways. Some of the names of the newer paradigms include constructivism, feminism, interpretavism, critical, emancipatory, poststructural, and postmodern (Crotty, 1998; Lather, 1991; Lincoln & Guba, 2000). We start our paradigm discussion with positivism because of its historical importance and the fact that many of the newer paradigms are a reaction against its philosophical assumptions and practices. Then, we will delineate the characteristics of postpositivism. Finally, we will present several emerging and contested paradigms such as critical and poststructural.

Positivism

Comte, a French philosopher who wrote primarily from 1830 to 1850, is typically credited for coining the word *positivism* (Coser, 1977), although Crotty (1998) argues that Bacon used the term much earlier. Regardless, Comte is known for his framing of a new scientific logic (Coser, 1977; Crotty, 1998; Ritzer, 1983). He wanted to analyze society and humanity with the tools and logic of the natural sciences that had, heretofore, only been applied to the study of natural phenomena. Comte sought scientific facts about society. For him these facts constituted the only viable answers to important questions about society. In the past, answers to these important questions were typically based on philosophical speculation that had not yielded a better society. Comte called this newly emerging scientific study of society sociology. Since his introduction of positivism over 150 years ago, the application of a rational, scientific, and fact-oriented framework for studying various aspects of humanity has become the modus operandi for social sciences.

Comte's proposed positivistic logic was clearly a revolt against the methodology of all previous philosophers who focused on understanding society (Coser, 1977). His revolt centered on the "fact" that there was no method. These metaphysical or unscientific studies, as Comte saw them, had not produced universal agreement on how to solve society's many dilemmas for the several thousand years they were in place, and, for Comte, this was unacceptable. Comte wanted to study society and to construct a better one based on the methodology and methods of the newly emerging natural sciences.

For positivists like Comte reality is fixed and there are laws that explain how the universe operates. If there is a real world that operates according to universal natural laws, then researchers must control for their bias and attempt to construct an investigation that allows these laws to reveal themselves through the data. Researchers must strive for objectivity and in a sense stand behind a one-way glass observing natural phenomena as it transpires.

Probably the most controversial assumption that positivists make is that knowledge is value free. Knowledge is seen as separate or apart from the social context in which it emanates. The scientific method, if followed carefully, is the only means to acquire that knowledge and any presuppositions that a researcher may have will be filtered out with the use of these methods. Positivists not only believe that truly objective research is possible, they also posit that it is the best approach to discover the world and then predict it.

Positivists do acknowledge the difficulty of achieving objectivity for two primary reasons: the possibility of bias and the difficulty encountered when trying to isolate a single variable for study from all other variables found in nature and society. Thus, it is difficult to make claims of certainty about what causes what. The positivist's answer to these two dilemmas is the use of a manipulative methodology and empirical methods. A manipulative methodology, such as an experimental or quasi-experimental design, alleviates the problem of multiple variables interference. Control and experimental groups, sampling of populations, and random assignment are all attempts to ensure that an investigation achieves objectivity, generalizability, and possesses the ability to ascertain relationships between the studied variables.

The implications of Comte's positivistic framework for studying humanity as individuals or in-groups have been profound. This has been particularly true in the United States where science is often not considered just another form of logic but rather is sometimes accepted as the only logic against which all other modes of thought are compared (Giroux, 1979). Besides Comte's claim that universal laws and facts that govern human behavior and society can be ascertained by the scientific method, another important assumption of positivism is that the universe operates in a linear, rational, coherent and stable fashion. The logical extension of this belief is that humans also operate in a stable coherent and rational manner.

The scientific method, undergirded by the paradigm of positivism, has contributed to an incredibly technologically-advanced society. However, at the beginning of the 20th century some philosophers began to question the use of positivism in studying humankind and the costs that its use had incurred socially.

The Emergence of Postpositivism

At the turn of the century in the United States, Dewey (1907, 1916), while a strong proponent of the scientific approach, began to question some characteristics of positivism especially as they related to the emerging social sciences. From an ontological perspective, Dewey questioned the existence of fixed and eternal truths. From a practical perspective, he argued that positivism gave flawed legitimacy to the methods of inquiry and proof that had been promulgated by the physical sciences and adopted by the social sciences.

During the 1930s in Germany, philosophers such as Adorno, Marcuse, Fromm, and Horkhiemer critiqued positivism and contributed to the development of a new paradigm of inquiry, postpositivism. Although they differed in how they viewed objectivity, subjectivity, and even the purpose of research, they agreed that positivism had exerted a type of hegemony, a preponderant influence or dominant authority, on people's understandings of the world and society as a whole (Benhabib, BonB, & McCole, 1993; Kelly, 1994; Wiggershaus, 1995). For this group, hegemony of positivistic thought had powerful and negative consequences for society in general. The critique of positivism continued with Heisenberg's uncertainty principle which questioned the certainty and objectivity of positivism; Popper's argument that science does not proceed in an inductive manner but rather in a hypothetical-deductive manner; Kuhn's embedding of science revolutions or paradigm shifts within broader historical contexts; and Feyerbend's focus on the absurd in science (Crotty, 1998).

Beginning in the 1960s and 1970s, minority groups and women in the United States questioned the powerful influence and consequence of positivistic thought on their own status. Women challenged the scientific findings regarding female mental and physical health (Harding, 1991). They became skeptical that male natural and social scientists could ascertain the mental, physical, and emotional issues of women's health when the latter typically developed their models based on studies of men. For example, Gilligan's (1983) classic work, *In a Different Voice*, contested Kohlberg's scheme of moral development because its conceptualization was based on male moral reasoning. Gilligan argued that women reason differently from men in solving moral dilemmas. Along the same lines, scholars of color began to critique how their own racial and ethnic groups had been constructed in supposedly scientific research and offered new epistemologies, or ways of knowing, drawn from their own lives. Patricia Hill Collins' (1991) classic "Black Feminist Thought" challenged positivistic thinking by offering a type of epistemology called "standpoint" that operated at the intersection of her race and gender. There are still ongoing critiques of how positivistic thought has fostered unequal power relations between researchers and those who are marginalized in the society and calls for responsible as well as respectful research (Lomawaima, 2000).

Although positivism has been the subject of criticism throughout much of the 20th and into the 21st centuries, most academics still acknowledge its profound influence today. Aronowitz (1995) argued that "scientificity" is the "permeation of the standard elements of the scientific attitude into all corners of the social world: seeing is believing; the appeal to hard facts such as statistical outcomes to settle arguments; the ineluctable faith in the elements of syllogistic reasoning" (p. 12). For Aronowitz, Giroux (1979), Eisner (1983), and other critical, feminist, and postmodern/poststructural thinkers, scientific thinking is a type of hegemony, and the "culture of positivism," is still all powerful in U.S. society even though a revolution in the social and natural sciences has occurred in the last twenty years. So, although positivism has been declared officially dead (Phillips, 1983; Popper, 1974), its philosophical assumptions still influence the social sciences through postpositivism and society.

From such early and later critiques of positivism, an alternative paradigm to positivism, postpositivism, began to emerge. Currently, there is some discussion that a single postpositivism paradigm does not exist. Rather, there are several different paradigms seen as opposing the paradigm of positivism. Carr and Kemmis (1986) argued that there are three forms of educational research: positivist, interpretive, and critical. Lather (1991; 1999) advocated a four paradigm typology: positivist, interpretativist, critical, and poststructural/postmodern and maintained that a researcher might adopt different orientations throughout a research process, based on the circumstances. Lincoln and Guba (2000) maintained that there are five paradigms, including positivism, postpositivism, critical theory, constructivism and participatory. Finally, Crotty (1998) saw positivism, postpositivism, constructivism, interpretivism, critical inquiry, feminism, and postmodernism as the paradigms now in use in the social sciences. We have distinguished among postivisim, postpositivism, constructivism, critical and feminist, and postmodern/poststructural.

We agree with Crotty (1998) and see postpositivism as a "humbler version of the scientific approach, one that no longer claims an epistemologically or metaphysically privileged position" (p. 40). So, although postpositivists react against the rigidity of positivism, there still lingers within this paradigmatic approach some of the same beliefs, values and assumptions about how the universe operates and what that means for research. Generally, postpositivists believe that laws governing the universe exist but are difficult to ascertain. Experimental designs are not always viewed as particularly helpful because they do not emulate the social world where people live. As a result, the use of quasi-experimental research designs and some qualitative forms of inquiry are preferred. While objectivity should be a constant goal for investigators, it is difficult to achieve since their beliefs and values are embedded in the entire research process.

Investigators operating within the postpositivistic paradigm may appear to be quite varied; there are those who practice quantitative methods exclusively and those who practice qualitative methods exclusively. You may wonder how such different research approaches could be found in the same paradigm. Although these researchers utilize different methods, they still hold some of the same assumptions about the world in which they conduct research. For example, qualitative researchers who draw from the grounded theory approach follow a somewhat mechanistic analysis approach just as that applied in an advanced statistical procedure. Both sets of complex research techniques assume that there are laws that govern the universe and that these laws can be ascertained through rigorous research. Although much qualitative research seeks to understand the world from the participants' worldview, that understanding can also produce models of cause and effect just as path analysis models can. In fact, historically, many early and some current anthropologists practice(d) a "fly on the wall" type of ethnography that parallels the one-way mirror approach of some positivists and postpositivists. Thus, those who operate within a postpositivistic paradigm still hold similar ontological, epistemological, and methodological assumptions, although their methods may differ from positivists.

Alternative Paradigms: Constructivist, Critical, Feminist, Postmodern/Poststructural

In 1991, Lather characterized the current state of educational research as "postparadigmatic diaspora." It is a decade later and we think that her claim still seems appropriate. We initiate our discussion of alternative paradigms with this phrase so that readers will consider the number of emerging paradigms as more than just a proliferation of ways of conducting research.

> Whatever the 'postmodern condition' is, it calls for an ability to locate oneself in the tensions that characterize fields of knowledge in a time of the loss of grand narratives and one best way of thinking, a time of multiplicity and competing discourses that do not map tidily onto one another, a time of unevenly legitimated and resourced incommensurabilities regarding the politics of knowing and being known. (Lather, 1999, p. 2)

We believe that the number of emerging paradigms and their critiques of the assumptions and procedures of both positivism and postpositivism warrant attention. These paradigms offer new visions of what science and research can do and be. However, because of space constraints we only briefly introduce readers to the following emerging paradigms: constructivist, critical, feminist, and postmodern/ poststructural.

Constructivism. Scholars working within the constructivist paradigm maintain that reality does not exist "out there" but is constructed by human beings in relation to each other (Crotty, 1998; Guba, 1990; Guba & Lincoln, 1994; Lincoln, 1990; Lincoln & Guba, 2000; Schwandt, 1998). Therefore, reality is contingent upon human meaning making. But, as Crotty notes, constructivism is not just about the human construction of meaning as if it were independent of phenomena in the world. Rather, it is human interaction with the world and how humans then make sense of that interaction. Thus, constructivists believe that there can be no objectivity. Researchers and those being researched, or the phenomena studied, engage in dynamic interaction that creates the meaning of findings. Thus, knowledge is always a human construction and never value free.

The purpose of a constructivist research project is not to predict the world or to control it as positivists and even postpositivists might desire (Crotty, 1998; Guba, 1990; Lincoln, 1990; Guba & Lincoln, 1994; Schwandt, 1998). Constructivists identify the myriad of mental constructions of the world, try to understand them, to locate some consensus among them, and to reconstruct the world based on these understandings. Drawing from the inductive nature of qualitative inquiry constructivists seek theories that arise from the data and help explain the many ways that humans conceptualize the world in which they live.

Constructivist research, therefore, diverges sharply from the precepts of positivism and postpositivism. As you read about other emerging paradigms such as critical, feminist, and postmodern/poststructural, you should note the similarities between constructivism and these others. However, you will also note where they diverge in some basic assumptions about the world and the purpose of research.

Paradigms that challenge the status quo: Critical, feminist, postmodern/poststructural. Although there have been many books written about each of these paradigms individually, we believe that critical, some feminist, and postmodern/poststructural paradigms of research share some important assumptions about the world, the purpose of research, and the position of investigators in the research process. The following discussion highlights these similarities. However, we warn readers that there are also important differences among these paradigms and that situating your research in any paradigm requires in-depth reading. In the following discussion, we highlight a few distinctions among critical, feminist and postmodern/poststructural research approaches but we cannot address all of them. Furthermore, many researchers who position themselves in the critical realm blur these paradigms.

The following are some common elements that link these three research paradigms. Although not fully embraced by every researcher operating from these stances, these assumptions are central to understanding them. They include an acknowledgment [1] that positivistic research has largely failed to capture the shifting complexities of people's ways of thinking and that it has contributed to further marginalizing oppressed peoples, [2] that a researcher's beliefs and values play a significant role in the conceptualization, implementation, and analysis of the research, [3] that knowledge is socially constructed and that facts should always be viewed within their historical, political, social and economic contexts, [4] that research has always been and is currently implicated in relations of power and has political and social consequences, [5] that unequal power relations are inherent in research and that researchers must attempt to alter that traditional hierarchical relationship between "researched" and researcher, [6] that oppression is complex and that focusing only on race, ethnicity, social class, gender, and/or sexual orientation simplifies the multiple positions and contradictions that individuals simultaneously inhabit, [7] that power and knowledge are intricately tied together through discursive practices, and, [8] that an explicit attempt to challenge oppressive social and economic practices must be made through the research process (Aggar, 1991; Anderson, 1989; Giroux, 1979; Harding, 1991; Harvey, 1990; Kincheloe & McLaren, 1998; Lather, 1991, 1999; Shacklock & Smyth, 1998; Thomas, 1993; Wexler, 1992). As can be easily seen, constructivists would embrace the first three assumptions we delineated. However, the following assumptions which focus on issues of power and oppression are more reflective of critical, feminist and postmodern/poststructural approaches to research. Thus, the overall goal of critical, feminist, and some postmodern/poststructural researchers is to challenge the inequities embedded in the social lives of research participants. This is a very different type of research goal than found in the prediction, control and understanding of positivism, postpositivism and constructivism.

Critical and feminist. Researchers working within a critical paradigm wish to explore how schooling is situated within historical, political, and social contexts and how schooling serves to both reinforce dominant relations of power as well as provide space for those relations to be challenged (Aggar, 1991; Anderson, 1989; Crotty, 1998; Gunzenhauser, in press; Kincheloe & McLaren, 1998; Lakes & Bettis, 1995; Popkewitz, 1990; Shacklock & Smyth, 1998; Thomas, 1993). Because critical researchers originally focused on how social class operated in schooling, they have been critiqued by feminists for ignoring the role of gender in oppression; by scholars of color for marginalizing the role that race and ethnicity play in oppression; and by postmodern/poststructual thinkers who questioned their use of Enlightenment ideals of progress and empowerment. As noted by Kincheloe and McLaren, the critical paradigm has been recently influenced by the writings of Foucault and Derrida, French postmodern/poststructural scholars. However, the goal of critical research is still to "produce(s), in our view, undeniably dangerous knowledge, the kind of information and insight that upsets institutions and threatens to overturn sovereign regimes of truth" (p. 260).

Feminist researchers have focused on how the subject position of female operates in society at large that is usually characterized as patriarchal in nature and have also explored how feminist researchers identity impacts the research process (Bloom, 1998; DeVault, 1996; Harding, 1991; Kirsch, 1999; Maher & Tetreault, 1993; Reinharz, 1992; Smith, 1987). Feminist theorists and researchers have argued that phallocentric ways of thinking have dominated traditional research and perpetuated the oppression of women and other marginalized groups. Thus, feminist researchers explore how gender remains hidden in common understandings of a phenomenon such as work. At the same time, many feminists have attempted to alter the traditional characteristics of the research act by advocating more collaborative research (between researcher and those being researched and among researchers themselves); focusing on the everyday realities of people's lives; and interrogating their own subjectivity in the research process.

Critical and feminist researchers are typically unabashed by their theoretical stance and their explicit research goal, and most critical and feminist research studies are replete with that information.

Postmodern/poststructural. Researchers working within a poststructural/postmodern paradigm operate from a very different worldview than researchers who still claim the tenants of the Enlightenment as forming their basis of research, which would include all positivists, postpositivists, constructivists, and many critical and feminist researchers. This genre of research challenges notions of universal Truths, the supremacy of rationality, and the goal of progress and focuses on ways that meaning is produced and struggled over (Britzman, 1997; Cary, 1999; Crotty, 1998; Kenway, Willis, Blackmore, & Rennie, 1994; Lather, 1991, 1999).

Drawing from Foucault, poststructuralists maintain that power and knowledge are intricately tied together in the concept of discourse that refers to how people speak about a phenomenon, or how they frame or understand it. Therefore, discourses construct how we may think and not think about something. For example, in Western culture dualistic or binary thinking is an acceptable way to construct an understanding of the world. Thus, there is scientific thought or nonscientific thought; rational or irrational thought; feminine or masculine; and good or bad. According to postmodern/poststructural thinkers and researchers, there is little awareness of and tolerance for ambiguities, omissions, and disruptions of such a dualistic way of thinking, and these disruptions, omissions, and pluralities of meaning are much more prevalent than acknowledged. Further, these pluralities of meaning are not given equal weight in society; dominant discourses wield much more power than those outside dominant society do. Poststructuralists would critique the hegemony of science (positivism and postpositivism) that still dominates the world of workforce education. Concepts such as validity and reliability continue to have the power to determine how a research project is conceptualized and whether it will be acceptable to committee members and advisors.

From Paradigms to Practice(s): Three Examples of Research in Workforce Education

Some of you may wonder why an introductory chapter in a book on research has devoted so many pages to exploring philosophy, theory and history in research. We position ourselves within alternative paradigm beliefs and maintain that research is embedded in particular social, political, economic and historical contexts. Furthermore, we believe that understanding the history of positivism, postpositivism, and the newly emerging paradigms will help you follow a discussion of their pragmatic differences.

In the remaining pages of this chapter we examine three workforce education studies that exemplify some of the paradigmatic differences we have discussed. We believe that the nebulous ideas and concepts presented in the first part of this chapter may solidify when viewed in the context of a study. All three examples are refereed publications that can be easily accessed for further perusal. We have chosen to present them in an order that parallels our discussion of paradigms. First, we detail a quantitative study that operates from the postpositivistic paradigm. Second, we examine another postpositivistic study, one that incorporates both quantitative and qualitative methods. Finally, we discuss a qualitative study that draws from the critical paradigm of research. We hope that the interrogation of these three studies enhances your understanding of the pragmatic implications of research paradigms.

A Quantitative Study

Dawes, Horan, and Hackett (2000) employed an experimental design to determine whether a published technology education program *caused* female students to consider nontraditional technical and scientific careers. Specifically, they stratified 169 seventh- and eighth-grade students according to grade, and then randomly assigned them to either a published technology education curricula or to a control curricula. The treatment was applied over a seven-week period. The researchers hypothesized that the treatment would foster female interest in at least three out of 21 possible technical and scientific careers. Valid and reliable pre- and post-test instruments were used to determine possible gains in either technical-scientific self-efficacy or career interest.

Quantitative researchers, such as Dawes et al. (2000), use theory to develop their hypotheses to test the relationship of variables through the use of instruments. To help examine the relationships among variables with respect to gender these researchers used a framework derived from self-efficacy theory. Specifically, they sought to determine causes and effects, and relationships. To accomplish this, they imposed a treatment on selected seventh- and eighth-grade technology education students. While this experiment was conducted in a natural rather than an artificial environment, the researchers attempted to detach themselves from their research *subjects* through the use of instruments and research proctors, to avoid bias.

The term "subjects" is especially symbolic for quantitative researchers conducting experimental or quasi-experimental research because its connotation suggests *subjecting* selected humans to a treatment. While most of us would consider the treatment imposed by Dawes et al. (2000) as helpful, the notion of treatment suggests a differential power relationship since researcher(s) make all of the decisions regarding the content of the treatment, how it is to be administered, and who receives it.

Because Dawes et al. (2000) adhered to accepted postpositivistic principles of validity and reliability, generalizability and prediction were outcomes that they sought. Further, they suggested their research effort contributed to the "truth" regarding whether a particular published technology education program *causes* female students to consider non-traditional technical and scientific careers.

A Qualitative Study Within Postpositivism: Grounded Theory

Ellibee (1997) sought to identify attributes of quality education-for-work curricula through interviews with curriculum practitioners. Although Ellibee conducted a qualitative investigation, her research can be considered postpositivistic because she employed a grounded theoretical perspective. This qualitative tradition, whose origins reside in the discipline of sociology, advocates a very technical and rational approach to data collection and analysis.

For example, in identifying and contrasting data incidents, Ellibee (1997) found an essential attribute relevant only "if at least half of the participants in at least three of the sites visited deemed it important" (p. 29). In fact, Ellibee presented a series of modified frequency charts as part of her data representation, an uncommon practice for most qualitative researchers. Ellibee also expressed the concern of representativeness shared by most quantitative researchers and embraced the position that a thorough understanding of one site cannot be accomplished without knowledge of other similar sites. Therefore, she employed a multi-case research design.

In an effort to avoid theoretical over-determination (for which critical, feminist, and postmodern/poststructural researchers are critiqued), Ellibee (1997) purported to begin her study without a theory even though she made initial research assumptions on what elements constituted quality education-for-work curriculum. While collecting data she constantly sought to develop a model in an effort to explain attributes of quality education-for-work curriculum. Further, she constantly compared the data collected from different sites and only stopped her project when she was no longer finding any additional information.

One of the primary implications of Ellibee's (1997) findings is that contextualized education-for-work curriculum is more effective than a fragmented, decontextualized approach, an assertion made by a variety of researchers working in different paradigms. Thus, while postpositivistic, constructivist, critical, feminist, and postmodern/ poststructural researchers may adhere to different principles and practices of research, their respective findings sometimes support one another.

A Critical Qualitative Study

The goal of critical researchers is to not only understand the world but also to alter existing inequities. Darrah (1994) found it problematic that much of the literature concerned with workplace skills conceptualized work as unambiguous, instrumental, rational, and generalizable. Drawing from critical theory he critiqued existing conceptualizations of skill requirements as still manifesting Taylorian values and emphasized the social nature of work and the human capacity to understand and change technology and organizations.

To explore how workers' skills are impacted by the context of their respective places of work, Darrah (1994) and other researchers affiliated with the Educational Requirements for the New Technology and Work Organization Project conducted four qualitative case studies. Each case represented a different sector of the economy (e.g., industrial, service). The first goal of this research project was to explore, describe, interpret, and explain the total complexity of skill requirements of workers in specific workplaces in an in-depth manner. To accomplish this goal, Darrah immersed himself in the lives of *participants* and their use of skills in the workplace. In a sense, the investigators became the instruments of the study. This aspect of the study could be found within any paradigms of qualitative research including feminist, constructivist, and some aspects of postpositivistic.

Through Darrah's (1994) critique of the dominant approach by workforce educators to conceptualize skill requirements, his use of particular references (e.g., Vallas, 1990), and his desire for workforce education curriculum to address the notion of agency, it is apparent that he drew from critical theory. However, Darrah was not explicit about his theoretical framework, which is somewhat of an anomaly among those who work within alternative paradigms.

Darrah (1994) wanted to provide an understanding of skill requirements from participants' perspectives. He wanted to learn from the participants and so interviewed them and observed them at work. He used a more inductive approach or emergent design. More specifically, Darrah [1] used natural settings as sites of his study, [2] placed more emphasis on meaning and process, [3] was more concerned with a holistic understanding of phenomena, and [4] tried to illuminate the contextual differences among skills in light of the different places of work in which they are found. Darrah not only found that the workplaces in different industrial sectors required different skills but he also found that each particular workplace environment required different specific skills; thus, troubling the notion of preparing workforce education students with narrow, specific, decontextualized skills. Further, this troubling was part of a critical researcher's attempt to challenge oppressive and dominant ways of thinking and living.

Conclusion

We end our discussion of research paradigms with our thinking of what it means to be a scholar in the new millennium. The uncertainty of the world of research alluded to at the beginning of this chapter is also found in our own field of workforce education and the institutions in which our programs are housed. Universities and their academic programs now face increased scrutiny from public governing bodies, decreased state revenues, and a rapidly changing political and social context (Aronowitz, 2000).

We believe that the uncertainty that envelopes the world of research and the liminal landscape of the university offer possibilities to rethink/reinvent/re-envision what it means to be a scholar and researcher. First, we maintain that opening up what constitutes research, in other words encouraging a paradigm proliferation, has and will contribute to the rethinking and possible rejuvenation of workforce education. At the same time that we celebrate the fact that there is room for differing ways of conceptualizing, implementing, and (re)presenting data, we acknowledge the need for all researchers to be thoughtful about their work. For us this means that researchers must see themselves not as technicians applying a set of methods and practices, but as scholars who acknowledge the philosophical assumptions that undergird their practices and who can situate themselves within the wide continuum of what constitutes research. Most importantly, scholars should be able to articulate the why of their research both paradigmatically and pragmatically. We believe that these types of conversations are central to promoting more thoughtful research and hopefully more thoughtful practices in workforce education.

References

Adams, N., Causey, T., Jacobs, M. E., Munnro, P., Quinn, M., & Trousdale, A. (1998). Womentalkin': A reader's theatre performance of teachers' stories. *Qualitative Studies in Education, 11,* 383-395.

Aggar, B. (1991). Critical theory, poststructuralism, postmodernism: Their sociological relevance. In W. R. Scott & J. Blake (Eds.), *Annual review of sociology* (pp. 105-131). Palo Alto, CA: Annual Reviews.

Anderson, G. (1989). Critical ethnography in education: Origins, current status, and new directions. *Review of Educational Research, 59,* 249-270.

Aronowitz, S. (1995). Bringing science and scientificity down to earth. *Cultural Studies Times, 1*(3), 12.

Aronowitz, S. (2000). *The knowledge factory: Dismantling the corporate university and creating true higher learning.* Boston: Beacon Press.

Benhabib, S., BonB, W., & McCole, J. (Eds.). (1993). *On Max Horkheimer: New perspectives.* Cambridge, MA: The MIT Press.

Bloom, L. (1998). *Under the sign of hope: Feminist methodology and narrative interpretation.* Albany, NY: SUNY Press.

Britzman, D. (1997). The tangles of implication. *Qualitative Studies in Education, 10*(1), 31-37.

Cary, L. (1999). Unexpected stories: Life history and the limits of representation. *Qualitative Inquiry, 5,* 411-427.

Carr, W., & Kemmis, S. (1986). *Becoming critical: Education, knowledge, and action research.* London: Falmer.

Collins, P. H. (1991). *Black feminist thought.* New York: Routledge.

Coser, L. (1977). *Masters of sociological thought: Ideas in historical and social context.* New York: Harcourt Brace Jovanovich.

Crotty, M. (1998). *The foundations of social research: Meaning and perspective in the research process.* Thousand Oaks, CA: Sage.

Darrah, C. (1994). Skill requirements at work: Rhetoric versus reality. *Work and Occupations, 21*(1), 64-84.

Dawes, M. E., Horan, J. J., & Hackett, G. (2000). Experimental evaluation of self-efficacy treatment on technical/scientific career outcomes. *British Journal of Guidance and Counseling, 29*(1), 87-99.

Devault, M. (1996). Talking back to sociology: Distinctive contributions to feminist methodology. *Annual Review of Sociology, 22,* 29-44.

Dewey, J. (1907). Education as a university study. *Columbia University Quarterly, 9,* 284-290.

Dewey, J. (1916). *Democracy and education.* New York: Macmillan.

Ellibee, M. A. (1997). A grounded theory of essential attributes of quality education-for-work curriculum. *Journal of Vocational Education Research, 22*(1), 21-38.

Eisner, E. (1983). Anastasia might still be alive, but the monarchy is dead. *Educational Researcher, 12*(5), 13-14, 23-24.

Gilligan, C. (1983). *In a different voice.* Cambridge, MA: Harvard University Press.

Giroux, H. (1979). Schooling and the culture of positivism: Notes on the death of history. *Educational Theory, 29,* 263-284.

Glesne, C. (1997). That rare feeling: Representing research through possibilities of vocational poetic transcription. *Qualitative Inquiry, 3,* 202-221.

Gregson, J. A. (1998). Reflecting on qualitative research and vocational education. *Journal of Vocational Education Research, 23,* 265-270.

Guba, E. (1990). *The paradigm dialog.* Newbury Park, CA: Sage.

Guba, E. G., & Lincoln, Y. S. (1994). Competing paradigms in qualitative research. In N. K. Denzin & Y. S. Lincoln (Eds.), *Handbook of qualitative research* (pp. 105-117). Thousand Oaks, CA: Sage.

Gunzenhauser, M. (in press). A promising rhetoric for post-critical ethnography. In G. W. Noblit, E. Murillo, & S. Flores

(Eds.), *Playgrounds of post-critical ethnography.* Mount Waverly, Australia: Hampton Press.

Harding, S. (1991). *Whose science? Whose knowledge? Thinking from women's lives.* Ithaca, NY: Cornell University Press.

Harvey, L. (1990). *Critical social science.* Boston: Unwin Hyman.

Kelly, M. (1994). *Critique and power: Recasting the Foucault/ Habermas debate.* Cambridge, MA: The MIT Press.

Kenway, J., Willis, S., Blackmore, J., & Rennie, L. (1994). Making 'Hope Practical' rather than 'Despair Convincing'; Feminist post-structuralism, gender reform and educational change. *British Journal of Sociology of Education, 15,* 187-210.

Kincheloe, J., & McLaren, P. (1998). Rethinking critical theory and qualitative inquiry. In N. K. Denzin & Y. S. Lincoln (Eds.), *The landscape of qualitative research: Theories and issues* (pp. 260-299). Thousand Oaks, CA: Sage.

Kirsch, G. (1999). *Ethical dilemmas in feminist research.* Albany, NY: SUNY Press.

Kuhn, T. S. (1970). *The structure of scientific revolutions.* Chicago: University of Chicago Press.

Lather, P. (1991). *Getting smart: Feminist research and pedagogy with/in the postmodern.* New York: Routledge.

Lather, P. (1993). Fertile obsession: Validity after poststructuralism. *Sociological Quarterly, 34,* 673-693.

Lather, P. (1999). *From competing paradigms to disjunctive affirmation.* Paper presented at the annual meeting of the American Education Research Association, Montreal, Canada.

Lakes, R. D., & Bettis, P. J. (1995). Advancing critical vocational education research. *Journal of Vocational Education Research, 20*(3), 5-28.

Lincoln, Y. (1990). The making of a constructivist: A remembrance of transformations past. In E. Guba (Ed.), *The paradigm dialog* (pp. 67-87). Newbury Park, CA: Sage.

Lincoln, Y. S., & Guba, E. G. (1985). *Naturalistic inquiry.* Beverly Hills, CA: Sage.

Lincoln, Y. S., & Guba, E. G. (2000). Paradigmatic controversies, contradictions, and emerging influences. In N. K. Denzin & Y. S. Lincoln (Eds.), *Handbook of qualitative research* (2nd ed., pp 163-188). Thousand Oaks, CA: Sage.

Lomawaima, K. T. (2000). Tribal sovereigns: Reframing research in American Indian education. *Harvard Educational Review, 70*(1), 1-21.

Maher, F., & Tetreault, M. K. T. (1993). Doing feminist ethnography: Lessons from feminist classrooms. *Qualitative Studies in Education, 6*(1), 19-32.

Phillips, D. C. (1983). After the wake: Postpositivistic educational thought. *Educational Researcher, 12*(5), 4-12.

Popkewitz, T. (1990). Whose future? Whose past? Notes on critical theory and methodology. In E. Guba (Ed.), *The paradigm dialog.* Newbury Park, CA: Sage.

Popkewitz, T. (1998). The culture of redemption and the administration of freedom as research. *Review of Educational Research, 68*(1), 1-34.

Popper, K. (1974). Autobiography. In P. A. Schilpp (Ed.), *The philosophy of Karl Popper.* La Salle: Open Court.

Reinharz, S. (1992). *Feminist methods in social research.* New York: Oxford University Press.

Richardson, L. (1994) Nine poems. *Journal of Contemporary Ethnography, 23,* 3-13.

Ritzer, G. (1983). *Contemporary sociological theory* (2nd ed.). New York: Knopf.

Shacklock, G., & Smyth, J. (1998). *Being reflexive in critical educational and social research.* Bristol, PA: Falmer.

Schwandt, T. (1998). Constructivist, interpretivist approaches to human inquiry. In N. K. Denzin & Y. S. Lincoln (Eds.), *The landscape of qualitative research: Theories and issues* (pp. 221-259). Thousand Oaks, CA: Sage.

Smith, D. (1987). Women's perspective as a radical critique of sociology. In S. Harding (Ed.), *Feminism and methodology* (pp. 84-96). Bloomington: Indiana University Press.

Thomas, J. (1993). *Doing critical ethnography.* Newbury Park, CA: Sage.

Tierney, W. (1997). *Academic outlaws: Queer theory and cultural studies in the academy.* Thousand Oaks, CA: Sage.

Vallas, S. P. (1990). The concept of skill: A critical review. *Work and Occupations, 17,* 379-398.

Wexler, P. (1992). *Becoming somebody.* Washington, DC: Falmer.

Wiggershaus, R. (1995). *The Frankfurt School: Its history, theories, and political significance.* Cambridge, MA: The MIT Press.

Chapter 2

Finding a Researchable Topic

Jay W. Rojewski and Edgar I. Farmer

It's been almost two weeks now. You spend, what seems like, every waking moment thinking about it. And yet, still nothing. In a cruel twist of fate, it seems that the more time you spend thinking about it the more elusive the answer becomes. Why can't someone just give it to you already and then you can be done with it!

Sound familiar? For graduate students trying to identify a research topic for their thesis or dissertation, the scenario it is probably all too familiar. Even well-seasoned scholars acknowledge that picking a research topic can be one of the most difficult hurdles faced by novice scholars. This task is made even more difficult when you realize its importance. Gall, Borg, and Gall (1996) noted that "the imagination and insight that goes into defining the research problem usually determines the ultimate value of a research study more than any other factor" (p. 47). Great! Just what you need, more pressure! Perhaps, but consider the alternative. An inability to select a "researchable" topic is probably the single biggest reason that students do not finish the dissertation; instead, acquiring the moniker *AbD*–All but Dissertation (Lanyon, 1995; Moore, n.d.; Satz, 1988). "The distance in time and space between the AbD and the PhD is seen by many graduate students as a journey penned by Dante's sadistic twin which catapults them into their own personal academic *inferno*" (Woodbury, 1993, p. 3). Thank goodness you're only writing a masters thesis, huh? Ahem. Not so fast. Read on.

It's interesting. Though many people, students and professors alike, have difficulty with selecting a research topic—you may be one of them yourself—the dissertation, particularly as it relates to process, has received insufficient attention in the professional literature (Butters, n.d./2000; Isaac, Koenigsknecht, Malaney, & Karras, 1989). Although empirical investigations are few it seems everyone has plenty of advice to share. Therefore, our aim in this chapter is to synthesize the available literature, both conceptual as well as empirical, on selecting a researchable thesis or dissertation topic. Several issues we address include possible reasons why topic selection is difficult, factors that affect topic selection, criteria to consider when making a tentative topic selection, and specific strategies people have recommended to make the selection process easier.

Reasons That Topic Selection is Difficult

What makes the task so difficult? After all, we are all intelligent people here, right? Why do we struggle and agonize over something that initially sounds relatively benign? It has been our experience that students try to refine a researchable topic without having a working understanding of the literature in their field. Without knowing what has already been done, what the current hot topics are, and projected issues and trends, defining a research topic is sort of like trying to force a square peg into a round hole—it might eventually fit but it ain't really worth the effort. Even if you succeed, in the end all you have is a chewed up peg. That's fine, you say, but what about my research topic?

The search for a topic is, in effect, a study of the literature. Unfortunately, it is a part of the overall research process that is often ignored or given short attention. We have seen too many graduate students jump into the topic development frenzy without a solid understanding of what is already known in their area. It is not unreasonable to spend anywhere from several weeks to several months or more reviewing the literature, thinking about potential problems, and narrowing your topic. The need to complete some preliminary background work and investigation of the literature before jumping into the study itself isn't unlike the *prep work* required before painting a room. If the cracks in the wall aren't filled in, the final product suffers.

We know that recommending preliminary library work, perhaps even a lot of it, goes against the expectations of, at least, some people who want a quick and painless solution. However, time spent up-front is well worth the investment. Knowledge of the field is critical, not only to understand what needs to be done in your interest area but also how to position your study with what has already been accomplished. What topics are considered most relevant? What areas of study represent the biggest contributions? Is there controversy or *inconsistencies* in the research? Does a *deficiency* appear in the literature on a particular topic? From a *historical* perspective, how has the field arrived at its present level of understanding the phenomenon you are interested in pursuing?

The task of identifying a research topic is also made difficult because graduate students are expected to think and act like *emerging scholars*, to have the ability and motivation to pursue independent study (Butters, n.d.). This expectation can seem to appear out of nowhere and takes more than a few people by surprise. This often-unanticipated expectation exists despite the fact that most students are rarely, if ever, mentored or treated as scholars during the completion of their coursework. Besides, the coursework is a known commodity, it is comfortable and students have a track record of successful performance. Not so with research. The tendency of many students is to postpone work on the thesis or dissertation because it represents the unknown and uncomfortable. So, consider a change of mindset from passive student to active learner/scholar, one who takes charge of the learning process.

Factors That Affect Topic Selection

Available Resources

An understanding of relevant literature is, perhaps, the single most important factor that influences the selection of a research topic. However, many other factors can and do affect the types of topics that are considered and the one that is ultimately selected.

Of course, money, or perhaps the lack thereof, is an important consideration (duh!). The thesis, dissertation, or any research for that matter, can become a costly endeavor if certain types of designs are used like surveys (for postage) or experimental designs requiring sophisticated equipment. However, having limited financial resources does not result in an automatic change of topic. Most universities have grant programs designed to financially support graduate thesis and dissertation research. There are also competitive grants available outside the university through government agencies and private foundations. If you are serious about your topic but don't have the cash consider these types of funding options.

The availability and access to other resources—access to research libraries, availability of computers, or ease of access to a major advisor—can also expand or limit the intended scope of an investigation (Emory University, n.d.; Miller, 1990). One issue that can alter topic selection is the major research advisor. Too often advisors have specific research agendas that their graduate students are required to work on through their own research. The opposite case may also hold true: An advisor gives you free rein on topic selection but is not very knowledgeable about your topic and can provide only limited guidance. Without reasonable access and predictable guidance from a major advisor, there is tendency, we think, to select a conservative or "safe" research topic rather than a riskier but also more interesting and viable study.

Knowledge and comfort level with data analysis techniques, whether it be quantitative or qualitative, is also something that will influence topic selection. "If your question is such that it will require hierarchical linear modeling and you have a tenuous hold on the eternal mysteries of the *t*-test, it's time for self-reflection" (Emory University, n.d.).

Time

In our experience, one of the most precious of all resources is the amount of time students can (or will) devote to the entire research process. The issue of time really refers to one of two things; time spent per day or per week on the investigation, and the length of time needed to complete the study. We recognize that some research topics and their resultant designs simply take more time to complete than others. This isn't necessarily a good or bad thing, it's just a fact. Over the years we have known students who only start to think about their research topic after the completion of their coursework. Suddenly they realize that time is slipping away from them and they frantically search for a topic that can be studied with relative speed and without undue pain. Unfortunately, if time frames are assigned *a priori* for the sole purpose of meeting a desired completion date, the scope of possible research topics even considered is prematurely narrowed.

At the same time we also wholeheartedly subscribe to the advice given by some wise (and probably really old) professor who recommended to "get your degree first and then set the world on fire!" In other words, it is possible to totally ignore the impact of time when selecting a topic, in which case a research topic requiring years to complete could easily be formulated. For every investigation, compromise can be achieved to maximize the scope of the intended study yet still consider and control for the length of time needed for completion.

The other time-related issue—amount of attention given to a research study over a period of time—is rarely considered in identifying a topic but can have a substantial impact on the quality of both the research topic and the end result. Devoting only a limited amount of time per week to a research study is problematic for both novice and experienced scholars alike. Students working part-time on a degree are usually pushed close to the limit on time to begin with and have little extra to spare. So, they squeeze out a couple of hours on weekends or an hour after the late news to work on their study. Hardly *quality* time. Faculty who have little or no assigned time to work on their research face a similar dilemma.

We know what the *time* problem is, what is the solution? Simply put, there is not an easy answer. In other words, we don't know. Oh, it is true, we could recommend the use of a day planner and diagram a complicated scheme for parsing out segments of each day to your research or suggest that you make research a top priority and then plan your life accordingly. But, we find that pat solutions like these are rarely useful. Rather, a purposeful and realistic assessment of time should be made that acknowledges the limitations imposed by other life responsibilities. From this assessment, alternative scenarios can be devised to gain a realistic appraisal of the amount of time that can be devoted to research each week and the length of time required to complete the project.

Important Factors in Topic Selection—Isaac et al. (1989)

The literature, although limited, provides some clues about factors that influence the selection of a research topic. The work of Isaac and his colleagues (1989) at The Ohio State University (OSU) is one of the most enlightening studies on this topic. In their investigation, Isaac et al. were interested in two things: [1] determining what graduate students considered important factors in selecting a dissertation topic, and [2] the relationship of student to advisor and dissertation committee. All OSU students who received the PhD during one calendar year were surveyed. The final data pool contained 438 useable responses, 299 males and 153 females. Students were asked to rate—on a five-point, Likert-type scale—the degree of importance of 11 factors on selecting a dissertation research topic. These factors were availability of equipment, lack of equipment availability, financial limitations, advisor's preference, personal preference, personal life experience, funding agency priorities, national political climate, likelihood of publication, current trends in the field, and likely impact on job prospects.

Isaac et al. (1989) found that "in all fields, the single most important factor in the choice of a topic was the student's *own preference*" (p. 362). The next most important factors overall were *trends in the field*, *own life experiences*, and *adviser's preference*. The order of importance attached to these factors varied by student's field of study. In education, *own life experiences* was second to *own preference*. Interestingly, while the factor *likelihood of publication* was an influence in all fields of study, the topic's potential *impact on job prospects* was considered unimportant ($\underline{M}$ = 1.13 on a 5-point scale) by doctoral graduates in education.

Two additional analyses were conducted on the data Isaac et al. (1989) obtained—a principal components analysis and cluster analysis. The principal components analysis was performed in an effort to determine whether a smaller number of underlying dimensions or factors could be used to represent the original 11 items. And indeed, three factors accounting for 56% of the total variance were identified and retained by the investigators. The first factor, accounting for 26% of the variance, represented *field-related* influences such as equipment and funding availability, advisers' preferences, and professional advancement concerns. Factor 2, a *personal interest* factor, accounted for 17% of total variance and included reasons such as personal preference and life experiences. The final dimension, a *political* factor (accounting for 13% of total variance), reflected *national politics* and *personal life*. The second supplemental analysis that Isaac et al. (1989) ran was a cluster analysis. They found that "the areas cluster nicely into the 'hard sciences' and 'other' areas. Thus, factors influenced in the hard sciences tend to be similar to one another, and so do those in the other areas" (p. 367).

So, now we know something about the factors that influence research topic selection. But what do we know about the time of topic selection in a graduate program? And what role does the advisor play in this final decision-making process? Thank goodness you asked. As luck would have it, Isaac et al. (1989) provide us with some insight. Just over half (52%) of the OSU survey respondents selected their research topic prior to the general comprehensive exams, while the remainder finalized their topic after comprehensive exams were completed. Not really much help here, although it is interesting to note that 60% of the students in education selected their topic after comprehensive exams were completed. Overall, doctoral advisors had little or no input on final topic selection for over one-third (37%) of graduates. Another third (31%) of the students indicated that they made their selection with input from their advisor or dissertation committee. Only 5% of students indicated that their adviser was solely responsible for the selection of a research topic. An interesting point: When broken down by field of study, 61% of those from education indicated they chose their own topic but only 17% of the students in the biological sciences indicated the choice was solely theirs.

Have you had enough of Isaac and his friends from OSU? Us, too. Let's move on and consider the types of strategies you can use to identify that ideal research topic.

Specific Strategies to Make Selection of a Research Topic Easier

It has been our experience that way too many people search for a research topic without a clear understanding of the literature. Doing so is like going on a trip with no clear destination in mind and no road map to help. You may eventually wind up some place that is nice and interesting. But, it is more likely that you will end up driving all over creation, spurred on by glimmers of a promising landscape, only to be disappointed when you crest the hill and find that thousands of other travelers have already beaten you to the best spots. Worse yet, you may find that the road you wanted to travel hasn't even been constructed yet—Sorry, no four-wheeling in the research literature. Rats! Now what?

There is simply no short-cut to understanding the literature. No *Cliffs Notes*® or *Research Literature for Dummies*® manuals available to cut your reading time but simultaneously increase your comprehension. [There are, however, reviews of literature and conceptual articles that basically serve the same purpose as these condensed manuals.] So, just what is the best strategy to finding a research topic?

We recommend that you start by identifying a general research area of interest. This topic can be rather broad, even somewhat vague. Wait, we can tell you're a bit confused. After all, you thought that finding a researchable topic was the whole point of this chapter. It seems rather disingenuous to advise students to find a topic by finding a topic. Well, technically, yes. But remember, here we are suggesting that you identity a broad area of interest. For example, you might have an *interest* in students with behavior problems and ways to minimize their disruption of class. Good. Now run with this broad topic to find specific issues or problems in need of investigation. Perhaps you *work* in a computer support lab and have seen students find unique ways to solve problems with new computer software. Sounds like the seed of a possible research study on reasoning or critical thinking skills.

While selecting a broad topic area can be difficult, remember that you are likely to change this focus once or twice before settling on a focused research topic. The point in selecting a tentative area of interest is to provide a critical starting point that allows you to identify useful descriptors that can be used for initial computer searches. This initial direction may be most helpful in getting you off square one.

Now, armed with a more or less vague idea of your research topic you need to camp out in the library or at a computer screen for a couple of weeks or so and start to read and organize the literature. We know. You're disappointed. You wanted us to simply hand over the *secret*, right? Unfortunately, we haven't found it yet, although we still pursue it as vigorously as Ponce de Leon searched for the fabled foundation of youth. In the meantime, we make do with reading the literature. But reading is not enough (you knew it was coming, didn't you?). You must actively read and organize the literature into some type of coherent package that helps make sense of the scores of articles and books you are likely to find on your broad areas of interest. Granted, this first, but all-important, step can be time-consuming and may result in more than one dead-end along the way. But it is <u>not</u> wasted time that could be better spent elsewhere.

How is it humanly possible to actively organize [and understand] the literature? Well, who wants to be a millionaire? Only one lifeline remaining, so let's ask a friend.

> Put succinctly, it means not just passively following the author's train of thought. More importantly, it means anticipating where the author's line of argument leads, considering alternative extensions, and constructing your own framework that covers these possibilities. . . . Some of the best ideas are born this way. (Krathwohl, 1994, p. 29)

Assuming that you trust our advice and are doing your best to read and actively interact with and organize the literature, what else? Well, consider some of the ideas listed in Table 2.1 as possible strategies for extending your topic search.

Criteria to Consider when Selecting a Research Topic

Okay, so you've got the big picture, initiated your strategies for topic identification, and you have narrowed your laundry list of possible research topics down to just a handful. Now what? What type of criteria can be used to determine whether a possible research topic is worthy of study? Help!?! Don't worry, we feel your pain and are here to help.

TABLE 2.1
Strategies to Consider When Selecting a Possible Research Topic

Strategies
Start with broad concepts first (Lanyon, 1995).
Identify a theory that can guide your thinking.
Start thinking about research topic areas early on. If in a graduate program, make classes and projects geared toward topic selection (Miller, 1990). Take note of topics in lectures, solicit professors' advice and recommendations, listen to scholarly presentations that may shed light on decision.
Use a variety of sources for identifying possible topics including past dissertations, theses, and published journal articles for recommendations about research. Find authoritative sources, comprehensive reviews of studies in areas of interest, encyclopedias of educational research (Crowl, 1996), broaden search beyond education to include psychology, sociology, etc.
Talk with friends and colleagues. Use the Internet—on-line mail lists, World Wide Web, chatrooms—for additional ideas. Look for practical problems at work, in personal experience, in media.
Draw a conceptual map of the studies you have found and see how they fit together. What information is still missing? What findings are unclear or inconsistent? (Creswell, 1994).
Consider replicating a past study by changing the population studied, modifying variables examined, or both (Crowl, 1996).

Any number of possible criteria or motivations may influence the selection of one research topic over another. As you consider the specific points we raise in this section remember that they are only selected criteria not an exhaustive list of the best or only criteria to consider. Obviously, your unique situation will dictate your use of these criteria, if at all, in your decision-making process.

Interest in topic vs. marketability. Arguably the most important criteria to consider when electing a research topic is level of personal interest in the topic (Crowl, 1996; Madsen, 1983). Will this topic hold your interest for the next 6 to 12 months, or even longer? You must have a passion for or a commitment to your selected topic. Being blasé just won't cut it.

Staz (1988) agrees that, in the long run, it is best to select a topic that will be enjoyable and of interest. However, she also suggests that individuals pursuing a career in higher education may have to temper their personal interest by the reality of job marketability. Potential candidates for the professorate might need to consider a topic deeply imbedded in theory that addresses the most current topics or issues in the field, or reflects individual areas of intended teaching and scholarship. For those not intending to teach in a university setting, Staz frankly admits that the "topic is probably less important...you can pick the one you love."

Contribution(s) to the literature. Useem (1997) views any research endeavor as "an active pursuit of new knowledge" (p. 215). As such, he believes that research must have some implication for the current state of the field; what other researchers are thinking and doing. In order to explain this potential contribution, a solid understanding of the literature is a must. What theory guides your study? What inconsistencies or deficiencies exist in the results of investigations within and tangential to your topic? Is there current interest in this topic in your field? (Staz, 1988; Woodbury, 1993).

So, how do you know if you have a topic that will make a contribution to the literature? Madsen (1983) gives this advice,

> Basically, a topic must have the potential to do at least one of the following: uncover new facts or principles, suggest relationships that were previously unrecognized, challenge existing truths or assumptions, afford new insights into little-understood phenomena, or suggest new interpretations of know facts that can alter man's perception of the world around him. (p. 25)

Focus. Don't try to investigate everything all at once! A good research topic is focused narrowly. The way topics become narrow is usually through a process of identifying broader issues from the literature and gradually reducing the scope of the idea until it becomes manageable from a research perspective. Initially, "broader topics are probably more helpful because the broader the topic is, the more numerous are the kinds of research questions that can be asked" (Crowl, 1996, p. 20). Eventually, however, a specific area of study needs to emerge. Nelson (1998) explained that

> one way to narrow your topic and to help yourself understand what is really being asked is to write a 30- to 50-word title for your proposed study. This effort may seem like overkill, but it will force you really to think through what it is you actually want to do.

So what is a sufficiently narrow topic? While the answer is to some degree a matter of personal opinion, a topic needs to be broad enough to find sufficient information but not so broad that it involves multiple issues or an overwhelming amount of information (Salgado, 1998).

Originality and creativity. The jury is out on this one. Some people stress the need for highly creative and novel approaches to the task of research topic development, while others argue for more conservative approaches such as identifying studies for replication. We don't have a specific preference. It's okay to be novel, unique, and creative. However, it is probably smarter for most novice researchers to take the tried and true approach toward research. Novelty, creativity, and uniqueness, while great buzzwords, usually raise the attention of faculty committees. You really don't need the added pressure at this point. Do you? Besides, it is much harder to uncover cutting-edge topics and to integrate them into the existing literature base.

Tractability. Useem (1997) advanced the notion of tractability, a combination of three components that he felt critical in evaluating potential research topics—*reach, clarity of research problem,* and *availability of data.*

Useem's (1997) first component, *reach,* has to do with the overall focus and scope of a research topic. He recommends, as we do, that research topics represent focused, narrow areas of the research literature. However, we have found that many first-time investigators balk at this approach. After all, "Where's the fame, the adulation, the Nobel prize for conducting narrow, constrained studies? Give me the big enchilada!" Hold on there, Poindexter. While we understand the sentiment, look at the issue from a different perspective.

The ultimate goal of research, indeed the entire scientific process, is to contribute to an ever-expanding body of information about specific topics and issues. Just like billions and billions of microscopic organisms gave their lives—although each contribution was miniscule—to make up the vast (but shrinking) oil fields found throughout the world. So too, great discoveries in science and related fields often come about as the result of innumerable smaller efforts that have laid the groundwork for understanding and progress. Think of your study findings as a brick. Some research topics represent bigger bricks, sometimes smaller ones. The point is that each brick is needed to construct the wall that represents a particular body of literature. Without your brick, regardless of size, the wall is weakened and our knowledge of the topic less complete. Besides, focused research topics are likely to be completed more quickly and represent an increased probability of completion.

The second component of Useem's (1997) notion of tractability has to do with the clarity of the research problem. Focus and clarity are really the hallmarks of exemplary research topics. First, pinpoint your area of interest (focus). Second, identify the specific issues within your area that you are interested in pursuing. This second task involves a clearly stated, succinct purpose and specific objectives or questions that support the purpose. Nelson (1998) declared that research topics should be reduced to a question that will guide all future steps in the research process. It should lead naturally to sub-questions, hypotheses, and a method. The topic should both guide and limit the literature review." So how is all of this accomplished? That's right, you know the drill— read, read, read! But as you do, consider these types of issues. Can you identify the specific connections between your variables or concepts of interest with those in the prevailing literature? Have you stated a clear purpose?

The final component of tractability is concerned with the availability of data. "Obtaining the right data in a timely manner can make or break a dissertation" (Useem, 1997, p. 214). While this point may seem obvious, don't forget to consider how data will be collected as you consider various research topics. Is the sample accessible? Can you actually "get" the types of answers or information you need to address your stated purpose and goals? You may have a great research topic, but if data is unavailable or impossible to retrieve, better go back to the drawing board. Ugghhhhh...

Cultural norms of the department. Don't you hate it? It always seems it boils down to politics. It's not what you know but who you know. Well, maybe. We often hear grizzled veterans—students who have *been there, done that*—counsel new graduate students about which faculty to avoid, classes to take, and what to expect during comprehensive examinations and the defense of the dissertation proposal. But other issues about how to maneuver through the bureaucracy imbedded throughout the university system, the types of topics deemed appropriate or acceptable by departmental faculty, and the general expectations of various faculty for thesis or dissertation research are equally important (Staz, 1988).

Okay, so you grudgingly acknowledge that this is important to consider. How do you find the answers to these things? Well, look at recently completed theses and dissertations in the department. How are research topics phrased? Is your type of topic and research design represented in one or more of the volumes you peruse? Also, talk with your research advisor and other members of the faculty to get a better sense of acceptable research topics. It can be different to obtain some of this information because many departmental norms are actually implicit assumptions rather than specifically identified expectations. Useem

(1997) suggests looking at the types of research completed by departmental faculty. What does their work look like? Are qualitative and quantitative paradigms represented? What theoretical backgrounds are represented by faculty? Are these theories compatible yours?

An Abbreviated Checklist

Mauch and Birch (1989) constructed a series of questions to guide researchers when trying to determine the relative strength of research topics. An abbreviated listing of the questions include the following:

1. Is there current interest in this topic in your field?
2. Is there a gap in knowledge that work on this topic could fill?
3. Is it possible to focus on a small enough segment of this particular topic to make it manageable?
4. Can you envision a way to study the topic that will allow conclusions to be drawn with substantial objectivity?
5. Is the data collection (i.e., test, questionnaire, interviews, etc.) acceptable to your advisor and in your department?
6. Is there a body of literature relevant to the topic?
7. Is a search of the topic manageable?
8. Are there large problems to be surmounted in working in this topic? Can you handle them? Do you want to handle them?
9. Are the needed data easily accessible? Will you have control of the data?

References

Butters, R. S. (n.d.). *Thinking about a dissertation topic.* Retrieved October 1, 2000 from the World Wide Web: http://www.problemfinder.com/ atopic.html

Creswell, J. W. (1994). *Research design: Qualitative and quantitative approaches.* Thousand Oaks, CA: Sage.

Crowl, T. K. (1996). *Fundamentals of educational research* (2nd ed.). Dubuque, IA: Brown & Benchmark.

Emory University. (n.d.). *Graduate student survival* guide. Retrieved September 24, 2000 from the World Wide Web: http://www.es.emory.edu/mfp/grad.html

Gall, M. D., Borg, W. R., & Gall, J. P. (1996). *Educational research: An introduction* (6th ed.).White Plains, NY: Longman.

Isaac, P. D., Koenigsknecht, R. A., Malaney, G. D., & Karras, J. E. (1989). Factors related to doctoral dissertation topic selection. *Research in Higher Education, 30,* 357-373.

Krathwohl, D. R. (1994). A slice of advice. *Educational Researcher, 23*(1), 29-32.

Lanyon, S. M. (1995). How to design a dissertation project. *BioScience, 45*(1), 40-42.

Madsen, D. (1983). *Successful dissertations and theses: A guide to graduate student research from proposal to completion* (2nd ed.). San Francisco: Jossey-Bass.

Mauch, J. E., & Birch, J. W. (1989). *Guide to the successful thesis and dissertation—Conception to publication: A handbook for students and faculty.* New York: Marcel Dekker.

Miller, P. W. (1990). Preparing for the comprehensive examination and writing the dissertation proposal: Advice for doctoral students. *Journal of Industrial Teacher Education, 27*(2), 83-86.

Moore, J. C. (n.d.). *Dissertation/thesis assistance.* Retrieved October 1, 2000 from the World Wide Web: http/www.dissertation-thesis.com/gs.html

Nelson, R. A. (1998). *Consideration in research topic selection* [Class handout]. Retrieved October 1, 2000 from the World Wide Web: http://www.jour.lsu.edu/manship/faculty/faculty.html

Salgado, K. (1998). *Narrowing a topic.* Retrieved October 1, 2000 from the World Wide Web: http://kong.sinclair.edu/screens/narrow.html

Satz, K. P. (1988, Fall). Choosing your thesis or dissertation topic. *The Graduate, 4*(2). Retrieved October 1, 2000 from the World Wide Web [reprint from University of California–Berkeley newsletter]: http://www.grad.Berkeley.edu:5900/publications/NEWS/Reprints/DISSTOPI.htm

Useem, B. (1997). Choosing a dissertation topic. *PS: Political Science and Politics, 30,* 213-216.

Woodbury, J. (1993, November). *A love/hate relationship: Dissertation topic to doctoral committee.* Paper presented at the annual convention of the Mid-South Educational Research Association, New Orleans, LA. (ERIC Documentation Reproduction Service No. ED 369 319)

Chapter 3

Conducting an Extensive Review of the Literature

Carol A. Wright

The literature review is a critical element of the research process. An extensive review can reveal both the existing knowledge and, perhaps more importantly, gaps in that knowledge and where your research will fit into evolving research efforts. Beyond subject content literature reviews can inform research design, reveal important research instruments, and connect you with others who share similar interests.

Understanding the Information Cycle

The key to successful information retrieval relies on the four phases of the information process—how information is produced, communicated, stored, and retrieved (Association of College and Research Libraries, 2000). Understanding this *information cycle* allows researchers to follow the *information trail* appropriate for their research question(s). Consider the range and value of information produced by the academic community, government agencies, consumer and community groups, professional associations, policymakers, special interest groups, and the media and popular press to your research question. Each of these information producers generates, communicates and disseminates information in a specialized way, and each has different strengths and advantages to inform the process. Some researchers characterize information paths as *patterns of discourse* or *conversations within communities* to reflect and emphasize important differences in the nature and dissemination of information. The notion of discourse patterns is a useful way to remain mindful of the varieties of information types and the relative value of information produced and disseminated both within and outside of academe.

Information Production and Dissemination

Academic / Research / Professional Sources

A primary responsibility of the academic community is to conduct original research or extend existing research so that knowledge is advanced. This information is communicated through the scholarly communication process, primarily academic journals. Published by professional associations, university presses, or traditional academic publishers, a prime criteria of scholarly journals is the peer review process. The most rigorous review is termed "blind" and refers to having experts provide anonymous feedback on the accuracy, conclusions, findings, methods, and effectiveness of communication. Neither author nor reviewer is known to the other. An editorial review is less rigorous and relies on editorial board members for manuscript review. Some editorial reviews also include external reviewers.

The degree of review anonymity and manuscript acceptance rate provides some indication of journal prestige. Standard evaluation criteria should apply to both scholarly and professional publications (Pyrczak, 1999). In addition to requesting reviewing criteria and procedures directly from publishers, comparisons of these criteria are available from directories and guides to journals (e.g., American Psychological Association, 1997; Cabell, 1994, 1995, 1998; Loke, 1990). Traditionally, academic journals have been available through print publications, but increasingly scholarly journals are becoming available in electronic-only formats as the peer review process becomes more stable in the digital environment (Kovacs, 2000; Tomlins, 1998).

All professional communities have literature concerned with issues of practice, member benefits, continuing educational opportunities, political issues that impact the profession, and more. These professional and *trade* publications are of professional interest, but are not usually subject to the same rigorous review process as research publications.

Dissertations

Dissertations represent research completed to satisfy the requirements for an advanced degree and are rarely published by the commercial press in their original version. Dissertations are most readily available from Dissertation Abstracts International, a cooperative program that gathers, abstracts, sells, and offers many titles through a digital dissertations project. Dissertations are a very valuable resource category because they represent current interests, thinking, and methods being employed by a new generation of researchers and can help identify potential future colleagues. They can also identify institutions where a concentration of research efforts may match your interests so that future employment or opportunities may be explored.

The 'Invisible College'

An informal but critical element of the scholarly communication process is sometimes called the *invisible college*. This refers to personal networks and communities of researchers interested in common questions, issues, and methods. While this level of communication has historically remained within the closed ranks of professional colleagues and academic mentors, the electronic environment of listservs, discussion groups, and e-mail has expanded this network to a potentially global scale. Researchers can easily establish contact others who share common interests permitting more extensive communication and collaboration to continue in more traditional, non-public forums.

Government Sources

The United States federal government is the largest publisher in the world. State and local of governments also publish extensively for all areas within their jurisdiction and authority. Responsibility to make information publicly available from executive agencies is assigned to the U.S. Government Printing Office. Be aware that the shift to electronic dissemination of information has not provided for a complete archiving of documents. This resulting gap in the public record may prove to be an obstacle to serious investigation of some areas. Government documents relevant to study in education can be found in testimony, legislation, statistics, agency reports, and special studies. Many aspects of education policy and workforce education have received intense federal and state attention, and a significant amount of pertinent literature is found in government publications. Central to successful retrieval of government documents is an understanding of the structure of government agencies and the legislative process.

Media and Popular Press

The media and popular press are responsible for investigating current events and for reporting and interpreting findings of the research community to the general lay population. The news information provided through print, digital, networked and broadcast outlets often represent sources of primary data. Authority and reliability of the media is based on reputation (Ward, 1997). These publications usually carry few of the traditional hallmarks of scholarly publication, such as being written by experts in the field, a statement of author's credentials, bibliographies, and abstracts, but they are valuable as the record of how important issues impact the general population, and how research findings and issues are presented to the public at large.

The Internet

The Internet provides opportunities for anyone to post information in any format. It has the potential to circumvent the established order and authority of scholarly communication patterns provided by commercial and academic publishers, and makes the process of critical evaluation of information more difficult for novices or casual searchers. Internet sites can provide an additional dimension to a literature search, but should not be relied on exclusively. Critical evaluation criteria must be stringently applied to web-based information (Pennsylvania State University Libraries, 1999). Web sites at the end of this chapter are examples of excellent resources for studies in education.

Information Storage and Retrieval

Information must be organized in a systematic fashion so that it can be efficiently retrieved. If this is not accomplished, the information is lost to any future access. Journal literature is indexed and abstracted by several groups, for example, professional organizations, commercial vendors, or, in the case of education and medical literature, the U.S. government. While some databases rely exclusively on keyword access [newspapers, for example], databases usually provide precise access through *controlled vocabulary* or *thesauri* whereby articles are assigned several subject headings or *descriptors* so that common topics are retrievable. The degree of precision in the structure of the controlled vocabulary and the consistency in application of subject terms varies significantly. Differences in vocabulary across databases are a critical variable that researchers must be vigilant to incorporate into an effective and successful search strategy.

Increasingly, digital access to retrieval tools and to full text resources is fundamentally altering habits and expectations surrounding the research process. Print journals are now frequently offered in digital versions for little or no additional cost. A small number of journals are available exclusively in digital format as peer review processes become more widely accepted in that environment. Digital resource access is controlled by complicated licensing and copyright arrangements. Litigation will continue to resolve ownership, access, and rights among publishers, vendors, and authors (Arms, 2000). Costs for databases and full text resources are sometimes staggering, making institutional ability to pay an issue (U.S. Department of Commerce, 2000).

Total reliance on electronic access is not a viable choice for most researchers since coverage is unevenly distributed among disciplines, and because electronic access has inherent time frame limitations relative to the entire body of literature. A comprehensive literature search will often require print indexes and abstracts, journals, reference resources, statistics, and more. The temptation to limit research to the use of electronic resources can be strong especially by learners who have significant logistical constraints. But, careful researchers will not allow availability and ease of electronic access to be the primary criteria to determine the nature and direction of their work.

Primary versus Secondary Resources

Primary sources are defined as uninterpreted sources of information, and can be a very important part of a literature search. Primary sources allow you to examine evidence firsthand without being affected by other opinions. Then, you are able to draw comparisons between your assessments and the conclusions of others.

Often, primary resources are described by their formats—letters and diaries as opposed to books, for example. However, it is more useful and accurate to consider records in relation to the original event as described by Stout (1991; see Table 3.1).

Uses of the Literature

Using the Literature to Select a Working Topic

A preliminary literature review is more similar to a scan than a detailed comprehensive examination. At this early stage the existing literature is your guide for determining the extent of research, present understandings, practices, and conclusions. It is also the most reliable way to examine dimensions of a topic that may not have been initially considered but can expand the idea generation process. This phase of a literature review should be a stimulating exploration of the entire field that helps to identify a *working topic*. The working topic is a flexible concept that required continuous adjustment as new information is

TABLE 3.1
Records Along the Time Line

	Primary resources		Secondary resources
Transactional records	Selective records	Recollections and reflections	Analysis
Laws; contracts; diplomas	Pictures; films; videos	Diaries; letters; oral history interviews; memoirs	Histories of events as books or articles
The document IS the substance of the action	A recording of the event as it happened	How participants / observers remembered it	Written by person who was not there
There is no interpretation	Not exactly what happened; just what the camera could see	Longer after the event; greater chance that story is altered	Historians examine evidence; write stories to explain what happened and why

gathered and incorporated. One effective technique to establish a working topic is to lay out significant ideas using a concept map to create a visual representation of the relationships among concepts.

Using the Literature to Select a Research Design

The literature includes detailed descriptions of research designs, methods, and instruments used in past studies. In addition to handbooks and research reviews, detailed descriptions are the best ways for novice researchers to determine possible approaches to sampling, interviewing, data collection, and interventions. This information is identified in databases that use searchable fields for methods or research design and contain search interfaces that support searching the full text of articles.

Using the Literature to Support the Process of Inquiry

During the process of establishing a working topic and formal research questions, researchers also generate a series of questions and subquestions to be answered during the investigation. These same questions also guide the literature search so that specific resources are identified. Table 3.2 is an example of the types of questions and appropriate resources that can be used to frame a research study.

Implementing Your Literature Search

Interdisciplinary Dimensions of Your Potential Topic

Before beginning with even a preliminary review of literature, first consider the disciplines that impact your broad concepts. For example, workforce education will almost certainly, in addition to education literature, require an examination of some combination of business, corporate, and psychology literature; government publications; literature from public policy agencies and think tanks; and more. Each discipline and *generators* of information will focus on different dimensions of a project. The resulting breadth will provide a comprehensive perspective. Premature exclusion of potential information generators and subject disciplines may result in an incomplete study of the topic.

Research as a Cyclical, Recursive Process

Research is not a linear process. Rather, it is a cyclical, recursive process that reflects the thinking process whereby new information results in new knowledge and understanding. The iterative nature of research causes ideas to be revisited as they are influenced by new information. Necessarily, then, reviews must be conducted not just once but multiple times throughout the process for different purposes. It is common to execute the same search in the same database at a later date to re-examine the same results from a more informed perspective.

The Research Log

A systematic way to record the search process and results must be developed to prevent you from missing large segments of the literature or from unnecessarily repeating the same search. Information recorded here should parallel your notes and search results and stand as documentation of your *process*. A research log or diary, should include:

- Databases used
- Search term vocabulary used in each database, update as necessary
- Combinations of search terms and exact search statements. (*Some databases with advanced features allow you to save your search history(ies) to be re-run at a later time.*)
- Remarks about the success of your search(es)
- Notes for a subsequent search

TABLE 3.2
Research Questions (and Sub-questions) and Related Resources

Sub-questions	Type of resource to answer sub-question
What is the definition of ...? What are major trends in ...?	Subject dictionary / encyclopedias Use for definitions or overviews of concepts and terms in the context of a specialized field
How many ...?	Statistical database or web site Use statistics to understand the scale of issues, to substantiate positions, and support claims
What is the overview of past research in ...?	Literature reviews / research summaries Identify patterns or conclusions of past work
What current research studies exist about ... ?	Scholarly research journals Use to identify current issues, past research, lit. reviews, professional practice and developments
Are there recent news stories about ... ?	Newspaper articles Use newspaper articles for current perspective on issues, and application of research to real situations
Is there recent legislation on ...?	Government documents Use government publications for information produced by Congress and government agencies
Are any professional groups interested in ...?	Directories of associations Use to identify professional, trade, or consumer associations to contact, extending the range of resources beyond library and Web, to create a networking base
What does the American public think about ...?	Opinion polls or surveys Finds how individuals/groups feel about issues

Developing Effective Search Strategies

Searching is *dynamic*. Your ability to evaluate and modify search results will result in a more effective and precise search. Remember that [1] search terms often vary among databases, [2] commands may vary, but search principles remain the same, [3] computers search for matches in words and phrases, NOT meanings, [4] computers do not hint when more is available, and [5] searches usually consist of a series of queries.

Common Search Strategies

The search process can be simplified by understanding that four common search strategies are effective across many databases.

Vocabulary selection. The incorrect use of search vocabulary is the single largest cause of a failed search.

1. Be deliberate in choice of keyword versus subject heading search.

Keywords can appear in any part of a record
Subject headings (or descriptors) are official terms used by each database to categorize records by topics. Use of each of these will yield significantly different results.

Search type	Best used when...	Disadvantages
Keyword	...unsure of subject headings ...searching for terms not used as a subject heading ...words can be anywhere in a record ...good for jargon terms	Retrieves *only* what is typed–exact spelling, misspellings, etc.
Subject heading	...headings accurately describe the topic ...cluster records by a common term	Are sometimes too broad

2. Use the appropriate search terms used by each database. Headings vary among databases to express the same concept.

EXAMPLE:

ABI Inform (business)	ERIC (education)	PsycINFO (psychology)
Vocational education Employment training programs In-service training Labor force + [Continuing education or training]	Worker education Adult education Industrial education Industrial training In-plant programs Workplace literacy	Apprenticeship In-service training Management training Business education Career development
Competency-based educational tests Competency tests	Competency-based education Performance-based assessment Teacher competency tests	Minimum competency test Achievement measures Educational measurement competence

3. Tips to determine correct vocabulary.
   a. Consult the on-line or print thesaurus for each database

   OR

   Do a preliminary keyword search to find a few useful articles. Note the heading(s) and sub-heading(s) used in the best matches for your topic. Often several terms are critical to the search.
   b. Reformulate your search using those headings
   c. Continually note additional terms and add them to your search

Combination of search terms. Most searchers know that the terms AND / OR / NOT are used to combine terms (you may be familiar with their formal name of *Boolean operators* or *Boolean logic*). However, it is common for beginning researchers to apply them incorrectly when formulating a search statement. Improper use of AND / OR / NOT is the second largest cause of a failed search.

AND >> narrows << search so that ALL search TERMS must be included in the search results.

OR <<expands >> search to include ANY SINGLE ONE of the search terms in the search results.

NOT eliminates unwanted search terms.

Truncation of variant endings. The ability to search for variant endings or variant spellings (called truncation or *wildcards*) in one search statement enhances search effectiveness and speed. The most common truncation symbols are the asterisk (*) and question mark (?).

EXAMPLE:

   Child?   retrieves children, childhood, Childreth.
   Comput? retrieves computers, computing, computed

Caution: Truncating too soon results in faulty results.

EXAMPLE:

   Bee?   retrieves beer, beet, beethoven, been, bees, etc.

Limiting search results. Once initial search results are retrieved it is often useful to limit those results. The most common *limit* commands are by date, by language, or by publication type. Use the help screen for specific commands for each database.

Search Features

Look for both the common and more advanced search capabilities to maximize your searching efforts.

Common search features	Advanced search features
"field" searching	on-line thesaurus
[author, title, publication, keyword]	search history list
mark search results	recombination of existing search
sort search results	statements
display format choices	save/re-execute search statements
email / save / print options	at a later date

Troubleshooting Techniques

After each search query, troubleshoot to modify the search for improved results.

If the problem is ...	Then you should ...
...you need more current articles	...limit by date
...you need articles only in English	...limit by language
...you need to retrieve variant endings *ex.* alcohol, alcoholics, alcoholism	...use *wild card* truncation symbol
...you need to determine appropriate subject headings for a particular database	...examine good articles retrieved ...determine assigned subject headings ...search again on those terms
...you need more search terms	...use synonyms, or more specific terms, using OR
...you have many irrelevant hits	...use NOT to eliminate those terms. But, remember some *desired hits* may be eliminated also.

Resources of Special Interest

Literature Reviews / Annual Reviews

Summaries of past research and handbooks of research are excellent tools to quickly and efficiently understand the state and direction of research and the fundamental trends in content and methods in a field. Extended reviews of research can be the basis for your review of research requiring only an updated search in the journal literature. Annual reviews are additionally useful because of their currency and ability to reflect trends over a period of time. Selected examples are:

Annual review of adult learning and literacy. San Francisco: Jossey-Bass, 2000. Annual. [A project of the National Center for the Study of Adult Learning and Literacy].

Annual review of psychology. Stanford, CA: Annual Reviews, 1950–.

Annual review of sociology. Palo Alto, CA: Annual Reviews, 1975–.

Handbook of research methods in social and personality psychology
New York: Cambridge University Press, 2000.

*Handbook of research on administration. (American Educational
Research Association,* 2nd ed.). San Francisco: Jossey-Bass, 1999.

*Review of research in education. (American Educational Research
Association).* Itasca, IL: Peacock, 1973–.

Overview Sources

At the initial stages of research, it is useful to consult overview
sources to understand the organization of the area under investigation.
These summaries provide structure to researchers and are valuable
during various phases of the process, such as for definitions of terms as
they are applied within the context of the discipline. A few excellent
overview sources are:

Guide to research for educators and trainers of adults (2nd ed.).
Malabar, FL: Krieger, 2000.

Handbook of adult and continuing education. San Francisco: Jossey-
Bass, 2000.

International dictionary of adult and continuing education. London:
Routledge, 1990.

International encyclopedia of adult education and training (2nd ed.).
Pergamon, 1996.

International encyclopedia of education (Vol. 12, 2nd ed.). New
York: Pergamon, 1994.

Databases

ERIC (Education Resources Information Center)
Sponsored by the U.S. Department of Education, ERIC is the primary
database for investigation of any aspect of education research or
practice. ERIC covers two types of literature, journals and documents.

Journals (in CIJE–Current Index to Journals in Education)
Scholarly, professional and practitioner journals, many peer
reviewed; since 1969.

Documents (in RIE–Resources in Education)
Non-journal literature such as full text curriculum guides, theses,
conference papers, professional standards, research reports, etc.;
since 1966. Not peer-reviewed.

Common ERIC search interfaces:
Ask ERIC: http://askeric.org/Eric/
From ERIC. Minimal search interface; searches are difficult to limit to publication types (journals, documents, etc). Free.

ERIC Wizard: http://searcheric.org/
Sponsored by the ERIC Clearinghouse on Assessment and Evaluation. Complete ERIC database with embedded thesaurus *Look up* feature plus many more search features than AskERIC. Free.

Commercial ERIC vendors (by subscription only)
Full ERIC database available by subscription from vendors such as Cambridge Scientific Abstracts or Silver Platter. Check subscriptions available at your institution.

EDRS–ERIC Document Retrieval Service (by subscription only)
Full text of most ERIC documents since 1993, complete ERIC indexes from 1966.

Education Complete (ProQuest)
More than 550 journals, 300+ full text, covering primary, secondary, and higher education, and behavioral sciences. Coverage varies often beginning in the 1990s.

PsycINFO (psychology)
Primary resource for psychology and related discipline, e.g., education, organizational management, and learning behavior. Includes journals, book chapters, literature reviews. Electronic version since 1987.

ABI/INFORM (business)
An extensive business-oriented database for industry trends, human resources, training, and more.

Dissertation Abstracts
Primary source for 1.4 million doctoral dissertations and selected masters theses from 1000+ North American and European universities. Over 1000 institutions are represented. Dissertations from institutions that don't participate can be requested for loan directly from the school.

Policy File (Public Policy Research & Analysis)
Documents and publications from public policy think tanks, university research programs, research organizations and publishers. Includes many hypertext links to original documents.

Government Publications

Congressional and legislative information
Thomas
From the U.S. government, includes major legislation, the Congressional Record, Bill summaries and status, "Hot Bills," etc.

Congressional Universe
Includes an index of congressional publications since 1970, legislative histories, congressional testimony, and more.

Federal government agencies
FirstGov
One-stop access to all online U.S. Federal Government resources, plus links to state and local information.

Statistical Resources

National Center for Education Statistics; http://www.nces.ed.gov
Includes Encyclopedia of ED Statistics (http://www.nces.ed.gov/edstats/); Digest of Education Statistics, Condition of Education Statistics, Projections of Education Statistics to 2008, Education Indicators: An International Perspective, and Youth Indicators 1996.

FedStats; http://www.fedstats.gov/
Links to statistical resources produced by more than 70 federal government agencies.

U.S. Census Bureau; http://www.census.gov/
A variety of social, economic, political and cultural statistics gathered by the U.S. government.

University of Michigan Documents Center
Contains an extensive collection of government statistics.
http://www.lib.umich.edu/libhome/Documents.center/

Statistical Universe
Index to statistical data in federal agency government publications, many full text.

Statistical Abstracts of the United States
The National Data Book contains a collection of statistics on social and economic conditions in the U.S. and selected international data.
http://www.census.gov/statab/www/

Citation Indexes (Cited Reference Searching)

Cited reference searching is useful to determine what newer works have cited an older work in their bibliographies. In contrast to the more typical retrospective search, cited reference searching lets you monitor the growth or acceptance of a research premise and update your research to identify more recent works that have cited an earlier know work. Discipline-related citation indexes are:

Social Science Citation Index, 1956–.

Science Citation Index, 1955–.

Arts and Humanities Citation Index, 1976–.

The on-line Web versions of these three indexes are found at the web site, *Web of Science,* since 1986.

E-mail, Listservs, and Newsgroups

Listservs and newsgroups provide a vehicle for informal communication, and support the formation of networks of scholars and professionals for communication in scholarly, pedagogical and professional activities. Several directories are of particular interest to educational research:

The Directory of Scholarly and Professional E-Conferences
http://www.n2h2.com/KOVACS/

AERA listservs (American Educational Research Association)
http://www.aera.net/resource/listserv.htm

EdWeb E-Mail Discussion Lists and Electronic Journals
http://edweb.gsn.org/lists.html

Data Sets for Research

Datasets are compilations of data elements that represent the characteristics of a systematically drawn sample of observations. Beyond primary datasets that are collected and compiled by individual researchers, secondary datasets collected and compiled by individuals or agencies may be of great value (see Chapter 16 for a detailed discussion of secondary data). Collections of datasets are available from various sources, the most notable being the Inter-university Consortium for Political and Social Research (ICPSR), located within the Institute for Social Research at the University of Michigan, ICPSR provides dataset access through institutional membership.

Examples of datasets for educational research include the Common Core of Data, Higher Education General Information Survey, National Assessment of Educational Progress, National Household Education Survey, Participation in Adult Education, and Integrated Postsecondary Education Data System (Pennsylvania State University Libraries, 2000). http://www.libraries.psu.edu/crsw/datasets/datasetsmain.htm

Selected Resources of Related Interest

Databases

America: History and Life
State and local historical journals, humanities and social science journals, book and media reviews, citations to published books, and dissertations.

Associations Unlimited
On-line directory of associations: International, national, regional, and state, with links to web sites.

Contemporary Women's Issues
Full text sources covering global information on women.

Ethnic NewsWatch
A comprehensive full text database of the newspapers, magazines and journals of the ethnic, minority and native press.

GenderWatch
A full text database focusing on the impact of gender across a broad spectrum including public policy, sociology and contemporary culture, education, business, and more.

PAIS (Public Affairs Information Service Bulletin)
Contemporary social and public policy issues.

Sociological Abstracts
Covers sociology, social work, and other social sciences; provides an international scope.

News Sources

Newspaper databases provide current perspectives, case study profiles, and primary source data. Many databases provide access to newspapers such as Academic Universe, ProQuest, and NewsLibrary.com

Aggregator Databases

Aggregator databases are collections of databases on a variety of subjects, packaged and sold together, with a common search interface for simplified user access. Sophisticated researchers must be familiar not only with primary content databases but also with the aggregator and vendor databases available at their institutions. Some examples are:

Academic Universe
Provides access to a wide range of news, business, legal, and reference information. Covers many news sources for 20 years. Court cases and statutes from all federal and state jurisdictions are included. Most resources can be searched in full text.

Proquest
Access to business, news, education, medicine, psychology, and more, depending on subscription.

UnCover
Over 15,000 journals on all subjects. Primarily a table of contents database with embedded document delivery available for a fee.

Materials Beyond Your *Home* Library

No matter how extensive any single library collection, there will almost always be a need to identify and obtain materials from other institutions. Several resources are exceptionally comprehensive in listing materials owned by many other libraries.

WorldCAT
Over 38 million records for books, periodicals, magazines, software, and more, including records for material as early as the 11th century.

WebCATS: Library Catalogues on the Web
Links to online catalogs with geographical, library type and vendor indexes. http://library.usask.ca/hywebcat/

Publishers Catalogs Home Pages
Includes over 6,000 U.S. and international publishers, with indexes by country, topic, or type of material. http://www.lights.com/publisher/

Selected Web Sites

American Psychological Association
Report of the "School–to–Work Task Force: How Psychology Can Contribute to the School–to–Work Opportunities Movement." http://www.apa.org/pubinfo/school/page29.html

Career and Work Links
Extensive links prepared by the Indiana Career and Postsecondary Advancement Center. http://icpac.indiana.edu/

CASAS (Comprehensive Adult Student Assessment System)
A national leader in adult education and training systems, provides essential tools and resources for assessment, instruction and evaluation. http://www.casas.org

Center on Education and Work (CEW)
At the University of Wisconsin–Madison CEW undertakes research, development, and activities to strengthen the connections among educational institutions, workplaces, communities, and families. http://www.cew.wisc.edu/cew/

Education World School Issues Center
Articles from Education World archive about school-to-work issues. http://www.education-world.com/a_issues/archives/sch_to_work.shtml

ERIC Clearinghouse on Adult, Career, and Vocational Education
A subset of the ERIC clearinghouse system focusing on career and vocational education. Located in Columbus, Ohio. http://ericacve.org/

International Career Development Library (ICDL)
Full-text resources for counselors, educators, workforce development personnel, and others who provide career development services. http://icdl.uncg.edu/

Making School–to–Work Opportunities Happen for Youth with Disabilities
   Sponsored by the National Transition Alliance for Youth with Disabilities. Overviews the School-to-Work Opportunities Act, disability resources, related legislation and Americans with Disabilities Act (ADA) Fact Sheet. http://www.dssc.org/nta/html/stw_fact.htm

National Association of Manufacturers Center for Workforce Success
Describes the Center's programs and projects, with links to workforce education-related sites. http://www.nam.org/workforce/

The National Center on the Educational Quality of the Workforce
A collaborative endeavor between the Wharton School and University of Pennsylvania's Institute for Research on Higher Education, to determine how better connections between employers, schools, students/workers, and public policy, would bolster economic competitiveness. http://www.irhe.upenn.edu/centers/ctrs-prog3.html

National Institute for Work and Learning
Seeks to bring work, education, government, and community together around a shared goal of creating effective collaborative relationships

among institutions to ensure that education and work are treated as lifelong pursuits. http://www.aed.org/ publications/sch2work.html

National Labor Management Association
School to Work links. http://www.nlma.org/ s2work.htm

National Leadership Institute for Workforce Excellence
Provides leadership development information, training, and tools for the leaders of the workforce development system. http://www.wibleadership.com/index.cfm

National Skill Standards Board
Sponsored by the U.S. Departments of Education and Labor to demonstrate pilot projects that serve as "living laboratories of a voluntary national skill standards system." http://www.nssb.org/ projects.htm

National STW Learning and Information Center
School–to–Work links for educators, employers, labor, parents and students. Links to partnerships, grants, legislation, resources, and more. http://www.stw.ed.gov/

Office of Vocational and Adult Education (OVAE)
From the U.S. Department of Education, identifies programs, grants, and events related to adult and vocational education, school-to-work; high school reform, community colleges, correctional education, tribal colleges and universities, community technology centers, empowerment zones and enterprise communities, and teacher development activities. http://www.ed.gov/offices/OVAE/

Pennsylvania School-To-Work Resources Center
Extensive state-wide and regional links. The Center, at Penn State, supports the Pennsylvania School-to-Work Opportunities Office, the Interagency Team, and the Local/Regional Partnership structure. http://www.pastw.psu.edu

References

American Psychological Association. (1997). *Journals in psychology* (5th ed.). Washington, DC: Author.

Arms, W. Y. (2000). *Digital libraries*. Cambridge, MA: MIT Press.

Association of College and Research Libraries. (2000). *Information literacy competency standards for higher education*. Retrieved from the World Wide Web: http://www.ala.org/acrl/ilcomstan.html

Cabell, D. W. E. (Ed.). (1994). *Cabell's directory of publishing opportunities in accounting, economics and finance.* Beaumont, TX: Cabell.

Cabell, D. W. E. (Ed.). (1995). *Cabell's directory of publishing opportunities in management and marketing* (6th ed.). Beaumont, TX: Cabell.

Cabell, D. W. E. (Ed.). (1998). *Cabell's directory of publishing opportunities in education* (Vol. 2, 5th ed.). Beaumont, TX: Cabell.

Kovacs, D. K. (2000). *The directory of scholarly and professional e-conferences.* Retrieved from the World Wide Web: http://www.n2h2.com/KOVACS/

Loke, W. H. (1990). *A guide to journals in psychology and education.* Metuchen, NJ: Scarecrow Press.

Pennsylvania State University Libraries. (1999). *Information literacy and you, evaluating your search.* Retrieved from the World Wide Web: http://www.libraries.psu.edu/crsweb/infolit/andyou/mod7/mod7main.htm

Pennsylvania State University Libraries. (2000). *Data sets for research.* Retrieved from the World Wide Web: http://www.libraries.psu.edu/crsweb/datasets/datasetsmain.htm

Pyrczak, F. (1999). *Evaluating research in academic journals: A practical guide to realistic evaluation.* Los Angeles: Pyrczak.

Stout, L. (1991). *Records along the time line.* Unpublished manuscript, University Park, Pennsylvania State University.

Tomlins, C. L. (1998). *Wave of the present: The scholarly journal on the edge of the internet.* New York: American Council of Learned Societies.

U.S. Department of Commerce, National Telecommunications and Information Administration. (2000). *Digital divide web site.* Retrieved from the World Wide Web: http://www.digitaldivide.gov/

Ward, J. W. (1997). *Search strategies in mass communication* (3rd ed.). New York: Longman.

Chapter 4

Elements of an Introduction Chapter

Saundra Wall Williams and James L. Burrow

The old communication adage applies—Tell them what you plan to tell them; Tell them; Tell them what you told them. That seems to be the philosophy guiding the development of a dissertation. There will certainly be some redundancy in your dissertation, but there is a purpose for that redundancy. The first chapter begins the formal writing process and "sets the stage" for the full research report that follows in subsequent chapters. It is the "tell them what you will tell them" phase of your research report.

Points of View Guide Your Writing

The first chapter of doctoral dissertations, as well as introductory sections to scholarly journal articles, are developed in response to several points of view. The introduction should indicate what these points of view are and why you are (and they should be) sensitive to them. First, remember that the first chapter of the dissertation is written in advance of the study as part of the research proposal. At many universities doctoral students are routinely asked to prepare and submit a proposal that includes significant elements of, if not the entire, first three chapters of the dissertation. Since Chapter 1 is most important for detailing the purpose(s) of your intended investigation, we remind you to work closely with your dissertation advisor and members of your doctoral committee. Regardless of how good you think your work is, the perspectives of these individuals are critical to your success.

The second point of view is personal. As researcher you need to be thoughtful, thorough, objective, and logical in your research plan. The introduction chapter provides a structure for clearly describing the critical decisions you have made about your research plan. Taking some time, up front, to think about each of the elements important to the success of your study should help you to write a clear description of the problem, purpose, and theoretical framework of your work. The clearer this information is initially the more defensible and less difficulties you should experience as you defend and then conduct your research.

A third point of view to consider while preparing Chapter 1 is the research consumer, people who will read your dissertation to determine its use and applicability in practice or to replicate or extend your work. Chapter 1 provides a "quick read" for research consumers to acquire an initial understanding of the purpose, context, and methods involved in your investigation. Your ability to effectively communicate the context and structure of your study will determine whether researchers and research consumers will continue with an in-depth review of your work.

Purposes of the Introduction Chapter

The first chapter of a doctoral dissertation should overview the study and is intended to answer three broad questions: [1] What is the purpose of the research? [2] What is the context of the research? [3] How will the research be conducted?

The actual organization of Chapter 1 will change depending on the type of research being conducted, the style manual used, and specific requirements of the institution where the research is conducted. However, several common elements will be included no matter how the chapter is structured including an rationale or context of the study, the specific purpose of the study and its significance, the research paradigm and design parameters, delimitations of the study, and, possibly, a definition of key terms (See Appendix).

The first chapter of your dissertation plays an important role in introducing the major elements of your investigation in a clear and meaningful way to readers. What you say in the 15 or so pages that will compose Chapter 1 has a direct relationship to the remaining chapters. Each succeeding chapter expands on the fundamental aspects of your study that has been established in the introductory section. Once readers understand the basic structure of your study, they will be better able to appreciate and understand an extended review of the relevant literature, the research design and method, sample, analysis of data, and conclusions drawn from completed investigation.

Common Elements of Chapter One

Introduction

The introduction section needs to be carefully crafted. It will normally be relatively short (typically 3-4 pages), but serves as the first opportunity to preview your study and interest the reader in the uniqueness of your research. According to Creswell (1994), the introduction "must (a) create reader interest in the topic, (b) establish the problem that leads to the study, (c) place the study within the larger context of the scholarly literature, and (d) reach out to a specific audience" (p. 42).

A common problem found in many introductions is providing too much information when readers are just beginning to learn about the study. The introduction should provide a *brief* frame of reference that can help readers understand the design adopted and, later, data interpretation. If the context is cast too broadly or provides excessive detail readers may have difficulty developing the appropriate perspective of the study. Remember that there will be adequate opportunity for detailed discussion of relevant literature, sample characteristics, methods, and analysis later in the dissertation.

On the other hand, the introduction needs to be precise. It should offer a clear context that explains the specific reasons for conducting the study its importance within the framework of previous research and relevant practice. A clear rationale detailing the need for the study and the potential value of expected findings must also be described. Care should be taken to avoid being overly dramatic or presenting a perception of researcher bias.

There is no single standard for structuring the introduction. However, a review of many studies suggests a sequence that guides the reader efficiently and effectively toward recognizing the issue under study. That sequence usually begins with a few paragraphs intended to attract readers' interest and attention in the issue to be studied. These paragraphs may describe a common problem faced by practitioners or present particularly meaningful or memorable statistics or other facts that highlight the issue.

Following the introductory paragraphs the issue or problem to be studied is presented. At this point the identification of the issue is not the formal and detailed problem statement or research questions that define the study. Those more precise statements will be included later. However, it is important that the issue under studied is evident to the reader. In other words, it should not be hidden in the introductory paragraphs nor should it be stated so generally that readers are unsure of the main issue. At this point it may be stated in a more practice-based or practical context than the formal statements that will effectively guide the research. But the intent of the study should be clear from these introductory sentences.

To complete the introduction, a preview of related research is presented. Because it is a part of the introduction and will be developed in greater depth in later sections, this research preview is typically limited to no more that two or three pages. The purpose of the literature preview is to establish connections between the current study and previous research. "Research-based knowledge, whether in the form of laws, theories, facts, information, or informed speculation, is always situated in a context" (Locke, Silverman, & Spirduso, 1998, p. 87). This preview identifies factors or variables important to the study, highlights key studies of those factors, and emphasizes major areas of agreement and disagreement as well as apparent deficiencies in the literature (Locke, Spirduso, & Silverman, 1993).

Purpose and Its Significance

It could be suggested that the most important part of planning and then reporting research is a clear purpose or problem. Questions or issues resulting from practice that become the focus for research are often complex. It will not be possible to address the many facets of an issue in one study. An individual study will need a narrow focus to be manageable and, ultimately, to become a meaningful part of a body of research contributing to the understanding of larger questions or issues.

Many beginning researchers struggle with moving from having a broad interest area to developing a clear statement of purpose. As with other parts of any dissertation or research article the actual structure and detail of the purpose and problem will vary depending on the research paradigm and preferences of individual researchers, graduate committees, and institutions. Whatever the structure, the statement that describes the purpose of your research should be clear and consistent throughout the dissertation.

The presentation of the purpose in Chapter 1 provides the first opportunity to define your investigation. Because of its importance and the meaning conveyed to readers, a purpose statement should be specific and concise, often one or two sentences and seldom more than a paragraph. The purpose statement describes the broader problem or issue that is the focus of the research, population, key variables or factors that were studied, and important elements of the research design

Following the purpose statement, a rationale for or significance of the purpose is developed. While the earlier preview of related research in the introductory section provides a context for the study in relation to other studies, the rationale offers the researcher's perspective about the importance of the study. Often, importance is stated in terms of improving practice, advancing theory, or answering questions posed in the literature. Creswell (1994) suggests that significance can be demonstrated from the viewpoints of researchers, practitioners, and policymakers. Locke et al. (1998) recommend calling attention to gaps in knowledge (deficiencies), conflicting findings (inconsistencies), or the need to refine previous studies. Whenever possible the statements of noted experts and research findings from the literature are cited to lend support to the significance of the current research.

Once again, since this is the introductory chapter, the rationale does not need to be lengthy. Usually a couple of pages is sufficient. However, the section must be logical and convincing. Readers should understand why the research has been conducted and its potential value to the area of study within the context of the research design.

In almost all quantitative studies the first chapter will introduce specific research questions that guide the study. Research questions are frequently, although not always, developed for qualitative studies as well. Since research questions are extensions and more precise specifications of the purpose, they are usually presented in the same section as the purpose statement. Alternatively, they can be presented in a separate section immediately following the purpose statement. Typically, since a rationale for the purpose has already been presented, there is little need for any discussion of the research questions (Krathwohl, 1988). In quantitative research reports statements of research hypotheses in their null or directional form or both are often presented in Chapter 1. If hypotheses are introduced, each should be clearly matched with the research question from which it was formulated. In qualitative studies the research questions take two forms. The "grand tour question" (Werner & Schoepfle, 1987) or a guiding hypothesis (Marshall & Rossman, 1994) is followed by subquestions (Creswell, 1994; Miles & Huberman, 1984).

Research Paradigm

The approach used to make research design decisions evolves from beliefs about the nature of the environment and the evidence to be studied. Two contrasting paradigms are available for designing studies: qualitative and quantitative (see Chapter 1). Increasingly, investigators have combined these two paradigms for a mixed methods approach (see Chapter 7). Each paradigm has a very different view of the research environment and the types of evidence necessary to study an issue or problem. Within each paradigm there are many alternatives for designing the study method, but the method needs to be consistent with the paradigm.

An important consideration for those who read your dissertation is whether or not an appropriate and strong research design was used. You will develop a very detailed description and discussion of the method later in the dissertation, but this initial presentation in Chapter 1 helps the reader understand how the study was structured.

There is often debate among scholars whether a qualitative or quantitative approach to research is appropriate. There is no need within your dissertation to specifically justify the choice of paradigms. That was a thoughtful decision you as researcher carefully made when planning the study. Rather it is important to identify the paradigm and provide adequate detail of the method used to conduct the study. While described at an introductory level the section should clearly identify the environment in which the study is completed, and data collection and analysis procedures. We discuss unique aspects of introducing each paradigm later in this chapter.

Delimitations and Limitations

Whenever specific design decisions have been made that narrow the scope of the study or pose a potential weaknesses, the investigator has an obligation to call them to the attention of readers. These cautions are usually a part of the first chapter of dissertation. They may be specifically discussed in a separate section or may be included within the preview of research design and methods.

Delimitations provide specific descriptions of decisions made about the sample, environment, variable characteristics or method that are narrower than would typically be anticipated from the general description of the research design. Delimitations of a study act as boundaries or parameters that may affect the replacability or generalizability of the investigation.

Limitations are procedural issues that suggest the need for caution in interpreting the findings. Often in "real world" research there are design elements that cannot be implemented in an ideal way or potential confounding variables. Here, then, readers are cautioned by clearly identifying any design "imperfections."

Definition of Key Terms

In a dissertation you must be precise and explicit in the terms and language you use. Defining key terms used in the study will help readers understand the context in which the words are being used, as well as any unusual or restricted meaning (Castetter & Heisler, 1977). A list of key terms can also help with keeping language consistent throughout the dissertation. Variables pertinent to the particular study design should be operationally defined, as well as terms that will help the reader more easily understand the research. Creswell (1994) provides guidance on the types of terms to define.

> 1. Define terms that individuals outside the field of study may not understand. 2. Define terms when they first appear so that a reader does not read ahead in the proposal operating with one set of definitions only to find out later that the author is using a different set. 3. Define terms introduced in all sections of the research plan. (p. 106)

Design Parameters of the Study

Chapter 1 introduces the research plan by describing the study's design. Researchers and consumers need to know how the study was designed and implemented to judge its quality and applicability. There are typically many methodological approaches that can be taken when addressing an issue or problem. Readers will want to now what methods were used to conduct the research and reasons for the choices.

A description of design parameters usually begins with the research question(s), identification of the people who are the focus of the study, and an outline of the methods used. While all studies will have a research plan the description will be quite different based on whether a qualitative or quantitative methodology is used. Those differences are explored next.

Introducing Qualitative Research Designs

Qualitative research methods allow you to uncover the meaning of a phenomenon for those involved with little disruption of the natural setting. Qualitative methods are seen as processes of systematic inquiry how people attempt to make sense of their experience and guide their actions, thoughts and attitudes about phenomena. Qualitative methods are well suited for research in education because these methods yield to the improvement of practice that comes from understanding the experiences of those involved. Qualitative methods, which include participant observations, interviewing, focus groups, and document analysis of texts, are all inductive techniques that allow for the development of theory on which hypotheses can be deduced and tested. (Granafaki 1996; Merriam & Simpson, 1995).

Chapter 1 of the dissertation should introduce the qualitative research design being employed in the study. This section should cover the assumptions and rationale for adopting a qualitative design, the type of qualitative design used, the role of the researcher, data collection and analysis procedures, and methods for verifying data (Creswell, 1994). These elements may seem to be an abundance of methodology information for Chapter 1, but remember that the first chapter of your dissertation needs to provide an understanding of the purpose, context and method of your investigation. Although these elements are usually detailed in a later section of the dissertation (often Chapter 3), they must be introduced and described in reasonable detail in Chapter 1.

Assumptions and Rationale for Qualitative Designs

When a qualitative design is being used Chapter 1 should provide the rationale and associated assumptions for selecting a qualitative design. A strong rationale should be made for the choice of a qualitative design in one or two paragraphs. The rationale and assumptions should link directly to both the purpose of the study and the research questions and must emphasize description, discovery, explanation, or exploration (Rudestam & Newton, 1992).

Type of Qualitative Design Used

Description of the qualitative design introduces readers to the specific method of inquiry used to address the research questions. There are nine common types of qualitative research: basic or generic, ethnography, phenomenology, grounded theory, case study, action, participatory, critical and feminist (Merriam, 1998; Merriam & Simpson, 1995). Each type of qualitative design has specific characteristics. Hence, the type of qualitative design chosen must reflect the rationale, purpose, and research questions of your study. For example, a summary of the design selected might address the discipline field where the design originated, a definition of the design, various data collection and data analysis processes associated with the design, and other special characteristics associated with the design (Creswell, 1994).

Role of the Researcher

The role of the researcher is a critical element in all types of qualitative research, since investigators are the primary instrument for data collection and analysis (Creswell, 1998; Merriam & Simpson, 1995). In this section of Chapter 1, give the reader a clear description of the specific role(s) you, as the researcher, played. For example, clearly describe your role in participant selection, data collection and data analysis. In addition, identify any viewpoints, biases, values, or judgements that may have had influence while completing the research.

Participant(s) in Qualitative Research

Research participants in qualitative studies could be people, an organization, or written, visual, or oral documents. When describing the research participant(s) in Chapter 1, you should answer five basic questions.

- Who are the participants in the study and where are they located?
- Why were participants selected to participate in the study?
- What are the characteristics of participants (e.g., race, gender, age, occupation, organization, etc.)?
- How many participants were included?
- Because all participants should remain anonymous, answer these questions without revealing the identity of participants.

Data Collection Procedures

There are three primary ways to collect data for qualitative research: participant observations, interviewing (individual and group), and document analysis (written, oral, or visual). In the Chapter 1 discussion of methods, give a brief description of the data collection procedure(s) used. Also give a rationale for and identify any parameters of the data collection procedure you chose.

The rationale must support and give reasons for the selected data collection method. The rationale is usually connected closely to the purpose of the study and research questions. It also may be guided by the participants of the investigation or the research environment. If more than one data collection method is used, describe and give a rationale for the choice and use of each one. For example, if you utilized participant observation and individual interviews, both these methods should be addressed in the Chapter 1 preview.

Data Analysis Procedures

There is no one specific way to describe the analysis of qualitative data. However, it is important to highlight the analysis procedures in Chapter 1. Briefly describe the activities you engaged in. If you conducted your data collection and data analysis simultaneously, then say so. A practical way to present the data analysis procedures is by summarizing them in a list, table, or matrix.

Methods for Verifying Data

The qualitative research design section of Chapter 1 should conclude with a summary of how you determined and maintained the quality of the research data through the data collection and data analysis steps. Elements of validity and reliability are important in any kind of research. In order for readers to believe and trust the findings of your study a brief discussion of internal validity, reliability, and external validity should be provided. If a combination of methods (triangulation) was used, it should be stated in this section. Verification of data should also state any limitations for generalizing the findings and delimitations for narrowing the scope of or replicating the study.

Introducing Quantitative Research Designs

Quantitative research evolves from the perspective that investigators are independent from the object of study and objective in observation, reporting, and analysis of information. Well-accepted, systematic, and scientific research designs and methods are used to address precise research questions.

The approach to developing answers to problems and issues in quantitative research is deductive. Research moves through a process of identifying variables and their relationships, subjecting the relationships to carefully designed and managed tests, and using findings to better understand and predict relationships. Because of the very structured and precise nature of quantitative research, researchers are expected to provide clear specification of elements in the research design. Chapter 1 introduces each of the elements of the design including the type of study, population and sample, variables, data collection methods, instrumentation, and data analysis procedures.

Type of Study

Quantitative studies are organized within two broad types: experiments and surveys. There are a range of experiments based on the identification and control of variables, assignment of subjects to experimental and control groups, and treatments. Each, however, requires that the conditions of the experiment and the treatment are clearly described. Surveys gather information without experimental control or manipulation. Data are gathered through questionnaires or interviews administered to a carefully identified and selected set of respondents. With surveys, researchers describe the purpose of the survey and the factors to be tested that influence survey design.

Population and Sample

The introductory description of the population and sample begins with identifying relevant characteristics of the individuals (or groups, organizations, etc.) who are the primary focus of the study and to whom the findings can be generalized. Then, sampling procedures and the size of the sample are identified. Procedures for assigning participants to treatment groups are also mentioned, if appropriate for the study.

Study Variables

A key to quantitative research is the identification and classification of research variables, that is, the characteristics or qualities being studied. Each variable should be introduced, described in adequate detail for understanding, and classified as independent, dependent, or other. Definitions and measures of variables should be consistent with use in related research. Any difference should be clearly and specifically identified with accompanying reasons for the change.

If research hypotheses have not been introduced in another section of Chapter 1, they can be included here. Hypotheses will describe the relationships to be studied among the identified variables.

Data Collection Methods

This limited preview of the research methods used in the study serves to demonstrate the systematic and objective approach of the researcher. It allows the reader to make an initial judgement about the quality of the research.

If a survey method is used, describe the important procedures used to administer the survey including any pre-testing and follow-up activities. With an experimental study, the type of experimental design needs to be identified. Then, operation of the experiment including time frame, introducing and managing the treatment, controls applied, and data collection procedures is overviewed.

Instrumentation

Whether a survey or experiment, instruments selected for data collection may also be discussed in Chapter 1. The introductory discussion includes a brief review of the nature and structure of each instrument, the relationship of study variables and the instrument's items, scale construction, the source of the instrument if previously developed, procedures used to design and test instruments, and validity and reliability criteria.

Data Analysis

Data analysis procedures range from simple to complex. The description in Chapter 1 should be reasonably straightforward leaving the more detailed discussion for later chapters. Readers will want to know the types of data that will be used to describe participants and variables and the way those descriptive data will be reported. The types of statistics to be used to make comparisons of variables and to test hypotheses may also be identified. A brief rationale for the decisions about statistical tests is usually included to describe the relationship between the nature of the data collected and the statistic(s) selected. In some dissertations—particularly those with an extended time frame, multiple measures, or complex relationships—the data analysis procedures are outlined and the statistical program(s) used is identified.

Concluding Chapter One

Chapter 1 should conclude with a summary (usually 1–2 paragraphs) of the information presented in the chapter. The elements of the introductory chapter—the problem or issue that led to the study, purpose of the study, research questions or hypotheses, theoretical framework, significance, research design, and limitations and delimitations—should be summarized in this section. The summary reminds the reader of key elements in the study and prepares for the transition to the remaining chapters.

Many researchers choose to provide a preview of the organization of the remainder of the dissertation at the end of Chapter 1. While quantitative studies often have a common organization and sequence of chapters there are some variations. Qualitative studies frequently are organized in quite different ways to fit the nature of the research design and the presentation, analysis, and discussion of data. It is helpful to prepare readers for detailed study of the investigation especially when the chapter organization and content is different than traditional organization. You can also provide a paragraph on the organization of the remainder of the study.

References

Castetter, W., & Heisler, R. (1977). *Developing and defending a dissertation proposal.* Philadelphia: University of Pennsylvania, Graduate School of Education, Center for Field Studies.

Creswell, J. (1994). *Research design: Qualitative and quantitative approaches.* Thousand Oaks, CA: Sage.

Creswell, J. (1998). *Qualitative inquiry and research design: Choosing among five traditions.* Thousand Oaks, CA: Sage.

Grafanaki, S. (1996). How research can change the researcher: The need for sensitivity, flexibility and ethical boundaries in conducting qualitative research in counseling/psychotherapy. *British Journal of Guidance and Counseling, 24,* 329.

Krathwohl, D. (1988). *How to prepare a research proposal.* Syracuse, NY: Syracuse University Press.

Locke, L. F., Spirduso, W. W., & Silverman, S. J. (1993). *Proposals that work: A guide for planning dissertations and grant proposals* (3rd ed.). Newbury Park, CA: Sage.

Locke, L. F., Silverman, S. J., & Spirduso, W. W. (1998). *Reading and understanding research.* Thousand Oaks, CA: Sage.

Marshall, C., & Rossman, G. (1994). *Designing qualitative research.* Thousand Oaks, CA: Sage.

Merriam, S. (1998). *Qualitative research and case study applications in education.* San Francisco: Jossey-Bass.

Merriam, S., & Simpson, E. (1995). *A guide to research for educators and trainers of adults* (2nd ed.). Malabar, FL: Krieger.

Miles, M., & Huberman, A. (1989). *A qualitative data analysis: A sourcebook of new methods.* Beverly Hills, CA: Sage.

Rudestam, K., & Newton, R. (1992). *Surviving your dissertation: A comprehensive guide to content and process.* Thousand Oaks, CA: Sage.

Werner, O., & Schoepfle, G. (1987). *Systematic fieldwork: Foundation of ethnography and interviewing.* Newbury Park, CA: Sage.

APPENDIX
Chapter 1 Checklist

The following checklist is provided as a review of the essential content of this chapter and as a resource to plan the development of Chapter 1 of your dissertation.

INTRODUCTION
• Does the Introduction preview the study and interest the reader in the uniqueness of your research?
• Is the issue or problem to be studied presented?
• Does a research overview establish connections between the current study and previous research?

PURPOSE AND SIGNIFICANCE OF STUDY
• Is there a specific and concise statement of the focus of the research, the population, key variables or factors that will be studied, and important elements of the research design?
• Is a specific rationale for the purpose provided?
• Is there a discussion of how this research will contribute to or enhance the current body of knowledge and practice in the field?
• If appropriate, are there specific research questions or hypotheses stated that are consistent with the issue being studied and the research design?

DELIMITATIONS AND LIMITATIONS
• Are critical delimitations and limitations identified?
• Was a rationale for the delimitations provided?
• Was the reader assured of how limitations would be addressed?
• Does the discussion of delimitations and limitations specifically describe how the generalizability will be affected?

DEFINITION OF TERMS

- Are important and unique terms used in the dissertation defined?
- Are the definitions stated with clarity and precision?

RESEARCH DESIGN (QUALITATIVE)

- Is a rationale for using the qualitative design provided consistent with the issue and environment of the research?
- What type of qualitative design was used in the study?
- What was the role of the researcher?
- Have the participants/subjects been described?
- What were the data collection and analysis procedures?
- What methods were used to verify the study?

RESEARCH DESIGN (QUANTITATIVE)

- What type of quantitative design was used in the study?
- Was the population and sampling procedures described?
- Are all variables identified and classified?
- Are important data collection methods identified?
- Did you describe how all instruments were developed?
- Are data analysis procedures and statistics appropriate for the research questions, hypotheses, and data?

SUMMARY OF CHAPTER 1

- Is there a summary of all the elements of Chapter One?
- Do readers know what will be presented in the remainder of the dissertation?

Chapter 5

Developing a Theoretical Framework

Gregory C. Petty

Begin your research with the end in mind. This is a good way to justify the development of a solid theory for your research. There are a lot of reasons to develop a theoretical framework and just as many methods for this development. As you begin your struggle to develop a good research plan several salient points can be made regarding the application of your research methodology. This chapter will focus on the development of this plan.

The obvious question to begin with is: Why do research? Of any kind? medical? scientific? geographic? educational? The answer lies within each of us, because the desire to know, in some cases to know for the sake of knowing, is why we do research. For some conducting research may be for the purpose of improving the lives of others. Developing a good idea and if possible having a passion for conducting research is a good start. Unfortunately, too many students seeking a topic for a thesis or dissertation cannot find a topic where the "So what?" question can be easily answered.

The problem is: How can I do good and accurate research? versus promoting my beliefs (also known as personal bias). Let's take a latter day wives' tale: Ear infections must be treated with antibiotics for 10 days. Research evidence: With the emergence of bacteria resistant to common antibiotics, there has been much written in the pediatric literature concerning either short or non-treatment of middle ear infections. The Dutch have been using an initial non-treatment approach for many years with good success and the rate of antibiotic-resistant S. Pneumoniae, a common cause of ear infections, is less than 1 per cent in the Netherlands in contrast to a 25% rate in Boston. The Dutch approach is to treat the ear pain with pain medication, acetaminophen, and for children less than two years of age, recheck them in the office in 24 hours and again at 48 hours. If not improved at either 24 or 48 hours antibiotics are started. For those children older than two, antibiotics are only used if there is no improvement in symptoms in 3 days. The success of the Dutch approach is based on the finding from many studies that up to 80 per cent of children with ear infection that are treated with a placebo recover (http://members.aol.com/tireswing/otitis.html#art1).

Interesting, you say. Good research, I say. This is an example of research with a good theoretical framework with findings and conclusions that are published for the purpose of improving the lives of many people by sharing this useful information (in this case via the Internet) to as many people (worldwide) as possible. As the example shows, good research applied with proper scientific methods can be used to dispel old or new rumors or fables. Unfortunately, exploration of new worlds and dispelling old wives tales are the jobs for other people and there are very few new worlds left for the rest of us to explore. Today we do good research to answer questions that we have regarding issues that impact our profession, our students, and our life.

Importance of Belief in Developing a Theoretical Framework

Forming a Sense of Conviction

Most people use strategies other than the scientific method to make sense of things or even to answer their curious minds. Philosophers, novelists, theologians and others seeking answers offer a coherent picture of the world and present a plausible scenario for the occurrence of events. They do not use the scientific method to organize their ideas and give us information, but they do contribute to our fixation of belief.

Charles S. Peirce (1839-1914), an American philosopher whose work had a strong influence on William James, the founder of experimental psychology in the US, suggested four distinct strategies for what he called the "fixation of belief." Peirce (pronounced "purse") described these strategies for the formulation of a sense of conviction as: [1] tenacity, [2] authority, [3] *a priori* method, and [4] the scientific method. Each strategy essentially contains a formula or guiding principle that, once it becomes inculcated as a habit of mind, influences whether we will draw one inference rather that another in a given situation (Peirce, 1966).

Peirce believed the most primitive method for fixing belief was tenacity. He said people cling stubbornly (tenaciously) to beliefs or claims just because they seem obvious or make "common sense". Of course clinging to an ideal is problematic because sometimes the belief is based on an illusion. Like an ostrich that buries its head in the sand, people who cling to false ideas (i.e., dogmatic or closed-minded people) go through life systematically excluding anything that might change their beliefs (Rokeach, 1960). Sometimes an entire society seems to have fallen victim to false ideas, and it is not easy to shake them loose or to open up dogmatic minds. For example, for centuries people considered it obvious that the earth is fixed and immobile, and that it is at the center of the universe. Elaborate explanations using myths to embellish this belief persisted until they were finally swept away by what has been characterized as the "witness of the naked eye"—that is by observational (i.e., empirical) astronomy (Boorstein, 1985, p. 305).

Method of tenacity. The method of tenacity still has an insidious hold on many people's belief. We have all been exposed to what we later learned was a myth, fabricated in ancient folklore and superstition. Today we are exposed to cyclic rumor, perpetuated it seems by the proliferation of the Internet and world wide, instant communication. It sometimes seems as if there are forces that strive to perpetuate facts that might change one's beliefs (Peirce, 1966).

As crazy as it seems many people accept weird or astounding allegations as factual, and once accepted, such beliefs feed on people's anxieties and uncertainties (Kimmel & Keefer, 1991; Rosnow, 1980, 1991; Rosnow & Fine, 1976). Carl Jung (1959), the eminent Swiss psychiatrist and psychologist, wrote about the old rumor of "flying saucers," unidentified flying objects (UFOs) piloted by extra terrestrials. As the story goes, benevolent superior beings from another planet have come to save humanity. We are also told of menacing creatures that, by threatening all earthlings, unify diverse ideologies against a common foe.

As people believe what they want to believe, they can become easy victims of hucksters who use fakery and showy methods to prey on human weaknesses. In the U.S., state and federal laws attempt to protect an innocent public from such trickery but new stories and accounts of shysters appear daily. According to Jung, belief in the UFO rumor is a way of expressing fears and uncertainties about the world situation and the universal wish for a redeeming supernatural force (Jung, 1959).

Method of authority. A second influence on beliefs viewed as at least minimally superior to the method of tenacity is the method of authority. With this method, Peirce asserts that certain claims (some true and others false) are accepted because someone in a position of authority says they are true. In the 15th century, the word of authority, the Pope, perpetuated beliefs that the earth not the sun was the center of all things. Nicolaus Copernicus was asked by the Pope to help with calendar reform. However, the Church rejected that idea, being at odds not only with "common sense" but also with the authority of ecclesiastical doctrine. The role of authoritative figures resulted in the false accusations of witchcraft in the 16th to 18th centuries resulted in atrocities of the most horrible kind. The word of authority was invoked for people to carry out their cruelties (Peirce, 1966).

Not all examples of authority are negative. Some examples on the benevolent side are; the physician who prescribes a drug or regimen to cure an illness; the electrician who advises replacing wiring that is about to blow out; and the mechanic who informs us that the spark plugs in our car are shot and need replacing. In these cases, we depend on the professional's honesty and the authority of their expertise. On the negative side are unscrupulous people who practice deceit in the name of authority, such as medical quacks, food faddists, and cult leaders (Gardner, 1957).

A priori method. A third method of influence, called by Peirce (1966) the *a priori* method, focuses on how we use our individual powers of pure reason and logic to know and explain our world. The a priori method has proven quite effective by mathematicians and philosophers. Peirce characterized this method as "far more intellectual and respectable from the point of view of reason" (p. 106) than either of the previous two. He maintained *a priori* is sometimes an effective defense against hucksters who depend on gullibility and that we can approach their dubious claims with a questioning mind. According to Gilovich (1991), a questioning mind assists us from being overly impressed even if the evidence seems to be immediately before us. He maintained that although the immediate source of a story may be quite credible, we might question the trustworthiness of the person with whom it originated. When we hear things described to us as secondhand, we may internalize whether or not they are third hand or even more distant from the original source.

Scientific method. The main characterization of the scientific method is empirical reasoning. The reasons for this are simple. Peirce recognized that the a priori method is constrained by the limits of pure reason. For example, if you claim that A causes B, and I disagree, do we just have to let it go at that? He argued that what we need is a way of drawing on nature to help us resolve matters of disagreement—the scientific method. By using the scientific method we can draw on independent realities to evaluate claims rather that depending on reason alone. Using empirical reasoning incorporated with the scientific method we can influence the fixing of belief (Peirce, 1966).

Begin with the End in Mind

Is the world really round? I grew up in Missouri, miles from any ocean, in country dotted with trees, crops, and rolling hills. I later served in the Navy, stationed in Rota, Spain, not far from where Christopher Columbus sailed to the new world. It was in Rota, from my ninth floor apartment balcony overlooking the Atlantic, that I understood what Columbus knew.

It is commonly thought that Columbus bravely set off to the New World not sure of whether he would sail right off the edge. The belief by the general population that the Earth was flat was promoted by the logical thinking of people who, like me, knew little of the ocean. Sailors and many others who lived by the sea knew full well that ships could sail right out of sight at about 15 miles from shore. And if you scrambled up a tall hill or to the top of a building you could still see the ship even though it was sailing away. Furthermore, when you first sighted an incoming ship you only saw the top of the mast. As the ship came closer you could see the sails and then the forecastle. The only logical reason for this fact was that the earth had to be round, or certainly spherical, like the moon. It was this knowledge and his experience with the sea, not to mention the incredible riches he envisioned would come from the effort, that steeled Christopher Columbus to setting out to the New World.

We also know today that Christopher Columbus was not the first to venture out to explore new worlds. Lief Erickson preceded him by at least two centuries. Pacific Islanders routinely traveled from island to island across miles of open ocean. However, we know about Columbus because he is well documented in the literature. His exploits were recorded and published in public reports and documents of the time and knowledge of his exploratory success were shared with other explorers.

That fact that Spain shot ahead with exploration and later in conquering the Caribbean and Americas was due, in large part, to Columbus's intuitive knowledge of the sea and the logic of his daily life.

Theory or Paradigm?

According to Babbie (1998), a sociologist, a theory is a systematic set of interrelated statements intended to explain some aspect of social life versus a paradigm which is a general framework or viewpoint that provides a way of looking at life and is grounded in sets of assumptions about the nature of reality.

As we begin to investigate theories for substantiating our research efforts via the scientific method, we must not forget that there are also a lot of ways to measure or evaluate things. Abraham Kaplan (1964) distinguished three classes of things that scientists measure. This classification system helps us recognize the types of measurements or truths that we use for research. Kaplan's first class is *direct observables,* those things than be observed simply and directly, like the color of an apple or the check mark made on a questionnaire. The second class is that of *indirect observables* which require "relatively more subtle, complex, or indirect observations" (p. 55). A person's check mark beside the category labeled "Female" on a questionnaire is an indirect observation of a person's gender. Journals or minutes of organizational meetings provide indirect observations of past social actions. The third class is *constructs* or *theoretical creations* based on observations not observed directly or indirectly. A good example of this is the measurement of intelligence or IQ. IQ is constructed mathematically from observations of answers given to a large number of questions on an IQ test.

Logic of Theory

Linking conceptualization to measurement and perceptions of belief is a major component of establishing a theoretical framework. An example of this logic is that of determining the work ethic. If you and I compiled a list of 100 indicators of work ethic and its various dimensions we might disagree widely on which indicators are the most salient for determining the presence or absence of work ethic. However, if we pretty much agree on some indicators, we could focus our attention on those, and we would probably agree on the answer they provided. But what if we don't really agree on any of the possible indicators? Perhaps we can still reach an agreement on whether men or women have a greater work ethic. If we disagree totally on the value of the indicators, one solution would be to study all of them. Now, suppose that women turn out to have a higher work ethic than men do on all 100 indicators. The ones I favor, as well as the ones you selected. We would then be able to agree that women have a stronger work ethic than men even if we disagree on the general measures and indicators of work ethic. This interchangeability of a large number of indicators has a special meaning to researchers. It means that if several different indicators represent the same concept, then all of them will behave the same way the concept would behave if it were real and could be observed. Thus, if women have a stronger work ethic than men, we should be able to observe that difference by using any reasonable measure of work ethic. This is the link and the fundamental logic of conceptualization and measurement (Babbie, 1998).

Terms Used in Theory Construction

Table 5.1 offers the definitions to several terms I think are important to understanding the construction and application of theory.

Scientific Method in Education

Borg (1963) introduced many of today's educational researchers to the newly developed application of the scientific method to education research. His book and teachings brought some respectability to this fledging science. His principles were sound and based on empirical research as discussed by Peirce (1966). Though his principles are well known to most researchers today, it is worthwhile to consider his techniques with a view to theoretical framework development.

Recognition of the problem. This is the awareness phase of a researcher's endeavor and is essential to the proper development of a theoretical framework. Beginning with the end in mind is a critical component for good research.

Definition of the problem in clear, specific terms. A well-defined problem helps focus a researcher's study on the theories surrounding its basis. An inability to clearly define a research problem reveals weaknesses in the theoretical framework, as well as the overall study.

Development of hypotheses. Development of hypotheses is the stage where one's research meets the requirement of testability, that is, whether or not it is empirically sound. Your study should demonstrate

TABLE 5.1
Terms Used in Theory Construction

Observation: Information gathering via seeing, hearing, and, less commonly, touching.

Fact: Some phenomenon that has been observed.

Law: Universal generalizations about classes of facts. The law of gravity is a classic example: "Bodies are attracted to each other in proportion to their masses and inversely proportionate to the distance separating them" (Kaplan, 1964, p. 91).

Theory: A systematic explanation for the observations that relate to a particular aspect of life.

Concepts: The "basic building blocks of theory," abstract elements representing classes of phenomena within a field of study (Turner, 1989, p. 5). The concepts relevant to a theory of work ethic, for example, include work and ethics. Kaplan defined concept as a "family of conceptions." He noted that the concept of compassion is a construct created from your conception or my conception of it, and the conceptions of all those who have ever used the term. It cannot be observed directly or indirectly, because it doesn't exist. We made it up.

Variables: Logical groupings of attributes. The variable *gender* is made of the attributes male and female.

Axioms or postulates: Fundamental assertions taken to be true on which a theory is grounded.

Propositions: Conclusions drawn about relationships among concepts, derived from the axiomatic groundwork.

Hypotheses: Specified expectations about empirical reality, derived from propositions.

---

the development of techniques and measurement instruments that will provide objective data pertinent to the hypotheses. This is also the point at which rival hypotheses can be presented to further clarify the theoretical rigor of your study.

Data collection. The collection of data should be centered on the principle of determining conceptualization through measurement. This empirical method should be tempered by the hypotheses that have been developed.

Data analysis. Today, most researchers use factorial designs that capitalize upon the strength of statistics, data processing, and the advent of computer applications to answer their research questions.

These techniques require strong connections with the theories forming the basis of the study.

Drawing conclusions relative to the hypotheses based upon the data. This is the end from which we began the study. In other words, the work, effort, and sound thinking initially applied to our theoretical framework will now pay dividends by helping us tie our findings to the major theories used in our framework. We will now answer the "So what?" question that research studies hope to answer.

Empirical Reasoning

Empirical reasoning was introduced into the behavioral sciences as the applications of the scientific method in physics and biology in the 19th century led to the development of psychology as a science. Trained in medicine and experimental physiology, Wilhelm Wundt (1832-1920) developed the first formal experimental laboratory to study psychological behavior. At Harvard University, William James (1842-1910), with a background in philosophy and physiology, taught a graduate course where students participated in psychological experiments. About the same time, other "traditional" scientists such as Francis Galton (1822-1911) demonstrated the application of empirical reasoning to behavioral questions that had been thought to lie completely outside its application (Forrest, 1974).

With roots in the so-called "hard sciences," empirical reasoning began to gain respectability. The word *empirical* refers to the use of experience or observation. In the context of the scientific method, empirical reasoning relies not on armchair theorizing, political persuasiveness, or personal position, but on observation and measurement. In empirical science, scientists have a choice of "keys," figuratively speaking that can unlock the door to a prescribed problem. A scientist decides on one key and then says, in essence, "Let's try it." The scientific method using empirical reasoning calls for a reliance on techniques that are available to anyone skilled enough to use them to open up the world for scrutiny and investigation. These shared reasoning techniques connect scientists working in different fields, even through they may use totally different empirical methods in their investigations (Conant, 1957).

Deductive Reasoning (Traditional Model)

I often ask students to "draw a picture" of their theoretical design, following the old axiom that "A picture is worth a thousand words." I ask my students to show the conceptual relationships of theory to their topic of interest. If the model can clearly or simply portray theory without loosing the credibility of its infrastructure, the diagram can serve to enlighten and communicate the essence of a research proposal.

The procedure for model development usually follows either a linear or bubble path. The key is to graphically depict a procedure or an overlapping relationship between theories and research topic. Some students find it helpful to put the bubbles inside a box such as the one in Figure 5.1. Actually, this figure is a box within a box. The student worked hours on this simple design but once finished had a better understanding of how the different theories interrelated.

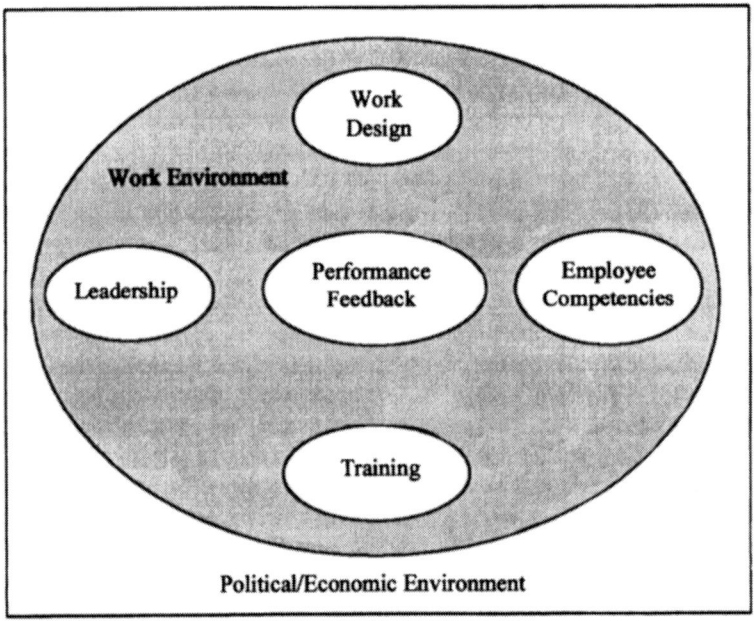

FIGURE 5.1. Leadership to initiate high performance workplaces.

Taken from Taylor, G.A. (1996). *Leadership practices for developing high performance public health agencies.* Unpublished doctoral dissertation, University of Tennessee, Knoxville.

Theory Based on Observation (Grounded Theory)

The process of grounded theory is called *inductive theory construction*. Inductive theory research begins by constructing a theory through the inductive method by observing aspects of social behavior and then seeking to discover patterns that may point to relatively universal principles (Glaser & Strauss, 1967). The result of this effort is the eventual development of a new theory ground in observation and documentation of facts. Beveridge (1950) made a clear distinction between inductive and deductive methods.

> Logicians distinguish between inductive reasoning (from particular instances to general principles, from facts to theories) and deductive reasoning (from the general to the particular, applying a theory to a particular case). In induction one starts from observed data and develops a generalization, which explains the relationships between the objects observed. On the other hand, in deductive reasoning one starts from some general law and applies it to a particular instance. (p. 113)

Theoretical Development

Theory Construction

The following steps are usually completed when constructing theory:
1. Pick a topic that interests you
2. It can be broad or narrower i.e., something you are interested in understand and explaining
3. Conduct an inventory of what is known or thought about it.
4. Write down your own observations and ideas
5. Learn what other scholars have said about it
6. Talk to other people
7. Read what others have written

The goal of developing theory is to have a sufficient blueprint to guide the completion of research study. You must, therefore, develop theoretical propositions. Propositions help determine what data to collect and the strategies to use when analyzing the data. These pathways to your research must be composed in plain English and developed from a comprehensive review of literature.

It is extremely important to fully develop and include rival theories when developing a theoretical framework. Rival theories can also take on the form of rival hypotheses or rival explanations (or alternative explanations). The use of rivals sharpens theoretical thinking and strengthens the research design. In quasi-experimental research, rival theories can help explain threats to validity. Campbell and Stanley (1963) discuss this concept in their discussion of quasi-experimental designs.

The model portrayed in Figure 5.2 begins with a solid review of available literature. Some students reveal components of their theoretical framework within their reviews of the literature without realizing it. Other students confuse rationale with theoretical framework or visa versa.

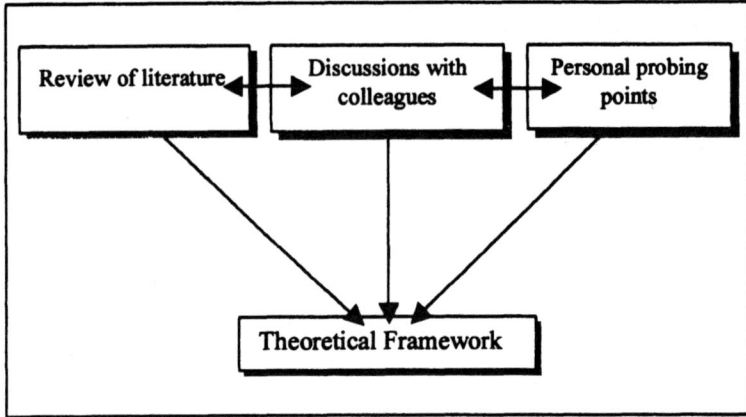

FIGURE 5.2. Model of theoretical development.

Forming a Theoretical Base

The following steps represent the fundamental components of an effective formulation of a theoretical base for research:

1. Collect environmental input (educated observation/familiarity)
2. Apply creative ideas/perceptions
3. Develop variables for initial pursuit/investigation usually from a review of the literature
4. Develop theoretical constructs (What can you manage to study?)
5. Develop a visual model depicting constructs
6. Develop yypothesis using deductive reasoning
7. Develop empirically testable hypotheses
8. Empirically test hypotheses

Rules of Theory Construction

A researcher's goal is to compile seemingly isolated facts and to manipulate these facts to show their relationship into a meaningful pattern. Therefore, theories must be built upon previously discovered facts to provide logical explanations for these recently discovered facts. All too often this process is not a prescribed set of events but is based on happenstance or seemingly random occurrence. Regardless, many researchers simply set out to discover new facts without constructing a theoretical framework that provides meaning to their efforts.

As you develop a theoretical base, assure that you apply the following rules of theory construction:

1. The statement of a theory shoud make explicit its postulates and the definitions of terms involved in these postulates, that is, write definitions of your variables.
2. The statement of a theory should make explicit the boundaries of its concern and the limitations under which it is proposed.
3. A theory should have internal consistency as a logical system (share with others before starting study).
4. A theory should be consistent with existing empirical data. (utilize documentation or logical arguments).
5. A theory should be capable of generating specific hypotheses and predictions.
6. A theory should be testable (prove or disprove).
7. A theory should become more complex only as indicated by evidence.
8. A theory should be quantifiable.
9. Unnecessary formulization should be avoided.
10. Oversimplification should be avoided.
11. Theorizing by means of models should be approached with care.

Theory Types for Developing Theoretical Frameworks

Hypothetico–deductive theory. Hypothetico–deductive theory requires the development of a testable theory, then the use of empirical checks to amend the theory. The validity of this form of theoretical development is dependent on the agreement between the deduced consequences and the phenomena to which it refers. The typical pattern for this type of theory is:

1. Define critical terms.
2. Develop a set of hypothetical statements concerning the presumptive relationships among the phenomena represented by the critical terms.
3. Determine a series of deduced consequences that are logically derived from the hypothetical statements.
4. Combine the constituents into an "if-then" relationship.

Functional theory. Functional theory is a provisional tool that focuses on observation and data-oriented explanations. It is less formal than other theory formulations and places less emphasis on highly structured conceptualizations and logical-deductive procedures. It is used by researchers who feel that a highly structured theory may bring about a termination of exploratory efforts and bind them to other facts.

Inductive theory. Inductive theory is the least common type of theory. It is considered an "after-the-fact" explanation of discovered facts, and evolves as facts are established and these facts are considered. The theory becomes a summarized statement about specific observations. Rivals to this form of theoretical development argue that the researcher starts with some expectations and that some informal theory governs the choices they make, therefore introducing bias or "hunches" into the explanation.

Model theory. Also called paradigm theory, this form of theory development is conducted through an integrated design that strives to simplify the theoretical structure to gain insight into some known phenomena. The procedure includes mathematical equations, verbal statements, symbolic descriptions and graphic presentations that are used to represent objects and to show relationships.

Theory Application

1. Specify the topic.
2. Specify the range of phenomena your theory addresses (range of application).
3. Identify and specify your major concepts and variables.
4. Find out what is known (propositions) about the relationships among those variables.
5. Reason logically from those propositions to the specific topic you are examining.

It is at this point that several important questions must be addressed: Where to go from here? So what? Who cares? How does my study fit into the "big picture?" Several strategies may be employed to answer the big questions about how to apply your theoretical model, but in general your framework should provide several important concepts including [1] understanding and belief, [2] making sense of things, and [3] having a coherent picture of our world

Why Use Theory? (Epilogue)

Researchers must be able to devise some mechanism for the classification of facts. A mass of assorted facts is ineffective and inefficient in conducting sound research. A theoretical framework provides a scheme for classifying facts.

More specifically, theory is not considered an end in itself but a framework for additional discovery and observation. According to Van Dalen (1966), the function of theory is to

1. determine the number and kinds of facts relevant to a study,
2. govern the kind of phenomena researchers study,
3. provide a framework within which and against which researcher observe, test, and interpret their observation,
4. classify phenomena,
5. formulate logical constructs,
6. summarize facts,
7. predict facts, and
8. reveal needed research.

When dealing with the phenomena involved with educational research it becomes impossible to acquire all data by direct observation and measurement. The researcher therefore, must create concepts to account for behavior that are not directly observable but to which they can attach empirical referents. These concepts include such things as knowledge, attitude, and so forth that, while not necessarily observable, manifest themselves in behavior. Also called logical constructs, hypothetical constructs or intervening variables are very helpful in guiding theoretical and experimental thinking.

The process of theorization is used to summarize knowledge within a given field. This process integrates pertinent facts into frameworks of knowledge that help explain certain phenomena. If the researcher interprets a theory as a generalization of data, then theories can also predict what should be observable where data are not available. This prediction enables researchers to direct the search for facts. In addition, theories lacking sufficient support will help focus attention on areas where knowledge is lacking. Therefore, suggesting new research problems and new avenues of inquiry.

In the past few years the growth of qualitative research in the literature has seemed to increase the presence, need, or expectation for a theoretical framework. Why? My best guess is that today's students are more sophisticated regarding their approach to research, and we have more technology (e.g., computers and the Internet) and technical expertise available at our fingertips, and society in general is becoming more complex and well educated.

As our research becomes better, it also becomes more complex. We therefore must develop good links of theory with the original research we conduct and share with the international research community. This end begins with a good start—a solid theoretical framework.

References

Babbie, E. R. (1998). *The practice of social research* (8th ed.). Belmont, CA: Wadsworth.

Beveridge, W. I. B. (1950). *The art of scientific investigation.* New York: Vintage Books.

Boorstein, D. J. (1985). *The discoverers.* New York: Vintage.

Borg, W. R. (1963). *Educational research: An introduction.* New York: McKay.

Campbell, D., & Stanley, J. (1963). *Experimental and quasi-experimental designs for research.* Chicago: Rand McNally.

Conant, J. B. (1957). Introduction. In J. B. Conant & L. K. Nash (Eds.), *Harvard case studies in experimental science* (Vol. 1, pp. vii-xvi). Cambridge: Harvard University Press.

Forrest, D. W. (1974). *Francis Galton: The life and work of a Victorian genius.* New York: Taplinger.

Gardner, M. (1957). *Fads and fallacies in the name of science.* New York: Dover.

Gilovich, T. (1991). *How we know what isn't so: The fallibility of human reason in everyday life.* New York: Free Press.

Glaser, B., & Strauss, A. (1967). *The discovery of grounded theory.* Chicago: Aldine.

Jung, C. G. (1959). A visionary rumor. *Journal of Analytical Psychology, 4,* 5-19.

Kaplan, A. (1964). *The conduct of inquiry: Methodology for behavioral science.* Scranton, PA: Chandler.

Kimmel, A. J., & Keffer, R. (1991). Psychological correlates of the acceptance and transmission of rumors about AIDS. *Journal of Applied Social Psychology, 21,* 1608-1628.

Kerlinger, F. N. (1979). *Behavioral research: A conceptual approach.* New York: Holt, Rinehart, & Winston.

Peirce, C. S. (1966). *Charles S. Peirce: Selected writings (Values in a universe of chance)* (P. P. Weiner, Ed.). New York: Dover.

Rokeach, M. (1960). *The open and closed mind.* New York: Basic Books.

Rosnow, R. L. (1980). Psychology of rumor. *Psychological Bulletin, 87,* 578-591.

Rosnow, R. L. (1991). Inside rumor: A personal journey. *American Psychologist, 46,* 484-496.

Rosnow, R. L., & Fine, G. A. (1976). *Rumor and gossip: The social psychology of hearsay.* New York: Elsevier.

Taylor, G. A. (1996). *Leadership practices for developing high performance public health agencies.* Unpublished doctoral dissertation, University of Tennessee, Knoxville.

Turner, J. H. (Ed.). (1989). *Theory building in sociology: Assessing theoretical cumulation.* Newbury Park, CA: Sage.

Van Dalen, D. B. (1966). *Understanding educational research.* New York: McGraw-Hill.

Chapter 6

Selecting an Appropriate Research Design

Fadia M. Nasser

Both qualitative and quantitative researchers *"think they know something about society worth telling to others, and they use a variety of forms, media and means to communicate ideas and findings."* (Becker, 1986, p. 122)

Recent years have seen an increased interest in qualitative methods for the study of research problems in different disciplines (Borg & Gall, 1989; Sofaer, 1999). This trend is evident in education, social science, psychology, and particularly in nursing research. Nonetheless, quantitative research still dominates and the merits of each type of research are still being debated. The major questions revolve around how qualitative and quantitative research approaches differ. Do they aim to say the same things but in different styles? This chapter addresses these questions by clarifying some of the major issues related to qualitative and quantitative research. In so doing readers may be helped to make informed choices between the two approaches.

Characteristics and Assumptions

Qualitative study is defined as a process of inquiry into understanding a social or human problem based on construction of a complex and holistic picture that is verbally formulated. Qualitative reports typically detail the views of informants elicited in natural settings. According to Creswell (1994), the characteristics of qualitative research are embedded in the characteristics of qualitative research problems. The problem in qualitative research usually involves [1] *immature* concept(s) owing to a visible lack of theory and/or previous research, [2] a notion that available theory may be inaccurate, inappropriate, incorrect, or biased, [3] a need to explore and describe the phenomena and to develop theory, and [4] a phenomenon that may not be suited to quantitative measures (Morse, 1991).

Merriam (1988) offered six key traits of qualitative research. First, qualitative researchers are concerned primarily with process rather than with outcomes or products. Second, they are interested in meaning, namely, how people make sense of their lives, experiences, and how they structure their world. Third, qualitative researchers are the primary instrument for data collection and analysis. Data are mediated through this human *instrument* rather than through inventories, questionnaires, or machines. Fourth, qualitative research involves fieldwork. Researchers physically go to the people, setting, site, or institution to observe or record behavior in its natural setting. Fifth, qualitative research is descriptive in that researchers are interested in process, meaning, and understanding gained through words and pictures. Sixth, the process of qualitative research is inductive meaning that researchers develop abstractions, concepts, hypotheses, and theories from empirical details gained through data collection and analysis. A more comprehensive list of attributes shared by many qualitative projects can be found in Burgess (1985) and Creswell (1998).

Assumptions at the core of qualitative research are significantly different from those that underlie quantitative research (Creswell, 1994; Merriam, 1988). From a qualitative approach reality is subjective and multiple as perceived by participants in a study (*ontological* assumption). Researchers are, therefore, required to interact with research informants to obtain relevant data (*epistemological* assumption). Hence, the resulting research is value-laden and biased (*axiological* assumption). The language used in qualitative research is informal, yet presented from a formal point of view through the use of an agreed-upon qualitative terminology (*rhetorical* assumption). As the qualitative research process is inductive it involves a mutual and simultaneous shaping of factors (themes) bound by context. Through the process of identifying themes, patterns, or theories are developed. The accuracy and reliability of results derived from qualitative research methods are secured primarily through verification (*methodological* assumption).

Most quantitative research examines social or human problems by testing a theory composed of variables that are measured by numeric values. Data are analyzed with statistical procedures to determine whether a theory's predictive generalizations hold true. Quantitative researchers tend to seek explanations and predictions that allow for generalization. To this end, quantitative methods include careful sampling strategies and experimental designs. In quantitative research researchers' *objectivity* is of utmost concern because their role is to observe and measure while avoiding personal involvement with the research participants.

Contrary to the assumptions of the qualitative approach, those of the quantitative approach view reality as objective, singular, and separate from researchers (*ontological* assumption). Thus, the object of study exists independently of researchers (*epistemological* assumption). Quantitative research is supposedly value-free and unbiased (*axiological* assumption). Language is formal and based on a set of conceptual and operational definitions. In the past, quantitative studies have been presented in impersonal voice and in accepted quantitative terminology (*rhetorical* assumption). Quantitative research generally involves a deductive process and is based on static design in which categories are defined *a priori*. Because quantitative research seeks to identify generalizations that can lead to predictions, explanations, and understanding, it is assumed to be context-free. Results of quantitative research are viewed as accurate and reliable in terms of validity and reliability (*methodological* assumption).

A review of the major elements of qualitative and quantitative research design is delineated in the next section. These elements should be carefully considered when choosing a research approach to apply in a particular study.

Research Problem

The core aspect to be considered when selecting a research design relates to the research problem. The problem in qualitative research normally needs to be explored because little information exists on the topic. Variables are largely undefined and researchers may need to focus on the context that shapes the way the phenomenon being studied is understood. Many qualitative studies are not based on a theoretical framework either because the theories available are inadequate or incomplete, or because such a framework simply does not exist. Therefore, information obtained throughout a qualitative study often contributes to an emergent theory.

In contrast, the problem in quantitative research generally evolves from an extant literature that offers a basis from which to build on.

Variables have been identified or constructed and accepted definitions are mostly attainable. Likewise, theories may exist that need to be further tested and verified.

Use of the Literature

One of the critical methodological differences between qualitative and quantitative approaches occurs in researchers' utilization of the professional literature. In spite of the predominately inductive nature of qualitative research methodologists report differing views on the use of the literature (Babchuck, 1997). According to Strauss and Corbin (1990):

> All kinds of literature can be used before a [qualitative] research study is begun both in thinking and getting the study off the ground. They can also be used during the study itself, contributing to its forward thrust. In fact, there should be some searching out of literature (but not just technical) during the research itself, an actual interplay of reading literature and data analysis. So, in effect, we read the published materials during all phases of the research. (p. 56)

Unlike Strauss and Corbin (1990), others regard the beginning stages of most forms of qualitative study as a period of pure and emergent discovery. Patton (1990) suggested that referring to the literature may be problematic as it can bias researchers' thinking and reduce openness to whatever emerges in the field. From this standpoint, researchers may well not even be aware of or sensitive to the literature considered pertinent to their topic as meanings and themes are initially unknown. Moreover, because one of the major objectives of qualitative research is to explore fairly unstudied directions the literature would presumably be scarce.

A variety of methods and approaches to obtaining data may be sought from a qualitative paradigm. This variety poses additional challenges to how and when researchers might choose to consult the literature in order to facilitate the discovery of themes and insights derived directly from the research setting.

In summary, when and how to use the scholarly literature in qualitative research simply depends, among other things, on the goal of the study, the chosen method of inquiry, and the perspective adopted by the researcher. In traditional forms of quantitative inquiry prior knowledge of the literature plays a major role in the investigation. Merriam (1988) noted, "While a literature review helps in problem formulation regardless of design, its prominence in inductive research may be considerably less than theory-testing studies" (p. 63). Thus, when applying a quantitative approach the literature is normally used deductively, as well as a basis for advancing research questions or hypotheses. The literature enables researchers to identify previous research and gaps in understanding. It further helps by suggesting theoretical and conceptual frameworks to guide the research and analysis and helps identify important variables and relationships among them. Hence, research questions and problem statements are often derived from the literature.

Theory Use

Qualitative and quantitative studies differ in both the place and use of theory. In qualitative research the term *theory* is less clearly defined than in quantitative research. In fact, the specific term used for theory varies by the type of qualitative design. For example, those conducting a *grounded theory* study use theory to refer to the outcome of their inquiry. In grounded theory studies researchers hope to discover theory as it emerges from data gained from study informants. In *critical ethnographic* studies researchers begin with a theory that informs their study. In *ethnographic* studies without a critical-theory component, existing theories of culture such as structural functionalism, symbolic interaction, social exchange theory and others (Goetz & LeCompte, 1984) may help shape research questions. For *case studies*, Lincoln and Guba (1985) refer to pattern theory that develops in the course of naturalistic or qualitative research as opposed to the deductive form found in most quantitative studies. Pattern theory refers to a pattern of interconnected thoughts or themes linked to a whole. According to Neuman (1991), pattern theory contains an interconnected set of concepts and relationships, uses metaphors or analogies, and consists of a system of ideas that inform its constituents, so that their relationships makes sense. Thus, a pattern theory forms a mutually reinforcing and closed system by specifying a sequence of phases or by linking parts to a whole. Alternatively, in *phenomenological* studies no preconceived notions, expectations, or frameworks guide the analysis of their data (Field & Morse, 1985). However, regardless of the design type, whether theories are called patterns, grounded theories, generalizations or holistic pictures (Merriam, 1988), the methodological use of some larger explanation should fit the logic of an inductive research process. Hence, in most qualitative studies, one does not test or verify a theory. Instead, consistent with the inductive model of thinking, a theory may emerge during data collection and analysis phases or be used relatively late in the process to compare research findings with other theories.

The construction of empirically–grounded theory requires a reciprocal relationship between data and theory. Data must be allowed to generate propositions in a dialectical manner that permits use of *a priori* theoretical frameworks but keeps the framework from becoming the sole container into which data is poured. Introducing theory into a qualitative study is more difficult because there are no standard terminology or rules to guide its use. Because most qualitative studies employ an inductive mode of development, theory tends to be introduced towards the end of the study. If theory is introduced at the beginning of a study, qualitative researchers subsequently modify or adjust the theory on the basis of informant feedback. Creswell (1994) advised researchers to [1] employ theory in a manner consistent with the type of qualitative design, [2] use theory inductively so that it does not become something to test, but rather to develop and shape through research process, [3] create a visual model of the theory as it emerges, and [4] if applied toward the end of the study, compare and contrast the theory with other theories.

In quantitative studies, hypotheses, research questions, or objectives are rooted in a theoretical body of knowledge by definition. Theory is used deductively and is introduced at the beginning of the study. The primary objective of quantitative research is to test or verify theory rather than to develop it. Accordingly, theory represents the conceptual framework for the entire study, a model for organizing the research questions or hypotheses and the data collection procedure. Creswell (1994) advocated dedicating a separate section in doctoral dissertations to the description of theory so that readers can clearly distinguish theory from other research components. This section should provide a complete explication of the theory(ies) used, how it is used and how it relates to the study at hand.

Theory use differs between qualitative and quantitative studies. The employment and placement of theory in qualitative research depend, among other things, on the method of inquiry (e.g., biography, phenomenology, grounded theory, ethnography, and case study) and the researcher's perspective. Regardless of the chosen method of inquiry and researcher's perspective, use of theory should be consistent with the inductive logic of qualitative research. Alternatively, quantitative studies apply an accepted definition and role for theory. Variables are related through hypotheses or research questions. Quantitative researchers usually employ theories deductively and, thus, tend to present them at the beginning of a study. The common format is presentation of theory, gathering of data to test it, and a return to the theory at the end of the study to determine whether conclusions confirm or refute it.

Statement of Purpose

Qualitative and quantitative statements of purpose address similar content, but their form and language differ because of the rhetorical and methodological distinctions between the two approaches. A good qualitative statement of purpose implies, if not explicitly expresses, the assumptions of the qualitative paradigm (Firestone, 1987; Merriam, 1988). A qualitative statement of purpose uses qualitative terminology (e.g., understand, describe, develop, or discover) that conveys an evolving, developing study. The purpose statement also clearly identifies key concepts being explored, indicates the specific qualitative method of inquiry, and identifies the unit of analysis (e.g., person, group, or site).

In quantitative research the statement of purpose differs considerably from its qualitative counterpart. A proper quantitative statement of purpose requires a solid understanding of the variables in terms of temporal order and measurement. Such a statement, therefore, begins by identifying proposed variables for the study, clearly defining the relationships among these variables, and specifying the mode of measurement for the respective variables. A common purpose of quantitative studies is either to interrelate variables or to compare samples or groups.

Questions, Objectives, and Hypotheses

In qualitative research reports one typically finds research questions rather than objectives or hypotheses. These questions assume two forms. First, a *grand tour question* (Werner & Schoepfle, 1987) or a guiding hypothesis (Marshall & Rossman, 1989) is followed by sub-questions (Miles & Huberman, 1984). The question format might be related to a specific qualitative design type. For example, ethnographic questions differ from questions asked in critical ethnography, phenomenology, or grounded theory (see Creswell, 1998). Second, a limited number of sub-questions are elaborated. Creswell (1994) suggested asking two grand-tour questions followed by no more than five to seven sub-questions. He also recommended that research questions begin with the words *what* or *how* so as to inform readers that the study aims to [1] discover (grounded theory), [2] explain or seek to understand (ethnography), [3] explore a process (case study), or [4] describe experiences (phenomenology). These concepts convey the language of an emergent research design.

Questions, objectives and hypotheses in quantitative studies represent pointed restatements of the purpose statement. In survey research these restatements typically take the form of research questions or objectives, while in experimental studies they are usually phrased as hypotheses. In either case, questions, hypotheses, or objectives are usually presented as either comparisons between two or more groups in terms of one or more dependent (outcome) variable(s), or as relationships between two or more independent (explanatory) and dependent variables. Questions, hypotheses, or objectives are phrased as testable propositions that are normally deduced from theory in a deductive methodological process (Kerlinger, 1979).

Terms /Variable Definitions

Terms and variables are defined in both qualitative and quantitative studies although differences exist in their scope and the methodological status. Because of their inductive, emergent methodological design, qualitative studies may initially include very few defined terms or variables while others may emerge during data collection. In a research plan, qualitative researchers may advance tentative definitions prior to refining them in the course of their study. Qualitative designs often do not include separate sections dedicated to the precise definition of terms.

Quantitative researchers generally operate within a deductive model that requires predetermined and fixed variable definitions. In addition, quantitative researchers work within a defined theoretical framework and rely on the scholarly literature. Consequently, quantitative research usually starts out with lists of variable definitions introduced early in the research plan and kept constant throughout the investigation. Redefinition of one or more research variables may be offered as part of the quantitative researchers' conclusions.

Research Method

No agreement has been reached as to a standard procedure for data collection, analysis, and reporting of qualitative research. However, investigators (e.g., Creswell, 1994, 1998; Marshall & Rossman, 1989; Wolcott, 1990a) point out that different assumptions guide qualitative and quantitative designs. In fact, an array of qualitative designs is available. A major characteristic shared by these designs is that researchers reflect on and express their role or experience in so far as they may have biased their interpretations or bring a unique view to data collection and analysis. Approaches to data collection include observations, interviews, documents, and visual materials.

The procedure by which information is recorded is also noteworthy. Qualitative researchers record comments about data collected, their thoughts about procedures related to forming categories or themes, and specific analytic approaches identified with particular qualitative design. Subsequently, the verification process that demonstrates internal and external validity and reliability should be described. Finally, the forms of narrative used and ways that it will be compared and contrasted with existing theories (if such theories exist) and with literature on the topic is indicated.

As with qualitative research, several types of quantitative research designs are available. Only two of these designs, survey and experimental design, are discussed here to give a sharper sense of the differences within the quantitative approach and between qualitative and quantitative approaches. A survey study begins with a discussion about the purpose of the survey design, the identification of the population and sample for the study, and the forms of statistical analysis to be employed. In an experimental design, researchers describe the participants in the study and how they were chosen, the variables or treatment conditions, and the criterion variable(s) within the specific experimental design. This section of the research report also includes descriptions of instruments used for pretests and posttests, and materials used in treatments. Threats to internal and external validity of research results and the statistical analyses used to test hypotheses are explicitly outlined.

Writing

One of the outstanding characteristics of scientific writing in the postmodern era is the use of metaphors and writing formats (Shapiro, 1986). Social scientific writing, in particular, uses metaphors at every level and depends upon a deep epistemtic code regarding the way "that knowledge and understanding in general are figured" (p. 198). Facts are considered interpretable only in terms of their place within the metaphoric structure.

There are many possible qualitative writing formats (Richardson, 1990). There is no single way that is more or less right for staging a text. The same material can be written for different audiences: positivists, interactionists, postmodernists, feminists, humanities professors, cultural studies scholars, policy makers, and so on, each preferring a different format. Qualitative researchers use ethnographic prose, historical narratives, first-person accounts, photographs, life histories, fictionalized facts, and biographical and autobiographical materials, among others (Dezin & Lincoln, 1994). Qualitative research can be endlessly creative in the transmission of findings. However, researchers do not simply leave the field with mountains of empirical data and then write up their findings. Qualitative interpretations are constructed on the basis of field notes and other sources of data. Interpretations can follow one of several forms including confessional, realist, impressionistic, critical, formal, literary, analytic, or grounded theory (Van Maanen, 1988). Although many qualitative researchers in the positivist tradition use statistical measures, methods, and documents as a way of locating a group of research participants within a larger population, they seldom report their findings in terms of statistical measures or quantitative methods (Denzin & Lincoln).

Quantitative researchers use mathematical models, statistical tables and graphs, and often write about their research in impersonal, third person prose. The final product is a positivist report written in standardized, technical, and formal language meant to transmit an aura of objectivity.

Evaluation

Judging the quality of research is an essential aspect in both qualitative and quantitative approaches. Nonetheless, different criteria are used to evaluate studies from these two paradigms. Multiple criteria for evaluating qualitative and quantitative research exist. For example, the qualitative criteria emphasized by Denzin and Lincoln (1994) stresses the situated, rational, and textual structures of ethnographic experience. Furthermore, as no single interpretive truth has priority and multiple interpretive communities exist, each group or school has its own evaluation criteria. Meanwhile, findings are usually presented in terms of the criteria of grounded theory (Strauss & Corbin, 1993). Concepts such as credibility, transferability, dependability, and conformability replace the accepted positivist criteria of internal and external validity, reliability, and objectivity.

Qualitative researchers use triangulation as a strategy to add rigor, breadth, and depth to the investigation. The new generation of qualitative researchers, those with post-structural or post-modern sensibilities, seek alternative methods for evaluating their work. The key notions concerning the evaluation criteria inventory include verisimilitude, emotionality, personal responsibility and ethic of caring, political praxis, and multi-voiced dialogues with respondents.

Flick (1992) argued that triangulation, a combination of multiple methods, empirical materials, perspectives and observers in a single study, is not a tool for validation but an alternative to validation. Wolcott (1990b) questioned the importance of validity in qualitative research while outlining some strategies he follows to satisfy the implicit challenge of validity. These strategies include to talk little and listen a lot, to record accurately, to begin writing early, to let readers see for themselves, to report fully, to be candid, to seek feedback, to try to achieve balance to ensure rigorous subjectivity, fairness, completeness, and sensitivity; and to write accurately. By applying these strategies, Wolcott arrived at the *thick* description that most qualitative researchers now consider a major criterion for the evaluation of qualitative work.

Other qualitative researchers focus on the generalizability of qualitative research findings. Schofield (1990) noticed an emerging consensus that generalizability is best thought of as a matter of the fit between the situation studied and other situations to which one might be interested in applying the concepts and conclusions of a study. This conceptualization makes thick description crucial because its elements can provide the information necessary for an informed judgment about the issue of fit. In addition, because of the nature and assumptions of qualitative research, and the fact that researchers are the main instrument for data collection, reliability becomes a problem. No agreement has yet been reached on the relevance and meaning of reliability in qualitative research.

The situation with qualitative research contrasts sharply with that of quantitative research. Reliability and internal and external validity (generalizability) are the major criteria for judging findings of quantitative studies. Quantitative researchers attempt to ensure a satisfactory level of reliability and validity by controlling the sources of irrelevant variance through the study design (appropriate samples, instruments, procedures, manipulations, etc.) or by statistical means (e.g., analysis of covariance). In other words, reliable and valid results are sought through careful design and selection of appropriate instruments used to collect data from representative samples. This does not mean, however, that these instruments are ethically beyond question. They may be racially, sexually, or culturally biased (Solitis, 1990), an issue that quantitative researchers must openly address.

Factors Affecting the Selection of the Research Approach

Given the differences outlined in previous sections, the underlying question guiding this chapter can now be answered. What factors affect the decision to select one of the two research approaches?

Several factors may affect the selection of a research approach and should be considered during the decision process (see Table 6.1 for a summary of these factors and constraints). Among the most influential factors are the nature of the problem and the researcher's training and experience. Whether certain problems are better suited for qualitative or quantitative studies remains open to debate. Meanwhile, there is considerable agreement that the nature of the problem is an important factor in selecting a research approach. Creswell (1994) recommended using a qualitative approach when the research problem needs be explored because little information exists about the topic, the variables are largely unknown, the context is important for understanding the phenomenon under study, and a theoretical base does not exist or is not sufficient. Sofaer (1999) enumerated a variety of situations in which the use of qualitative methods is useful. She indicated that qualitative research methods are valuable for describing complex phenomena, tracking unexpected events, illuminating the experience and interpreting events by informants with widely differing stakes and roles, giving voice to those whose views are rarely heard, conducting initial explorations prior to developing theories, generating and even testing hypotheses, and moving toward explanations. On the other hand, the problems in quantitative research emerge from the literature so a substantial body of the literature exists upon which the researcher can build. Variables may be known and theories may exist that need to be empirically tested or verified.

The researcher's training and experience are also a substantial factor when selecting a research approach. A researcher trained in technical, scientific writing statistics, or computerized statistical programs, and familiar with the quantitative literature may tend to choose the quantitative approach. Alternatively, the qualitative approach incorporates a more literary style of writing than does the quantitative approach. Library experience is important when searching for illustration of good writing. Experience in using qualitative computer software is also helpful for researchers choosing a qualitative approach.

An additional factor stresses the psychological attributes of the researcher. Researchers may prefer quantitative approach because it offers low-risk, fixed research methods potentially having minimal ambiguities and possible frustrations. Researchers may also prefer the

TABLE 6.1

Factors and Criteria Considered When Selecting an Appropriate
Research Design

Factor	Qualitative	Quantitative
Research problem	• Should be explored • Little or no information about nature of problem(s) exists • Variables are largely unknown or undefined • Lack of theoretical basis	• Arises from literature • Information of problem usually exists • Variables are defined • Strong theoretical bases exist
Researcher: *Training and experience*	• Qualitative methods (assumptions; collection, coding, and analysis of data) • Qualitative literature (library search, journals, etc.) • Qualitative software	• Quantitative methods • Quantitative literature • Statistical software
Researcher: *Psychological attributes*	• Willingness to engage in unstructured/ambiguous tasks • Willingness to take risks and deal with ambiguity • Comfortable with intensive interaction with participants in natural settings • Readiness to engage in lengthy research process • Inclination to constructivism • Comfortable with assumptions of qualitative approach	• Comfortable with structured, clear guidelines and rules • Low tolerance of ambiguity • Unwillingness to intensively interact with participants • Tendency toward relatively short research processes • Tendency to positivism • Comfortable with assumptions of quantitative approach
Focus of study	• Description • Meaning based on participants' perspectives • Theory development • Outcome as process not product • Context shapes understanding of phenomenon • Particularities–details (generalization is not an issue)	• Explanation • Prediction • Description • Theory testing; verification • Outcomes as product • Inference and generalization

quantitative approach because it requires shorter time. Alternatively, qualitative designs call for researchers who are willing to take the risk inherent in an ambiguous procedure and a lengthy research process.

The audience of the study should also be taken into consideration when selecting a research approach. The research approach should be sensitive to the audience's needs. Hence, the approach of choice must be one that audience(s) of a study will understand and support as a valuable and legitimate method.

The contents of this chapter may leave the misleading impression that researchers should always choose either one of the two research approaches: this is not the message I intended to convey. On the contrary, it is important to stress that when investigating complex phenomena in the social and behavioral domains a single approach often may prove to be inadequate to address the research problem properly. In such cases, a mixed design combining elements from both approaches can be devised to appropriately collect the relevant information and to arrive at adequate research findings. The strategies for planning and implementing combined-designs deserve special address.

References

Babchuck, W. A. (1997). *The rediscovery of grounded theory: Strategies for qualitative research in adult education.* Unpublished doctoral dissertation, University of Nebraska–Lincoln.

Becker, H. J. (1986). *Doing things together.* Evanston, IL: Northwestern University Press.

Borg, W. R., & Gall, M. D. (1989). *Educational research: An introduction* (5th ed.). New York: Longman.

Burgess, R. G. (1985). Issues and problems in educational research: An introduction. In G. R. Burgess (Ed.), *Issues in educational research: Qualitative methods* (pp. 1-17). London: Falmer Press.

Creswell, J. W. (1994). *Research design: Qualitative and quantitative approaches.* Thousands Oaks, CA: Sage.

Creswell, J. W. (1998). *Qualitative inquiry and research design: Choosing among five traditions.* Thousands Oaks, CA: Sage.

Denzin, N. K., & Lincoln, Y. S. (1994). Entering the field of qualitative research. In N. K. Denzin & Y. S. Lincoln (Eds.), *Handbook of qualitative research* (pp. 1-17). Thousands Oaks, CA: Sage.

Field, P. A., & Morse, J. M. (1985). *Qualitative nursing research: The application of qualitative approaches.* Rockville, MD: Aspen.

Firestone, W. A. (1987). Meaning in method: The rhetoric of quantitative and qualitative research. *Educational Researcher, 16*, 16-21.

Flick, U. (1992). Triangulation revisited: Strategy of validation or alternative? *Journal for the Theory of Social Behavior, 22*, 175-198.

Goetz, J. P., & Lecompte, M. D. (1984). *Ethnography and qualitative design in educational research.* New York: Academic Press.

Kerlinger, F. N. (1979). *Behavioral research: A conceptual approach.* New York: Holt, Rinehart, & Winston.

Lincoln, Y. S., & Guba, E. G. (1985). *Naturalistic inquiry.* Beverly Hills, CA: Sage.

Marshall, C., & Rossman, G. B. (1989). *Designing qualitative research.* Newbury Park, CA: Sage.

Merriam, S. B. (1988). *Case study research in education: A qualitative approach.* San Francisco: Jossey-Bass.

Miles, M. B., & Huberman, A. M. (1989). *Qualitative data analysis: A sourcebook of new methods.* Beverly Hills, CA: Sage.

Morse, J. M. (1991). Approaches to qualitative–quantitative methodological triangulation. *Nursing Research, 40*, 120-123.

Neuman, W. L. (1991). *Social research methods: Qualitative and quantitative approaches.* Boston: Allyn & Bacon.

Patton, M. Q. (1990). *Qualitative evaluation and research methods* (2nd ed.). Newbury Park, CA: Sage.

Richardson, L. (1994). Writing: A method of inquiry. In N. K. Denzin & Y. S. Lincoln (Eds.), *Handbook of qualitative research* (pp. 516-529). Thousand Oaks, CA: Sage.

Schofield, J. W. (1990). Increasing generalizability of qualitative research. In E. W. Eisner & A. Peshkin (Eds.), *Qualitative inquiry in education* (pp. 201-233). New York: Teachers College Press.

Shapiro, M. (1986). Metaphor in the philosophy of the social sciences. *Cultural Critique, 2*, 191-214.

Sofaer, S. (1999). Qualitative methods: What are they and why use them? *Health Service Research, 4*, 1101-1118.

Solitis, J. F. (1990). The ethics of qualitative research. In E. W. Eisner & A. Peshkin (Eds.), *Qualitative inquiry in education* (pp. 247-258). New York: Teachers College Press.

Strauss, A., & Corbin, J. (1990). *Basics of qualitative research: Grounded theory procedures and techniques.* Newbury Park, CA: Sage.

Van Maanen, J. (1988). *Tales in the field: On writing ethnography.* Chicago: University of Chicago Press.

Werner, O., & Schoepfle, G. (1987). *Systematic fieldwork: Foundation of ethnography and interviewing* (Vol. 1). Newbury Park, CA: Sage.

Wolcott, H. T. (1990a). *Writing up qualitative research.* Newbury Park, CA: Sage.

Wolcott, H. T. (1990b). On seeking and rejecting validity in quantitative research. In E. W. Eisner & A. Peshkin (Eds.), *Qualitative inquiry in education* (pp. 121-152). New York: Teachers College Press.

Chapter 7

Mixed Method Research Designs

Ernest W. Brewer

In my experience as a professor, researcher, and journal editor, I have observed few instructors teach students to use mixed methodologies. In fact, most texts and classes deal with either quantitative or qualitative methods, not expanding beyond one basic approach (Bernard, 2000; Goodwin, 1995; Leary, 1995; Marshall & Rossman, 1999; McBurney, 1994; Miles & Huberman, 1994). Moreover, many committee chairs and members do not believe they have enough expertise in both areas to guide students or to conduct personal research using both qualitative and quantitative methods. Some, due to the research topic or perhaps just out of conviction, place their emphasis on one methodology or the other. Therefore, they typically advocate that students use one method—one all committee members agree upon. Usually, this is the methodology of the members' professional research. These personal observations are confirmed by Strauss and Corbin (1998), who stated, "A researcher's own preference, familiarity, and ease with a research mode inevitably will influence choices" (p. 33)

From this development there has come what some authors have described as the *paradigm war* (Mertens, 1998; Miles & Huberman, 1994; Tashakkori & Teddlie, 1998), with researchers on each side of the quantitative–qualitative battle, each group claiming to have the superior method. However, there appears to be a growing number of researchers calling for use of a combination of quantitative and qualitative designs. This may well be the beginning of a more reasoned approach, since each method has specific strengths and weaknesses.

In this chapter, the terms of the paradigm debate are defined, a brief historical overview of the two traditional research methodologies is presented, and the various purposes of research designs are discussed. Finally, the use of mixed methodologies and a discussion of the advantages and disadvantages of mixed designs are explored.

Definitions of Terms

Although definitions have been offered by others in this text, I define a few basic terms to establish a common background of understanding. These terms are presented in Table 7.1.

TABLE 7.1
Basic Terms Related to Mixed Methods

Constructivist: An individual who believes that reality is mainly subjective. Constructivists generally ask questions that can best be answered through qualitative research.

Mixed methods: An approach that applies both qualitative and quantitative methods to an investigation.

Mixed models: An approach that applies qualitative and quantitative methods to each phase of a research study.

Paradigm: A way of viewing the world that is basic to a particular research design. Paradigms influence researchers' questions or hypotheses, research methods, and outcomes and interpretations.

Positivist: A researcher who views the world as objectively real and, therefore, quantifiable.

Qualitative design: A study characterized by narrative data and the collection of data from relatively few cases, usually in natural settings.

Quantitative design: A study characterized by numeric data and the collection of data from a large number of participants.

Scientific research: The investigation of a problem under specified circumstances to discover a definitive answer or answers to a problem. Research may occur in either natural or controlled environments, and requires that researchers (a) recognize their assumptions and limitations in conducting a study, (b) objectively develop and follow a design that facilitates the gathering of sufficient and appropriate data, (c) conduct and evaluate appropriate analyses, and (d) arrive at sound conclusions.

Triangulation: The convergence of multiple sets of data to interpret a single problem.

Historical Overview of Traditional Research Methodologies

Two traditional research methodologies have derived from different paradigms, and generally one or the other has dominated in various scientific disciplines (Creswell, 1994; Mertens, 1998; Neuman, 2000; Tashakkori & Teddlie, 1998). Both basic and applied research, including evaluation studies (Gay & Airasian, 2000), have employed a quantitative approach (Creswell, 1994; Reinard, 1998) and found it useful for detached, objective investigations. On the other hand, disciplines that have asked subjective questions—studies of the human *experience* of the objective world—have turned to qualitative research.

Quantitative Research

Positivists have generally relied upon quantitative research to address their hypotheses (Bernard, 2000; Gay & Airasian, 2000; Tulloch, 2000). Their world is an objective place, one where researchers attempt to determine, for example, the best teaching method for a particular class or a cure for a specific illness. This perspective had its origins in rationalism and empiricism and derived from the thinking of such philosophers as Aristotle, Bacon, Locke, and Kant (Brewer, Campbell, & Petty, 2000; Brewer & Marmon, 2000). Quantitative researchers assume that variables within a single research problem can be isolated for examination and that all else remains intact (Salomon, 1987). To solve research problems, positivists collect numerical data on their observations (Reinard, 1998). From their perspective, controlled investigations garner hard data that provides reliable evidence for solutions to problems. Types of studies within this broad category include quasi-experimental, experimental, correlational, causal-comparative, and quantitative (see Chapter 10). Quantitative design is also the choice for meta-analyses and for many single subject studies. The methodologies for these studies are typically either survey or experimental.

According to some researchers (Gall, Gall, & Borg, 1999; Patten, 1997; Reinard, 1998), quantitative research is characterized by deductive reasoning, large random samples, use of formal instruments, and the collection and analysis of numerical data. Quantitative studies isolate variables for study; participation often is anonymous. The total research design is developed prior to initiation of the study. Gay and Airasian (2000) reported that educational researchers have often combined basic and applied designs, although each has its own characteristics and purposes.

Quantitative studies have been divided into two categories: *basic* research and *applied* research, although methods are identical for both (Reinard, 1998). Fraenkel and Wallen (1996) enumerated those identical factors to include a preference for [1] precise hypotheses and definitions stated before the research begins, [2] numerical data, [3] precise explanations of research procedures, [4] control over extraneous variables, [5] control for procedural bias, [6] statistical statement of findings, and [7] random selection of appropriate participants. Since both basic and applied research methods collect numeric data, use similar research designs, and require objectivity, it may be difficult to determine whether a study is an example of one or the other. The key is to understand the purpose of a particular study. A brief discussion of each category follows.

Basic research is also called pure research or academic research. It is used to investigate theory or to advance fundamental or theoretical knowledge of either the physical or social world. According to Neuman (2000), explanatory research is the most common form of basic research, that is used to explain, describe, and sometimes predict the occurrence of phenomena. Theoretical research methods generate, verify, expand, or contradict current theoretical assumptions or beliefs. There is little emphasis on application of knowledge gained.

The ultimate purpose of applied research is to use findings to solve real-world problems. These problems may deal with behavior and attitudes, policy, or natural phenomena. Types of applied research include action research, social impact assessment, and evaluation studies (Neuman, 2000). Applied research has a theoretical framework but is not theory focused. Examples of appropriate applied research questions include: "Which of three methods of teaching basic concepts of statistics is most effective?" "Why did the number of auto fatalities increase nationally during the past 12 months?" "Is this training program achieving the purpose for which it was designed?"

Qualitative Research

Constructivists have relied on qualitative research to solve research problems (Marshall & Rossman, 1999; Mertens, 1998; Taylor & Bogdon, 2000; Tesch, 1990). Working from a paradigm that views reality as a construct of individual or group experience, constructivists ask different types of research questions. Research issues are considered complex and multi-textual, require inductive thinking, and involve exploration and discovery. To answer these types of research questions has called for different methods such as observations in natural settings, field experiences, and open-ended interviews. This approach to data collection contrasts with positivists' preference for controlled settings and close-ended queries. Constructivists favor a holistic approach because they see reality as systemic, that is, composed of interrelated parts that can not be isolated for examination without changing the whole (Salomon, 1987). Qualitative investigations are interested in how people interpret their own experiences. Research methods include grounded theory, ethnographic studies, historical research, and phenomenological studies (LoBiondo-Wood & Haber, 1998).

Characteristics of all qualitative studies include a preference for [1] definitions that may change as the study progresses, [2] narrative data, [3] assumptions of reliability of inferences, [4] purposive sampling, [5] less than precise discussion of procedures, [6] reliance on the researcher to be alert to and to control for procedural bias, [7] narrative discussion of results, and [8] logical analysis in controlling or accounting for extraneous variables (Fraenkel & Wallen, 1996). A qualitative approach can be used for either interpretive or critical research studies. The approach employs an holistic approach to problem-solving and emphasizes inductive processing and the collection and analysis of narrative data. The researcher's initial plan often is incomplete with no initial hypotheses. The plan is flexible and mainly descriptive. When possible, the "laboratory" is the field setting. "Qualitative researchers tend to spend a great deal of time in the settings they study" (Gay & Airasian, 2000, p. 19).

Summary of Quantitative and Qualitative Research Characteristics

Many contrasts exist between quantitative and qualitative methods. Gay and Airasian (2000) and Patten (1997) presented the following summative characteristics to differentiate these methods:

1. Reasoning for quantitative research is deductive; for qualitative it is inductive.

2. The purposes for quantitative are testing of theory and hypotheses, establishing facts and using them to predict; for qualitative research purposes include describing complex levels of reality and gaining an understanding of human experiences.

3. Quantitative research focuses on large samples, using formal instruments to collect numeric data, and controlled studies that isolate variables of interest. Qualitative research focuses on examining the full context and on face-to-face human interactions.

4. Quantitative research designs are structured and are developed prior to initiation of the study; qualitative designs begin with an idea that evolves during the research.

5. Data analysis in quantitative studies is statistical; qualitative analysis involves interpretive analysis of narrative data.

6. Quantitative researchers seek to collect data that is representative of a specified population and where results are generalizable to that population. Qualitative researchers seek to find the unique, rather than the common, and have little interest in the generalizibility of results.

Understanding the Paradigm War

A paradigm may be thought of as a lens through which one views the world. This lens represents a viewers' philosophical assumptions, affecting the perception and interpretation of what is seen. Positivists have long scorned the qualitative work of their constructivist colleagues and vice versa (Bernard, 2000; Mertens, 1998). In fact, the prominence of one approach in a particular academic discipline has frequently resulted in either the eclipse or demise of the other in that area of study. Perhaps, however, another issue has helped fuel this debate.

Ethnographic studies had a recognized place in early history. These *pre-scientific* studies, precursors to modern qualitative research, were relatively unsystematic observations and vulnerable to naiveté and personal bias. Examples include the recorded observations of Native Americans conducted by explorers from the 16th through early 20th centuries (see Brinton, 1891; Brownell, 1864; Morton, 1846; Wissler, 1938). Although such studies were simply preludes to true scientific investigations, they may have led some to view even modern-day qualitative research with cynicism. Thus, numerous authors (e.g., Bernard; Denzin & Lincoln, 1994; Strauss & Corbin, 1998) have noted a lack of professional respect between the two methodologies.

According to Wimmer and Dominick (2000), most researchers have come to understand the futility of the paradigm war and to recognize that both qualitative and quantitative methodologies are necessary "to fully understand the nature of a research problem" (p. 49). Those authors reported that convergent triangulation was frequently discussed in the research conducted on the field of communications.

Mixed Studies

During the past two decades, numerous researchers have moved beyond paradigm wars to a new paradigm that allows for integrating both perspectives (Creswell, 1994; LoBiondo-Wood & Haber, 1998; Strauss & Corbin, 1998). This view, leading to mixed studies, has resulted in the creation of two subcategories: *mixed methods* and *mixed models* (Tashakkori & Teddlie, 1998). An important point to remember is that mixed studies designs may call for data collection from different sources simultaneously or throughout two or more phases of the same study (Strauss & Corbin). In this section, I consider this issue and its potential for 21st century scientific research.

Mixed Methods

In mixed methods approaches, a single research issue is addressed by incorporating multiple forms of data collection in the research design. For example, a mail survey might also include field observations or open-ended telephone interviews. Generally, mixed methods supplement quantitative data taken from a larger sample with qualitative data from a smaller representation of the population. According to Miles and Huberman (1994), the purpose for employing this type of mixed design could be to add depth to the information gathered in the mail survey, to uncover any weaknesses in the quantitative data, or possibly to complement the objective data. Other mixed methods are also possible such as [1] addressing both quantitative and qualitative research questions, [2] quantifying narrative findings (i.e., counting the number of times various themes arise in interviews), and [3] qualifying some of the quantitative findings (e.g., writing a narrative profile of the mean participant based on the statistical data).

To summarize, when using mixed designs researchers perform both qualitative and quantitative techniques either *sequentially* or *simultaneously*. Another possibility is using a multiple-phase design where data is first collected and analyzed from either a qualitative or quantitative design. The next phase of data collection and analysis uses techniques from the remaining paradigm. Finally, data from both phases are integrated and summarized.

Mixed Models

Mixed models research combines quantitative and qualitative data collection techniques throughout the entire research plan. The purpose of mixed models research is the same as for the mixed methods approach. However, mixed models is more complex and offers interesting opportunities such as investigating both the objective and subjective worlds of human phenomena (e.g., everyday life in a war zone).

Tashakkori and Teddlie (1998) discussed a way of conducting a mixed model design that did not require incorporating both qualitative and quantitative methodologies into the same research plan. With respect to time frame, their idea utilized two types of mixed model designs: *simultaneous* (also referred to as parallel) and *sequential*. Each contained both qualitative and quantitative techniques within the data collection and analyses phases and in inferential statistics. General hypotheses research could be fitted into these mixed model designs. According to Tashakkori and Teddie, qualitative and quantitative studies could be conducted by using either simultaneous (parallel) or phased (sequential) investigations, rather than by incorporating both basic types of research in the same research project.

Simultaneous (parallel) designs. LoBiondo-Wood and Haber (1998), Tashakkori and Teddlie (1998), and Morse (1991) each discussed simultaneous, or parallel, models. Morse described simultaneous designs as ones that gather quantitative and qualitative data from different samples within a population. The two sets of data are collected independently, and are analyzed and compared afterward. Triangulation can be achieved through the convergence of findings from the two data sets. Thus, simultaneous designs consist of two independent studies (one qualitative and one quantitative) conducted at the same time, using two samples from the same population, with each methodology having equal status. Triangulation, if achieved, results from the convergence of data (Denzin & Lincoln, 1994; Tashakkori & Teddlie). The choice of a simultaneous design might depend on convenience, the availability of funding, concerns regarding contamination of data by conducting one study first then returning for the second phase, or hope of one using one set of data to complement the other.

In contrast to Morse's (1991) approach of using separate research samples, LoBiondo-Wood and Haber (1998) described several different designs that used the same research sample. One design called for conducting a qualitative study to serve as the foundation of the study with quantitative data being collected to provide complementary information. Another model involved the collection of quantitative data followed by the use of qualitative methods to collect data that would complement the basic findings. Strictly speaking, LoBiondo-Wood and Haber's simultaneous models were rapid sequential designs using the same sample for each portion with one basic method dominating and the other being used to for data triangulation.

Sequential designs. A sequential research design might include the collection of numerical data in the first phase of a study followed by field observations and open-ended interviews. The data from each phase would be analyzed and interpreted separately. Then, findings from each phase would be compared. Inferential findings would also be reported for the completed study. LoBiondo-Wood and Haber (1998) discussed sequential studies that involved the use of one method followed by the other, using the same sample. As with their simultaneous models, the first set of data dominated.

Creswell (1994) discussed the issue of dominance in mixed studies and noted two possibilities. One was using qualitative and quantitative data more or less equally throughout the study. Creswell termed this *equivalent status design.* The second possibility was the use of one methodology, qualitative or quantitative, for most of a study but with some inclusion of the other. Creswell termed this type *dominant-less dominant design.* For example, a quantitative study might examine two modes of instruction in a college freshman algebra course, a traditional classroom and on-line delivery. Data collection might include demographics, homework grades, and pre- and post-tests. If a researcher conducted e-mail interviews with a few students from each class and reported the narrative data that would constitute a dominant-less dominant study.

Triangulation

Triangulation always includes comparisons of multiple data sets for determining the consistency of evidence (Mertens, 1998). Some confusion could result from the variety of ways that this term is used, since researchers do not agree on its definition. Denzin and Lincoln (1994) identified four categories of triangulation.

1. *Data triangulation:* Use of a variety of data sources in a study.
2. *Investigator triangulation:* Use of several different researchers or evaluations.

3. *Theory triangulation:* Use of multiple perspectives to interpret a single problem.
4. *Methodological triangulation:* Use of multiple methods to study a single problem. (pp. 214-215)

My personal definition of triangulation corresponds to Denzin and Lincoln's (1994) fourth point, that is, methodological triangulation. Creswell (1994), referred to methodological triangulation as "triangulation in the classic sense of seeking convergence of results" (p. 175). This definition is shared by numerous other researchers (e.g., Babbie, 2000; Flick, 1998; Greene, Caracelli, & Graham,1989; Jick, 1979; Neuman, 2000; Tulloch 2000; Wimmer & Dominick, 2000). However, others (e.g., Berg, 1989; Frankfort-Nachmias & Nachmias, 1996; LaBiondo-Wood & Haber, 1998) defined triangulation studies according to Denzin and Lincoln's (1994) methodological triangulation, that is, to include all mixed methods studies.

Triangulation is one possible outcome of using a mixed methods approach or a mixed models design. If data from independent methodologies confirms the findings for a particular research question, then triangulation is said to have occurred. That finding, however, must never be assumed beforehand.

Other Types of Triangulation

When multiple databases view a single problem from different angles and meet at a particular location, *convergent triangulation* has been reached. Jick (1979) described this phenomenon using the analogy of sailors measuring distance by using multiple methods. Neuman (2000) called this a *triangulation of measures* and noted that it substantially increased researchers' confidence in their findings because the same results are viewed from multiple angles. Another type, *triangulation of observers*, includes multiple interviewers or field observers to gain depth of perspective and to correct biases of a single observer. Newman also recognized *triangulation of theory* utilization of several theoretical perspectives to plan a research study or for the interpretation of results. This type of triangulation could increase creativity in synthesizing information and in developing new perspectives.

The different methodologies may confirm findings, increase the depth of knowledge gained, or even refute one another. In the latter case, it becomes the researcher's task to conduct additional analyses or to draw inferences from the existing analyses to understand the variant findings. It could also be seen as an alert that further studies are needed.

Across-methods triangulation. Campbell and Fiske (1959) devised the term *multiple operationalism* when attempting to confirm the validity of specific findings. They argued that an apparent validation of findings could result from variance in the method employed rather than from the variable under investigation. Thus, obtaining confirmatory results using multiple methods provides assurance of the validity of those findings. This design, according to Jick (1979), represents the most often used form of triangulation and the one most trusted when congruent results are obtained.

Within-methods triangulation. Within-methods designs use various techniques within one basic method. An example might be the use of both a questionnaire that is administered immediately following course completion and a mailed questionnaire to determine students' experience with a college course. In such a case, the use of multiple techniques serves to cross-check findings and to increase external validity (Denzin, 1989; Jick, 1979).

Triangulation study designs represent a continuum from simple to complex (Jick, 1979). A modest, straight-forward mixed study is useful for validating a scale of a research instrument and also the instrument's reliability. *Convergent triangulation* can strengthen confidence in research findings, and a complex design such as a mixed models plan can also add depth to findings by supplying multiple levels of information.

Even when data convergence does not occur, the use of mixed methodologies is recommended because it provides for "complimentarity" of the data obtained from one source, adding depth. This can provide greater understanding of the research topic, especially for theory confirmation and development (LoBiondo-Wood & Haber, 1998; Strauss & Corbin, 1998; Tashakkori & Teddlie, 1998).

Presentation of Three Studies

It may be helpful to consider several examples of mixed design studies. Three studies are presented in this section that represent a variety of mixed methodologies. Two are sequential studies and one is a simultaneous equal-status triangulation study. At the end of each presentation, I provide a brief observation of the study.

Tulloch's (2000) Study

In *The Meaning of Age Differences in the Fear of Crime: Combining Qualitative and Quantitative Approaches,* Tulloch (2000) conducted a two-phase study that used basic quantitative approaches in the first phase and qualitative approaches in a second, smaller phase.

Phase 1. The first phase of Tulloch's (2000) study involved participants from New South Wales, Australia and from Tasmania. There were 11 focus groups from both rural and urban settings in Australia and 4 focus groups from Tasmania, for a total of 148 subjects. The initial research procedure called for asking close-ended questions centered on interviewees' feelings of safety when they were alone in their own homes. Participants were asked to rate their perceived risk for specific crimes. Using a 5-point Likert-type scale, respondents were presented a set of statements regarding the increase of societal violence in Australia. The close-ended questions were followed-up with open-ended, probing questions. Verbal transcripts comprised the data for the follow-up questions. In the focus groups, individuals first completed written forms to provide demographic information. The focus groups then discussed questions similar to those in the individual interviews. Thus, both quantitative and qualitative data were gathered from individuals and from the focus groups.

Tulloch (2000) also conducted a path analysis on the data to model the relationship of predictors with fear of crime. She determined that the greatest predictors for perceived fear were age, gender, and size. The dominant data set was qualitative. Tulloch found that both age and gender were predictors of perceived risk.

Phase 2. Tulloch (2000) conducted a follow-up after the findings of her primary study had been analyzed. Based on Phase 1 findings, Tulloch determined that there were differences based on age and gender in the perceptions of being at risk of violent crime and on participants' experiences and behaviors (victimization perceptions). Phase 2 sought to determine "how people use social categories in their narratives about crime threat" (p. 460). In this study, social self-concept was the variable of interest. Qualitative analysis was conducted to examine the narrative data of representatives from distinctive social groups rather than to obtain data from a wide range of persons. The first study dealt with participants' experiences of fear of crime when they were alone at home. This second study dealt with participants' experiences when traveling alone via public transportation. The procedure was similar to that used in the first phase.

Phase 2 uncovered some divergent findings. For example, a focus group of gay participants reported that their physical appearance and behavior resulted in being victimized. This contrasted with other young male participants who felt least vulnerable and were more likely to be the aggressors. Another discrepant finding was that aggressors could be older females.

> One young male recounted that he was 'minding my own business sitting having a smoke' at a bus stop when he was confronted by a handbag-waving 'loony' old woman who swore at him, telling onlookers that if he hit anyone she would hit him. She followed him on and off the bus and chased him home. (Tulloch, 2000, p. 464)

Another participant reported that an elderly female retaliated when three young males annoyed her as they were riding on public transportation. After the third provocation, she pulled out a knife and threatened them. Tulloch reported that the three perpetrators left immediately.

Tulloch's (2000) study provides an excellent example of a sequential study using a dominant-less dominant design. One sees both the complimentarity of two approaches (qualitative and quantitative) and the relative weakness of Phase Two due to the omission of a quantitative component from a larger population. Interesting as the divergent incidents are, without quantitative data it is not known whether or not they represent anything beyond anecdotal information.

Aldriage, Fraser, and Tai-Chu's (1999) Study

In this comparative-interpretive study, *Investigating Classroom Environments in Taiwan and Australia with Multiple Research Methods,* Aldridge, Fraser, and Tai-Chu (1999) sought to identify and understand cultural similarities and differences in diverse educational settings. Diverse methods were used to gain a deeper understanding of the variables under study.

The first part of the Aldridge et al. (1999) study was quantitative and provided an overview of the population with a sample of 2,960 students. Participants completed demographic and attitude questionnaires. Based on that information, researchers designed some of their interview questions to determine socio-cultural differences in students' expectations of desirable learning environments. This phase of this study consisted of field observations and in-depth interviews with teachers and "at least three students from each of eight classrooms" (p. 50). Different observation and interview techniques were used in the two countries to permit cross-validation of the information. Data were found to be complementary.

The quantitative part of the study (Aldridge et al., 1999) indicated weaknesses that the investigators attributed to cultural differences. One such weakness was reflected in differences found on the student attitude scale. These differences guided investigators to formulate some of the interview questions used to explore the diverse expectations of students based on cultural factors. Another shortcoming was identified during the interview phase: the Chinese translation of the attitudes scale did not always convey the full meaning of the original (English) text. A third difficulty was that the questionnaire contained some questions that were foreign to the experience of Taiwanese students, such as, "I discuss ideas in class."

Since the purpose of Aldridge et al.'s (1999) study was to gain an understanding of learning environments in two diverse settings, the qualitative information was considered dominant. Analysis revealed that each environment was determined by socio-cultural factors including expectations regarding the behavior of children and young people, teachers' behavior toward students, and the education system.

The first part of the study served two purposes. It validated the instruments used in each cultural setting, and it provided an overview of each culture. Investigators used that information to guide their field observations and interviews. In addition to providing information needed for gathering qualitative data, the quantitative data corroborated multiple aspects of the qualitative findings such as student involvement and task orientation. Convergent triangulation was achieved on those aspects of the study.

Floyd's (1993) Study

Floyd's (1993) study, *The Use of Across-Method Triangulation in the Study of Sleep Concerns in Healthy Older Adults,* is an example of simultaneous, equal-status research. The purpose of this study was to identify and evaluate the sleep patterns and sleep concerns of older adults. Research questions were formulated to determine the influences of age, gender, and sleep concerns on participants' sleep patterns. Floyd's study used the same participants for both qualitative and quantitative aspects. Criteria for selection included an ability to articulate experiences with sleep and an appropriate representation of males and females.

The 173 participants were randomly assigned to different data collection procedures. One group completed the qualitative instrument first and then completed the quantitative instrument. The other group completed instruments in the reverse order. In the interviews, participants responded to semi-structured questions such as, "What do you do to handle aspects of sleep that bother you?" (Floyd, 1993, p. 73). In addition, three quantitative instruments were used to determine participants' level of activity, health status, sleep patterns, and other relevant information. Floyd used *t* tests to compare frequency and intensity scores on the two instruments and found that the order of instrument completion had no significant effect on responses.

Four themes were identified through the qualitative interviews: physical discomfort, external environmental factors, emotional discomfort, and sleep pattern changes. Triangulation of quantitative and qualitative data sets revealed that approximately one-half of all participants were troubled to some extent by sleep concerns. Consistently, 54.8% of females and 45.2% of males reported concerns.

One possible disadvantage with a study like Floyd (1993) is that participants' responses to the second instrument (either interview or questionnaire) can be influenced by experiences with the first instrument. This problem can be circumvented by selecting two groups of participants, perhaps a larger one for the quantitative study and a relatively small group for interviews. However, Floyd elected to use the same participants for both parts of the study and to subdivide them. One subgroup completed the questions first; the other completed interviews first. The fact that the order of data collection was not significant validated the selection method and answered a question that could not have been considered if a different route had been taken (e.g., using separate samples for each data set).

Disadvantages and Advantages of Mixed Studies

Employing a combination of research methods has both advantages and disadvantages. Thoughtful decisions must be made on need and the availability of resources. Before addressing the advantages and disadvantages of mixed studies, I present Reinard's (1996) personal challenges that should be considered before undertaking any research.

Personal Challenges

Reinhard's (1996) five challenges apply equally to designers and administers of mixed research studies.

1. *Orderly thinking:* Faithful, systematic research requires an organized approach.
2. *Clear writing:* Communicating a complex design to others (e.g., funding sponsors. research participants, consumers) requires precise, organized writing.
3. *Objectivity:* A lack of prejudice for one research technique over another is necessary to proceed with objectivity.
4. *Organization and orderly process:* A need exists for orderly thinking and clear writing.
5. *Astute reasoning in developing the research methods:* Logic is necessary for *effective,* complex designs. (p. 12)

After reviewing these, an individual should consider whether or not mixed methodological would be appropriate. But before doing that, one should also evaluate the disadvantages and advantages presented in the following paragraphs.

Disadvantages of Using Mixed Studies

Some disadvantages of mixing methods involve the challenges I have mentioned previously. Since complexity is increased with mixed studies, researchers must be especially careful. Keeping studies free of bias in participant selection and interviewing can be difficult. If quantitative data is examined prior to a field study and interviews, for example, researchers could have difficulty remaining bias-free. On the other hand, fine-tuning the design of a supplemental research phase might be facilitated by an understanding of the findings obtained during the primary phase.

In addition to personal challenges, some studies may present difficulties because of circumstances only indirectly related to the purpose of the study. Polit and Hungler (1991) noted four items that some researchers consider disadvantages to mixed methods: [1] higher possible costs, [2] a lack of training of those directing or conducting the study, [3] certain professional journals may lean towards one method or other, and [4] epistemological biases of some research consumers. When considering mixed methods, Morse (1991) pointed out that the greatest threat to the validity of mixed methods is the use of the same sample. She felt that the sample for a qualitative aspect of a study should be separate from the sample of a quantitative component.

In addition to these general disadvantages, certain circumstances— grant proposals, dissertations and theses—can pose other difficulties. When applying for competitive funding, certain issues must be considered when combining methodologies. Writing a proposal requires careful explanation of the purposes for each technique used and, in multi-phase studies, for the separate phases of the study. There should be a clear justification for combining methods beyond the general purpose of providing more confidence in the research findings. While such a goal is useful, it ordinarily would not justify the additional funding needed. In fact, this type of rationale could be interpreted as a revelation of the investigator's insecurity or lack of experience. To ease the problems of requesting funding for phased studies, Strauss and Corbin (1998) recommended breaking down multi-phase research plans into a series of proposals with a specific purpose for each. In this manner, findings from the previous phase/s can be used to justify using a different research technique in the next phase.

In their text, *Secrets for a Successful Dissertation,* Fitzpatrick, Secrist, and Wright (1998) strongly advised graduate students not to embark on mixed methods studies. The authors stated that one of them had done so and encountered monumental difficulties. Among the obstacles they discussed were:

1. The process is time and labor intensive.
2. Conducting two types of research can be doubly expensive.
3. The candidate may lack adequate research skills for the two methods.
4. The candidate's committee may raise more questions concerning results.

Nevertheless, there is a wide range of topics for dissertation and thesis investigation, and candidates have varied experiences and resources. Therefore, I tend to disagree with Fitzpatrick et al. (1998), depending on the topic, student, and committee. I would encourage the "right" student to do a mixed methodological study. Mixed methodologies can add credibility and importance to a proposed study, as well as enhance students' research skills.

Advantages of Using Mixed Studies

There are multiple advantages to using mixed methodologies rather than relying on only one method. Not infrequently, a study benefits from more than one of these advantages.

Complement other findings. Greene et al. (1989) mentioned that complementarity of results can be a positive outcome of mixed studies.

Expand information. Results of mixed studies sometimes increases the scope of knowledge about a problem. This may be the case when different techniques yield conflicting data, as well as when undiscovered aspects or previously unmentioned information is reported (Creswell, 1994).

Overcome bias. Qualitative techniques used in isolation are open to observer bias, and this weakness can be overcome by using quantitative data as a balance. Fine and Elsbach (2000) noted two types of bias that can affect qualitative data. "What one 'observes' is filtered through one's experience (bias is interpretive), and one's presence in a situation inevitably affects—to a greater or lesser extent—how participants respond (observer bias)" (p. 53). This observation was supported by Wimmer and Dominick (2000) who noted that field studies were vulnerable to reactivity (observer bias). Use of multiple observers or interviewers can also be used to correct bias.

Uncover need for further study. Firestone (1987), referring to use of only one method, stated that a need exists to to assess findings for strength and stability. In two-phase studies, the risks of these weaknesses are minimized. For example, in the second phase of Tulloch's (2000) study, information from an elderly woman and gay participant was at variance with Phase One quantitative findings. Even though the results had come from a mixed study, the qualitative data appeared to need further investigation. If only the second phase had been conducted, Tulloch would have been blinded to its inadequacy.

Confirm hypotheses. Triangulation studies are advantageous for hypothesis testing. Frankfort-Nachmias and Nachmias (1996) advocated using mixed studies whenever feasible for theory building.

Show development. Sequential design may show development of the phenomenon under investigation.

Add texture. Findings from one technique may be enriched by those of the alternate technique—uncovering paradoxes, contradictory findings, or other information.

Summary

Many studies could be enhanced by using mixed methodologies including theory development, reliability studies, and validity studies. Reichardt and Rallis (1994) discussed two interesting studies that might have benefited from mixed methodologies. In the first, Whittingham's (1986) research included a listing of the best ski resort cities in the United States. Cities such as Detroit, Buffalo, and Chicago were among the top 10, whereas Denver, Winter Park, and other Colorado resorts were not mentioned. Had researchers also completed a field study their embarrassing error might have been avoided. Following the

Whittingham report another researcher, Kliewer (1986), conducted interviews with some of the top 10 listed resort managers. He learned that the Detroit slopes were built on a landfill and relied on artificial snow. Another manager reported that the slope was mainly a hill designed to prepare skiers for higher slopes. Kliewer later interviewed Whittingham and learned that he had relied on usage data alone and had not taken into account the quality of the sites. Thus, his report had resulted in a listing of 10 high-density population areas! This illustration highlights one of the possible research errors when only one methodology is employed.

Another, more famous research error resulting from use of a single methodology is found in Margaret Meade's (1928) famous study, *Coming of Age in Samoa: A Psychological Study of Primitive Youth.* Meade relied on field observations and interviews to investigate sexual activity in a society with which she was unfamiliar. She wrote that promiscuous behavior was the norm among preadolescents and adolescents in Samoa. What Meade did not realize was that the young females whom she interviewed were embarrassed by her questions and that they saw her intense focus on sexual behavior as strange. They believed the researcher was obsessively preoccupied with sexual behavior and decided to tell her whatever they believed she wanted to hear. Findings of this widely acclaimed study were later discovered to be a hoax. Again, the error might have been avoided had multiple methodologies been employed in addressing this research issue.

Fortunately, the concept of enhancing research efforts through triangulation may be coming to the forefront. As noted, some researchers (e.g., Creswell, 1994; Tashakkori & Teddlie, 1998; Wimmer & Dominick, 2000) are seeing the value of using multiple approaches to the same research issue. Tashakkori and Teddlie even spoke of the paradigm war as a phenomenon of the past, claiming that "the triangulation of methods [Denzin and Lincoln's (1994) methodological triangulation] was the intellectual wedge that eventually broke the methodological hegemony of the mono-method purists" (p. 41). Stated succinctly, it ended the paradigm war.

References

Aldridge, J. M., Fraser, B. J., & Tai-Chu, I. H. (1999). Investigating classroom environments in Taiwan and Australia with multiple research methods. *Journal of Educational Research, 93*(1), 48-62.

Babbie, E. (2000). *The practice of social research* (9th ed.). Belmont, CA: Wadsworth.

Berg, B. L. (1989). *Qualitative research methods for the social sciences.* Needham Heights, MA: Allyn and Bacon.

Bernard, H. R. (2000). *Social research methods: Qualitative and quantitative approaches.* Thousand Oaks, CA: Sage.

Brinton, D. G. (1891). *The American race: A linguistic classification and ethnographic description of the native tribes of North and South America.* New York: Johnson Reprint.

Brewer, E. W., Campbell, A. C., & Petty, G. C. (2000). *Foundations of workforce education: Historical, philosophical, and theoretical applications.* Dubuque, IA: Kendall/Hunt.

Brewer, E. W., & Marmon, D. (2000). *Characteristics, skills, and strategies of the ideal educator.* Boston, MA: Pearson Education.

Brownell, C. D. W. (1864). *The Indian races of North and South America.* Hartford, CT: Scraton Hurlbut.

Creswell, J. W. (1994). *Research design: Qualitative and quantitative approaches.* Thousand Oaks, CA: Sage.

Campbell, D., & Fiske, D. W. (1959). Convergent and discriminant validation by the multitrait-multimethod matrix. *Psychological Bulletin, 54,* 297-312.

Denzin, N. K. (1989). *The research act* (3rd ed.). Englewood Cliffs, NJ: Prentice-Hall.

Denzin, N. K., & Lincoln, Y. S. (Eds.). (1994). *Handbook of qualitative research.* Thousand Oaks, CA: Sage.

Fine, G. A., & Elsbach, K. D. (2000). Ethnography and experiment in social psychological theory building: Tactics for integrating qualitative field data with quantitative lab data. *Journal of Experimental Social Psychology, 36*(1), 51-76.

Firestone, W. A. (1987). Meaning in method: The rehetoric of quantitative and qualitative research. *Educational Researcher, 16*(7), 16-21.

Flick, U. (1998). *An introduction qualitative research.* Thousand Oaks, CA: Sage.

Floyd, J. A. (1993). The use of across-method triangulation in the study of sleep concerns in healthy older adults. *Advanced Nursing Science, 16*(2), 70-80.

Fitzpatrick, J., Secrist, J., & Wright, D. J. (1998). *Secrets for a successful dissertation.* Thousand Oaks, CA: Sage.

Fraenkel, J. R., & Wallen, N. E. (1996). *How to design and evaluate research in education* (3rd ed.). New York: McGraw-Hill.

Frankfort-Nachmias, C., & Nachmias, D. (1996). *Research methods in the social sciences* (5th ed.). New York: St. Martin's Press.

Gall, J. P., Gall, M. D., & Borg, W. R. (1999). *Applying educational research* (4th ed.). Reading, MA: Addison Wesley Longman.

Gay, L. R., & Airasian, P. (2000). *Educational research: Competencies for analysis and application* (6th ed.). Upper Saddle River, NJ: Merrill.

Goodwin, C. J. (1995). *Research in psychology: Methods and designs.* New York: Wiley & Sons.

Greene, J. C., Caracelli, V. J., & Graham, W. F. (1989). Toward a conceptual frames of mixed-method evaluation designs. *Educational Evaluation and Policy Analysis, 11*(3), 255-274.

Jick, T. D. (1979). Mixing qualitative and quantitative methods: Triangulation in action. *Administrative Science Quarterly, 4,* 602-611.

Kliewer, T. D. (1986). America's top skiing mecca? Why, Detroit! *Denver Post,* December 12, 1A.

Leary, M. R. (1995). *Behavioral research methods* (2nd ed.). Pacific Grove, CA: Brooks/Cole.

LoBiondo-Wood, G., & Haber, J. (1998). *Nursing research: Methods, critical appraisal, and utilization* (4th ed.). St. Louis, MO: Mosby.

Marshall, C., & Rossman, G. B. (1999). *Designing qualitative research* (3rd ed.). Thousand Oaks, CA: Sage.

McBurney, D. H. (1994). *Research methods* (3rd ed.). Pacific Grove, CA: Brooks/Cole.

Meade, M. (1928). *Coming of age in Samoa: A psychological study of primitive youth for Western civilization.* New York: Morrow.

Mertens, D. M. (1998). *Research methods in education and psychology: Integrating diversity with quantitative and qualitative approaches.* Thousand Oaks, CA: Sage.

Miles, M. B., & Huberman, A. M. (1994). *An expanded sourcebook: Qualitative data analysis* (2nd ed.). Thousand Oaks, CA: Sage.

Morse, J. M. (1991). Approaches to qualitative-quantitative methodological triangulation. *Nursing Research, 40*(1), 120-123.

Morton, S. G. (1846). *Some observations on the ethnography and archaeology of the American aborigines.* New Haven, CT: B. L. Hamlen.

Neuman, L. W. (2000). *Social research methods: Qualitative and quantitative approaches* (4th ed.). Needham Heights, MA: Allyn & Bacon.

Patten, M. L. (1997). *Understanding research methods: An overview of the essentials.* Los Angeles: Pyrczak.

Polit, D. F., & Hungler, B. P. (1991). *Nursing research: Principles and methods* (4th ed.) Philadelphia: Lippincott.

Reichardt, C. S., & Rallis, S. F. (1994). The relationship between the qualitative and quantitative research traditions. In C. S. Reichardt & S. F. Rallis (Eds.), *The qualitative–quantitative debate: New perspectives* (No. 61). San Francisco: Jossey-Bass.

Reinard, J. (1998). *Introduction to communication research* (2nd ed.). Boston: McGraw Hill.

Salomon, G. (1987). Transcending the qualitative-quantitative debate: The analytic and systemic approaches to educational research. *Educational Researcher, 16*(7), 10-18.

Strauss, A., & Corbin, J. (1998). *Basics of qualitative research: Grounded theory procedures and techniques* (2nd ed.). Thousand Oaks, CA: Sage.

Tashakkori, A., & Teddlie, C. (1998). *Mixed methodology: Combining qualitative and quantitative approaches* (Applied Social Research Methods Series, Vol. 46). Thousand Oaks, CA: Sage.

Taylor, S. J., & Bogdon, R. (2000). *Introduction to qualitative research methods: The search for meanings* (2nd ed.). New York: Wiley & Sons.

Tesch, R. (1990). *Qualitative research analysis types and software tools.* New York: Falmer.

Tulloch, M. (2000). The meaning of age differences in the fear of crime: Combining quantitative and qualitative approaches. *The Centre for Crime and Justice Studies, 40,* 451-467.

Whittingham, R. (1986). *Sports places rated: Ranking America's best places to enjoy sports.* Chicago: Rand McNally.

Wimmer, R. D., & Dominick, J. R. (2000). *Mass media research* (6th ed.). Belmont, CA: Wadsworth.

Wissler, C. (1938). *The American Indian: An introduction to the anthropology of the New World.* New York: Oxford University Press.

Chapter 8

Case Study Research

Derek Mulenga

This chapter examines the main tasks involved in designing and conducting case study research and provides an example of how to apply these tasks to case study research in education. The chapter has five main sections. First, the nature and characteristics of case studies are discussed, along with a brief history of the design. The second section looks at the main types of case studies, drawing heavily on the work of leading experts on case study research including Bassey (1999), Stenhouse (1985), Stake (2000), and Yin (1994). The third section describes the tasks contains in the three phases of designing and implementing case studies. The underlying assumption of this design is that case study research, whether a single-case analysis or comparative investigation, is primarily a "structured" (i.e., the same general questions are asked of each case in order to guide data collection) and "focused" (i.e., the study deals with only certain aspects of the cases) method. Studies presented in the fourth section illustrate how the main tasks inherent in case study investigations are implemented. The final section offers several conclusions about designing and implementing case study research.

What is Case Study Research?

Case study research has become increasingly popular as a form of qualitative inquiry in education and other disciplines. The design excels in examining complex phenomena through a detailed contextual analysis of a limited number of events or conditions and their relationships. And yet, case studies are neither new nor essentially qualitative. Although the disciplines of anthropology and sociology are usually credited with shaping the concept as we know it today, case study research has been influenced by a variety of sources including history, social work, law, medicine, and journalism (Hamel, 1993).

It is important to note that many researchers conducting doing case study research call their work by other names such as "fieldwork," "field study" or "ethnography." The use of different labels contributes little to an understanding of what researchers do. There is also some debate whether the case study is an approach or a method. The critical question, then, is, "What is a case study?"

First, a case study is not a methodological choice. Rather, it is primarily characterized by an interest in individual cases. This interest in an individual or single case is the driving motivation behind the use of a case study approach. The specific methods used to study individual cases are of secondary significance.

Stake (2000) identifies three features of a case. First, a case may be simple or complex. It may be an incident, a person, or a group of employees in a factory. A focus on one specific thing is what makes up a case study. "The time we spend concentrating our inquiry on one may be long or short, but while we so concentrate, we are engaged in case study" (p. 436). Second, the case is a bounded, functioning specific, that is, a purposive, integrated system with working parts. For example, a school as a case is a functioning (or dysfunctioning) combination of students, teachers, learning, teaching, and other aspects. Third, the behavior of the case is patterned; there is a certain order and coherence to it. One may be interested in the internal workings of a case, within the boundaries of the case or other aspects outside it's boundaries. It is also important to recognize that interest may be in a population of cases more than in any individual case, particularly if one cannot understand this case without studying other cases. Thus, it is possible to study a comparison of cases. Finally, the way a case is defined is not entirely independent of researchers' paradigm or methods of inquiry. Two researchers with different paradigms may see the same school (the case) differently. The definition of a case changes in different ways under different methods of research.

Short of Stake's (2000) proposed features of a case study, there is no agreed upon definition. A case study is both a process of inquiry and a product of that inquiry. Sturman (1997), writing in the second edition of *Educational Research, Methodology and Measurement: An International Handbook*, offered this definition:

'Case study' is a generic term for the investigation of an individual, group or phenomenon. While the techniques used in the investigation may be varied, and may be both qualitative and quantitative approaches, the distinguishing feature of the case study is the belief that human develop a characteristic wholeness or integrity and not simply a loose collection of traits. As a consequence of this belief, case study researchers hold that to understand a case, to explain why things happen as they do, and to generalize or predict from a single example requires an in-depth investigation of the interdependencies of the parts and patterns that emerge. (p. 94)

In his now classic book, *Case Study Research: Design and Methods*, Robert Yin (1994), a leading expert on case study research, emphasized the "real-life context" of case studies, as opposed to contrived contexts found with surveys or experiments. He defined case study as empirical inquiry examining contemporary phenomena within real-life contexts, especially when the boundaries between phenomenon and context are not clearly evident. Yin noted three key features of case study research: [1] examination of many variables in given situation as one, [2] reliance on multiple sources of evidence, with data needing to converge in a triangulating fashion, and [3] benefits from the prior development of theoretical propositions to guide data collection and analysis.

Another leading authority on case study is Robert Stake. In *The Art of Case Study Research*, Stake (1995) defined case study as "the study of the particularity and complexity of a single case, coming to understand its activity within important circumstances" (p. xi). Stake elaborated on this definition by pointing out that a case is both a bounded and integrated system. The system's parts may not be working well or the purposes may be irrational, but it is a system nonetheless.

Clearly, the term case study has many meanings. However, there is some agreement that the quintessential characteristic of a case study is the purpose of deriving holistic understanding of a particular, unique, and bounded system. Case study, therefore, refers to the collection, analysis, and presentation of detailed information about a specific phenomenon. Typically, emphasis is placed on *exploration* and *description* rather than on discovery of universal, generalizable truths.

Types of Case Studies

In the literature on case study research there are a number of classifications or types of case studies described, depending on one's research goals. Here, I review the main approaches advocated by Stenhouse (1985), Yin (1993), and Stake (2000).

Stenhouse (1985) identified four broad styles of case study; ethnographic, evaluative, educational and action research. He described ethnographic case studies as

> A single case . . . studied in depth by participant observation supported by interview, after a manner of cultural or social anthropology . . . Of ethnographic case study it may be said that it call into question the apparent understanding of the actors in the case and offers from the outsider's standpoint explanation that emphasize causal or structural patterns of which participants in the case are unaware. (p. 49)

Stenhouse saw the other three types of case studies as being concerned with different aspects of educational action. In evaluative case studies, a single case or collection of cases is studied in depth in order to inform educational actors with knowledge needed to judge the merit or worth of policies, programs, or institutions.

Yin (1993) categorized case studies into three main types or approaches; exploratory, explanatory, and descriptive. Each one of these approaches can be either a single or multiple-case design, where multiple-case studies are replicatory, not sampled cases.

An exploratory case study is aimed at defining specific research questions or hypotheses for subsequent (not necessarily case) study (Yin, 1993). Fieldwork and data collection may actually be undertaken prior to the definition of specific research questions and hypotheses. This type of study has often been considered a prelude to some types of social research. However, the framework of the study must be created ahead of time. Pilot projects are very useful in determining the final protocols used. Survey questions may be dropped or added based on the outcome of a pilot study

Selecting cases is a difficult process, but the literature provides guidance (Yin, 1989). Generally, it is recommended that case selection offer the opportunity to maximize what can be learned, knowing that time is limited. Hence, cases that are selected should reflect easy and willing participants.

An explanatory case study presents data that informs cause-effect relationships, that is, explaining which causes produce which effects (Yin, 1993). Explanatory cases are suitable for doing *causal* studies. In very complex and multivariate cases, analysis can make use of pattern-matching techniques.

In 1985, Moore and Yin examined the reasons that some research findings get translated into practical use while others do not. They used a funded research project as their *unit of analysis*, where the topic was constant but the project varied. The outcomes of their work were explained by three rival theories, i.e., a knowledge-driven theory, a problem-solving theory, and a social-interaction theory. Knowledge-driven theory means that ideas and discoveries from basic research eventually become commercial products. Problem-solving theory follows this same path, but originates not with researchers, but external sources that identify problems. Social-interaction theory claims that researchers and users belong to overlapping professional networks and are in frequent communication.

A descriptive case study presents complete description of a phenomenon within its context (Yin, 1993). Descriptive cases require that investigators begin with a descriptive theory or face the possibility that problems will occur during the project. The descriptive theory must cover the depth and scope of cases being studied. The selection of cases and unit of analysis are developed in the same manner as the other types of case studies.

Finally, Stake (1995, 2000) identified three types of case studies; intrinsic, instrumental, and collective. An intrinsic case study is undertaken to better understand *the* particular case.

> Here, it [the intrinsic case study] is not undertaken to primarily because the case represents other cases or because it illustrates a particular trait or problem, but because, in all its particularity and ordinariness, this case itself is of interest. (2000, p. 437)

The purpose of an intrinsic case study is not to understand some abstract construct or generic phenomenon. Similarly, the purpose is not theory building although this is not completely ruled out. Rather, an intrinsic case study is undertaken because of an intrinsic interest in, for example, a particular vocational education teacher or vocational curriculum.

Stake (2000) categorizes an investigation as being *instrumental* when a particular case is examined mainly to provide insight about an issue or to redraw a generalization.

> The case is of secondary interest, it plays a supportive role, and it facilitates our understanding of something else. The case is still looked at in depth, its contexts scrutinized, its ordinary activities detailed, but all because this helps the researcher to pursue the external interest. (p. 437)

The choice of an instrumental case is made to advance understanding of a topic of interest. For example, a researcher may be interested in the impact of new curriculum guidelines on teacher performance and success. To understand "teacher performance," a particular teacher in a specific school may be studied. The case, the selected teacher, need not be typical of other cases (other teachers in the school). Because researchers generally have several interests, a line that distinguishes intrinsic and instrumental case study does not exist. Rather, a zone of combined interest separates them.

The third type of case study Stake (2000) identifies is the collective case study which involves jointly studying a number of cases in order a to understand a phenomenon, population, or general condition. It is essential that instrumental case studies are extended to several cases. Since single cases may or may not be known in advance to manifest some common characteristic, cases are selected because of the belief that understanding them will lead to a better understanding or better theorizing about a larger collection of cases. Elsewhere, Herriot and Firestone (1983) have referred to Stake's collective case study as *multi-site* qualitative research.

Stake (2000) correctly noted that the three types of case studies should be viewed as heuristic rather than determinative categories. Case studies do not fit neatly into any of the typologies suggested by Stenhouse (1985), Yin (1993), or Stake. In fact, within the burgeoning literature on case study methodology, there are a number of other types of case studies. For example, in *Naturalistic Inquiry*, Lincoln and Guba (1985) classify case studies into four categories according to function and purpose. Similarly, Ragin (1992) conceptualizes case studies into two by two categories, as empirical units or theoretical constructs, and general or specific in nature.

Finally, while law and medical schools have been using the case study method as a method of instruction for decades, it is now widely used in variety in humanities and social sciences. Schools of business, such as the Harvard Business School, have been the most aggressive in implementing case-based or *active* learning as a primary method of teaching. The main advantage of the case method as a teaching strategy is the transfer of responsibility for learning from teachers to students, whose role, as a result, shifts away from passive absorption toward active construction (Boehrer, 1990).

Designing Case Studies

Just as there are different purposes for research (description, explanation, prediction) and different modes of theory-building (heuristic induction of possible theories, empirical testing of competing theories, and exploratory probes of new-theories), there are many types of research designs possible when using a case study approach. Designs are usually adapted to fit different purposes including single case studies, comparative case studies, and case studies for most and least likely cases as examples.

Before discussing specific procedures and tasks involved in designing and implementing a case study, it is important to note that, to a certain extent, the field of study will influence design. In anthropological and educational studies, researchers work from a predominantly qualitative, descriptive standpoint. In contrast, researchers in economics and related *hard* social sciences may approach their research from a more quantitative perspective.

Still, in designing any case study, theoretical perspectives need to be made explicit. The three most commonly adopted perspectives are individual, organizational, and social theories. Individual theories focus primarily on individual development, cognitive behavior, personality, learning and disability and interpersonal interactions of a particular individual. Organizational theories focus on bureaucracies, institutions, organizational structure and functions. Social theories focus on urban development, group behavior, cultural institutions, or market place functions. Of course, a theoretical perspective may be derived from multiple levels and focuses.

Within the literature, the design and implementation of case studies is commonly described in the form of phases, stages, or tasks. Obviously, this is a simplification process because research is a creative activity and every inquiry has its own unique character. Even so, Yin (1994) identified five components of design that are important for case study research:

1. Clearly stated research questions,
2. Propositions of the study, if any,
3. The selected unit(s) of analysis,
4. The logic that links collected data to propositions, and
5. Criteria used for interpreting findings

In addition to these basic components, Yin also stressed the importance of clearly articulating theoretical perspectives, determining the goals of the study, selecting participant(s), selecting the appropriate method(s) of data collection, and providing some consideration to the structure and style of the final report.

The study's questions are most likely to be "How" and "Why" questions, and their definition must be completed first. Propositions are sometimes derived from the "How" and "Why" questions, and are helpful in focusing the goals for the study. Not all studies need to have propositions. An exploratory study, rather than having propositions, would have a stated purpose or criteria on which success is judged. The unit of analysis defines the case, and primary unit of analysis, which could be groups, organizations or countries. Linking data to propositions and criteria for interpreting findings are the least developed aspects in case studies (Yin, 1994).

Bassey (1999) proposed seven stages in the research design process.

1. Identifying the research as an issue, problem, or hypothesis.
2. Asking research questions and drawing up ethical guidelines.
3. Collecting and storing data.
4. Generating and testing analytical statements.
5. Interpreting or explaining the analytical statements.
6. Deciding on the outcome and writing the case report.
7. Finishing and publishing.

Bassey noted, "The procedures described here will only rarely be in accord with the processes of actual studies" (p. 65). More often than not, the actual process is iterative.

Drawing upon the work of Yin (1994), Bassey (1999), and Stake (2000), I propose using three phases of case study design and implementation. The first phase is *research design* which is composed of four tasks; specifying research objective(s), developing a research strategy, selecting cases, and specifying data requirements. The second phase focuses on the *implementation* of the case study including preparation for data collection, field data collection, and the organization and storage of data. The third phase consists of *analyzing, interpreting and drawing theoretical inferences* from case studies. This last phase involves communicating the outcomes of the study including preparing the report.

Phase One: Design

Task 1: Research focus. The first task in the design phase is to identify and select a clear research focus that can be referenced over the course of the study. A clear research focus is closely coupled with a well-reasoned research problem and one or more objectives. A research focus is established by forming questions about a particular situation or problem, and then determining a specific purpose for the study. Case study research generally answers one or more questions that begin with "How" or "Why." Questions are targeted to a limited number of events or conditions and their interrelationships.

The statement of the problem should be embedded in a well-informed assessment of the research literature that identifies gaps and acknowledges contradictory theories or inadequate evidence. In short, a convincing argument needs to be made that the proposed research will significantly contribute to our understanding of the issue or topic of interest. The literature review, purpose of the case study, and an early determination of potential audiences for the final report will guide how the study is designed, conducted, and publicly reported.

Several important points to remember during the design phase of a case study include:

1. *Formulate clear and realistic research objective(s).* Initial efforts to formulate research objective(s) for a study often lack sufficient clarity or are too ambitious. Unless these defects are attended to and corrected, a study will lack clear focus, and however desirable these objectives appear, will seldom be possible to design a productive study to achieve them.

2. *Delimit the scope of the phenomenon to be studied.* Experience also indicates that better results are achieved if the "class" of the phenomenon under investigation (e.g., an intervention) is not defined too broadly. Most successful studies, in fact, work with a well-defined, smaller-scope sub-class of a general phenomenon. Instead of trying to develop a general theory for an entire phenomenon in one investigation, formulate a typology of different kinds of interventions and choose one type or "sub-class" of interventions for successive studies (Bennett & George, n.d.).

Task 2: Develop a research strategy. Having formulated research objective(s) that often evolve as design work continues, the second task requires the development of a research strategy to achieve stated objective(s). Developing a strategy requires early consideration of the elements that will be used in analyzing cases, including context, conditions, parameters, issues, and/or variables of the case.

A related task in developing a research strategy is to determine whether objectives can best achieved by using a single case or multiple-case design. Single cases are typically used to confirm or challenge a theory or to represent a unique or extreme case (Yin, 1994). Single-case studies are also ideal for revelatory cases where investigators may have access to a phenomenon that was previously inaccessible. These types of studies can be holistic or embedded, the latter occurring when the same case study involves more than one unit of analysis.

Single-case designs require careful investigation to avoid misrepresentation and to maximize investigators' access to the evidence. Single case designs can fall prey to mistakes such as selection bias or over-generalization of results. Multiple-case designs usually follow a replication logic. This should not be confused with sampling logic where the selection of a population is made to allow for later inferences. Each individual case study consists of a "whole" study, where facts are gathered from various sources and conclusions drawn on those facts. When using multiple cases, each case is treated as a single case. Conclusions drawn for each case are used as information that contributes to the whole study. Exemplary case studies carefully select cases and carefully examine the choices available from among many research tools available in order to increase the validity of the study. Careful discrimination at the point of selection also helps erect boundaries around the case.

Researchers must determine whether to study cases that are unique in some way or cases considered "most similar" or typical, and may also select cases to represent a variety of geographic regions, a variety of size parameters, or other parameters. A useful step in the selection process is to repeatedly refer back to the purpose of the study to focus attention on where to look for cases and evidence that will satisfy the purpose and answer research questions. Selecting single or multiple cases is a key element, but a case study can include more than one unit of embedded analysis. For example, a case study may involve study of a single type of school in a district (e.g., vocational education school) and a specific school (e.g., Vocational School #7) in that district. This type of case study involves two levels of analysis and increases the complexity and amount of data gathered and analyzed.

A key strength of the case study method involves using multiple sources and techniques in the data gathering process. Researchers must determine in advance the evidence they will need to gather and what analysis techniques to use in order to answer the research questions. The data that is gathered is normally qualitative, but it may also be quantitative. Tools to collect data can include surveys, interviews, documentation review, observation, and even the collection of physical artifacts.

Task 3: Select cases. Researchers with limited experience often find it difficult to decide what cases to select. This difficulty usually arises from a failure to specify a research objective that is clearly formulated and not overly ambitious. Cases should be selected not simply because they are "interesting," "important," or easily researched using readily available data. The primary criterion for case selection should be relevance to the research objective, whether it includes theory testing or heuristic purposes.Research objectives must also be integrated into decisions on whether the strategy will include one or several cases, case comparisons or within-case analysis. The cases must be selected to provide relevant data required to answer research problems and questions. The universe or sub-class of events must also be well developed to be able to select cases.

Important criticisms have been made about the selection of cases in small N studies by scholars who have been influenced by the rich experience of statistical methods for analyzing large N samples. Although it is not possible to fully summarize the debate on selection bias, it is instructive to highlight major points. For a detailed critique of selection bias, you are referred to Collier and Mahoney (1996).

1. Selection bias in case studies is potentially a greater problem than is often assumed, as it may not just understate relationships (the standard statistical problem), but may overstate them.

2. Case study designs with no variance in the dependent variable do not inherently represent a selection bias problem.

3. Case study researchers sometimes have good reasons to narrow the range of cases studied, particularly to capture heterogeneous causal relations, even if this increases the risks of selection bias; and,

4. Case study researchers do not "over-generalize" from their cases as often as is commonly assumed; instead, they are frequently careful in providing circumscribed "contingent generalizations" that subsequent researchers then over-generalize.

Validity and reliability. Throughout the design phase, researchers must ensure that their study is well constructed to ensure construct validity, internal validity, external validity, and reliability. Construct validity is especially problematic in case study research, and has been a source of criticism because of potential investigator subjectivity. Yin (1994) proposed three remedies to counteract this problem: using multiple sources of evidence, establishing a chain of evidence, and having a draft report reviewed by key informants.

Internal validity (especially important with explanatory or causal studies) demonstrates that certain conditions lead to other conditions and requires the use of multiple pieces of evidence from multiple sources to uncover convergent lines of inquiry. Campbell (1956) was the first to apply the term "triangulation" to research methodology. Triangulation has been generally considered a process of using multiple perceptions to clarify meaning, verifying the repeatability of an observation or interpretation (Stake, 2000). Internal validity is a concern only in causal (explanatory) cases. This is usually a problem of inferences in case studies, and can be dealt with using what Campbell (1975) called "pattern-matching." Pattern-matching is a technique for linking data to research propositions. Campbell (1975) showed, through pattern-matching, that an observed drop in Connecticut traffic fatalities was not related to lowering the speed limit. His study illustrated some of the difficulties in establishing criteria for interpreting the findings.

External validity reflects whether or not findings are generalizable beyond the immediate case or cases; the more variations in places, people, and procedures a case study can withstand and still yield the same findings, the more external validity. Techniques such as cross-case examination and within-case examination, along with a review of relevant literature, help ensure external validity.

Reliability refers to the stability, accuracy, and precision of measurement. Reliability is achieved in many ways in a case study. One of the most important methods is development and use of a protocol. A case study protocol contains more than a survey instrument, it also contains the procedures and general rules that should be followed in using the instrument. Protocol needs to be created prior to data collection: It is essential in a multiple-case study, and desirable in a single-case study. Yin (1994) presented the protocol as a major component in asserting the reliability of case study research. A typical protocol should have the following sections:

1. An overview of the case study project (objectives, issues, topics being investigated) should communicate the general topic of inquiry and purpose of the research.
2. Field procedures (credentials, access to sites, sources of information) involve data collection issues and must be properly designed. Since, researchers do not control the data collection environment (Yin, 1994), as in other research strategies; hence the procedures become all the more important.
3. Case study questions (specific questions that the investigator must keep in mind during data collection).
4. A guide for case study report (outline, format for the narrative).

Other ways to improve reliability and validity of case studies are:

1. *Prolong the processes of data gathering on site.* This will help to insure the accuracy of findings by providing more concrete information on which to formulate interpretations.
2. *Conduct member checks.* Initiate and maintain an active corroboration on the interpretation of data between researchers and those who provided the data. In other words, talk to your participants.
3. *Collect referential materials.* Complement the file of materials from the actual site with additional document support. For instance, an investigator conducting a case study of "teaching in a vocational education school" may support the initial propositions of the study with historical accounts of former teachers as well as examples of empirical research dealing with teaching in vocational schools.

4. *Engage in peer consultation.* Prior to composing the final draft of the report, researchers should consult with colleagues in order to establish validity through pooled judgment.

Task 4: Specify data requirements. The case study method will be more effective if a research design includes a specification of the data to be obtained from the case(s) being analyzed. Specifications should address issues of "What?" "How?" "When?" The specification of data requirements should be integrated with the other three design tasks identified previously.

When a single case study or a case comparison is undertaken, specification of the data requirements should take the form of general questions to be asked of each case. This is a way of standardizing data requirements so that comparable data is obtained from each case. Case study methodology is no different in this respect from survey research with large N samples. Unless one asks the same question from each case, the results cannot be compared, cumulated, and systematically analyzed.

A problem sometimes encountered in case study research is that data requirements are inadequately formulated or missing altogether. Simply listing general questions to be asked of each case is inadequate if the questions do not reflect what is needed to satisfy the research objective of the study and to make the kind of contribution to theory that is intended.

Integrating the four tasks. Several observations must be made about these four design tasks. First, in any given study these tasks should be viewed as comprising an integrated whole. These tasks are interrelated and interdependent. For example, the way in which Task 2 is performed should be consistent with the specifications of Task 1. Similarly, the selection of cases in Task 3 must be appropriate and serviceable from the standpoint of determinations made for Task 1 and 2. And finally, the specification of data requirements in Task 4 must be guided by the cumulative decisions made for Task 1, 2, and 3.

Second, a satisfactory integration of the four tasks usually cannot be accomplished on the first try. A good design does not come easily. Considerable iteration and re-specification of the various tasks may be necessary before a satisfactory research design is achieved. Researchers may need to gain familiarity with the phenomenon in question by undertaking a preliminary examination of cases before selecting one or several for intensive examination.

Third, despite researchers' best efforts, the formulation of a design is likely to remain imperfect in one respect or another. These

s may emerge and become evident after the investigation is
ase 2 or even Phase 3 of the study. If these defects are
earchers should consider halting further work and
redesigning the study, even if this means that some of the case studies
will have to be redone. In drawing conclusions from the study,
researcher s (or others who evaluate the results) may be able to state
some useful lessons for a better design in future studies of the problem.

Phase Two: Implementation

The second phase involves implementing the design as described in
Phase One. The main tasks in the second phase are preparing for data
collection, field data collection and organization, and data storage.

Task 1: Prepare to collect data. Once data requirements are clearly
specified, the next logical and interrelated task is to decide which
specific methods and techniques of data collection will be used. Case
study has no specific methods and techniques of data collection (and
analysis) that are unique to it as a research approach. The selection of
data collection methods is guided by the research questions and the
availability of possible sources. Depending on whether a single or
multiple case study approach is selcted, researchers can choose to
collect data from one or any combination of sources (Bassey, 1999;
Stake, 1995, 2000; Tellis, 1997; Yin, 1994).

Documents can include letters, memoranda, agendas, administrative
documents, newspaper articles, or any document considered germane to
the investigation. In the interest of data triangulation, documents serve
to corroborate evidence obtained from other sources. The main
strengths of documents include their stability (i.e., they can be reviewed
repeatedly), and unobtrusive and broad coverage (Yin, 1994).
Documents are useful for making inferences about events. The
problems presented by documents include gaining access and
retrievability, biased selectivity, and possible reporting/author bias.
Documents can also lead to false leads, particularly in the hands of an
inexperienced researcher.

Archival documents can be service records, organizational records,
lists of names, survey data, and other such records. Investigators must
be meticulous in evaluating the origin and accuracy of records before
using them. Even if records are quantitative, they might still not be
accurate. In many respects, the strengths and weaknesses of archival
documents are the same as those mentioned for documents. Privacy and
access are usually major concerns with archival material.

Interviews are one of the most important sources of case study information. There are several forms of interviews including open-ended, focused, and structured or survey. In an open-ended interview, key respondents are asked to comment about certain events. They may propose solutions or provide insight into events. They may also corroborate evidence obtained from other sources. Researchers must avoid becoming dependent on a single informant, and seek the same data from other sources to verify authenticity. Focused interviews are used in situations where a respondent is interviewed for a short period of time, usually answering set questions. This technique is often used to confirm data collected from another source. Structured interviews are similar to surveys, and are used to gather data in cases such as neighborhood studies. Questions are detailed and developed in advance, much as they are in surveys. Problems generally associated with interviews also apply here, e.g., bias due to poor questions, response bias, incomplete recollection, and reflexivity (Yin, 1994).

Direct observation occurs when a field visit is conducted during the case study. It could be as simple as casual data collection activities, or as complex as involving detailed formal protocols to measure and record behaviors. This technique is useful for providing additional information about the topic being studied. Reliability is enhanced when more than one observer is involved. Glesne and Peshkin (1992) recommended that researchers should be as unobtrusive as wallpaper. Some of the problems/weaknesses associated with interviews, such as reflexivity and bias, are also applicable to direct observation. In addition, direct observation is often time-consuming and costly.

Participant-observation makes researchers active participants in the events being studied. This often occurs in studies of neighborhoods or groups. The technique provides some unusual opportunities for collecting data, but could face some major problems as well. Researcher could alter the course of events as part of the group, which may not be helpful to the study.

Physical artifacts can be tools, instruments, or some other physical evidence that may be collected during the study as part of a field visit. A researcher's perspective can be broadened as a result of the discovery. It is important to keep in mind that not all sources are relevant for all case studies (Yin, 1994). Investigators must be capable of dealing with all of them, should it be necessary, but each case will present different opportunities for data collection.

There are some conditions that require case researchers to start collecting data before study questions have been defined and finalized (Bassey, 1999; Yin, 1994). This is likely to be successful only with experienced investigators. Another important point to review is the benefit of using rival hypotheses and theories as a means of adding quality control to the case study. This improves the perception of the fairness and serious thinking of the researcher.

It is important to provide good training programs for researchers and research assistants, establish clear protocols and procedures in advance of the fieldwork, and conduct a pilot study in advance of moving into the field to remove obvious barriers and problems. The training program should cover the basic concepts of the study, terminology, processes and methods, and teach data collectors how to properly apply the techniques being used in the study. The program should also train researchers to understand how gathering data using multiple techniques strengthens the study by providing opportunities for triangulation during the analysis phase of the study. The program covers protocols for case study research including time deadlines, formats for narrative reporting and field notes, guidelines for collection of documents, and guidelines for field procedures to be used.

Researchers need to be good listeners who can hear exactly the words being used by those being interviewed. Qualifications for researchers also include being able to ask good questions and interpret answers. Good researchers review documents looking for facts, but also read between the lines and pursue collaborative evidence elsewhere when that seems appropriate.

Researchers need to be flexible in real-life situations and not feel threatened by unexpected change, missed appointments, or lack of office space. They need to understand the purpose of the study, grasp relevant issues, and be open to contrary findings. Researchers must also be aware that they are going into the world of real human beings who may be threatened or unsure of what the case study will bring.

After training, a pilot site needs to be selected and a pilot test conducted using each data gathering method so that problematic areas can be uncovered and corrected. Researchers need to anticipate key problems and events, identify key people, prepare letters of introduction, establish rules for confidentiality, and actively seek opportunities to revisit and revise the research design in order to address and add to the original set of research questions.

Task 2: Collect and store data. Researchers must collect and store multiple sources of evidence comprehensively and systematically, in formats that can be referenced and sorted so that converging lines of inquiry and patterns can be uncovered. Researchers need to carefully observe the object of study and identify causal factors associated with the observed phenomenon. Renegotiation of arrangements with the objects of study or addition of questions to interviews may be necessary as the study progresses. Case study research is flexible, but when changes are made, they are documented systematically.

It is advisable to use field notes and databases to categorize and reference data so that it is readily available for subsequent reinterpretation. Field notes record feelings and intuitive hunches, pose questions, and document the work in progress. They record testimonies, stories, and illustrations that can be used in later reports. They may warn of impending bias because of special attention give to a participant, or give an early signal that a pattern is emerging. They assist in determining whether or not the inquiry needs to be reformulated or redefined based on what is being observed. Field notes should be kept separate from the data being collected and stored for analysis.

Maintaining the relationship between the issue and the evidence is mandatory. Data may be entered into a database, while other data physically stored. Regardless, researchers must document, classify, and cross-reference all evidence so that it can be efficiently recalled for sorting and examination over the course of the study.

Organizing data. Because case study research generates a large amount of data from multiple sources, systematic organization of the data is important to prevent researchers from becoming overwhelmed by the amount of data and to prevent them from losing sight of the original research purpose and questions. Advance preparation assists in handling large amounts of data in a documented and systematic fashion. For example, noting the date, time, and place of every interview and creating back-up files/copies helps to store and organize data efficiently. It is also advisable that researchers prepare databases to assist with categorizing, sorting, storing, and retrieving data for analysis.

Developing a database. With available computer technology and qualitative data analysis software such as *Atlas, Ethnography,* and *NUDIST,* data organization and processing has become relatively manageable. In fact, it is now feasible to develop good databases using word processing applications such as Microsoft Word and WordPerfect. The development a database may take the form of four common components: notes, documents, tabular materials and narratives:

1. *Case study notes* are the most common component of a case study database. These notes take a variety of forms. They may result from an investigator's interview, observations, or document analysis.

Notes may be handwritten, typed, on audiotapes, or on computer disks, and they may be assembled in the form of a diary, on index cards, or in some less organized fashion. It is critical that case study notes must be stored in such a manner that other persons can retrieve them efficiently. Notes can be divided into major subjects as outlined in the case study protocol. However, any classificatory system will do, as long as the system is evident to an outside party. The only essential characteristics of the notes are that they be organized, categorized, complete, and available for later access.

2. *Case study documents* may also constitute a large component of the database. One helpful way is to have an annotated bibliography of these documents. Such annotations should facilitate storage and retrieval, so that later researchers can inspect or share the database. Documents also require a large amount of physical storage space. In addition, the documents may be of varying importance to the database, and investigators may want to establish a primary file and a secondary file for such documents. The main objective, again, is to make documents readily retrievable for later inspection or perusal.

3. *Tabular materials* may consist of surveys and other quantitative data either collected from the site being studied or created by the research team. Such materials also need to be organized and stored for later retrieval. For example, a survey may have been conducted at one or more of the case study sites as part of the overall study. In such situations, tables of the results may even be stored in computerized files.

4. *Narratives* may also be a formal part of the case study database. Researchers may compose open-ended answers to the questions in the case study protocol. Each answer or narrative represents an attempt by the researcher to integrate the available evidence and to converge upon the facts of the matter or their tentative interpretations. These narratives may serve directly as the basis for the final case study report.

Ethical considerations. The ethical considerations for qualitative research are well documented (Bassey, 1999; Christians, 2000; Punch, 1994). Researchers must adhere to rules that protect human participants. In addition, researchers must be truthful. This means not intentionally trying to deceive others. Researchers, in taking data from persons, should do so in ways that recognize those persons' initial ownership of the data and should respect them as fellow human beings who are entitled to dignity and privacy. Issues of observation and reporting should be discussed in advance. Agreements or contracts should be heeded. It is particularly important that study participants receive drafts of how they are presented, quoted, and interpreted and for researchers to listen well for signs of concern (Stake, 2000).

Phase Three: Analysis

The analysis aspect of case study methodology is, according to Tellis (1997), the least developed, and hence, the most difficult. Part of problem is that case study research produces a great deal of raw data, and trying to make sense of it can be overwhelming. In cases where data are quantitative, analysis is usually easier to process and analyze.

In their influential book, *Qualitative Data Analysis*, Miles and Huberman (1994) suggested analytic techniques such as rearranging the arrays, placing the evidence in a matrix of categories, creating flowcharts or data displays, tabulating the frequency of different events, using means, variances, and cross tabulations to examine the relationships between variables, and other such techniques to facilitate analysis.

Bassey (1999) emphasized the generation and testing of analytic statements as an integral and important aspect of data analysis. He suggested an *iterative* process consisting of four related stages:

1. Generation of draft analytical statements based on raw data that give concise answers to the research questions.
2. Formulation of tentative propositions or hypotheses based on careful analysis (reading and re-reading) of data.
3. Careful testing (and amendment where necessary) of the statements against the data.
4. Formulation of possible interpretations or explanations that attempt to answer the "Why" and "How" questions based on the evidence.

Bassey pointed out that:

> The likely result of a first testing of the analytical statements is that some stand, some need modifying and others lack verity and are rejected. Analysis and data testing is an iterative process that continues until the researcher feels confident that the analytical statements are trustworthy. (p. 71)

Yin (1994) suggested that every investigation should have a general analytic strategy for analysis. He presented three methods for general use: pattern-matching, explanation-building, and time-series analysis. In general, analysis relies on the theoretical propositions that led to the study, and then, the evidence is based on those propositions. If the propositions are not present, then researchers are encouraged to develop a case description, which would be a framework for organizing the case study. In other situations, the original objective of the case study may help to identify some causal links that could be analyzed.

Trochim (1989) suggested pattern-matching as one of the most desirable strategies for analysis. This technique compares an empirically-based pattern with a predicted pattern. If the patterns match, internal reliability and validity are enhanced. If the case study is an explanatory one, the patterns may be related to the dependent or independent variables. If a descriptive study, the predicted pattern must be defined prior to data collection. Yin (1994) recommended using rival explanations as pattern-matching when independent variables are involved. This requires the development of rival theoretical propositions, but the overall concern remains the degree to which a pattern matches the predicted one.

Elsewhere, Bennett and George (1997) proposed a method similar to pattern-matching called "process-tracing." Ideally suited to case studies that compromise the "method of structured, focused comparison," the general purpose of process-tracing is to generate and analyze data on the causal mechanisms, or processes, events, actions, expectations, and other intervening variables, that link putative causes to observed effects. Within the general method of process-tracing there are two very different approaches. The first, "process verification," involves testing whether observed processes among variables in a case match those predicted by previously designated theories. The second, "process induction," involves the inductive observation of apparent causal mechanisms and heuristic rendering of these mechanisms as potential hypotheses for future testing. Put simply, process-tracing attempts to identify the intervening causal process, the causal links, between an independent variable(s) and the outcome of the dependent variable.

Explanation-building is considered a form of pattern-matching, in which building an explanation of the case carries out the analysis of the case study. This implies that it is most useful in explanatory case studies, but it is possible to use it for exploratory cases as well as part of a hypothesis-generating process. Explanation-building is an iterative process that begins with a theoretical statement, refines it, revises the proposition, and repeats this process from the beginning. This is known to be a technique that is fraught with problems. One of those problems is a loss of focus, although keeping this in mind can protect the investigator from those problems.

Time-series analysis is a well-known technique in experimental and quasi-experimental analysis. It is possible that a single dependent or independent variable could make this simpler than pattern-matching, but sometimes there are multiple changes in a variable, making starting and ending points unclear.

Yin (1994) encouraged researchers to make every effort to produce an analysis of the highest quality. In order to accomplish this, he presented four principles that should attract the researcher's attention:

1. Show that the analysis relied on all the relevant evidence.
2. Include all major rival interpretations in the analysis.
3. Address the most significant aspect of the case study.
4. Use prior, expert knowledge to further the analysis.

Stake (1995) recommended categorical aggregation as another means of analysis and suggested developing protocols for this phase of the case study to enhance quality of the research. He also presented ideas on pattern-matching along the lines that Yin (1994) presented. Runkel (1990) used aggregated measures to obtain relative frequencies in a multiple-case study. Stake (1995) favored coding data and identifying the issues more clearly at the analysis stage. Eisner and Peshkin (1990) placed a high priority on direct interpretation of events, and lower on interpretation of measurement data, which is another viable alternative to be considered.

Thus, although the specific tactics and procedures for analyzing data may differ, the process generally involves careful and systematic examination of raw data, searching for meaningful patterns and deriving analytic statements/theoretical propositions with reference to the original research objectives and questions. Throughout the analysis process, researchers must remain open to new opportunities, new insights, conflicting explanations, and corroborating evidence. In all cases, researchers should treat the evidence fairly to produce analytic conclusions answering the original "How" and "Why" of the research questions.

Regardless of the purpose and design, the analysis phase *can* be seen as having four related components: defining the analysis, organizing and classifying data, making connections and sense of the data and communicating the outcomes/results. The emphasis on each of these iterative processes will vary according to philosophical and epistemological assumptions, purposes, skills, and resources.

Preparing the case study report. There is no standard format or style for a case study report. This largely depends on the type of case study being reported. A theory-seeking or theory-testing case study will typically have a more scholarly and structured format with an empirical statement, clearly stated research objectives/questions, specific findings and (tentative) generalizations. On the other hand, an evaluative case study may respond to agreed-upon terms of reference supported with evidence that lends confidence to findings and recommendations.

In the many forms a case study report can take, it should report the data in such a way that it transforms a complex issue into one that can be understood, allowing readers to question and examine the study and reach an understanding independent of the researcher. Boehrer (1990) noted that the case study is a story that can be told; it presents the concrete narrative detail of actual, or at least realistic, events. Generally, case study reports are extensively descriptive, with the most problematic issue often referred to as being the determination of the right combination of description and analysis.

Typically, authors address each step of the research process, and attempt to give as much context as possible for the decisions made in the research design and for the conclusions drawn. Researchers pay particular attention to displaying sufficient evidence to gain readers' confidence that all avenues have been explored, clearly communicating the boundaries of the case, and giving special attention to conflicting propositions.

This contextualization usually includes a detailed explanation of the theoretical positions, of how those theories drove the inquiry or led to the guiding research questions, of the participants' backgrounds, of the processes of data collection, of the training and limitations of the coders, along with a strong attempt to make connections between the data and the conclusions evident.

Techniques for composing the report vary but include handling each case as a separate chapter or treating the case as a chronological recounting. Some researchers report the case study as a narrative that tells the story of how the research was designed and conducted. Others may adopt a descriptive style where a picture is drawn in words of the case or cases based on careful probing and thoughtful analysis. During the report preparation process, critically examine the document looking for ways the report is incomplete or inaccurate. Representative audience groups can be used to review and comment on the draft document. Based on comments, the revisions can be made.

Merriam (1988) offered several suggestions for consideration when presenting case study data, particularly in cases where there are many stakeholders:

1. Prepare specialized condensations for appropriate groups.
2. Replace narrative sections with a series of answers to open-ended questions.

3. Present "skimmer's" summaries at beginning of each section.
4. Incorporate headlines that encapsulate information from text.
5. Prepare analytic summaries with supporting data appendixes.
6. Present data in colorful and/or unique graphic representations.

There is one other issue that is related to style that I think is important. Since all research, from its conception to interpretation and dissemination is influenced by the social identity, beliefs and values of the researcher, I believe that researchers should be truthful and explicit about their identity and ideological stance. To this end, I see no difficulty in a researcher making *polemical* statements, for example, as part of the beginning or ending of a report.

Finally, before a researcher accepts the euphoria of finishing the case study report, it is instructive to take heed of Michael Bassey's (1999) suggestion that a colleague should be invited to conduct an audit. Simply stated, this involves asking a professional colleague to spend a few hours reading the report, and sampling parts of the case record in relation to the report. The case record consists of interview transcripts, observation reports, journal writings and other documents containing data collected. The auditor can ask the following key questions:

1. What *claim to knowledge* is made, as expressed in the abstract and the report?
2. Is the *theoretical framework or conceptual background* given by the author appropriate?
3. Was the *collection of data* appropriate, sufficient, and ethical?
4. Was the *analysis and interpretation of data*, as reported, appropriate, sufficient, ethical?
5. Does the evidence of the report, as examined in answer to questions 2 to 4, *substantiate the claim* to knowledge made in answer 1?

An Example of A Case Study

The following example is included to show how some of the key tasks in the three phases discussed previously are accomplished. An example, an explanatory case study undertaken expressly to determine a cause-effect relationship between two variables, is an investigation conducted by Mills, Cervero, Langone and Wilson (1995). The central problem addressed in this study was that planning practices of county agents within the Cooperative Extension System (CES) produced educational programs that served the interests of some constituents at the exclusion of others. The study was undertaken because, although there was some indication that ongoing debate between traditionalists and expansionists may affect the kinds of programs offered, there was no research-based evidence to about how such abstract policy between competing traditionalist and expansionist interests within the CES organization affects programs that county agents construct.

The overall purpose of the study was to show how the personal and organizational interests of CES agents were causally related to the educational programs that they planned. The study articulated a well-developed theoretical framework anchored in an extensive review of literature spanning 30 years. The main assumption of the investigators was that competing interests would be expressed through the social context in which county agents worked, thereby influencing programs.

The overall research design was a "qualitative case study" which they defined as "a form of inquiry for studying a particular phenomenon within its natural setting using multiple sources of evidence" (Mills et al., 1995, p. 4). The case unit in the study was the "typical program planning practices of county extension agents in Georgia Cooperative Education System." Using Yin's (1989) typology, the study used a multiple-case design or what Merriam (1988) called "cross-site or multi-site" case study designs that involve collecting and analyzing data from several single cases.

The sample of cases consisted of six individual county extension agents and four district program development specialists. A typical case approach was used (Patton, 1990). The strategy devised by the investigators was to identify "information-rich cases that represent the actual everyday planning practices of county agents in Georgia" (Mills et al., 1995, p. 5). To assist in identifying the cases, district program development specialists were used as key informants due to their insight into planning practices of agents.

Data collection sources included in-depth interviews with agents and specialists; documents; reports; correspondence; meeting minutes; and organizational plans and charts. In interviews, county agents were asked to describe how they planned extension programs, including what decisions were made, who was involved, and so forth. Data analysis was conducted in two phases. In the first phase, the entire interview transcript for each of the six county agents and the four development specialists was analyzed and coded using a modified form of analytic induction. This phase focused on identifying factors embedded in the social context of agents' planning practice. The second phase focused on how these contextual factors affected the educational programs that agents constructed.

The results of data analysis were presented into two sections. The first section described the contextual factors (organizational culture and structure, available resources, and power relationships) that affected planning practices. The second part discussed how these factors affected the program planning practices of the agents. The last part of the study discussed the implications/significance of the results. The study also offered tentative conclusions and theoretical generalizations "about mechanisms through which interests affect the educational programs constructed in *any* adult education organization" (Mills et al., 1995, p. 15).

The style and format of the case study report was obviously dictated by the primary audience: academics in the field of adult education. As such, the organization and tone of the report adhered closely to requirements of an academic journal, the *Adult Education Quarterly*, "committed to the dissemination of research and theory" in adult education.

Conclusion

Case study has become a major part of research methodology. Although primarily associated with the qualitative research tradition, particularly in education, case study is not, as Stake (2000) correctly points, about methodological choices but *what* is to be studied. As a method, it is especially responsive to research questions of "Why" and "How?" and offers a flexible yet integrated framework for holistic examination of a phenomenon in its natural state.

The case study can accommodate different epistemologies and has application to a wide range of disciplines, especially in the educational, social, and behavioral sciences. Case study design can be customized to address a wide range of research questions and types of cases and to incorporate a variety of data collection, analysis, and reporting techniques.

The data collection processes of case studies tend to be more complex than processes used in other research designs. Researchers require a versatility that permits data collection from multiple sources, the creation of a well-organized and high-quality controlled database, and maintenance of a chain of evidence.

Because case study is exceptionally useful for building explanations, generating theory, and examination of typical and atypical phenomena, it is particularly appropriate for applied research related to contemporary issues and problems in the real world. It can, however, also be used to test hypotheses and modify existing theory, a purpose most closely associated with the positivist orientation. There appears to be a growing trend away from considering case study exclusively and reflexively in a qualitative context to a more expansive view of case study as an adaptive research structure that can accommodate qualitative and quantitative perspectives, techniques, and standards.

References

Abramson, P. R. (1992). *A case for case studies*. Thousand Oaks, CA: Sage.

Bassey, M. (1999). *Case study research in educational settings*. Buckingham, England: Open University Press.

Bennet, A., & George, A. L. (1997, October). *Research design tasks in case study methods*. Paper presented at the MacArthur Foundation Workshop on Case Study Methods, Belfer Center for Science and International Affairs (BCSIA), Cambridge, MA: Harvard University.

Boehrer, J. (1990). Teaching with cases: Learning to question. *New Directions for Teaching and Learning, 24,* 41-52.

Campbell, D. T. (1956). *Leadership and its effects upon the group.* Columbus: Ohio State University, College of Commerce and Administration, Bureau of Business Research.

Campbell, D. T. (1975). Degrees of freedom and the case study. *Comparative Political Studies, 8,* 178-193.

Christians, C. (2000). Ethics and politics in qualitative research. In N. K. Denzin & Y. K. Lincoln (Eds.), *Handbook of qualitative research* (2nd ed.). Thousand Oaks: Sage.

Coffey, A., & Atkinson, P. (1996). *Making sense of qualitative data: Complementary research strategies.* Thousand Oaks, CA: Sage.

Collier, D., & Mahoney, J. (1996). Insights and pitfalls: Selection bias in qualitative research. *World Politics, 49*(1), 56-91.

Eisner, E. W., & Peshkin. A. (Eds.). (1991). *Qualitative inquiry in education: The continuing debate.* New York: Teachers College Press.

Feagin, J. R., Orum, A. M., & Sjoberg, G. (Eds.). (1991). *A case for the case study.* Chapel Hill: The University of North Carolina Press.

Glaser, B. G., & Strauss, A. L. (1967). *The discovery of grounded theory: Strategies for qualitative research.* Chicago: Aldine de Gruyter.

Glesne, C., & Peshkin, A. (1992). *Becoming qualitative researchers: An introduction.* White Plains, NY: Longman.

Goetz, J. P., & LeCompte, M. D. (1984). *Ethnography and qualitative design in educational research.* Orlando, FL: Academic Press.

Guba, E. G., & Lincoln, Y. S. (1981). *Effective evaluation.* San Francisco: Jossey-Bass.

Hamel, J. (1993). *Case study methods.* Thousand Oaks, CA: Sage.

Herriot, R. E., & Firestone, W. A. (1983). Multisite qualitative policy research: Optimizing description and generalizability. *Educational Researcher, 12*(2), 14-19.

Kennedy, M. M. (1979). Generalizing from single case studies. *Evaluation Quarterly, 3,* 661-679.

Lincoln, Y. S., & Guba, E. G. (1985). *Naturalistic inquiry.* Thousand Oaks, CA: Sage.

Maxwell, J. A. (1992). Understanding and validity in qualitative research. *Harvard Educational Review, 62,* 279-300.

Merriam, S. B. (1988). *Case study research in education: A qualitative approach.* San Francisco: Jossey-Bass.

Merriam, S. B. (1998). *Qualitative research and case study applications in education.* San Francisco: Jossey-Bass.

Miles, M. B., & Huberman, A. M. (1994). *Qualitative data analysis: An expanded sourcebook* (2nd ed.). Thousand Oaks, CA: Sage.

Mills, D. P., Cervero, R. M., Langone, C. A., & Wilson, A. L. (1995). The impact of interests, power relationships, and organizational structure on program planning practice: A case study. *Adult Education Quarterly, 46*(1), 1-16.

Moore, G. B., & Yin, R. K. (1985). *Identifying advanced technologies for education's future.* Washington, DC: COSMOS.

Patton, M. Q. (1987). *How to use qualitative methods in evaluation.* Newbury Park, CA: Sage.

Patton, M. Q. (1990). *Qualitative evaluation and research methods* (2nd ed.). Newbury Park, CA: Sage.

Punch, M. (1986). *The politics and ethics of fieldwork.* Thousand Oaks, CA: Sage.

Ragin, C. C. (1987). *The comparative method: Moving beyond qualitative and quantitative strategies.* Berkeley: University of California Press.

Ragin, C. C. (1992). Case of "What is a case?" In C. C. Ragin & H. S. Becker (Eds.), *What is a case? Exploring the foundations of social inquiry.* Cambridge, England: Cambridge University Press.

Runkel, P. (1990). *Casting nets and testing specimens: Two grand methods for psychology.* New York: Praeger.

Stake, R. E. (1995). *The art of case study research.* Thousand Oaks, CA: Sage.

Stake, R. E. (2000). Case studies. In N. K. Denzin & Y. S. Lincoln. (Eds.), *Handbook of qualitative research* (2nd ed., pp. 435-454). Thousand Oaks, CA: Sage.

Stenhouse, L. (1985). Case study methods. In J. P. Keeves (Ed.), *Educational research, methodology, and measurement: An international handbook.* Sydney: Pergamon Press.

Strauss, A. L., & Corbin, J. (1990). *Basics of qualitative research: Grounded theory procedures and techniques.* Thousand Oaks, CA: Sage.

Sturman. (1997). Case study. In J. P. Keeves (Ed.), *Educational research, methodology, and measurement: An international handbook* (2nd ed., p. 94). New York: Pergamon.

Tellis, W. (1997). Introduction to case study. *The Qualitative Report, 3*(2). Retrieved February 1, 2001 from the World Wide Web: http://www.nova.edu/ssss/QR/QR3-2/tellis1.html

Trochim, W. (1989). Outcome pattern matching and program theory. *Evaluation and Program Planning, 12,* 355-366.

Williams, C. L. (1991). Case studies and the sociology of gender. In J. R. Feagin, A. M. Orum, & G. Sjoberg (Eds.). *A case for the case study.* Chapel Hill: The University of North Carolina Press.

Wolcott, H. F. (1990). *Writing up qualitative research.* Thousand Oaks, CA: Sage.

Yin, R. K. (1989). *Case study research: Design and methods* (Rev. ed.). Newbury Park, CA: Sage.

Yin, R. K. (1993). *Applications of case study research.* Newbury Park, CA: Sage.

Yin, R. K. (1994). *Case study research: Design and methods* (2nd ed.). Thousand Oaks, CA: Sage.

Chapter 9

Focus Group Research

Lee Jones and Barbara W. Farmer

A focus group may be described as an extended interview session in which about 10 subjects are encouraged to express their opinions concerning a particular topic or issue with the assistance of a trained facilitator; who is responsible for keeping the group on-task and recording their responses (Westbrook, 1990).

The two major techniques used by researchers to collect qualitative data are participant observation and individual interviews (Madriz, 2000). Focus groups, or group interviews, possess elements of both techniques while maintaining their own uniqueness as a distinct research method (Morgan, 1988). According to Frey and Fontana (1993), qualitative data collection research methods can be placed on a continuum; focus groups use more familiar settings than other research techniques but less familiar settings than field research or ethnographic studies. The focus group is a collective rather than an individualistic research method that focuses on multiple voices of participants' attitudes, experiences, and beliefs.

Focus groups, a form of group interview, capitalizes on communication between research participants in order to generate data, explicitly using group interaction as part of the method. David Morgan (1996) indicated that focus group research is a technique that collects data through group interaction on a researcher-selected topic. People are encouraged to talk to one another; asking questions, exchanging anecdotes, and commenting on each other's experiences and points of view (Kitzinger, 1994). Morgan (1996) identified three essential components of focus group research: [1] devoted to data collection, [2] interaction via group discussion is the primary source of data, and [3] the investigator's role in creating group discussion for data collection purposes is acknowledged. The method is particularly useful for exploring the participants' knowledge and experiences, and can be used to examine what they think, how they think, and why they think that way (Kitzinger, 1995). According to Ledingham (1999), focus groups work best when addressing specific issues or problems or when conceptual approaches need to be tested to determine their likelihood of success.

This chapter offers insights into focus groups as an increasingly used qualitative research method and provides practical steps to conduct focus group research. For novice researchers, this information can possibly "turn on the light" for a "can do" attitude to encourage you to engage in this methodology. For veteran researchers, it might serve as another attempt to confirm that which you already know.

History and Present Popularity

The term *focus group* was coined by Merton, Fiske, and Kendall (1956) to be applicable in situations where researchers or moderators have a need to ask very specific questions about a specific topic. According to Morgan (1988), the use of focus groups has undergone three distinct phases: [1] first used by social scientists during the 1920s to develop survey questionnaires; [2] next used by market researchers, between World War II and the 1970s, to understand people's wants and needs; and [3] lastly, since that time and into the present, used to gain understanding on issues ranging from health and sexual behavior to TV preferences and other social issues.

Focus groups were originally used in communications studies to explore the effects of films and television programs on viewers. Industries from film studios to banking, from jury selection to fast food and public relations, as well as across a wide variety of disciplines (e.g., education, political science, public health) have used focus groups to test marketplace strategies, audience reaction to a particular plot or character, the response of jurors to courtroom arguments, and resolutions to issues involving key public figures or policy.

Over the past decade, focus groups and group interviews have re-emerged as a popular technique for gathering qualitative data, both among sociologists and across a wide range of academic and applied research areas. Morgan (1996) posited that focus groups have more recently been used as both a self-contained method and a method used in combination with surveys and other research methods, particularly individual in-depth interviews. Part of the present popularity of focus groups may be due to their unique advantages for addressing such contemporary issues as empowerment and diversity, as well as giving a voice to marginalized groups.

According to Stewart and Shamdasani (1990), focus groups are often used very early in a research project and are frequently followed by other types of quantitative research that provide data from larger groups of respondents. The technique can be used, however, at virtually any point in the research process, either for exploration or following the analysis of a quantitative survey to facilitate interpretation of the results. Their flexibility allows them to be adapted to a variety of settings and cultural practices. Some of the more common uses of focus groups are to [1] obtain general background information about a topic of interest, [2] generate research hypotheses that can be submitted to further research and testing using more quantitative approaches, [3] stimulate new ideas and creative concepts, and [4] diagnose the potential for problems with a new program, service or product. In the area of program development and evaluation, focus groups have become an important tool for post-program evaluation, needs assessment and strategic planning.

Advantages and Disadvantages of Focus Groups

Focus groups provide a number of advantages for researchers. The technique is a way to gather data from a group of participants who interact directly with the researcher or a designated facilitator (or group moderator). Compared with individual interviews, the clear advantage of a focus group is that it makes it possible for researchers to observe the interactive processes occurring among participants. Madriz (2000) believes that they involve both "vertical interaction" (interaction between researcher and interviewees) and "horizontal interaction" (interaction among group participants). Focus groups have the ability to capture the power of participants' interaction by capitalizing on relationships and, consequently, generating insights that might not otherwise emerge from the group discussion (Dreachslin, 1998). The plurality of actors involved in a group makes the process of interviewing more active and dynamic.

The multivocality (Madriz, 2000) of the group situation validates individual participant's experiences with others of similar socioeconomic, gender, or racial/ethnic backgrounds. Madriz believes that within focus group interaction, empathy and commonality of experiences are promoted while fostering participant self-disclosure and self-validation. Focus groups, too, may be one of the few research tools available for gaining data from children or for securing data from individuals who are not particularly literate (Stewart & Shamdasani, 1990).

While focus group research holds several distinct advantages, critics of the method point to several disadvantages. For example, acceptance of qualitative techniques including focus group interviews has been slow, due most likely to the positivistic legacy of most social science research that traditionally has relied on numbers as the most accurate measure of social reality. Even traditional interview techniques with highly structured questionnaires have been historically viewed from a critical positivistic eye. The most direct criticism has focused on how the nature of the questions asked and the choices given to research participants are impacted by the researcher's framework, viewpoints, and beliefs (Krueger, 1994).

Another disadvantage is that the setting where participants meet is often outside the setting where the social interaction actually occurs. Therefore, the range of behavioral information that can be gathered through group interviews is narrower and is—with some exceptions—limited to verbal communication, body language, and self-report data (Madriz, 2000).

Relationship of Focus Groups to Other Data Collection Methods

Focus Groups Compared to Other Methods

A benefit of comparing focus groups to other research methods is a more sophisticated understanding of focus groups' strengths and weaknesses. Comparisons to other methods have concluded that the real strength of focus groups is not simply in exploring what participants have to say, but in providing insights into the sources of complex behaviors and motivations (Morgan & Krueger, 1993).

When compared to individual interviews, focus groups usually have two advantages. First, focus groups can be less time consuming, thereby requiring less interview time per participant. Second, interaction among participants can also have intrinsic value. In general, the use of focus groups as an alternative to individual interviews has become rather popular especially in marketing contexts, but also in the social sciences and in applied evaluation (Goldman & McDonald, 1987; Krueger, 1994; Lunt & Livingstone, 1996; Morgan, 1993).

Focus Groups Combined With Other Methods

There are times when research is too complicated to be analyzed solely with quantitative measures or too complex to be fully understood using a single evaluative tool. Triangulation (looking at measurement from multiple angles) is the systematic use of a variety of carefully chosen research methods in an effort to compensate for the weaknesses of any one method. According to Tashakkori and Teelie (1998), mixed method studies are those that combine qualitative and quantitative approaches to form a single research methodology for a particular study or series of studies (see Chapter 7). Though there is no single formula to follow, mixing research tools is sometimes central to valid qualitative evaluation. Triangulation, or mixed method studies, functions as a vital safeguard to minimize bias and maximize the amount and quality of data gathered (Westbrook, 1990).

The most frequently used techniques to be combined with focus groups appear to include in-depth, individual interviews or surveys (Morgan, 1996). Although frequently considered to be more of a quantitative tool, surveys can have a qualitative function; the trick is to focus on allowing as much leeway as possible in responses (Westbrook, 1990). Studies that combine focus groups and surveys are one of the more commonly used ways in combining qualitative and quantitative methods. However, combing these two methods raises complex issues since they produce different kinds of data.

Morgan (1993) presented a conceptual framework to clarify these issues and distinguished four ways to combine qualitative and quantitative methods in general and focus groups and surveys in particular. These four combinations are based on the method that receives the primary attention while relying on the secondary method as either a preliminary or follow-up method. The four most common combinations of focus groups and other research techniques are:

1. *Surveys as the primary method and focus groups as the secondary method in a preliminary capacity.* This design is often the preferred choice when developing the content of questionnaires. Fuller, Edwards, Vorakitphokatorn, and Sermsri (1993) described the benefits of focus group research for fine-tuning survey questionnaires for an intended population, finding that focus groups were helpful in detecting problems in comprehension and interpretation. Surveys are limited by the questions asked; therefore, focus groups are used to provide data on how respondents talk about intended survey topics (Morgan, 1993). According to Westbrook (1990), surveys are useful for exploring areas that contain a minimum of jargon but are particularly useful for research involving the affective domain because they provide the anonymity often required for more meaningful communication.

2. *Focus groups as the primary method with surveys as the secondary method providing preliminary input that guide their application.* Research studies using this design frequently use what Morgan (1993) calls the broad but "thin" data from surveys to assist in selecting samples for focus groups or topics for detailed analysis.

3. *Surveys as the primary method with focus groups used as the secondary method to provide follow-up of participants to assist in interpreting survey results.* This use of qualitative follow-up methods is to reconnect with survey respondents for acquiring illustrative material that can be quoted in conjunction with quantitative findings. Though these designs are the second most frequently used among the four combinations they have yet to receive systematic methodological attention (Morgan, 1993, 1996).

4. *Focus groups as the primary method and surveys as the secondary method to provide follow-up data.* This combination is the least used of the four (Morgan, 1996). If observation or interviews have revealed concern about a specific reaction or situation, then a survey can sometimes be used as follow-up to obtain more detail about that situation. Westbrook (1990) posited that surveys do not allow the researcher to follow someone's train of thought, question them about straight facts, or gain an in-depth understanding of a situation. Morgan (1996) posited that researchers conducting focus group

studies seldom use this combination to avoid any implication or suggestion that quantitative data are necessary to verify the results of qualitative research.

Focus groups have also been found to be useful in combination with individual in-depth interviews. Many consider this combination a more straightforward approach since both are qualitative techniques. However, it is important not to assume that the two are interchangeable. The individual interview is viewed as offering greater depth while focus groups offer greater breadth. Studies using individual interviews may possibly be followed by focus groups to check the conclusions from initial data analysis. Studies using focus groups may be supplemented by the more specific opinions and experiences generated in individual interviews. Therefore, combining individual and group interviews poses minor difficulty for the researcher. According to Brewer and Hunter (1989), multiple methods of research are now frequently used in the social and behavioral sciences as a matter of course. In particular, Morgan's (1996) stated that over 60 percent of the empirical research using focus groups during the past decade, as revealed by a content analysis of the materials from *Sociological Abstracts*, combined the technique with other data collection methods. The likelihood that research using triangulation or various combinations of data collection methods will continue to be one of the major uses of focus groups is quite obvious by the increased usage, and it will continue to be one of the most practical ways of bringing together qualitative and quantitative methods.

When to Use Focus Groups

Since there are many ways of conducting focus groups, investigators must choose to use focus groups in a particular way. Another issue for researchers to consider is the assessment of the focus group project by an outside reviewer as to whether things were done properly and in an effective fashion. The emerging consensus, particularly among sociologists and other social scientists, is that these issues, in choosing to use focus groups in particular ways and their effectiveness, can be resolved through an emphasis on research design. The emphasis on research design forces researchers to determine whether or not to follow the "status quo" that has guided past practice of focus groups in the number of participants, the type of setting, structured versus less structured discussions, etc. (Morgan, 1996). Dick (1998) explained that highly structured focus groups, one variant of focus groups, use a structured process to increase the [1] quality of information received, [2] time economy of the procedure, and [3] unstructured content so the information is gained from participants rather than being determined by the questions asked. The emphasis on research design also causes researchers to investigate whether to use smaller or larger groups, rather than strictly adhering to the 6 to 10 homogeneous participants rule. Emphasis placed on these issues of research design would require researchers to produce definitive principles that would replace the status quo that has guided past practice (Morgan, 1992).

Focus groups can be used at different points or times during a research project—at the preliminary or exploratory stages of a study (Kreuger, 1988), during a study, perhaps to evaluate or develop a particular program of activities (Race et al., 1994), or after a program has been completed to assess its impact or generate further avenues of research (Gibbs, 1997). Appropriately used, focus groups can be particularly effective in generating or producing important information about consumer attitudes toward a variety of topics (Greenbaum, 1998), can be helpful in planning and implementing the marketing of products (Greenbaum, 2000), and can be useful in gaining insights into participants' shared understandings of everyday life and the ways in which they are influenced by others in group situations (Gibbs). They can be used either as a method to stand alone in their own right or as a complement to other methods, especially for triangulation (Morgan, 1988) and validity checking.

To aid in selecting focus groups as the qualitative type or data collection most appropriate for a given study, Greenbaum (1998) identified nine different uses of the focus group technique: [1] new product development studies, [2] positioning studies, [3] habits and usage studies, [4] packaging assessments, [5] attitude studies, [6] advertising/copy evaluations, [7] promotion evaluations, [8] idea generation, and [9] employee attitude and motivation studies. Of these nine uses, some are more applicable to the field of marketing (new product development, positioning, packaging assessments, and advertising/copy evaluations studies), while others (habits and usage, attitude, and employee attitude and motivation studies) may be more applicable in the fields of education and sociology.

Focus groups are far reaching in their use including communication studies, education, public health and marketing. Programs run by the U.S. Army Family Advocacy staff use focus groups to complement parenting, child safety, relationship or violence prevention programs. They use focus groups involving participants from the soldiers' families, NCOs, commanders and family-serving professionals as a practical way to bring all representative participants together to create and market family advocacy programs. Ultimately, however, goals of the research should drive the selection of the most effective usage of focus groups.

Organization of Focus Groups and Data Analysis

In order to maximize the effectiveness of focus group research, a planned process must be developed and implemented. This process should involve a minimum of the following stages: [1] preparation or design, [2] group session(s), and [3] analysis and write-up, with appropriate phases to facilitate each stage.

Preparation Stage

The preparation stage usually includes the following sequence of activities: [1] establishing research goals/questions; [2] selecting a moderator if a more experienced person is needed or desired to conduct focus groups; [3] determining the population from which participants will be selected and designing a screening process; [4] determining the exceptional details (Greenbaum, 1998) of the groups (e.g., number of groups that will be conducted, timing of the sessions, and geographical location and facility), and [5] determining the costs involved, particularly as to how deeply costs will impact the entire process.

At this point the assumption is that focus group methodology has been decided as the most appropriate means of gathering data to answer established research questions (e.g., "What strategies or techniques can you identify for administrators and teachers to implement a global perspective in their academic programs?" "What are some advantages for educators in having a global perspective integrated in the curriculum?" "Are there 'pitfalls' to consider if educators implement a global perspective in the classroom?").

Selecting a moderator or facilitator can be crucial to the data collection process. If someone other than the investigator is selected for this role, a skillful person is needed who can [1] maintain an on-going discussion on the specified topic without stifling participants' responses, and [2] guide the group through the successful interactions needed to gather desired data.

An experienced group facilitator can help to ensure that the discussion flows between and among group members, rather than one-on-one with the facilitator. A moderator or facilitator can be helpful in suggesting the best way to conduct research that provides answers, have resources to handle the administrative aspects of the project (i.e., recruiting, facility selection, etc.), moderate effectively (i.e., seek input from all, not invoke personal biases, etc.), and interpret results in a way that provide solutions to the issues addressed. Subject-matter experts are most frequently used in education-related focus groups. Therefore, it is imperative that the selection of a moderator or facilitator is given a priority equal to any other step in the process, particularly if the researcher relinquishes her/his role to a professional moderator.

Participants in focus groups—just as in survey research—should be randomly selected from individuals deemed crucial to your organization or research project. Those who aren't representative of the target group should be screened out; concentrate on depth—not numbers (Ledingham, 1998). Once the type of participants needed for the study has been determined, locating and recruiting them can be time consuming, especially if the topic under consideration has no immediate benefits or attractions to them (Gibbs, 1997). It is likely that people with specific interests will have to be recruited by word of mouth (Burgess, 1996), through the use of key informants, by advertising or poster campaigns (Holbrook & Jackson, 1996), or through existing social networks (Gibbs). Incentives such as travel or child care expenses, gift certificates, or presents might serve as motivation for participation.

Most researchers recommend homogeneous grouping to capitalize on participants' shared experiences. Investigators must be careful that diverse opinions and experiences are not stifled within a homogeneous group. However, it can also be advantageous to bring together a diverse group to maximize the exploration of different perspectives within a group setting. If a group is too heterogeneous, either in terms of gender and class, or professional and lay perspectives, the differences between participants can have a considerable impact on their contributions (Gibbs, 1997). Kitzinger (1995) posited the importance of being aware about how the hierarchy within groups may affect results (a nursing auxiliary, for example, is likely to be inhibited by the presence of a consultant from the same hospital).

Focus groups can be naturally occurring (e.g., people who work together) or may be drawn together specifically for the investigation (Kitzinger, 1995). Naturally-occurring groups allow friends and colleagues to relate each other's comments to incidents in their shared daily lives or challenge each other on contradictions to these incidents.

At this point, the exceptional details (Greenbaum, 1998) of the groups can be determined. The recommended number of people per group is usually six to ten (MacIntosh, 1993), but it is not uncommon for researchers to use upwards of fifteen or as few as four people. Overly large focus groups are cumbersome, difficult to moderate and often produce meaningless output characterized by unfocused discussion. On the other hand, groups that are unduly small can limit the range of discussion or may quickly exhaust the subject. Ledingham (1998) noted that a skillful and experienced moderator could often handle a slightly larger group or generate a lot of depth out of a smaller one. Numbers of groups vary according to project needs, some studies using only one meeting with each of several focus groups (Burgess, 1996), while other groups meet several times (Gibbs, 1997). Neutral locations can facilitate avoiding either negative or positive associations with a particular site or building (Powell & Single, 1996). There are no strict guidelines for location of focus groups.

It is imperative that researchers count the costs of engaging in focus group research. Expenses can range from minor to major depending upon the geographical location of participants in relationship to the researcher's home base, the types of incentives used to motivate group participation, rental fees of meeting facilities, hiring a professional moderator, hiring subject matter experts, and the number of sessions conducted. The degree to which these types of expenses are accounted for can either support or sabotage a well-designed research project. To offset some expenses, investigators may be able to generate funds from a supporting organization or through grant writing to solicit funding. Time is another important factor that can impact the cost of the project; it, too, must be calculated in a manner that supports total implementation.

Running Group Sessions

Group sessions can be regarded as having the following phases: [1] introduction, [2] questioning to tap contextual information and key information required, and probing for follow-up or to elicit more specific information (Dick, 1998), [3] participant discussion in response to the questions and group interaction, and [4] summation.

Prior to gathering participants for actual discussions, it is advantageous to meet each participant face-to-face. If this is not possible, communicate with participants about the purpose of the focus group, what will occur during the meeting, and how data will be used. Confidentiality of input should also be clearly communicated.

Introductions, participants introducing themselves to the group, should be made as each session starts. It is also important that participants know the investigators and their roles. A brief overview of the session and its purpose should then be offered. This brief overview should be followed by [1] a more thorough review of the purpose of the research study, [2] ground rules for discussion, and [3] affirmation from participants that they understand. The groundwork for having the discussion flow successfully is set during opening remarks and sets the climate in which discussion takes place. Sessions should be conducted in a relaxed and comfortable setting with participants sitting in a circle. Refreshments may be served as well as provisions made for other comforts. Focus group sessions range from a single 1-2 hour meeting to a series of meetings over several days or weeks.

Predetermined interview questions provide a framework for guiding the discussion, probing interesting issues in greater depth, and promoting follow-up discussion on participants' statements. Questions are intended to elicit the information that is being sought and to direct the discussion to help ensure that enough contextual information is collected. As the discussion progresses toward closure, participants can become partners in interpreting the information being shared. Final wrap-up may include a closing exercise that allows participants to share a summary closing comment. Though the discussion has been either videotaped, audio taped, or facilitated by note takers with the assumption that the data will be analyzed later, soliciting participants' assistance in the interpretation of the information—however limited—can be more time efficient and cause them to feel more like partners than informants. This is a decision that investigators make in the preparation phase. Group facilitators ask participants either to summarize the main ideas they feel have emerged from the discussion or generate a summary of the discussion or ask participants to suggest changes to clarify the consensus of the group. In either event, the end result is a summary and interpretation of discussion that is captured via video, audio, or print and transitioned into hard copy. Upon completion of the group discussion, extend thanks and appreciation to participants and, if appropriate, offer them a copy of any subsequent report.

Analysis of Data and Write Up

In analyzing data from focus groups, investigators compare participants' input on similar themes and determine how this input relates to the variables within the sample population, realizing that it is important to try to distinguish between individual opinion and actual group consensus. According to Kitzinger (1995), the only distinct feature of working with focus group data is the need to indicate the impact of the group dynamic and analyze the session in ways that take advantage of the interaction between participants. The researchers' role in data analysis falls along a continuum from the assembling of raw data on one end to interpreting comments on the other end. The analysis process involves a consideration of participants' words, tone, nonverbal communication, frequency of participation, intensity, and specificity of responses. Strategies for reducing the quantity of data and extracting the most useful data that relates to the research topic must also be used.

When coding scripts from group discussions, it is helpful to use special categories for certain types of narrative, such as jokes and anecdotes, and types of interaction, such as questions, deferring to the opinion of others, censorship, or changes of mind. Kitzinger (1995) believed that a focus group research report that is true to its data should include at least some illustrations of the discussion between participants rather than simply presenting isolated questions taken out of context. Investigators need to capture a sense of what participants said with an identifier of who said what (e.g., single father comment), while also capturing the general flow—or commonly expressed ideas—and recording any characteristic language (e.g., nonverbal cues or specific phrases expressed by participants).

Focus groups are labor intensive and analyzing data from group discussions can take an inordinate amount of time. It is impossible to note immediately all problems raised during discussions; the direction of discussions are far too unpredictable, with problems being raised in quick succession (Jong, 1998). Videotaping or audio recording is suggested to facilitate these difficulties. Videotaping is a powerful way to capture the participants' perceptions and review participant reaction and response for those unable to attend group sessions. To avoid participants being inhibited by the videotape, inform them of taping prior to the session. Moreover, the facilitators should get written permission from members of the focus group before videotaping them.

Most discussion on the "how-to" of analyzing focus groups has occurred within broader discussions of the method. Although it is true that many of analytic issues in focus groups are the same as in other qualitative methods, it is also true that focus groups raise some unique issues, such as the ongoing debate about the correct unit of analysis for focus group data, the group, participants, or participants' utterances (Carey & Smith 1994, Gamson 1992, Morgan 1995, 1996).

Conclusions

Focus groups, as a qualitative methodology, have been increasingly and consistently gaining a solid reputation as the method of choice for many researchers. The depth of data extracted from focus group discussions enhances and promotes their use in fields of study that have traditionally rejected their implementation. Focus groups are an integral part of our professional and personal lives over a wide range of endeavors. They have become a valuable tool for social researchers and other professional, regardless of their particular fields of inquiry (Frey & Fontana, 1993; Morgan, 1998).

References

Brewer, J., & Hunter, A. (1989). *Multimethod research: A synthesis of styles.* Newbury Park, CA: Sage.

Burgess, J. (1996). Focusing on fear. *Area, 28,* 130-136.

Carey, M. A., & Smith, M. (1994). Capturing the group effect in focus groups: A special concern in analysis. *Qualitative Health Research, 4,* 23-27.

Dick, B. (1998). *Structured focus groups.* Retrieved from the World Wide Web: http//www.scu.edu.au/schools/sawd/arr/focus.html

Frey, J. H., & Fontana, A. (1993). The group interview in social research. In D. Morgan (Ed.), *Successful focus groups: Advancing the state of the art* (pp. 20-34). Newbury Park, CA: Sage.

Fuller, T. D., Edwards, J. N., Vorakitphokatorn, S., & Sermsri, S. (1993). Using focus groups to adapt survey instruments to new population: Experience from a developing country. In D. Morgan (Ed.), *Successful focus groups: Advancing the state of the art* (pp. 89-104). Newbury Park, CA: Sage.

Gamson, W. A. (1992). *Talking politics.* Cambridge, UK: Cambridge University Press.

Gibbs, A. (1997). *Social research update.* Guilford, England: University of Surrey, Department of Sociology.

Goldman, A. A., & McDonald, S. (1987). *The group depth interview: Principles and practice.* Englewood Cliffs, NJ: Prentice Hall.

Greenbaum, T. L. (1998). *The handbook for focus group research* (2nd ed.). Thousand Oaks, CA: Sage.

Greenbaum, T. L. (2000). *The practical handbook and guide to focus group research* (Rev.ed.). Lexington, MA: Lexington.

Holbrook, B., & Jackson, P. (1996). Shopping around: Focus group research in North London. *Area, 28*(2), 136-142.

Holstein, J. A., & Gubrium, J. F. (1995). *The active interview.* Thousand Oaks, CA: Sage.

Jong, M. D. (1998). Focus groups or individual interviews: A comparison of text evaluation approaches. *Society for Technical Communication, 45*(1), 77-88.

Kitzinger, J. (1994). The methodology of focus groups: The importance of interaction between research participants. *Sociology of Health and Illness, 16,* 103-121.

Kitzinger, J. (1995). Introducing focus groups. *British Medical Journal (International), 311,* 299-302.

Krueger, R. A. (1994). *Focus group: A practical guide for applied research.* Thousand Oaks, CA: Sage.

Lederman, L. C. (1990). Assessing educational effectiveness: The focus group interview as a technique for data collection. *Community Education, 39,* 117-127.

Ledingham, J. A. (1998). Ten tips for better focus groups. *Public Relations Quarterly, 43*(4), 25-28.

Lincoln, Y. S., & Guba, E. G. (1985). *Naturalistic inquiry.* Thousand Oaks, CA: Sage.

Lunt, P., & Livingstone, S. (1996). Rethinking focus groups in media and communication research. *Journal of Communication, 46*(2), 79-98.

MacIntosh, J. (1981). Focus groups in distance nursing education. *Journal of Advanced Nursing, 18,* 81-85.

Madriz, E. (2000). Using focus groups with lower socioeconomic status Latina women. In N. K. Denzin & Y. S. Lincoln (Eds.), *Handbook of qualitative research* (2nd ed.). Thousand Oaks, CA: Sage.

Merton, R. K., Fiske, M., & Kwndall, P. L. (1956). *The focused interview.* Glencoe, IL: Free Press.

Morgan, D. L. (1988). *Focus group as qualitative research.* Newbury Park, CA: Sage.

Morgan, D. L. (1992). *Designing focus group research.* Thousand Oaks, CA: Sage.

Morgan, D. L. (1993). *Focus groups and surveys.* Paper presented at the annual meeting of the American Sociological Association, Pittsburgh, PA.

Morgan, D. L. (1996). Focus groups. *Annual Review of Sociology, 22,* 129-152.

Morgan, D. L. (1998). *The focus group guidebook.* Thousand Oaks, CA: Sage.

Munodawafa, D., Gwede, C., & Mubayira, C. (1995). Using focus groups to develop HIV education among adolescent females in Zimbabwe. *Health Promotion, 10*(2), 85-92.

Powell, R. A., & Single, H. M. (1996). Focus group. *International Journal of Quality in Health Care, 8*(5), 499-504.

Stewart, D. W., & Shamdasani, P. N. (1990). *Focus groups: Theory and practice.* Newbury Park, CA: Sage.

Tashakkori, A., & Teddlie, C. (1998). *Mixed methodology: Combining qualitative and quantitative approaches.* Thousand Oaks, CA: Sage.

Walkinson, S. (1998). Focus groups in feminist research: Power, interaction, and the co-construction of meaning. *Women's Studies International Forum, 21,* 111-125.

White, G. E., & Thomson, A. N. (1995). Anonymized focus groups as a research tool for health professionals. *Qualitative Health Research,* 5(2), 256-261.

Chapter 10

Designing Quantitative Research

Theodore Lewis

Many questions in education can be resolved best by resorting to scientific methods of inquiry. For such inquiry, the raw material of educational thought (variables) must be represented numerically. Class rank, academic achievement, learning style, gender, ethnicity, attitude toward mathematics, or satisfaction with how a class was taught, are examples of concepts that can be expressed numerically to become amenable to quantitative manipulation and analysis. Each of these examples can be measured against an appropriate scale. Just as temperature can be measured by the calibrated height of mercury in a tube, a student's level of satisfaction with the curriculum can be expressed on a graduated satisfaction scale. American educational institutions at all levels rely heavily on the use of a simple four-interval scale as the basis for expressing student academic performance. Course grades earned throughout high school, or in college, can be summarized and represented by a single point on this scale, referred to as grade-point-average (GPA).

Four basic types of measurement scales are used in educational research, namely, *nominal*, *ordinal*, *interval*, and *ratio*. Numbers in nominal scales are not quantities but place holders. However, they can be counted to provide frequency measures, and could be the basis of statistical analyses that show relationships between variables. Typical use of a nominal scale would be a study where two types of teaching methods are compared. Here, one method can be assigned the number 0 and the other the number 1. Similarly, males in a study could be assigned the number 1 and females the number 0. Ordinal scales are used to represent rankings (e.g., class rank). High school graduates in a study may have their class rank entered as an item of data. Interval scales represent quantities to a limited degree. GPA is computed on the basis of an interval scale with points 0.0–4.0. Unlike mercury in the thermometer which rises proportionally in relation to temperature, scales in education respond to human judgment which cannot be precisely calibrated. Thus, the grades that teachers or professors issue to students have built-in error. Three judges evaluating an ice skating performance (typically on a 10-interval scale) may differ in the scores they award. Interval scales do not have absolute zero points, where there is complete absence of the trait being measured. Even where one fails a course, it cannot be assumed that nothing was learned. This means that the GPA of two students cannot be meaningfully expressed as a ratio. A student whose GPA is 4.0 has twice as high an average as a student whose GPA equals 2.0 but has not necessarily learned twice as much. Still, these scales do provide good information from which intelligent practical inferences can be made, and the challenge for researchers is to use proper safeguards in their construction.

Ratio scales are the only scales that assume an absolute zero point, thus allowing two points on the scale to be expressed meaningfully as fractions of each other. But true ratio-level variables in education are probably non-existent. Zero on an IQ test does not equate with absence of brain activity so the scores on such tests are not really of ratio quality. This caution holds even for tests where the final score is obtained by counting the number of correct items such as on a multiple-choice test. The scores lend themselves to ratio treatment, but again not with the precision of true science. The ratio scales that apply in education are not peculiar to the field. They include concepts imported from the physical world such as time or speed. Thus, years of teaching experience, hours of professional development, typing speed, or time taken to solve a problem can be treated as ratio level. Other examples of general variables include salary and age. Generally speaking, a researcher in education, is probably better off forgoing the assumption that a variable measuring a purely educational concept can be treated at the ratio level, though it seems a good candidate and to opt instead for interval measures.

Faith in numbers could represent false hope mainly because, as with nominal variables, the numbers used in educational research often do not reflect tangible quantities or cannot be yielded by direct observation and measurement. In many other cases, though, as with SAT score, GRE score, or grade point average, the numbers have some integrity, being reflective of given standards. Then there are cases (e.g., measures of satisfaction or interest) where quantities are self-reported, and where great caution must be taken in ascribing meaning to them since the scores yielded may not be stable over time or across individuals. A student may feel better about a teacher two weeks after the end of a course, than on the day when he/she learned of the course grade. Course ratings by students may differ, if given on one day rather than the other.

In resorting to quantitative approaches then, it is important for educational researchers to be of the disposition that numbers do not yield scientific exactness that validate research findings merely by their use. Numbers mean little if the research questions they support are not interesting. To be of worth, good quantitative studies in education, like good science, should begin with as thorough an understanding of the problem as is possible, and should combine insightful questions with impeccable data gathering procedures, measurement instruments that yield stable results over time and are truly reflective of the characteristic being scaled, analysis methods suited to the research questions being resolved, and interpretations of findings that are bold and intuitive.

Nature of Science

Researchers in the social sciences who wish to approach their study design as a disciplinary scientist would, needs to understand that there is much diversity in how science is done, and much variation in approach from one discipline to the next. The methods and approaches that are used depend upon a host of factors such as whether the particular field is theory-driven or data-driven, whether the approach to inquiry is observational or experimental, or whether the field is data-rich or data-poor. For example, physics is a theory-driven field that relies on calculation. Geology relies on observation and description. Scientists in all fields are trying to arrive at truth and they take care to document their inquiry processes, and to subject their findings to rigid validating tests before publishing them. There is no one method of doing science and verifying results. What is key though is that the investigative processes of the scientist, whatever they are, are documented and can be retraced and replicated.

Despite variation among scientific disciplines in how inquiry is done, there is a set of underlying practices—a research cycle—that are common to most. According to Kneller (1997) this cycle begins with identification of a problem, generation of a hypothesis, making inferences, testing data, getting feedback, changing of hypothesis based on this feedback, and repeat of the process. The process is inherently messy, given to trial and error, and heavily dependent on the ability of scientists to question their data.

Finding Problems

Problem finding is the most creative aspect of research. This point is worth reiterating, especially in the context of a discussion of quantitative research design, since there is a mistaken tendency to judge the merits of quantitative studies, not by the quality or importance of the questions they seek to resolve, but by the sophistication of the statistical methods employed. Quantitative methods ought to be the servant not the masters of problems. In science, problems come about in a number of ways including the quest to resolve anomalies with respect to well established laws or theory; interest in reconciling conflicting theory ("How did the universe begin?") or seeking to unravel puzzles of nature (e.g., architecture of human genes, causes of diseases, or an ability of some materials to conduct electricity at very low temperatures). Good scientific problems arise from nagging curiosity. For example, one puzzle that has been preoccupying scientists is the existence of certain life forms in the harsh environment of boiling springs. How is it possible that these life forms can thrive in such extreme environments? What can we learn from them that can have worldly applications?

While social scientists are interested in problems of a different order than natural scientists, some basic principles of scientific problem finding may yet apply. For example, anomalies that defy conventional wisdom may be worth investigation (e.g., "Why do children from some inner city schools excel in academics?").

Problems are areas of scholastic tension that are given to contest, debate, or controversy; or that are clouded with doubt or ignorance. Possible problem sources in education or training include:

1. *Controversial practice.* Examples are home schooling, curricular tracking, emergency certification of teachers, or the use of school vouchers.

2. *Efficacy of reforms or other interventions.* Issues relating to standards-based reforms, high stakes testing, tech-prep, or career academies.

3. *Efficacy of intellectual models.* Models of how teachers adopt innovation or how children or adults learn.

4. *Testing theory.* Efficacy of vocational maturity theory, multiple intelligence theory, theories of human motivation, or human capital theory.
5. *Challenging commonplace belief systems.* Is learning style a viable concept? Do adults and children learn differently? Do minority students require ethnic-specific pedagogic strategies?
6. *Efficacy of specific innovations.* Does computer use in classrooms lead to increased student understanding of concepts?

Problem Statement

Stating the problem is a prerequisite early step of quantitative research, as indeed it is for other types of research. The researcher spells out the particular area of difficulty onto which the study is embarking and provides the rationale for so doing. Maybe there is much that is unresolved still in this particular area of inquiry—much that is not known. Perhaps there is still ongoing controversy. Or maybe the lawmakers have gone out on a limb in this area, making policy and providing funding without the basis of definitive empirical studies. The problem statement must make the case that the study to be undertaken adds an increment of understanding in a sphere of knowledge that is still unsettled.

Hypotheses

A hypothesis is a conjecture or prediction about the relationship between variables. Hypotheses may be based upon hunch, theory, or previous research. A good hypothesis should yield testable predictions, should account for known facts, and should predict new facts.

Examples:

• Girls will perform better in science if they are taught by female teachers in single sex classes.
• Children who are home schooled will score higher than other children on high stakes tests.
• Companies that invest in the training of their workers will yield higher rates of productivity than those companies that do not.

Research Questions

Once a hypothesis is established, researchers have an obligation to also consider rival hypotheses. It is common in quantitative research design for both the primary hypothesis *as well as plausible rival ones* to be restated or expanded into research questions. For example, the main hypothesis about the relationship between the gender of science teachers and the performance of girls may have rivals relating to socio-economic status and whether or not science classes are coeducational. Thus, research questions for the study could include the following:

1. Do girls taught by male teachers score higher than girls taught by female teachers?

2. Do background factors (specifically socio-economic status and reading level) account for variation in science achievement among girls?

3. Does the composition of classes (coed or single-sex) account for variation in science achievement among girls?

These research questions must account for all variables in the study and, taken together, they dictate the lines along which data analysis will proceed. Individual research questions become organizers for the reporting of the methodological approach and the discussion of results.

Inferences

The reasoning that leads to hypothesis formation may be of five basic kinds, namely retroduction, hypothetico-deduction, deduction, induction, and analogical.

Retroduction. Retroduction is the explanation of anomalies, such as forming a hypothesis about why a particular set of schools in inner cities produces high achieving children.

Hypothetico-deduction. This is, first, forming a hypothesis and, then, predicting conclusions from the hypothesis, as in this example:

Hypothesis: Girls perform less than do boys in science because they do not have female science teachers as role models.

Deduction: Girls who are taught science by female teachers will out-perform girls who are taught by male teachers and will achieve to the same degree as boys.

Deduction. This kind of inference begins with general knowledge followed by prediction of particular results. For example, given knowledge that a school is under-funded, a researcher may predict that many of its teachers will be dissatisfied with their jobs and that the students will perform below state norms.

Induction. This is the opposite of deduction and involves inferring a general regularity from the particular. For example, inferring from productivity increases due to particular training programs in selected companies that investment in human capital is a component of corporate productivity.

Analogical reasoning. This is reasoning by borrowing using the principle of transfer. For example, principles from the corporate world are often applied to schools; thus, we may hypothesize that schools which conform to principles of Total Quality Management would yield higher achievement than schools that do not.

Hypothesis Testing

Educational researchers use probabilistic methods to test whether hypotheses relating to their research problem are tenable. The primary assumption of such methods is that the populations from which samples of participants are drawn are normally distributed. Statistical tests try to eliminate any possibility that an observed phenomenon is just a chance occurrence and not due to any particular intervention. We know from daily life that if we take any two oranges from a bin at a grocery store and weigh them each, one would be heavier than the other. We could have no explanation for this difference except chance. In the same way, if all ninth graders in a particular state took the state test of math proficiency, and we were to compare the mean scores of any two school districts taken at random, one would invariably be larger than the other purely by chance. For a researcher who has hypothesized that children in school districts that have embraced standards-based curriculum will score higher than school districts that did not, and whose study compares two such contrasting districts, the question becomes, what magnitude of difference rules out pure chance? Statistical logic allows us to imagine that the differences between every possible pair of school districts can be plotted and would be distributed normally. Where does the difference from the pair of districts in the study lie? The convention is that if the difference lies in the region of the distribution where only 5% of all differences are found, then it must truly be special. If such a small probability of occurring randomly exists, then the reason for differences must be the use of standards-based curriculum.

Researchers can choose a statistical test that has a distribution that can be fitted to that of the population in the study. This could be the *F*-distribution (analysis of variance, ANOVA), or the Student's *t*-distribution (*t*-test). The required value of the test statistic at the 5% probability level (*p* value = .05) is identified from a table of critical statistical values ahead of time so that calculated values for the study sample at hand can be compared. The size of the statistic at the 5% probability level varies according to sample size.

It should be noted that the logic of determining when a finding is important and not a chance occurrence can be employed for all statistical tests used in educational research, not just when comparing means but for other statistics as well such as correlations. Thus, a researcher might be interested in whether there a correlation exists between the years of teaching experience of technology education teachers and the technological literacy scores of ninth grade children. Here, all possible correlations from hypothetical samples of the same size as that of the study can be drawn and the coefficient for the study in question located to see if it falls in the critical 5% region.

Effect Size

The fact that one finds significance should not be the end of analysis since differences in studies might come about merely as a statistical artifact. Especially, such a result may be due merely to the sample size being large. Very small differences between groups or very small correlation coefficients that would have no meaning in the real world can be found significant if the sample size is large enough. Hence, if there is a statistically significant difference in findings then the researcher should probe further to determine whether the difference is *practically significant* or substantively meaningful for applied purposes. For this an *effect size* can be computed which provides an estimate of the <u>magnitude of difference</u>. A commonly used unit of measure for effect size is the average standard deviation of the groups. Say the difference in the mean ninth-grade test scores between two schools in adjoining school districts is statistically significant, and the actual mean difference is 20 points. And, say that the average standard deviation of the two schools taken together is 10 points. Then by dividing the point differential by this composite standard deviation the effect size is 2.0. Thus, the mean of one school is roughly two standard deviations away from the mean of the other. School board members of the lower performing school may find such a difference to be cause for alarm.

Variables

Variables are the raw material of problems. If interested in whether the gender of teachers of science makes a difference in the achievement of girls, then *teacher gender* and *science achievement* become primary variables of interest. This problem may suggest other variables that can influence science achievement, and that must be kept in mind such as the socioeconomic status (SES) of students and their reading proficiency. For this study then, a researcher will need male and female science teachers and an appropriate test of science achievement. Information about the SES of each girl in the study, as well as reading levels will also need to be collected. Researchers are obligated to review the literature relating to their problem thoroughly. One important reason for this is to identify variables, particularly those that can plausibly contribute to the explanation of particular phenomena. Thus, the researcher here includes socio-economic and reading level data on students in the study to be able to rule these in or out as reasons for the relatively low performance of girls in science.

It might be useful to think of variables not in isolation but as families. This way of thinking makes for a more pleasing design. For example, reading proficiency is but one facet of literacy. Thus, the entire family of literacy indicators might deserve consideration in the study design.

A Typology

There is no one way to cluster variables, but one typology is provided in the following:

Demographic variables—gender, race, socio-economic status, income, religion, age, occupation, level of education, and so forth.

Affiliation variables—professional organization membership.

Personal attributes/Traits—learning style, whether introvert or extrovert; intelligence.

Academic/literacy indicators—high school GPA, SAT score, math achievement score, reading level.

Attitudes—to authority, to religion, to work, to school, to minority groups, to innovation or change, and so forth.

Perceptions—about the curriculum, about technology, about the importance of professional development.

Beliefs—about what works in classrooms, about how children and adults learn, about the value of professional development.

Interventions—types of teaching method, types of curriculum, educational technology.

Categorical Versus Continuous Variables

For analysis purposes, variables may be classified in terms of their elasticity. That is, while some can be fitted on a numeric continuum (continuous variables), others must be sorted into categories (categorical variables). For continuous variables, each participant in a study can be assigned a numeric score that is a point on a continuum. Examples of such variables are age, math achievement score, SAT score, or monthly income. Included among this categorization of variables are all measures that can be fitted to a Likert-type scale.

For categorical variables, each participant in a study is assigned to a category. Examples are gender (male, female), region (east, west, north, south), and curriculum type (vocational, academic). The prototypic categorical variable requires nominal scales of measure but, while all nominal variables are by nature categorical, it is possible to convert variables that ordinarily require ratio or interval scales of measure into categories. For example, monthly salary, a ratio level variable that is naturally continuous, could be divided into categories (e.g., 1000–1999, 2000–2999, 3000–3999). Each participant is not assigned his/her actual salary but a salary range. Age could likewise be treated as categorical. The reason why such conversion becomes necessary is that some types of data are more sensitive than others. Some people are reluctant to provide their actual salary or age but would respond to a salary range or an age range. Such compromises result in data loss. It is clearly more pleasing to collect data in a manner that is consistent with the highest level of measurement scale to which it conforms.

Design

Quantitative designs require that all variables for which data are to be collected be identified, operationalized ("How will variables be measured?) and specified (What scale of measure will be used?). It is also very important that each variable be tracked through a study and accounted for at the end. Did it make a difference or not? Researchers should have a rationale for the inclusion of each class of variable or for individual variables. A rationale may originate from prior studies, from observation of practice, or from intuitive sense, and should be argued as part of the conceptual framework of the study. In the initial listing of variables, it is useful to categorize them generally in terms of the role they would likely play, based upon the way the research questions for the study are framed. Some may be treated as independent variables and others as dependent variables. Some may be treated as both.

Dependent (Criterion) Variables

Some variables are used as the standard against which groups are compared or against which other variables are made to relate. They are referred to as criterion or dependent variables. For example, if an investigator wishes to determine which of two types of schools (public vs. private) is performing better, he/she will need to operationalize what is meant by school performance so that the comparison can be made. Criteria might include percentage of graduates who have gone on to college in a specified time period or the mean scores of ninth graders on the state test in mathematics and science. These criteria would be dependent variables. A researcher could decide to use one only or all. In another case, you might be interested in identifying what factors can help predict the starting annual salary of a college graduate. Here, the point of focus is the salary of each participant. Salary is the criterion or dependent variable.

Independent Variables

Criterion variables owe their magnitude to other variables which are called independent variables. In the first example given above, the hypothesis is that percentage of students who go on to college and the mean scores of ninth graders in mathematics and science, *depend* upon the type of school one attends. School type (public vs. private) is the independent variable. In the second example, we may hypothesize that beginning salary (criterion or dependent variable) depends upon one's college major, gender, and job type (e.g., manufacturing or service). College major, gender and job-type are all independent variables.

Operationalizing Variables

Once identified as a component of a study, variables should be operationalized. That is, how they are to be measured needs to be spelled out. Thus, in one example given above, the hypothesis was that school-type determined school performance. School performance had to be operationalized, and that required spelling out of measures. Another example might be a study where training is hypothesized as yielding productivity. The variable "productivity" has to be operationalized first before it can be measured, and before data can be collected. In this case productivity might be operationalized as company earnings per capita.

Specifying Variables

To specify a variable is to say how it will be measured after it has been operationalized. In the productivity example, provided above, earnings per capita may be measured by a ratio of company earnings over size of workforce, or that value may be standardized by computing it's log. Some variables are straightforward and can easily be specified, while others require thought in their construction. For example, there are pre-existing instruments for measuring job satisfaction, organizational commitment, intelligence, and mathematics achievement. Some demographic variables (e.g., gender, ethnicity) can simply be self-reported. But some variables, particularly those that measure affect, are not of straightforward character and require the creation of suitable and valid measures. A study requiring an examination of attitudes toward technology may require the creation of a measurement instrument. That instrument may be comprised of a number of questionnaire items, each requiring a response via a Likert-type scale that progresses from a low to high degree of agreement as shown in the 3-item example in Table 10.1.

TABLE 10.1
Technology Attitude Instrument

Items	Scale
1. Technology improves the quality of human life	1 2 3 4
2. Technology makes jobs and work more interesting	1 2 3 4
3. Technology improves the quality of human interaction	1 2 3 4

Here, the variable "Attitude to Technology" can be determined by assigning participants either their total score on the three items or the average score. Creating and specifying variables by clustering questionnaire items is a common occurrence in quantitative research.

Control

The most difficult task of the quantitative researcher is to get results that are free of error and not open to alternative explanation due to the effect of *extraneous* variables. If graduates of Catholic schools are shown to score higher on college entrance tests than graduates of public schools, then you want to be sure that factors other than a schooling effect are not *confounding* the results. It may be, for example, that children of higher socioeconomic status (SES) are more likely to go to Catholic schools. To be able to say that it is the school and its curriculum that is at play, and not social class, the researcher must screen out the effects of SES. Options available to do so include elimination, inclusion, manipulation, randomization, and statistical control (see Pedhazur, & Schmelkin, 1991).

In elimination, variables are neutralized and made constant. So, when comparing children from Catholic and public schools, only students of comparable SES are included in the study. Others are excluded. Using students only within a prescribed SES range assures the investigator that SES will not be the reason for any differences that are found. In like vein, studying white female students only in a given study eliminates the chance that race and gender are factors influencing findings. Studying eighth graders only eliminates the chance that any differences found are due to developmental stage. But, a disadvantage of control by elimination is that researchers are limited in the population where study results can be generalized. Thus, from the examples discussed above, researchers may generalize only to eighth graders or to white female students.

With inclusion, researchers consciously include variables in a study that have potential for helping to explain findings. In doing so, they may resort to a statistical process that can indicate if a rival variable not included in the advanced hypothesis has significant effect. Or indeed, the researcher may be able to parcel out the effects of the suspect variable, saying to what degree it has influence. In comparing Catholic school and public school graduates, a researcher includes students from across the SES spectrum and, in addition to checking for a school effect, checks for and measures any SES effect. Thus, the researcher can see if SES was benign or active. Control of this order can then be had through multiple regression analysis.

Control by manipulation is possible only in experimental type studies. All other factors in the study constant are held except for the independent variable to be manipulated. Thus, in a given study, one group of participants may be exposed to inquiry-based teaching and another to traditional pedagogy. The remaining conditions of the study must be the same for both groups including such factors as the experience of teachers, school climate, and availability of resources in support of the curriculum.

Randomization is possible in true experiments. Each participant in the study is given the same chance of being exposed to interventions. If one group is to receive computer-based instruction and the other traditional instruction, then at the beginning of the experiment there must be a random way for each subject to get into one group or the other (perhaps via a coin flip or through assignment via a table of random numbers). Randomization does not eliminate error due to effect of extraneous variables; rather, it distributes the possibility of such error evenly across all participants.

Statistical control allows estimation of the degree to which extraneous variables affect findings. For example, in comparing two methods of teaching where student performance is used as the criterion, it may be that differences between students can be partially explained by their level of intelligence. The effects of intelligence must be isolated and this can be done statistically. To do so, each student's intelligence score will have to be known. A statistical method, such as regression analysis or analysis of covariance, is used to check for any effects of intelligence. If there is significant effect, its magnitude can be measured and separated out of the findings.

Questions

The choice of quantitative research depends on the kinds of questions researchers pose. One can consider a typology of such questions.

Comparison questions. These are questions that ask whether X is more efficacious than Y (e.g., "Is one type of teaching method more effective than another?"). Where two groups are involved and their means are to be compared, a *t*-test or ANOVA could be employed as the appropriate statistical method. For more than two groups, ANOVA would suffice.

Impact questions. These are questions that ask whether intervention X makes a difference (e.g., "Did the introduction of computers into the classroom lead to increased reading scores?"). One way to resolve an impact question is to convert it into comparison form. In this case, the scores of students who experienced computer-assisted reading can be compared with students who had an alternative form. Here again, ANOVA can be employed to resolve the basic question of difference. Impact questions may also be resolved by taking into account other possible factors that can explain difference between groups. For example, in the case in question here, other factors that may plausibly help to account for variation in reading scores might be gender, socioeconomic status, or prior reading level. Researchers need to disentangle the impact of the intervention of interest (computer-assisted reading) from the rival ones. To do this, at least two very good statistical methodology options exist; namely. analysis of covariance (ANCOVA) and regression analysis. What these two approaches have in common is the ability to isolate the unique contribution of an intervention to the size of a predetermined criterion. So that even if prior reading ability or gender are significant, factors in determining a student's reading achievement score after instruction, one can still determine whether computer-assisted instruction was a uniquely significant factor in the size of that score.

Relational questions. These are questions that seek to establish associations between variables. The simplest relation is between two measures. For example, a researcher might be interested in whether there is a measurable relation between students' reading achievement scores and their science achievement scores. This basic question can be resolved by computing a correlation coefficient, that expresses the degree of affinity between the two scores. This coefficient may vary in size from -1.00 to 1.00. Researchers need to be aware that whether or not two variables are significantly correlated depends on sample size. If the sample is quite large, even a very small relation may show to be statistically significant. But computation of effect size may show such significance to be of no practical use.

Relational questions in the social sciences are usually complex, requiring simultaneous consideration of more than two measures. For example, the researcher may be interested in the following question: "What are the factors which determine whether or not students will drop out from college by the end of the freshman year?" Here, there are many plausible factors to consider, including gender, ethnicity, socio-economic status, and the presence of specific campus interventions such as peer mentoring. Problems of this order can be resolved by multiple regression analysis, allowing estimation of the relative and absolute effects of each factor in question.

Latent traits/beliefs questions. These are questions that are investigative in nature. They seek to unearth hidden clues that can help explain behavior. Several examples are [1] understanding the value orientations of teachers with respect to curriculum and instruction, and [2] understanding the factors that determine whether a student survives or drops out of the freshman year in college. The use of factor analysis to explore questions of this order is explored later.

Types of Designs

Design depends upon the question(s) to be resolved. Some kinds of questions are resolved best by correlational research designs and others by experimental designs.

Experimental Designs

Experiments in education can be quite rigorous, especially if randomization is employed as the means of control. Basic elements of an experiments are [1] experimental variable or treatment, [2] dependent variable, [3] treatment group, [4] control group, [5] pre-test, and [6] post-test.

Example: A researcher conducts an experiment to determine whether method of instruction makes a difference in students' understanding of physics concepts (as measured by a post-test). One group had a hands-on laboratory experience. A second group completed a simulation exercise using a piece of computer software. A third group got no instruction but was simply asked to read the relevant chapter. Students from all three groups were given a pre-test to check their prior knowledge of the material. Experimental design nomenclature would apply in this case as follows:

Experimental variable—the type of teaching method (simulation or lab)
Treatment group—both the simulation group and the lab group
Control group—group that reads only
Dependent variable—physics achievement test score
Pre-test—Test of prior knowledge administered before instruction

Here, the mean scores from the three groups could be compared, and ANOVA or a simple *t*-test could be employed to determine whether there is significant difference among them.

As indicated earlier in this chapter, to have rigor in educational experiments researchers must pay attention to control. Without adequate attention to control the following kinds of error may have crept into the experiment just described:

1. The practical conditions of the experiment may not have been uniform for each group. For example, one group may have been exposed to more instructional time than the other.
2. Students may have self-selected instead of being randomly assigned to groups.

3. Different teachers may have taught the lab and computer environments.

4. The post-test score could have been affected by students prior knowledge of physics.

These potential opportunities for error in experimental designs are sources of internal invalidity (or threats to internal validity). This means, that we can not be certain that the effects of variables other than the treatment were accounted for. For experiments, randomization is the most stringent form of control. But even when it is employed, researchers should still deliberately try to equalize the experimental conditions for all groups, and should still try to remove threats to internal invalidity as far as is possible. These threats may be classified as follows:

History. This is error introduced due to changes that occur over time, during the course of a study, that affect the results in untoward ways. For example, students in a study may become exposed to relevant information from sources (such as television) other than the particular treatment group to which they belong.

Maturation. Participants may change psychologically during the course of an experiment.

Testing. Some students may become test-wise; they do better on the post-test having learned from the pretest.

Instrumentation. The test used to measure participant knowledge may not be valid or reliable (The instrument was not pilot-tested).

Statistical regression to the mean. Individuals with high degrees of prior knowledge have less room for improvement in their scores after experimental treatment than persons with less. This phenomenon raises a caution against the use of gain scores (post-test minus pre-test scores) as dependent variables in studies, since those with low prior knowledge are likely to show greatest gain.

Differential selection. Experimental and control group participants may not come from the same general pool.

Experimenter effect. The experimenter may confound results by not being neutral with respect to all groups in a study.

Whatever the method of control employed, the design of studies should be checked against each common threat to internal validity.

Quasi-Experiments

Since it is not always practicable to conduct true, randomized experiments in education, quasi-experiments may be considered. These are experiments conducted in natural settings such as schools or workplaces. Without being able to resort to randomization, it is still possible to infuse control into the design. This may be done by insuring that the groups to be compared share as much as possible in common except on the primary "treatment." For example, a researcher may be interested in tracing high school graduates into the labor market to see whether their job prospects vary according to the curricular track they pursued. Thus, students must come from the academic track on the one hand and vocational track on the other. Here, curriculum track is the analog of treatment in a controlled experiment. The dependent variable could be wage data, perhaps current monthly earnings. One control could be that the graduates were members of the same cohort, graduating at the same time. Other controls could be of a statistical nature. For example, data on gender, social class, and ethnicity could be collected and these variables could be controlled statistically. Studies of this type, where the treatment condition is determined after the fact rather than manipulated by researchers, are also called *ex-post facto* or causal-comparative designs.

A second example of a quasi-experimental study would be the case where a proportion of freshman students at a community college followed the advice of academic counselors and formed study groups while others did not. It becomes possible to study the effects of joining study groups on academic achievement by comparing the grades of students who joined or did not join them. Such a study would also be ex-post facto because school administrators must allow students free choice in whether or not to join study groups.

Since quasi-experiments fit more readily into the cut and thrust of educational practice, the main caution with respect to such designs is that they need not be shoddy. They can be the basis of gaining critical evaluative data for the making of educational decisions.

Correlational Designs

Correlational designs are based on the strength of relationships between variables. In the simplest form of correlational studies, the degree of correspondence between two variables may be measured. For example, a researcher may explore the connection between socioeconomic status and academic achievement. To do this, he/she will have to collect data from participants on these two measures, then compute a correlation coefficient. If the correlation is perfect, meaning that two variables influence each other positively to the exclusion of all others, then the correlation coefficient will be 1.00. If the relationship is perfect, but negative, then the coefficient is –1.00. Thus, the correlation between two variables may lie somewhere between 1.00 and –1.00, such as .50, or –.30.

The principle of correlation can be exploited where the purpose of research is to disentangle complicated social phenomena, where multiple related variables impinge on each other simultaneously. Here's an example. A researcher wishes to determine what factors determine science achievement in the 12th grade. The dependent or criterion variable is 12th grade science achievement score as determined by a standardized state test. Independent variables include gender, 5th grade reading achievement score, 5th grade math score, socioeconomic status, gender, and type of curriculum (traditional vs. innovative). In a study such as this, there may be correlation among the independent variables in varying degrees. For example, there may be significant correlation between 5th grade math score and gender. Further, several of the independent variables may independently correlate with the dependent variable. Thus, both socioeconomic status and type of curriculum may separately correlate with science achievement score.

It is possible for the researcher to determine which of the independent variables, acting alone or in concert, significantly influence 12th grade science achievement score. Multiple regression analysis can compute the correlation between an entire set of independent variables and a single dependent variable, and it can also be used to isolate the relative contribution of each independent variable towards the size of the dependent.

Path analysis uses the same principle of correlation as multiple regression, but seeks to fit relations between independent and dependent variables in terms of causal links. For example, a researcher may hypothesize that socioeconomic status predicts 5th grade reading score which, in turn, predicts science achievement score in the 12th grade. Separate populations of students can be studied to test such a model. For each group, correlations would be computed first between socioeconomic indices and 5th grade reading score, then between 5th grade reading score and 12th grade science achievement score.

Latent traits/beliefs questions were set forth above as a category of question suited to quantitative designs. Such questions can be resolved by factor analysis methods. Underlying these methods is the principle of correlation. One investigation used factor analysis to study the instructional thoughts, beliefs, and preferences of HRD practitioners (Lewis & Peasah, 1998). In this study, factor analysis was the primary method of data analysis. One question studied was whether HRD practitioners are disposed toward the needs of their trainees (humanism) or that of employers (corporatism) as they consider the nature of their jobs. Items reflective of these two basic dispositions were randomly dispersed in the study questionnaire. Responses were via a Likert-type scale ranging from 1 ("weak" belief) to 10 ("core" belief). Results showed that indeed, items reflecting "humanism" and "corporatism" tended on the basis of correlation to form relatively discrete clusters, with the intensity of clustering being stronger among the former. Items clustering together to form "humanism" included the following:

1. The purpose of training is to improve the desire of workers to continue learning
2. The trainer's job is to help workers to realize their fullest potential
3. An important purpose of training is to keep workers intellectually challenged

Items clustering to form the "corporatism" cluster included:

1. The test of the content of training programs should be workplace relevance
2. Trainers should keep their sights on the bottom line
3. The job of the trainer is to help the organization/client offer a better service/product.

Clusters that are yielded in factor analysis do not reveal their thematic logic readily. Researchers have to examine the structure of clusters, seeking to determine the predominating content of the related questionnaire items, and the underlying idea(s). It is useful if the researcher has hypothesized cluster logic ahead of time, rather than assuming a scatter shot approach to items hoping for clusters to thus reveal themselves.

Items that cluster to form a factor in factor analysis studies can be treated as a composite by computing a "factor score." This factor score can then be treated as either an independent or dependent variable, typically in regression analyses, in further analysis of the data.

In typical educational studies, the variable list is mixed. Some variables may be continuous and others dichotomous. Some standard educational research textbooks provide tables to help guide the choice of correlation method for particular combinations of variables. But such tables, while useful for working with dissimilar pairs of variables, are not very helpful where large numbers of them may have to be correlated simultaneously, as in factor analysis or multiple regression analysis. While the Product-moment correlation (Pearson's r)—which is best suited for correlation continuous variables—would work in cases of a mixed variable list, pay close attention to the options that standard statistical software (such as the Statistical Package for the Social Sciences–SPSS) offer, and choose the coefficient that seems the best fit given data.

Categorical variables (e.g., gender, teaching method, ethnicity) must be converted to numeric form for statistical analysis purposes. Where the variable is dichotomous (consisting of only two levels), it can be dummy coded. Thus, one category could be coded 1 and the other 0 (e.g., for the variable gender, coding could be male=1, female=0). Where there are more than two categories, effect coding must be used. Here, each of the categories of a variable is treated as a sub-variable in its own right and dummy coded. For example, the variable ethnicity may have three categories, Caucasian, African, and Hispanic. Each of these levels is treated as a separate variable. Thus, a Caucasian participant in such a study is coded 1 (for the sub-variable "Caucasian"), 0 for African, and 0 for Hispanic. Say a hypothetical study of determinants of math achievement score has five basic variables, namely gender, ethnicity (with sub levels Caucasian, African, and Hispanic), math achievement score, reading achievement score, and homework (in hours per week). The variable ethnicity will have to be replaced by its three subsets. Each participant in the study would have three bits of data for ethnicity, one for each category. The data for one person in the study who is Hispanic and female may look like this: gender=0; Caucasian=0; African=0; Hispanic=1; math score=85; reading score=80; homework=8. As can be seen from these data for one student, the units of data do not all reflect real quantities. The data for gender and ethnicity are nominal. But it is still possible, as shown here, to treat such data statistically.

Non-Parametric Statistics

The research designs that have been discussed above are premised on the assumption that scores in the populations from which samples are drawn are normally distributed. Inferences about populations can be made from such samples. The statistical tests of significance that are yielded by techniques such as ANOVA, factor analysis, or regression analysis are referred to as parametric statistics. These techniques also assume that equal interval scales of measurement, particularly interval and ratio scales.

When these assumptions are not met, research designs must be based on nonparametric statistical methods. One of the more commonly used non-parametric statistics is chi-square. It is applied when dealing with categorical data for which there are frequency counts, proportions, or percentages. The test could be whether data are distributed differently for one group as opposed to the next, or whether there is a relationship between variables. An example is a study in which the labor market status of male and female graduates of a two-year vocational program is compared to see whether there is a statistically significant difference in their profiles. There could be four measures: working full-time, working part-time, at school, and not working. Data could be as shown in Table 10.2.

TABLE 10.2
Gender Differences in Labor Market Status

Status	Male	Female
Working full–time	90%	80%
Working part–time	5%	7%
Not working	3%	5%
At school	2%	8%
Total	100%	100%

The chi-square test will resolve whether the labor market profiles of the two groups are different. These data could also be expressed as raw frequency counts. A single chi-square value would be computed and compared with the table value at $p \leq .05$ to determine significance.

A different case might be where two groups of teachers, traditional and innovative, are asked to rate three sets of curriculum materials. There are 100 teachers in the study, 50 traditional and 50 innovative. They are asked to examine the materials, then indicate whether or not they would use them in their classes assuming availability. The data could be as shown in Table 10.3. In the case of Table 10.3 each row responds to a separate issue and reflects a count of the entire sample, chi-square has to be computed in each case. Each row is tested thus, "Is there a statistical difference between traditional and innovative?"

TABLE 10.3
Comparison of Teacher Preferences (Frequency Data).

Teacher preference	Traditional		Innovative	
	Yes	No	Yes	No
Set 1	30	20	20	30
Set 2	40	10	10	25
Set 3	20	30	30	20

A county may look at the percentage of students who successfully met the state requirements in reading, math, and science, then wish to compare that data to statewide data. Results are as shown in Table 10.4.

TABLE 10.4
Comparison of State and County Data

Subjects	County	State
Reading	75%	80%
Math	60%	70%
Science	50%	60%

In such a case where data are compared to a known distribution (in this case the state distribution), the researcher can use a chi square goodness of fit test to see if there is significant comparison.

Once data are frequencies, percentages, or proportions, a nonparametric analog of the correlation coefficient (e.g., a phi coefficient) can be computed to express the relationship. In Table 10.5, the hypothesis that a correlation exists between school type and academic achievement can be tested, using percentage of 12th graders passing the state reading and math tests as the achievement measure. Frequency scores can also be compared using the Kruskal Wallace test, which is the nonparametric analog to ANOVA. Usage is appropriate when comparing more than two groups and asking the question whether significant differences exist in their distribution.

TABLE 10.5
Comparison of Percentage of Students Meeting State Requirements

Subject	School type	
	Public	Private
Reading	60%	50%
Mathematics	75%	70%

Nonparametric statistics are not commonly used in educational research, but the reason is that insufficient emphasis is placed on their use in graduate programs. These statistical techniques are invaluable in dealing with everyday situations where head-counts and percentages are common forms in which one finds data. Graduate students who become equipped with these tools have a significant advantage in that they thereby increase the range of research situations they can address.

Conclusion

In this chapter, I have taken an intuitive look at the question of designing quantitative studies. The approach has been straightforward, helping student researchers and others to understand some of the critical factors that must be taken into account, and suggesting the content knowledge with which one must be equipped to be able to conduct such studies competently. To be a good quantitative researcher requires that students take an array of courses in educational statistics. The student should also become familiar with at least one of the education statistical packages (such as SPSS). Even students who feel that their work will be in the qualitative realm should get solid grounding in the quantitative realm, if only to become good, critical consumers of published quantitative research.

References

Kneller, G. F. (1997). A method of inquiry. In J. Hatton & P. B. Plouffe (Eds.), *Science and its ways of knowing* (pp. 11-25). Upper Saddle River, NJ: Prentice-Hall.

Lewis, T., & Peasah, K. (1998). An investigation of the instructional thoughts, beliefs, and preferences of selected HRD practitioners. *Journal of Industrial Teacher Education, 35*(2), 6-28.

Pedhazur, E. J., & Schmelkin, L. P. (1991). *Measurement, design, and analysis: An integrated approach.* Hillsdale, NJ: Erlbaum.

Chapter 11

Survey Research

Roger B. Hill

One of the most prevalent types of research associated with theses and dissertations is survey research. This type of research uses questionnaires or similar types of instruments for data collection with responses in either written or oral interview format. Students who choose to use survey research must deal with several issues including selection of an instrument and the processes of collecting data with that instrument. In some instances the necessary decisions are quite straightforward, but other cases require more complex decisions, trade-offs, and defense of the chosen course of action.

Several criteria that indicate appropriate use of survey research can be identified. One of these is the size of the sample indicated by the design of the study. In qualitative research designs it is not unusual to have participant numbers in the single digits. For quantitative work sample size often ranges from twenty or thirty to several hundred respondents. Use of a questionnaire or some form of survey instrument provides a reasonable solution for dealing with data collection when large sample sizes are involved.

The nature of the data to be collected is another factor influencing the decision to use survey research. Content of a questionnaire must be of a type that can be expressed in written or oral form using relatively concise items. For questionnaires that will be self-administered content must be expressed in a way that respondents can understand the items without clarification or extensive explanation. When data is needed from respondents and the topic of study is not conducive to written expression for instrument items other forms of research are indicated.

Issues related to the availability of potential respondents can influence choices about using survey research for a study. Participants in a study must be accessible and willing to provide needed information. If the context of a research project is such that a large geographic region is involved or other constraints to accessibility are present, use of a questionnaire is often a good choice. An example of limited accessibility would be respondents who are members of an intact group in a school or other institution that restricts direct contact with outside individuals. Accessibility to data extends to the willingness of sample members to respond to a questionnaire. Even when an instrument is placed in their hands, if respondents are unwilling to provide accurate answers the desired data is unattainable.

Advantages and Disadvantages

As is the case with any method of inquiry survey research has advantages and disadvantages. The positive aspects of survey research are relatively low cost, ease of managing the data collection process, and the ability to accommodate samples that are removed from the researcher by institutional structures, geography, or some other barrier.

Costs of survey research are primarily associated with developing or purchasing copies of the questionnaire, mailing or delivering the questionnaire to respondents, providing for return of the questionnaire responses, and any follow-up communication that might be required. In some instances, questionnaires are created by the researcher and administered through some direct contact with respondents so duplication costs are the primary expense. In other cases, a published questionnaire is selected and must be purchased; delivery and return costs add to expenses. Incentives that might be included with the questionnaire to encourage participation can also contribute to costs. Considering even the more expensive options that might be chosen, costs per sampling unit are less than research methods that require direct observation, extensive interviewing, and other time-intensive data gathering techniques.

Although low cost is listed here as an advantage of survey research, expenses that can be incurred should not be underestimated by new researchers. Costs of obtaining an appropriate questionnaire, especially if being purchased commercially, and mailing expenses can easily exceed $1,000. Care should be taken to develop an estimate of the costs associated with data collection procedures being contemplated so that expenses are anticipated. Budgets of graduate students and other new researchers are often tight and unexpected expenses can add a burden that is better avoided. If cost estimates exceed available resources, grants or other kinds of financial aid are sometimes available through universities, professional associations, or other sources.

Survey research is well suited for situations where breadth over depth of information is needed as an end result of research being conducted. Some types of studies are designed to represent a broad geographical region or numerous types of respondents. In these situations, questionnaires can be delivered or administered by a third party or delivered directly to respondents for completion. Instructions can be provided in concise written form, and since the data is usually recorded on paper it can be managed using common filing and document handling techniques.

Another circumstance where survey research techniques are usually most appropriate is where sensitive topics are involved and respondents have concerns about anonymity. Questionnaires can be distributed and completed using methods that allow participants to respond truthfully even when information is being shared that would be potentially embarrassing or involve some risk. This characteristic of survey research can facilitate its approval by institutional human subjects research offices at universities as well as contribute to the accuracy of data collected.

Use of survey research also has disadvantages that should be considered. These include limitations on the type of data that can be collected and adverse respondent attitudes toward providing requested data. Choices made by the researcher can minimize these issues but sometimes problems arise that are difficult to anticipate.

Care should be taken when choosing or designing a questionnaire to be sure the time needed to complete the instrument is reasonable for the circumstances in which it will be used. If it is too long or complex for the intended respondents accurate data may not be generated. A lengthy instrument can also reduce response rates and increase costs of administration.

Respondent attitudes toward questionnaires also can adversely impact success of survey research. If members of a sample either do not take the process of completing the instrument seriously or they have a negative attitude toward the activity, data might not accurately reflect the issues of interest to the researcher. How the questionnaire is presented can have an influence on respondent attitudes. Whether administered by someone in person or using the mail, consideration should be given to minimize potential problems in this area.

Survey research provides little opportunity for follow-up questions or probing of responses. This is not always a problem but in some instances unanticipated results can raise questions or indicate a lack of clarity in responses gathered. Care taken in construction of survey instruments or questionnaires can minimize this problem but it sometimes arises anyway and the researcher might wish that follow-up questions could be asked.

One final challenge to be mentioned regarding possible disadvantages of survey research is the reduction of complicated issues to limited response formats. Independent variables associated with a study are often represented by demographic data on an instrument and some type of instrument scale frequently is used as an indicator of dependent variables of interest. In both instances these variables can involve complex issues that are difficult to represent using the kinds of response items required when a questionnaire is being used.

Types of Surveys

Data collection for survey research can be conducted by using a written questionnaire or by asking a series of questions in an oral interview. Usually one or the other of these techniques is used but in some instances a combination of both can be applied.

Written questionnaires usually consist of a series of items with scaled responses providing answer options that can be checked or circled by persons completing the instrument. Open-ended items can be used but coding this type of response can be difficult and lack of clarity usually precludes comparisons between participants.

It is important for written questionnaires to use words that can be clearly understood by participants in the study. If special terms are used they must be recognized by respondents or defined in a way that will not bias answers. Reading level should be appropriate and directions for marking responses should be clear.

Survey research data can also be collected using an oral interview process. Questions can be asked of respondents either in person or using information technology such as telephone, computer conferencing, or dedicated video conferencing equipment. Use of interviewing to collect data is usually more time-consuming than using a written questionnaire but the technique provides opportunity to gain clarity in responses. If open-ended items are needed interviewing allows follow-up questions to be asked that assure a more accurate recording of participant answers.

Sometimes the topic being researched will influence the decision to use either a written questionnaire or an oral interview. If the topic is sensitive, perhaps dealing with personal issues, a written questionnaire managed in a way that assures anonymity is sometimes more acceptable to respondents. In the past anonymous random-dialed telephone surveys provided opportunity for people to be interviewed without worrying about being individually identified. With modern technology almost any electronic communication channel allows users to identify the parties participating. For that reason, a written questionnaire administered in a group setting might provide a greater sense of security for participants and thereby enhance accuracy of responses when data is of a sensitive or potentially embarrassing nature.

Another format for written surveys that is appropriate for some types of research involves use of a web site and the World Wide Web. Technical expertise is needed to prepare materials for delivery using the Web but that expertise is readily available in most college and university settings. Instrument items can be coded using HyperText Markup Language (HTML) or converted to web page format using features now included in most word processors. Responses can be sent to the researcher using an e-mail form or other web-based delivery strategy. An alternative is to develop a CGI script that is installed on a Web server to generate both the questionnaire items as well as to record the responses of end users.

Using the Web to manage data collection for survey research is dependent upon respondents having access to computers connected to the Internet. Participants will also need to be proficient enough in using the computer and Web browser software so that items can be read and responses entered. Administration must be controlled so that selected respondents participate and other Internet users are kept out. A key advantage of using the Web to conduct survey research is the ease of assuring anonymity if the data is collected in a computer lab or other location where computers are not exclusively used by a single user.

Survey research data is typically gathered using response options that are either scaled or open-ended. Scaled responses are more common and one of the significant decisions when designing response options is the wording and number of choices to be provided. Wording for available responses should be carefully considered and should match the corresponding instrument item. Readability should match the reading level of other sections of the questionnaire and all possible responses should read coherently when matched with the instrument item.

If the item is one that respondents would be reluctant to mark an absolute answer to, options should provide opportunity for responses that allow expression of some uncertainty. Instead of Disagree and Agree, the options [1] Disagree, [2] Tend to disagree, [3] Tend to agree, and [4] Agree provide possible answers for the person who resists an absolute answer in one direction or the other. As in this example, when possible responses represent a progression between a lesser and greater level, the options should be listed from left to right in lower response to higher response order.

Whether or not to provide a middle or "neutral" response is another issue for consideration. Some instruments improperly include a middle position in scaled response options to accommodate respondents who do not have a directional stance on an issue. In practice, selection of a neutral response might result from lack of understanding of the issue, reluctance to provide an honest answer, or inapplicability. Using a neutral position on a Likert-type response scale is also not logical since it does not represent a unit of increase on a continuum. Providing a "NA" or Not Applicable response option in a column adjacent to the Likert scale is a better way to accommodate responses to items that are not applicable. When using a commercially-developed instrument or one developed by another person someone else will have determined the response options, but these issues should be considered during the instrument selection process.

Some instrument items will require a middle position response. When asking respondents whether the quantity of something is too little, too much, or about right, the middle response position is needed. Instrument items that measure a situation that respondents find either comparable to something else or satisfactory should have a middle option as an answer choice.

The number of response options to provide for instrument items should be from two to seven. Distinguishing more than seven levels of response is not likely to be achieved by respondents and in most instances four or five levels are sufficient. If response options are too prolific, respondents can become either annoyed or frustrated as they complete the questionnaire. For researcher-developed instruments, final judgment about the number of response items should be based on pilot testing of the instrument.

Open-ended response items provide opportunity for participants to frame their own answers to questions asked. When this type of survey instrument is used, it is important to provide clearly stated questions and accurate recording of responses. If questions are asked using an interview process, clarification can be provided if an item is not understood. For written questionnaires with open-ended responses respondents may not have opportunities to seek clarification so clear statement of instrument items is very important.

When using open-end response items in an interview format, gathered data can be inaccurate due to inability of participants to provide information or unwillingness to answer. Respondents will sometimes not be able to provide answers whether open-ended or scaled responses are used. Reasons range from not knowing the answer to failure to properly understand what is being asked.

With open-ended responses, especially those asked in an interview format, unwillingness to provide an accurate response is a prominent concern. Two issues should be considered in this regard. One of these is the desire on the part of the respondent to provide an answer that is socially acceptable or pleasing to the person asking questions. An interview is an interaction between two people and responses can be influenced by the perceptions of both parties and the verbal and nonverbal communication conveyed. Potentially embarrassing or sensitive topics can also be difficult to deal with in an interview setting using open-ended questions. If the respondent is called upon to formulate a response that might be damaging, the result will sometimes either be an inaccurate answer or a refusal to respond.

When open-ended survey responses are being used, it is important to assure confidentiality and to avoid judging or indicating expectations of the researcher. Self-administered questionnaires should be used in place of or to supplement interviews when person-to-person social interaction will interfere with accurate data collection.

Use of Existing Instruments

When a decision has been made to use survey research, the researcher must determine whether to use an existing instrument or to develop a new instrument. In most instances, consideration should be given to using an instrument that already exists if it has produced scores in prior research that were valid and reliable. A starting point in this process is to identify what already exists.

Questionnaires that are available commercially and those developed by other scholars provide two categories of existing instruments for survey research. *Mental Measurements Yearbook* (Impara & Plake, 1998; Plake & Impara, 1999), *Tests in Print* (Murphy, Impara, & Plake, 1999), and *Test Critiques* (Keyser & Sweetland, 1984-1994) are three sources for information about existing commercially-available research instruments. *Mental Measurements Yearbook* is produced by the Buros

Institute and includes test descriptions, one or two professional reviews for each entry, and references to relevant literature. To be included a test must be commercially available, printed in English, and either be widely used or recently developed or revised.

Tests in Print, also produced by the Buros Institute, provides an extensive bibliography for tests that are commercially available and still in print. It also serves as an index for the *Mental Measurements Yearbook* by showing the volume(s) where a researcher can locate test critiques and other information. References to other literature related to each test entry are provided along with guidance for acquiring copies of tests listed.

Test Critiques is a ten-volume collection of critical test reviews. Entries are arranged in alphabetical order by test title. The set of ten covers the years of 1984–1994 and was published by Test Corporation of America. The instruments included in this reference include psychological, educational and business tests. Entries include critiques of test score validity and reliability with an emphasis on practical information.

Another valuable resource to assist in locating existing instruments is the ERIC Clearinghouse on Evaluation and Assessment located at http://ericae.net on the World Wide Web. This Web site provides a test locator that is a joint project of the ERIC Clearinghouse on Assessment and Evaluation, the Library and Reference Services Division of the Educational Testing Service, the Buros Institute of Mental Measurements at the University of Nebraska–Lincoln, the Region III Comprehensive Center at George Washington University, and Pro-Ed test publishers. Search engines are provided to locate tests, test reviews, and commercial test publishers. Tests include both commercially-marketed materials and researcher-developed instruments that have not been commercially published.

Most university libraries provide a number of other types of reference books that can assist researchers in locating previously developed instruments for use in survey research along with critiques and acquisition information. Beyond these references, instruments that are not commercially published are usually found in conjunction with reviews of related literature. Dissertations and other manuscripts published to report research typically include either copies of selected instruments or a description of them. These sources also should provide a report of how an instrument was used, some evidence of test score validity and reliability, and in some cases an overview of other similar instruments that were considered for use but not selected.

Researcher-Developed Instruments

When an existing instrument cannot be located or is not available due to cost or other issues, an alternative solution is to develop an instrument. The additional work necessary to follow this option should not be underestimated. Developing an instrument that produces valid and reliable scores is a time-consuming and sometimes resource intensive activity.

Several key issues should guide instrument development. The first is developing a questionnaire that matches the problem statement and research questions of the study. If the materials developed do not accurately capture needed data, the basis for any analysis that follows will be flawed and results will not be trustworthy. It is essential for researcher-developed instruments to be carefully crafted to target the data that will answer research questions being examined.

The process of developing an instrument that matches the needs of a study can involve reviewing other similar instruments, consulting experts in relevant fields of study, and using expert panels to review instrument items, sometimes over several iterations. In other instances, the process might be less intensive, using items developed by the researcher with little external consultation. Each situation is different and good judgment and sound advice should guide decisions made about the instrument-development process.

It is important to develop an instrument that participants in the study will respond to. A questionnaire can include all of the needed items with excellent wording and thorough coverage of research questions, but if respondents choose not to complete it the data collection process will falter. Length, organization on paper, and clarity of instructions can all play a role in respondent participation.

In the initial phase of developing an instrument decisions must be made about the format of items, how responses will be captured, and how the items will be organized. Items can be designed as brief statements with a scaled response or as questions with multiple-choice responses. Early consideration should be given to how the results will be analyzed and reported. For example, if the researcher envisions working with ordinal data in the analysis and reporting of results, the survey instrument must be designed so that responses are ordered along a single dimension representing a rating for the item.

Instrument items should be clearly stated and logically arranged. Short items are preferable to lengthy ones, and language or terminology that respondents would not understand should be avoided. Care should also be used to present only one decision point in each item. Consider this example: *"On how many holidays did you stay home from school this year?"* Respondents must determine the meaning of "holiday" in this item. It is unclear whether the item is asking about legal holidays or just days when school was not in session. Respondents must also determine what is meant by "stay home." Does this mean literally stay at home or does it include going shopping or doing other activities during part of the day away from school?

The wording of items on researcher-developed instruments should be consistent with that of a questionnaire rather than an opinionnaire. Scholarly research should be situated on a sound theoretical or conceptual base and this should be reflected in the instrument used to gather data. Rather than asking, "What do you think about 'xyz'," it is better to ask respondents to rate 'xyz' based on their experience or observation. Thoughtful construction of instrument items should frame responses so they are more than opinions that might change from day to day depending on a person's mood or other superficial criteria.

If multiple-choice items are to be used on an instrument, decisions must be made about possible answers to be provided. In some instances, this process will be as simple as listing the range of options to indicate an opinion from bad to good or disagree to agree along the selected response continuum. In instances where nominal data is being gathered, and the choices are not ranked or ordered, development of the instrument should include a phase where items are pilot tested in an open-ended format. Based on frequency of appearance the responses provided can then be used to develop multiple-choice options for closed format questions.

Arrangement of instrument items should be thoughtfully considered. Related items can be grouped together or items can be randomly arranged throughout the instrument. The key to this decision is the desired perception on the part of respondents. If the instrument is presented as covering several issues or topics, the related items should be grouped so that consideration can be focused on that issue before moving to the next one. If applicable, order the items from easy to hard or from least to most intrusive. For instruments that are presented as being related to a single construct items should be randomly arranged even if subscales or subsets of related instrument items are embedded.

Care should be taken with regard to instrument items that are closely related. If global and specific questions on an issue are used, global questions should come first. Avoid leading questions or items that have possible responses that would eliminate the need for questions that follow. Questions should focus on a single concept. "Double-barreled" questions that include two constructs that might influence a respondent's answers should be avoided.

The number of instrument items needed to capture responses related to each construct being examined should be carefully determined. In most instances four or five items will be needed to provide reliable data. Too little variability will usually result from responses if only one or two instrument items relate to a single construct.

The overall appearance of the survey instrument is very important. It should be attractive, easy to read, and as brief as practical considering the content to be included. Colored paper or colored ink on white paper can be used but care should be given to color combinations selected. Print color should contrast with background color to assure readability. Color triads such as blue, yellow, and red or orange, green, and purple are attractive to the eye but red text on a blue background tends to "vibrate" and can be difficult to read.

Selection of a typeface and justification of text is another consideration. A serif typeface with left justification is generally the most readable kind of text. San serif typefaces provide a pleasing contrast when used for headings, labels, or instructions. Serif typefaces have small finishing strokes at the ends of main character strokes and a common example is Times Roman. San serif typefaces, like Arial, appear heavier and bolder than serif type of the same size. Full justification can be used as an alternative to left justification, but multi-line text should never be center justified with a jagged edge on both sides of the block of text.

Guidance for completing and returning a questionnaire can be included in accompanying correspondence but instructions should also be provided on the instrument. A return address and the requested return date should be printed on the instrument if possible. If instruments are being mailed and are to be numbered to track responses, a small code in the footer can provide an unobtrusive means of identifying non-respondents so follow-up mailings can be sent, but participants should be notified of their presence and use.

Documenting the Process

Careful documentation should be maintained when developing an instrument for use in survey research. Notes should be maintained to describe how initial instrument items were developed, how they were pilot tested or reviewed, and what steps were taken in developing the final version of the instrument.

When reporting a study that used a researcher-developed instrument greater detail is needed to describe not only the instrument but how it was produced. Care should be taken to note what other instruments were reviewed and how those influenced the items included on the researcher-developed instrument. Caution should be exercised to avoid violation of copyright laws when constructing instrument items and the discussion of any other instruments should clearly communicate how they were used.

In most instances, some type of panel review or pilot testing will have been used to inform the instrument development process. The methods for selecting panel members or pilot test participants should be clearly described. Readers will be interested to see what expertise was involved or how pilot test participants were similar to members of the survey research sample. Iterations of revisions should also be described so it is clear how the final version of the instrument was developed.

An appendix in the report of a study will sometimes contain a copy of the instrument used in the research, especially if the questionnaire is not readily available. For researcher-developed materials not included in an appendix, a careful description of the instrument should be provided along with some sample items. Efforts should be made to assure that those reading about the instrument have a clear description of both the development process and the end product.

Demographic Data

In some instances a form to gather demographic data will need to be developed for use with a commercially-produced instrument, but it will always need to be produced with researcher-developed questionnaires. This is an important part of the survey data collection process because it often represents the independent variable(s) identified for use in the study. If demographic data is not accurately and consistently gathered, other efforts to conduct a viable research project can become futile.

Two major considerations for gathering demographic data are placement and presentation of the items on an instrument and wording of the demographic questions and response options. It is important to only gather information that is necessary for the study. Survey instruments should be kept as brief as possible and collection of extensive demographic data can impede this objective.

It is best to place demographic items at the end of a questionnaire or survey instrument. If they are placed at the beginning they can distract the respondent's attention from the survey items that require thoughtful answers. Depending on the nature of the survey they can also sensitize survey participants to identity issues that could impact honesty in replies to potentially embarrassing items on the questionnaire. By placing demographic items at the end of the instrument these concerns will be minimized. If fatigue is a factor as respondents complete the instrument demographic items at the end of the survey signal the end of the process with questions that require less thinking.

Wording of demographic items and response options is also an important consideration. Item stems should be clearly stated and not subject to various interpretations. For example, asking how many years of education have been completed would not be a good way to determine the level of education achieved. Persons who have "compressed a four year bachelor's program into six years" will not have a clear response option if education is measured in time spent enrolled in school. Level of education should be determined by listing various benchmarks (e.g., less than high school diploma, high school degree or GED, 2 years of college or Associate's degree, a bachelor's degree, some graduate work) for persons to choose from.

Multiyear categories for items such as age, years of work experience, or other measures of a time-rated condition should be avoided when possible. It is better to provide a blank for respondents to enter numerals for age as of last birthday and number of years working. If categorization of continuous variables is used on commercially-produced instruments or surveys developed by others, the categories should correspond to those in a review of literature. Prior research that has identified benchmarks or stages of development can provide a rationale for multiyear categories. It is usually better, however, to gather data for continuous variables without *a priori* categorization.

Prior research should also guide development of response items for occupations, ethnicity, income, and other similar independent variables. Using Holland's occupational types (Gottfredson & Holland, 1996) to classify occupations, for example, allows new research to connect with a broad array of prior work that has used that classification system. Efforts should be made to identify categories from research that are related to the study being undertaken. If no prior research can be found, a conceptual rationale should be developed for categories used for gathering demographic data.

Validity and Reliability

Validity and reliability are issues that require attention for both newly developed and pre-existing instruments being used for survey research. Validity is the characteristic of instrument *scores* that indicate the instrument is accurately measuring what it is supposed to measure. Reliability is the characteristic of producing consistent measurements over time.

Regardless of the source of the instrument used in survey research, explanations in written reports should describe how content validity, criterion validity, and construct validity have been assessed. Since validity relates to scores—not to instruments—it is important to address this concept regardless of how well an instrument has functioned in previous research studies. Procedures used to establish reliability should also be reported. Techniques used with questionnaires might include test-retest, parallel forms, or calculations of internal consistency (e.g., Cronbach alpha).

If data collection involves an interview process, details should be provided regarding the techniques used. When interviewing is used the interviewer functions as a part of the measurement instrument. Care must be given so that variation in answers is due to differences in respondents and not caused by differences in how data was obtained. If persons other than the researcher are to conduct interviews, training should be carefully delivered and documented.

Interviews should be based on a complete script used by the person conducting the interview. Wording of questions should be carefully designed to provide consistent meaning to all participants and any guidance regarding possible responses—examples or choices suggested—should be the same for all respondents. The steps taken in carefully crafting the interview process address the same concerns as those procedures to show validity and reliability in a printed questionnaire do. Whether data is gathered using a self-administered written questionnaire or an oral interview, accurately measuring what is supposed to be measured and producing consistent measurements over time are important features.

Developing a Rationale for Instrument Selection

Regardless of whether a commercial or researcher-developed instrument is used, any report of survey research should provide a clear rationale for why a particular instrument or data collection process was chosen. For purposes of a thesis or doctoral work this material is usually presented in the latter portion of Chapter 2 or 3 in the completed written report of the research project. If the review of literature, usually contained in Chapter 2, covers the various instruments that might be applicable to the planned study, the chosen instrument along with a rationale for its selection can be included there.

Otherwise, the rationale for selection of a particular instrument will likely be included in Chapter 3 along with a description of the research design and procedures.

The rationale for selecting a particular questionnaire or interview process should grow out of a discussion of prior related research. Instruments that have been used previously should be described along with a brief overview of earlier studies in which they were used. It is important to describe the theoretical or conceptual base for each instrument and to explain what dependent variables were measured. In each instance the characteristics of a particular instrument should be commented on with regard to fit with the research questions or important constructs considered in the study being reported.

If previous research has been reported that provides a comparison of several relevant instruments, those findings can be especially helpful. Whether the instrument selected for use is included or not, studies that provide such a comparison often identify important features to be considered. For example, Furnham (1990) reported a comparison of seven different scales designed to measure Protestant work ethic. He identified five interpretable factors that these instruments measured when used collectively but reported that each existing instrument by itself was essentially one-dimensional. He recommended development of a multidimensional measure for Protestant ethic.

When previous research has identified inadequacies in existing instruments the rationale for developing a new instrument or choosing an alternative method for gathering data is enhanced. Attention should be given to addressing weaknesses identified, and details should make it clear that the new instrument is an improvement over what was already available. If an existing instrument chosen for use has not been included in a comparative study, key features leading to its selection can be highlighted.

The criteria for judging an instrument for survey research should involve more than its prior use in research that has been published. Numerous studies have been conducted using procedures that essentially measured respondents' perceptions and opinions rather than their attitudes, actions, and observations. Opinion polls and similar survey research are appropriate for publication in newspapers and other outlets for general consumption. For scholarly research, however, instruments and procedures should be thoughtfully designed with clear connections to prior scholarly work. Data collection tools and strategies should capture data that reflect thoughtful responses and the essence of reality—not superficial impressions that are transient and disconnected from a theoretical or conceptual base.

The reasons for selecting a particular format for data collection in survey research should also be presented. If a self-administered questionnaire is to be used as compared to one that is completed in a group setting, reasons for this decision should be evident. Explanation should also make it clear why a written questionnaire was chosen rather than an oral interview or an oral interview rather than a written questionnaire. Readers should be presented with the essential thought processes that determined the data collection technique to be used.

Survey Administration

Procedures for administering data collection in survey research are obviously different depending on whether a written questionnaire or oral interview is used. Variations also exist within each of these categories. Self-administration, researcher-administered, and third party administered questionnaires all have certain unique facets to consider.

For self-administered questionnaires careful attention should be given to packaging and delivery of the instrument. A cover letter should be prepared to provide a brief explanation of the study and why participation is important. Also, assurance should be given that data will not be reported in a manner such that individual respondents are identified. Pertinent details like requested return date, who is conducting the research, how results will be reported, and who to contact in case questions arise should be included.

If research is being conducted as an institutional activity, use of official stationary should be used. Associating the study with a respected or esteemed institution such as a recognized university or business can encourage participation. If graduate student research that is not part of a sponsored project is involved, departmental policies should be checked prior to using university letterhead. In some instances it will be allowed, but in other cases it is not permissible.

When developing a cover letter the opening paragraph is especially important. Try to capture the curiosity and interest of the reader without being flippant or cute. If the project can be related to an interest or concern of the recipient, participation will be encouraged. Any personal benefits that participants receive should also be described.

Database software is sometimes used to manage contact information for survey participants. A computerized mail merge can be used to generate personalized cover letters for each person being asked to complete a questionnaire. Attention to details of this nature increases the likelihood recipients will look at the materials. Each letter should also be signed by hand using blue ink so that the contrasting ink color will call attention to the individual care given to the correspondence. If individual signatures by hand are not practical, consideration should be given to using an ink jet printer to apply a scanned signature in blue ink. Using commemorative postage stamps on each outgoing envelope further enhances the personal touches that promote participation.

Another technique that can be used to encourage participation in a survey research activity is the use of an incentive. This could consist of enclosing an uncirculated dollar bill or some other token of appreciation. The intent is to obligate the recipient so that they complete and return the questionnaire enclosed with the incentive.

A mailing envelope should be included to be used in returning the self-administered questionnaire. Be sure to provide adequate postage on it and use a regular postage stamp rather than a business reply or postage metered envelope. Respondents will be reluctant to discard an envelope with a postage stamp attached since that is tantamount to throwing away money.

It is a common practice to write a code number on the return envelope to keep up with responses. If this technique is used, be sure to explain how confidentiality is being managed so that participants are not dissuaded from returning a questionnaire. It is usually helpful to use some technique to target follow-up correspondence to non-respondents.

Two aspects related to time should be considered when questionnaires are to be sent and returned using the mail system. Time of mailing and return due date are both issues to think about. Consideration should be given to anything that is known about the schedule of activities for research participants when determining time of mailing. Materials should be sent so that they arrive near the beginning of the workweek, not on a Friday, and so that the beginning of holiday periods is avoided. If events such as the beginning or end of an academic term are possible factors, these should be considered also.

The return date requested should be set so that a reasonable amount of time is provided for completion of the instrument, but procrastination is discouraged. If too much time is indicated, the questionnaire might be set aside for later and then lost in the shuffle of materials the participant is dealing with. A due date for return mailing ten days from anticipated time of receipt is generally appropriate for completion of most questionnaires. It is important to indicate the date return is requested in a prominent way on the questionnaire. Bold print or use of color can be used for emphasis. Bright colored paper stock can also be useful to enhance the visibility of the questionnaire should it be placed with other materials on a desk or other workspace.

Nonrespondents

Regardless of the efforts made some persons approached to respond in a survey research project will choose not to participate. A follow-up strategy will be needed to encourage non-respondents to reply. At least two iterations of follow-up should be considered. Approximately one week following the requested return date a brightly colored post card can be mailed to nonrespondents. If a tracking system is not used to identify nonrespondents, this reminder can be sent to all participants so that it arrives at approximately the same time the instrument is due.

Four weeks after the original due date a second follow-up should be sent to nonrespondents. This mailing should include another cover letter and a duplicate copy of the questionnaire printed on another color of paper stock. The cover letter should present a carefully worded final appeal for participation. By printing the questionnaire in an alternate color it will be easy to determine if data being compiled is from an early respondent or a late respondent. In some instances a statistical comparison of early and late responses is used to evaluate inferred differences between respondents and non-respondents.

Another technique that can be used to determine if respondents fairly represent the entire sample is to use telephone calls or some alternate means of communication to contact a representative group of non-respondents to get their answers to items on the questionnaire. These are then compared to responses from participants who returned questionnaires to make sure answers are similar. In survey research it is important to verify that the responses being used in data analysis are representative of the entire sample selected for use in a study.

Group Administered Questionnaires

In some instances survey research is completed using group-administered questionnaires. In those cases, respondents are accessible to either the researcher or an associate and the questionnaire is completed during an arranged session. This procedure is often used in conjunction with an academic class, professional meeting, or other activity that brings potential research participants together as a group.

For group-administered questionnaires some of the concerns to be considered vary depending on whether the researcher administers the data collection process or someone else does. Typically, the researcher will be familiar with all aspects of the study and is well-equipped to explain instructions and provide other information to respondents. Even though a sense of confidence might lead the researcher to administer the survey without it, a set of procedures should be developed and carefully followed when administering a questionnaire with a group. This will provide documentation for the process that can be included in the report of the study. Developing a set of procedures for administration also facilitates consistency when more than one group administration of the instrument will be used.

When an associate or third party administers a questionnaire with a group detailed instructions should be provided. This is especially important if more than one person will gather survey data when multiple group administrations are involved. Each group completing a questionnaire should be provided equivalent instructions and guidance so that responses are not biased by differences in administration.

Written notes or documentation should be maintained for the process of administering questionnaires to each group. Any abnormal occurrences or factors that could have a bearing on results should be noted. Particularly when several groups are participating in a study it will be difficult for those administering the questionnaires to recall later all the details needed to assure that results were not adversely impacted by differences in administration of the instrument.

For survey research involving multiple groups and several different persons assisting with administration, careful instructions should be provided for collection and return of instruments. The very best of procedures for administering a questionnaire will have little value if completed instruments are not returned to the researcher. In most instances a labeled manila envelope can be used to keep instruments together both before and after administration. Sufficient information should be provided on the label so that if it is misplaced someone finding it will know how to return it. A large colored envelope can be used to provide a package that is less apt to be misplaced.

Ideal circumstances will sometimes allow the researcher to deliver and pick up the questionnaire materials through personal contact with those who administer the data collection. Opportunity for both verbal and written feedback on the administration process is provided in this case. If that is not possible, mailing materials or using some type of delivery service is a customary option. Prepaid shipping materials and clear instructions should be provided when this method is used.

Concluding Remarks

The use of survey research by graduate students will continue to be a frequent occurrence. When applied with care and attention to detail the new knowledge generated can be beneficial and enlightening. Samples representing populations that would be difficult to gather data from in any other way can be surveyed. Especially considering the limited financial resources available to most graduate students, the moderate costs of most types of survey research are appealing.

For both graduate student research as well as that conducted by more experienced scholars, the advent of the Internet and the World Wide Web will continue to provide a new vehicle for implementing survey research. Software needed to develop online forms and other applications that can be used to gather online data continues to become more user-friendly and accessible. While the proliferation of online surveys will likely generate some of the same constituent reactions that excessive use of telephone surveys have, appropriately designed systems will still provide useful tools for serious researchers.

As technology advances beyond the Internet as we know it today, new communication tools will provide further vehicles for gathering survey data. The basic principles, however, will remain constant. Regardless of the specific methodology used, it will still be important for research participants to clearly understand what is being asked of them and how they are to respond. It will be important for answers to reflect differences in respondents rather than differences in stimuli generated by the survey process. Assurances of confidentiality will be an issue and incentives to participate will need to be clear.

Survey research will play a key role in scholarly work long into the future. By developing clear understanding of underlying principles and adopting good practices graduate students will equip themselves to shape that future. The potential benefits to both the academic community and society are worth it.

References

Furnham, A. (1990). A content, correlational, and factor analytical study of seven questionnaire measures of the Protestant work ethic. *Human Relations, 43,* 383-399.

Gottfredson, G. D., & Holland, J. L. (1996). *Dictionary of Holland occupational codes* (3rd ed.). Odessa, FL: Psychological Assessment Resources.

Impara, J. C., & Plake, B. S. (Eds.). (1998). *The thirteenth mental measurements yearbook.* Highland Park, NJ: Gryphon Press/Buros Institute of Mental Measurements.

Keyser, D. J., & Sweetland, R. C. (Eds.). (1984-1994). *Test critiques* (Vols. 1-10). Kansas City: Test Corporation of America.

Murphy, L. L., Impara, J. C., & Plake, B. S. (Eds.). (1999). *Tests in print V*. Lincoln, NE: Buros Institute of Mental Measurements.

Plake, B. S., & Impara, J. C. (Eds.). (1999). *Supplement to the thirteenth mental measurements yearbook.* Highland Park, NJ: Gryphon Press/Buros Institute of Mental Measurements.

APPENDIX
On-line Resources for Survey Research

RESEARCH METHODS KNOWLEDGE BASE

1. http://trochim.human.cornell.edu/kb/survey.htm
   The Web site provides a Web-based textbook that addresses all of the topics in a typical introductory undergraduate or graduate course in social research methods. The specific Web address provided is the URL for the section that covers survey research.

2. *ERIC/AE Test Locator,*   http://ericae.net/testcol.htm
   An excellent resource for locating both commercial and researcher-developed survey instruments.

3. *American Statistical Association Survey Research Methods Section*
   http://www.amstat.org/sections/srms/whatsurvey.html
   Be sure to have Adobe Acrobat Reader installed before visiting this site on the Web (Acrobat Reader is available free of charge from Adobe at http://www.adobe.com/products/acrobat/readstep2.html). The particular Web address provided will present a page where several useful survey research brochures in pdf format can be downloaded.

TUTORIAL ON SURVEY RESEARCH

1. http://dmsweb.badm.sc.edu/grover/survey/MIS-SUVY.html
   A management science professor at the University of South Carolina produced this Web site. It is targeted at information systems research but provides materials that might be of interest to others. An extensive reference list is included.

USING THE INTERNET FOR QUANTITATIVE SURVEY RESEARCH

1. http://www.swiftinteractive.com/white-p1.htm
   A communication sciences professor at the University of Connecticut produced this Web page. It provides some interesting information about using the Internet for survey research.

INTERNET SITES RELATED TO SURVEY RESEARCH

1. http://www.srl.uic.edu/srllink/srllink.htm
   The Survey Research Laboratory at the University of Illinois at
   Chicago provides this page with numerous links related to survey
   research.

2. *Princeton University Survey Research Center*
   http://www.princeton.edu/~abelson/index.html
   A variety of links to resources relevant to survey research are provided.

3. *The Work Ethic Site,* http://www.coe.uga.edu/workethic
   This Web site provides two examples of online survey instruments used
   in survey research. The instruments are delivered using a Common
   Gateway Interface (CGI) script written in Perl. Data is collected in an
   ASCII file for analysis purposes.

Chapter 12

Assessing Validity and Reliability for Data Collection Instruments

Gene W. Gloeckner, Jeffrey A. Gliner,
Suzanne M. Tochterman, and George A. Morgan[*]

This chapter focuses on measurement validity and measurement reliability. First, however, we need to clarify some ambiguity that surrounds these two terms. The terms *validity* and *reliability* are used in a variety of ways within the field of research. The general definition of the terms is the same, but the use of the terms within different portions of a research paper, thesis, or dissertation varies.

Defining Validity and Reliability

The term validity asks the question, "Are you really measuring what you think you are measuring?" The term reliability asks the question, "How consistent is that measurement?" An example might be useful here. Most of us have bathroom scales. If our bathroom scale measures weight accurately then we can say that the scale is a valid measurement instrument. However, if our bathroom scale measures 5 pounds underweight each time, then clearly it is not a valid measurement tool. However, it would be reliable. That is, it provides us with a consistently

---

[*]Portions of this chapter were adapted with permission from Gliner, J. A., & Morgan G. A. (2000). *Research methods in applied settings: An integrated approach to design and analysis.* Mahwah, NJ: Erlbaum.

wrong measurement. Given this example it should be clear that validity is the most important measurement of the two. If an instrument is not valid then measurements made by the instrument or process are incorrect. If a measurement is not valid, then reliability has no real meaning or value. On the other hand, if a measure is not consistent it cannot be valid. Looking again at the bathroom scale, suppose that first the scale registers four pounds too low, then a minute later registers the correct weight, and then another minute later weighs three pounds too high. The scale is unreliable so cannot be an accurate or valid measure because you would not know which weight to use. Thus, both reliability and validity are important, but validity is critical.

A second example is more timely. In the election of 2000, the state of Florida used a measuring device that is now famous called the "butterfly ballot." The ballot and process used to collect peoples' votes resulted in tens of thousands of votes being either undercounted, not counted, or double punched (voters apparently indicating that they wanted to vote for two persons for president). People who knew that they could only vote for one person and that they wanted to vote for one person produced many of the questionable ballots. The measuring instrument was not valid. One party argued that recounting the votes by machine was all that was needed. The other party argued that although that would be a reliable count, it would not be a valid count. Then, the world watched as our country tried to find a *valid* way of measuring peoples' vote for president. You can be assured that the days of the butterfly ballot are over.

Internal and External Validity

Making the whole validity issue even more complex is the fact that even within the research field, the term validity is used in a variety of ways. There is, for example, internal validity. *Internal validity* measures whether an experiment is really measuring what the researcher thinks it is measuring. Internal validity poses the question, "Did the independent variable make the difference or were there other factors which caused the dependent variable to vary?"

There is also external validity. *External validity* asks the question, "If a study found a difference with a certain group and setting, is that result generalizable to a larger audience and other settings?" Again, the 2000 presidential election provides a good example. One external validity question for any election process is "Can a researcher generalize data collected from exit polling to actual voting? Using exit polling data during the presidential election of 2000 the major networks declared Al Gore the winner of the state of Florida, then hours later declared George Bush the winner, then hours later determined that the results were too close to call. Clearly in some cases exit polling can successfully be generalized and in other cases it cannot successfully be generalized to the actual vote count. Election 2000 proved to be an embarrassing example of researchers' inability to currently generalize the findings of a sample (exit polls) to a larger population (the actual vote count). In the end the U.S. Supreme Court validated the election result.

Table 12.1 shows the relationship between measurement reliability and validity (the topic of this chapter) and internal and external validity. The table also points out that measurement reliability and validity refer to each of the particular instruments used in a study, while research validity refers to the results of the study as a whole. Internal and external validity are two main aspects of research validity. Hopefully, this table will help you understand and remember this important distinction.

TABLE 12.1
Similarities and Differences Between Measurement and Research Reliability and Validity

	Reliability	Validity
General definition	Stability or consistency	Accuracy or correctness
Related to a specific measure, test, or instrument	**Measurement reliability** Participants get the same or a very similar score from a test, observation, rating, etc.	**Measurement validity** The score accurately reflects or measures what is was designed or intended to measure.
Related to a whole study	**Research reliability or replication** If repeated, study would produce similar results.	**Research validity** Results of the study are accurate and generalizable.

Key dimensions of the validity of a study are:
• *Internal Validity*
• *External Validity* |

Correlation Coefficient

Before we discuss validity and reliability in depth a review of *correlation coefficients* will be helpful because it is the measure most often selected to evaluate validity and reliability. There are several types of correlation coefficients, but the interpretation of most is similar. A correlation coefficient is usually expressed as the letter *r* and indicates the *strength of a relation*. The values of *r* range from –1.00 to +1.00. A value of 0 is viewed as no relation between two variables or scores, whereas values close to –1.00 or +1.00 are viewed as very strong relationships between two variables. A strong negative relationship, often referred to as an inverse relationship, indicates that the relatively *higher* a person's score is on one variable or test, the *lower* that person's score is on a second variable or test. On the other hand, a strong positive relationship indicates that people who score high on one measurement also score high on a second measurement. In the literature, validity coefficients are relatively low while reliability coefficients are positive and quite high. When looking at validity measurements, a significant correlation is usually all that is needed to provide some, perhaps weak, support. However, when calculating reliability coefficients we would expect a *positive* and relatively high *r* value (.70 or above).

Table 12.2 provides guidelines for evaluating the strength of support for reliability and validity provided by correlation coefficients of various sizes. Please read the table notes carefully. They provide important information and qualifications.

Measurement Validity

Measurement validity looks at the quality of a measuring instrument used and whether that instrument is measuring what the researcher thinks the instrument is measuring. It poses the question, "Does the instrument really measure what we think it is measuring?" The current view of measurement validity is that it is an evaluation of *scores* on a particular test with a particular type of participants and how these *scores* will be interpreted. Thus, when we address the issue of validity with respect to a particular test, we are addressing the issue of the *validity of the scores* on that test for a *particular purpose*, and not the validity of *the* test or instrument, per se. Therefore, any particular test might be used for a number of purposes. For example, specialty area scores on the Graduate Record Examination might be used to predict first year success in graduate school. However, they also could be used

TABLE 12.2
Evaluating Measurement Reliability and Validity Coefficients

Correlation coefficient	Support for reliability	Support for validity
+.90	Very good[a]	Strong but[d]
+.80	Good[b]	Strong but[d]
+.70	Adequate[b]	Strong but[b]
+.60	Minimal[b]	Strong
+.50	Not acceptable	Strong
+.30	Not acceptable	Medium
+.10	Not acceptable	Weak
−.10	Not acceptable[c]	Weak[e]
−.30	Not acceptable[c]	Medium[e]
−.50	Not acceptable[e]	Strong[e]
> −.50	Not acceptable[e]	Strong but[d,e]

Note. Statistical significance is not relevant for measurement reliability, only the size and direction of the correlation. On the other hand, the strength or level of support for measurement validity is based on Cohen's (1988) effect size guidelines for correlations, with the qualification that the correlation first be judged statistically significant. Thus, a correlation of +/−.20 would provide weak to medium support for validity if *r* was significant, but no support if *r* was not significant.
[a]Useful for decisions about individual selection, placement, an so forth.
[b]Useful for research, but probably not for decision about individuals
[c]Check data for probable errors in coding or conceptualization
[d]If a validity coefficient is quite high (e.g., > +/−.70), you are probably measuring the same or very similar concepts, rather than two separate ones.
[e]Criterion and convergent construct validity would be expected to produce positive correlations, unless the concepts are hypothesized to be negatively related (e.g., anxiety and GPA).

as a method to assess current status in a particular undergraduate major. While the same test is used in both instances, the purpose of the test is completely different for each situation. Think about those bathroom scales mentioned earlier. A bathroom scale is usually a fairly valid device to measure the weight of people. However, using the same scale to measure the weight of cattle or insects would be a challenge and would be an inappropriate (invalid) use of the device.

Even though *an instrument may be consistent (high reliability), it may not be valid.* For example, one could construct a device for measuring a length of 12 inches. However, suppose that the device actually measures 13 inches. The device will be consistent but not valid because it does not measure what it is suppose to measure. Although measurement validity is clearly critical to establishing quality research instruments and designs, validity is not easily measured. As a reader of research, you have probably noted that there is often information in research articles about reliability, but often little if anything on validity. This is because validity is much more difficult to measure.

We discuss four different types of validity; face validity, content validity, criterion validity, and construct validity. Note, however, many researchers do not consider face validity to be a scientifically recognized type of measurement validity.

Face Validity

An instrument is said to have face validity if the content appears to be appropriate for the purpose of the instrument. The key word is "appears." Face validity does not actually describe the content. For example, you might find an instrument that was used in a master's thesis and you think you can use it for your research project because it "looks like" it gets at the concept that you want to measure. Others have used the instrument and it appears to have some validity (face validity). In other words, face validity simply implies that the items in the instrument appear to measure what they were intended to measure. Obviously, there are no statistical tests to support face validity.

Content Validity

Content validity is the type of validity that students are most familiar with. Content validity is involved in every test you take as a student. Content validity poses the question, "Does the test you are given really measure the content that you have been given?" One possible way to insure a content valid exam would be to have the course videotaped. Then a question could be written about every minute of the class. The instructor could also look at the textbooks being used and write a question about every page of the books. Students would not like this much, because the test would be almost as long as the course. Therefore, we have to use human judgment and a sample of the content. The instructor might write 10 questions about each lecture session or a few questions from each chapter of the text. A large test bank could be developed and randomly selected questions from the test bank could be used. Most likely, however, the instructor will simply think about the course and the emphasis he or she has placed on different portions of the course. The instructor might even do a content analysis of the material and insure that there are questions on each major topic in the class. What is key to good content validity is that the test be a good representation of the desired content.

Content validity has become a major issue with the recent academic standards movement. Many states and public schools are under pressure to develop tests that measure whether students have reached specific standards at given grade levels. These tests are often developed in the following manner. First, the standard is studied and questions are written around the standard. Content experts review the questions and are asked to indicate whether the questions are representative of the standard. Experts are also asked questions about the age appropriateness of the questions and whether the questions are written clearly or not. But again, the content validity is determined by human beings using their collective judgments. To the delight of many students, there is no statistic that demonstrates content validity. However, the converse is true. Students are often dismayed because there is little more than a difference of opinion between you and your instructor when arguing the content validity of a test question.

One correlational measurement that can be used for content validity is the point biserial correlation which is based on an assumption that students who do well on a test should do well on most questions. If several students got every question right but one, it seems logical that the instructor might want to look at the one question that the best students missed. If several students who did very poorly on the test got that same question right, it would seem to raise validity issues around the question. This is the concept behind the point biserial measurement of validity. Positive correlations mean that, in general, students who did well on the test did well on this item. Negative correlations mean that students who did well on the test missed the item and students who did poorly on the test did well on this item. Although this measurement of validity does provide some data, it is not unusual for a point biserial correlation to be relatively high but the item may be invalid because of miswording or other error. Likewise, if everyone gets the question right, the point biserial correlation is equal to is zero, because the question does not help to predict who would do well or poorly on the exam. Clearly, professors do not want to disregard important questions because everyone got the questions correct. In fact, most instructors want their students to get most of the questions right. Therefore, the point biserial has limited value, but at least instructors can review the questions that have a negative correlation. In addition, this method is only applicable when the instrument is a test with right and wrong answers and a total score. The bottom line, is that there **is no good statistical measurement for content validity.** Content validity is usually based on human judgment.

Criterion–related Validity

When people mention measurement validity, they are usually referring to *criterion validity*, which refers to validating an instrument against some form of external criterion. This validation procedure usually involves establishing a correlation coefficient between the instrument and the external or outside criterion. The key to criterion validity is being able to establish an outside criterion that is measurable. Common examples of criterion validity involve instruments that are intended to screen and select applicants for a school or an open position. There are two types of evidence for criterion validity, predictive evidence and concurrent evidence.

Predictive evidence. When we try to determine how someone will do in the future based on a particular instrument, we are usually referring to predictive evidence. Tests such as the Scholastic Aptitude Test (SAT), the Graduate Record Examination (GRE), and the Law School Aptitude Test (LSAT) are examples of instruments that are used to predict future performance. For example, the GRE is often required for students attempting to enter graduate school. If the GRE provides good predictive evidence, then students who score high on this test will perform better in graduate school than those who do not score high. The criterion in this case would be some measure of how well students perform, usually grades obtained during the first year. To establish predictive evidence in his example, college students would take the GRE. Then, when finished with their first year of grad school, correlations would be established between GRE scores and grad school grades. If the correlation was relatively high, then predictive evidence is good. If the correlation is low, then the test has problems for prediction of future performance. See Table 12.2 again for guidelines to use in interpreting support of validity.

A problem with predictive evidence is that often not all of the participants who were evaluated on the original instrument can be evaluated on the criterion variable. This is especially the case in selection studies. For example, we may have GRE scores for a wide range of applicants. However, not all of these students will be admitted and attend. Therefore, our criterion variable of first semester grade point average (GPA) will not only have fewer participants than our predictor variable, but will represent a more homogeneous group (those selected for admission). Therefore, the range of scores of those who could participate in the study for both the predictor and criterion variables is restricted, leading to a lower correlation coefficient (Anastasi, 1988).

Another example from the human resource (HR) field might be helpful. HR professionals often use commercially available instruments to predict the success of employees. In fact, vendors often make rather outlandish claims regarding the predictive validity of their instruments. Emotional intelligence has received a great deal of publicity in recent years. Some of the claims attributed to instruments designed to measure emotional intelligence are directly related to criterion validity. Take, for example, the statements, "Workers will be more productive if they have high ratings on emotional intelligence tests." Using predictive validity techniques, we can check this claim. We could require an emotional intelligence test of all workers and then collect performance measures on the employees at six-month intervals. Once these data are collected, we could run a correlation between emotional intelligence scores and performance scores. Then, we could say with confidence that emotional intelligence either is or is not a significant predictor of job performance.

There are two major drawbacks to predictive validity. You may recall the first, which was the collected data may not be representative of the entire group. We might, for example, screen people based on their emotional intelligence scores and say 25% aren't hired because of low scores and 25% more leave the company before performance measures can be taken on them. The reduction in the range of scores reduces the correlation coefficient, and thus, emotional intelligence could have a larger predictive value for job performance than measured by the study. A second drawback with predictive evidence is that in order to establish validity, the researcher must wait until those who were tested initially can be measured on the criterion. Sometimes this wait could take years. Therefore, a second type of criterion validity, concurrent validity, was developed to deal with this problem.

Concurrent evidence.   Similar to predictive evidence, concurrent evidence also examines the relationship between an instrument and an outside criterion. However, it is sometimes too expensive to wait for the time between when the predictor test is taken and measurement of the criterion. Suppose we were interested in seeing whether GRE scores from college were good predictors of first year grades in graduate school. However, we do not wish to wait the time it takes for students to complete their first year of graduate school. To determine concurrent evidence, we could use current first year grad students, have them take the GRE, and then determine if their GRE scores correlate with their grades (present grades since they are now first year grad students). If there is a relatively high correlation, we can have some confidence in using the instrument as a predictor for success in graduate school. However, concurrent evidence is not the same as predictive evidence, and one may not wish to place as much confidence in this procedure. Also, restricted range problems, similar to those pointed out under predictive evidence, are present. In this example, we must assume that there is little change in students between college and their first year in graduate school because the target for the GRE is college students. If there are substantial changes between college and grad school, the validity of the instrument should be questioned. The best situation would be to obtain both predictive and concurrent evidence, although, in fact, this rarely occurs.

There is good news for the HR field here. Concurrent validity works fairly well for companies who want to assess criteria associated with job performance if the company does not screen out many applicants (say for manufacturing or maintenance jobs) and does not have a high turnover rate. Such company could assess current workers who also have job performance ratings. The correlations between these assessments and job performance provide concurrent evidence for validity.

Concurrent evidence also can be obtained by substituting another instrument for the criterion, especially if it is difficult to measure the criterion. In HR studies, we could decide that percent increase in pay is a good measure of job performance, and thus, run a correlation between emotional intelligence and percent increase in pay. However, Cromack (1989) points out that the instrument substituted for the criterion can never be more valid than the criterion. One must be cautious when substituting an instrument for a criterion, since in many cases the substituted instrument or measure has not been validated against the criterion of interest. This can be a problem in the HR field because dollar amounts or percent increase in pay is often used as a measure of worker performance. While pay increase may represent performance, it is often associated more with other variables such as length of time with the company, equity increases, or unusual bonuses.

The major drawback to criterion validity is finding and measuring a suitable criterion. Correlation helps us determine if our predictor variables are valid and it allows us to measure the strength of those predictor variables. Most criterion validity correlations are in fact quit small. Many HR departments use a variety of criteria to help them predict job performance with each predictor adding to their ability to predict successful employee trends. For example, a HR office might measure emotional intelligence, general intelligence, use a scale of previous job satisfaction, an inventory on general happiness, and then use all four of these measures to predict job performance and to help make hiring decisions. If this procedure were used, the most likely statistic to run would be multiple regression analysis.

Construct Validity

The last type of measurement validity that will be discussed, certainly the most complex, is *construct validity*. Constructs are hypothetical concepts that cannot be observed directly. Intelligence, achievement, and anxiety are all considered constructs. While we cannot observe a construct directly, most agree that constructs exist through observable behaviors. We cannot directly observe anxiety, but under certain circumstances we may observe anxious behaviors, such as sweating or pacing, that are specific to a particular context, like immediately before an important examination. Therefore, it is common to create instruments to measure particular constructs, such as a test that measures anxiety or emotional intelligence. When applying construct validity to an instrument, there is a requirement that the construct, which the instrument is measuring, is based on an underlying theory. Often, especially in applied disciplines, there is little theory to support the construct. As Cronbach (1990) points out, sometimes a test is used for a long time before a theory is developed. Therefore, construct validation is a process, a relatively slow one, where an investigator conducts studies in the attempt to demonstrate that the instrument measures a construct. Three types of evidence that are important for achieving construct validity are convergent evidence, discriminant evidence, and factorial evidence.

Convergent evidence. Convergent evidence is determined by obtaining relatively high correlations between your measure and other measures that theory suggests should be related to it. In order to demonstrate construct validity, one develops hypotheses about what the instrument should predict if it actually measures the construct. Let's use emotional intelligence for an example. Emotional intelligence is a fairly new construct in human resource development and is composed of self-awareness, self-management, social awareness, and social skills (Goleman, 1994). We could develop an instrument that measures these four aspects of emotional intelligence and see if we could validate each of the sub-sections using published instruments measuring each of the four aspects. For example, to validate the portion of emotional intelligence measuring self-awareness. We could use the *Mental Measurement Yearbooks* (1938-2000) to find other measures of self-awareness, and then we could correlate the scores from the these instruments with the self awareness sub-score from our emotional intelligence instrument.

Discriminant evidence. Discriminant evidence is provided by obtaining relatively low correlations between our scale and measures that theory suggests should *not* be related to it. Discriminant evidence can also be obtained by comparing two groups that should differ on our scale and finding that they do, in fact, differ. Again, let's use the emotional intelligence idea for an example. If we are interested in validating social awareness, we could find a tool that measures social ineptitude. We hope that there is not a positive correlation between the measurements of social awareness and social ineptitude. If there was, we would have to question the validity of the social awareness instrument. We would expect, in fact, a negative correlation between measurements of social awareness and social ineptitude.

Factorial evidence. Factorial evidence is provided when a construct is complex, and several aspects (or factors) of it are measured. If the clustering of items, usually done with factor analysis, supports the theory-based grouping of items, factorial evidence is provided. Again, emotional intelligence can be used in an example. Let us say that emotional intelligence is composed of self awareness self management, social awareness and social skills. Then if we have an instrument with for example, 10 items about each of these four aspects of emotional intelligence, a factor analysis ought to group or factor the 40 items into four groups or factors corresponding to the four concepts.

A second example, taken from the mastery motivation literature (Morgan et al., 1993) may be helpful. The Dimensions of Mastery (DMQ) questionnaire was designed to measure five aspects or domains of mastery motivation: persistence at object-related tasks, gross motor tasks, social mastery motivation with peers, social mastery motivation with adults, and mastery pleasure. Factor analysis supported the grouping of items into these five clusters; thus, providing factorial evidence to support the theory of five aspects to mastery motivation.

Construct validity is never actually achieved. It is a continuing process of experimentation and modification leading to the refinement of an instrument that measures a specified construct. In truth, most construct validity is based on human judgment. This may help to explain why so many people are passionately for or against measurements such as IQ, workplace success, social skills, and so forth. However, the alternative is to throw up our hands and say human constructs cannot be measured, even though we know they exist.

Table 12.3 provides a summary of the types of evidence for measurement validity, the usual statistic computed to provide the evidence, and the criteria used to decide the degree of support provided by the evidence. Remember also that Table 12.2 provides more specifics about the strength of the evidence for measurement validity.

Measurement Reliability

What is reliability? When a person is said to be reliable, we have certain conceptions about that person. For example, the person always shows up for meetings on time, therefore, that person is a reliable person. Or, the person always gets the job done, therefore, she or he is a reliable person. When we use tests or other instruments to measure outcomes, we also need to make sure that these instruments are reliable. Reliability always refers to consistency. The importance of reliability for research cannot be overstated. If our outcome measure is not reliable, then we cannot accurately (validly) assess results of our study.

An Example

In order to understand the importance of measurement reliability and its underpinnings, it is best to start with an example. Suppose a researcher is interested in determining if quality of life for persons in a "Work and Family Balance Program" is different than quality of life for workers who do not participate in the program. In order to determine whether the intervention (Work and Family Balance Program) is effective, a randomized experiment using a pretest-posttest control group design is developed. In this design participants are randomly (R) assigned to one group or the other. One group receives the intervention (X), let's say for six months, and the other group does not receive the intervention ($\sim$X). Both groups receive a pretest (O_1) using an instrument that measures quality of life. After the six month period, both groups are administered the same instrument (O_2) as a posttest. The design can be shown as:

$$R \quad O_1 \quad X \quad O_2$$
$$R \quad O_1 \quad \sim X \quad O_2$$

TABLE 12.3
Summary of the Types of Evidence for Measurement Validity

Type of evidence	Usual statistic	Support for validity depends on
Face Do the items look valid?	None	Agreement that items look valid
Content Are all aspects of constructs represented in appropriate proportions?	Usually none	Good agreement by judges about the epresentativeness of the content
Criterion Does the test accurately predict an outside criterion?		
• *Concurrent*–Test and criterion are measured at the same time.	Correlation	Effect size[a]
• *Predictive*–Test predicts some criterion in future.	Correlation	Effect size[a]
Construct Based on theory, do variables accurately measure constructs of interest?		
• *Convergent* Based on theory, variables predicted to be related are related.	Correlation	Effect size[a]
• *Discriminant* Variables predicted not to be related are not related.	Correlation, *t* test, or ANOVA	Effect size[a]
• *Factorial* Factor analysis yields a theoretically meaningful solution.	Factor analysis	Meaningful factor structure consistent with content evidence

[a]The strength of support for validity (weak, medium, strong) is based on Cohen's (1988) effect size guidelines (see also Table 12.2).

Quality of life (the dependent variable) is measured with a particular measurement tool called the Quality of Life (QOL) inventory. Both the intervention and control groups are measured using the QOL prior to the intervention, and then, again after the intervention has been completed. Therefore, each participant in the study will produce a QOL score prior to and after the intervention period. If the QOL inventory has a range of scores between 0 and 100, then each participant will receive both a pretest and posttest score within this range. Of course, we hope that the posttest scores in the intervention group are higher than those of the control group. Assuming random assignment, the groups should be equivalent initially. This is a solid design that should yield meaningful findings. However, it is possible that the study is weak in other respects. The issue here is whether the QOL inventory measures quality of life consistently (reliably) in this study with each group of participants.

Test Scores

We call any score that we obtain from any individual on a particular instrument, an *observed score*. If Miss Jones scores 49 on the QOL pretest, then Miss Jones' observed score is 49. If we were to give Miss Jones the QOL a second time, her observed score probably will be different from 49. It might be 53 or 43. If we gave the QOL to Miss Jones a third time, the score probably will be different from either of the scores received from the two previous test administrations. Since Miss Jones' score will not be the same each time we give the QOL, and, since we must give Miss Jones a second QOL assessment *after* the intervention, how do we know if the change in Miss Jones' score from pretest to posttest is due to the intervention, or perhaps due to something else? Stated another way, how do we know whether the change in Miss Jones' score is due to *systematic* variation (variation due to the intervention) or *unsystematic* variation (variation due to other factors). To understand this problem, we need to consider classical test theory.

According to classical test theory, an *observed* score is made up of a *true score* and *error*. If we could subtract the true score from the observed score, we could determine how much of the score is due to error. We never actually know the amount of the observed score that is due to the true score, or the amount of the observed score that is due to error. If we were to measure the person thousands of times and take the average of all of those measurements, then the average score would be very close to the individual's true score. Unfortunately, we rarely measure a person more than a couple of times on any given instrument.

Since we rarely measure a person multiple times with any instrument, the researcher may have trouble showing that the intervention in the study was what caused the difference instead of a measurement error. Let's look at the Miss Jones example again. Suppose Miss Jones is in the intervention condition, and her QOL score increases from 49 (pretest) to 53 (posttest). How do we know whether this increase is due to an increase in Miss Jones' true score (systematic variation) or merely to an increase due to error (unsystematic variation)? The solution is to choose a test with high reliability. We have not considered specific methods of determining reliability at this point, but we have stated that reliability is a measure of consistency. How does reliability relate to observed scores and true scores? Measurement reliability is expressed as a coefficient. The reliability coefficient is the *ratio of the variance of true scores to the variance of observed scores* (Ghiselli, Campbell, & Zedeck, 1981). In other words, the higher the reliability of an instrument, the closer that true scores will be to observed scores for that instrument.

While the correlation coefficient r can vary from -1.00 to $+1.00$, *to say that a measurement is reliable, one would expect a coefficient between $+.70$ and $+1.0$.* Others have suggested even stricter criteria and argue for stricter interpretation of reliability. It is not uncommon, for example, to require very high reliability scores in the engineering fields where error variance is much smaller than in the social sciences. Remember that Table 12.1 provided suggestions about how to interpret reliability coefficients of different magnitudes.

Note that although correlations of $-.70$ to -1.00 indicate a strong (negative) correlation, they are totally unacceptable regarding reliability. Such a high negative correlation indicates that persons who initially score high on the measure later score low and visa versa. A negative reliability coefficient probably indicates a computational error or terrible inconsistency in the measuring instrument.

Methods to Assess Reliability

There are four methods that researchers use to assess reliability: test-retest, parallel forms, internal consistency and interrater. Each of these methods provides useful and somewhat different information about reliability. You should obtain and discuss as many of the types of reliability as possible.

Test-Retest Reliability

Cronbach (1990) refers to the coefficient for test-retest reliability as a *coefficient of stability*. Test-retest reliability is easy to understand. There is support for reliability if the test is given more than once to the same person, and that person's scores are very similar, if not equal. To determine test-retest reliability on an instrument, a sample of persons who are not study participants but fit the target population need to be found. The instrument is administered at two different times. Then the reliability coefficient (correlation) is calculated. If the coefficient is high, the investigator could state with confidence that there is support for reliability. If the coefficient is low (*r* is below .70) the instrument could be modified or changed. Then the test-retest procedure would be repeated. The researcher could also abort the use of the instrument all together and alter the nature of study.

Certain considerations must be taken into account in order to determine test-retest reliability. The first point is that test-retest reliability is *not established during a study*. The reliability coefficient must be established ahead of time, prior to the study, using a period of time when little related to the substance of the instrument should be happening between the two administrations of the instrument. This is especially important in experiments because the intervention is intended to change the behavior.

With standardized instruments, test-retest reliability has already been established for the instrument of choice, so the investigator need not worry about having to determine reliability for the study. In many cases, more than one reliability coefficient has been obtained for a particular instrument. However, the investigator needs to make sure of the following criteria when selecting an instrument:

1. The reliability coefficient is high (e.g., *r* > .80) or at least marginally acceptable (e.g., *r* > .60).

2. The length of time used to establish test-retest reliability is similar to the length of time used in the study. Note that as the length of time increases between administrations, reliability decreases.

3. The sample used to determine reliability of the instrument is similar to the sample in the current study.

Parallel Forms Reliability

One of the problems with using the same instrument for both the pretest and posttest is that participants may use the knowledge gained on the pretest to alter their posttest score. This problem, often referred to as testing or carryover effects, creates considerable problems because it becomes impossible to determine if the change in scores is due to the intervention or to knowledge obtained on the pretest. One way of avoiding the potential problems with carryover effects is to create a design without a pretest, for example, a posttest-only control group design. However, this design can only be used if participants can be randomly assigned to groups. A quasi-experimental approach is more likely in applied settings, where a pretest is needed.

In order to counteract the testing problem, some tests have a second or parallel version that can be used as a posttest in place of the instrument used for the pretest. *Parallel forms reliability* (called the coefficient of equivalence) involves establishing the relationship between two forms of the same test. This type of reliability is easy to establish, since it involves having a sample of participants take the two forms of the same instrument, usually with very little time elapsed between the two administrations. Then, a correlation coefficient is calculated for the two sets of scores, similar to test-retest reliability. A reliability coefficient of $r \geq .80$ would be expected for parallel forms reliability.

Internal Consistency Reliability

Often, in addition to obtaining test-retest reliability or parallel forms reliability, we want to know that the instrument is consistent among the items (i.e., the instrument is measuring a single concept or construct). Rather than correlate different administrations of the same instrument, investigators can use the results of a single administration to determine internal consistency. The most common methods of determining internal consistency are the split-half method, the Kuder-Richardson (KR-20) method and Cronbach's alpha. These methods are often referred to as *inter-item reliability* and can be used only when one has data from several items that are combined to make a composite score.

Split-half methods. Split-half methods of obtaining internal consistency reliability involve correlating two halves of the same test. The term split-half is a general term to describe a number of different methods of correlating two separate halves of a test. For example, one could correlate the first half of the test with the second half, or compare odd items with even ones. A third, highly recommended, method is to randomly sample half of the test items and correlate them with the remaining items.

One of the problems with obtaining split-half reliability is that when dividing the test into two halves, the number of items is reduced by 50%, as compared to a test-retest reliability or alternative forms reliability. This reduction in size means that the resulting correlation coefficient will probably *underestimate* reliability (Suen, 1990). Therefore, once the reliability coefficient is established by calculating the correlation coefficient, r, it is necessary to adjust the size of r by using the Spearman-Brown formula. If you computed the correlation coefficient between the first and second halves of the test and find that $r = .70$, the Spearman-Brown formula adjustment would change r from .70 to .82.

Kuder-Richardson (K-R) 20. If an instrument measures a single theme or trait, you may wish to determine how all of the items are related to each other. If each item is scored dichotomously—such as pass or fail, true or false, right or wrong—then *K-R 20* is the appropriate method of determining inter-item reliability.

Cronbach's alpha. If each item on the test has multiple choices, such as a Likert scale, then *Cronbach's alpha* is the method of choice to determine inter-item reliability. Cronbach's alpha currently is the *most commonly used index of reliability* in the area of educational and psychological research (Daniel & Witta, 1997), in part because it takes only one administration of the instrument and can be done using the data from the actual study.

A more important reason for using alpha is related to construct validity. Researchers assume that alpha provides support for their concepts. However, one of the problems with Cronbach's alpha is that while it is a measure of internal consistency, it does not necessarily measure homogeneity, or unidimensionality. In other words, people often determine Cronbach's alpha, and assume that since it is at a high level (e.g., $r = .85$) that the test is measuring only one concept or construct. Unfortunately, Schmitt (1996) points out that even though the overall item correlations may be relatively high, they could be measuring more than one factor or dimension. This can lead to problems because one of the assumptions of Cronbach's alpha, as an index of reliability, is that it is measuring only one construct. We caution that if only Cronbach's alpha is used to report reliability without information indicating [1] the existence of only one underlying dimension, and/or [2] other indexes of reliability, then reliability has not been adequately assessed.

Interrater (Interobserver) Reliability

The previous methods to establish reliability were accomplished by examining scores on some instrument. However, sometimes the measurement tool is observation performed by judges. This is usually the case with observations, interviews, and qualitative research. When observation is the instrument, then reliability must be established among the judges to maintain consistency. This type of reliability is

referred to as interrater reliability. Although there are numerous ways
to determine this form of reliability, the common theme is that two or
more judges (observers) score certain episodes of behavior and some
form of correlation is performed to determine the level of agreement
among the judges.

An example might be helpful here. Gloeckner (1983) studied
aspects of teacher clarity. Teachers were videotaped then three
observers rated teacher behaviors that had been shown to be
associated with clear teaching. Sample behaviors included [1]
repeating important points, [2] using visual aids, [3] pausing so
students had time to think about questions, [4] summarizing the
lesson, and so forth. Observers were trained on tapes that were not
part of the experiment. During the first training sessions, inter-rater
reliability was around $r = .60$. After several days of training,
however, observers were able to increase the inter-rater reliability to
$r = .88$. During the training sessions, observers reviewed the
videotapes in 30-second intervals and reviewed and discussed how
each observer coded the video portion. Through this discussion
process observers became more consistent with what each believed
was a clear teaching behavior. Only then did the observers begin
coding the videotapes used in the experiment.

Percentage agreement methods.   Percentage agreement methods
involve having two or more raters, prior to the study, observe a
sample of behaviors which will be similar to what would be observed
in the study. Suppose that rater A observes 8 occurrences of a
particular behavior and rater B observes 10 occurrences of the same
behavior. A percentage is then computed by dividing the smaller
number of observations by the larger number of observations of the
specific behavior. In this case, the percentage is 80. One of the
problems with this method is that although both observers may agree
that a behavior was elicited a particular number of times, this does not
mean that each time the behavior occurred that both judges agreed.
For example, suppose that the behavior of cooperation was the
dependent variable for a study. Prior to the study, two judges were to
observe a classroom of students for particular instances of
cooperation. One observer (judge) said that there were eight examples
of cooperation. A second observer said that there were 10 examples
of cooperation. The percentage agreement would be eight divided by
ten or 80%. However, it is possible that the eight instances observed
by one judge were not the same instances observed by the second
judge. The percentage would be inflated in this particular instance.
Ottenbacher (1986) suggested using a point-by-point basis of

establishing inter-rater reliability. In this approach, each behavior would be rated as an agreement or disagreement between judges. The point-by-point method would be easiest to perform if the behavior is on a videotape that could be played for the judges. To calculate percentage agreement in the point-by-point method, the number of agreements between the two judges would be divided by the total number of responses (agreements plus disagreements). A problem with this method is that it ignores chance agreements when few categories are used (Bartko & Carpenter, 1976). An additional problem with these percentage agreement methods is that they are most suited to situations with only two raters.

Intra-class correlation coefficients. Often, when performing a study using observations of behavior as the dependent variable, more than two observers are needed. *Intra-class correlation coefficients* (ICC) allow researchers to calculate a reliability coefficient with two or more judges. (For an excellent review of ICC type methods see Bartko & Carpenter, 1976). One criterion that must be satisfied in order to use an intra-class correlation coefficient is that the behavior to be rated must be normally distributed. As an example, each rater might be rating instances of cooperation on a 1-5 scale. ICCs are computed using analysis of variance methods with repeated measures to analyze inter-rater reliability. A second advantage of the ICC method of computing inter-rater reliability is that if judges are selected randomly, then the inter-rater reliability can be generalized beyond the sample of judges that took part in the reliability study.

Kappa. The method of calculating intra-class correlation coefficients when data are nominal is the Kappa statistic. Similar to ICC, Kappa can be computed with two or more raters. Kappa also corrects for chance agreement. While data for using Kappa are often dichotomous, for example, present or absent, it is not uncommon to have more than two nominal categories.

Summary on Reliability Methods

We have discussed four methods of assessing reliability. These methods and the statistics usually used to assess reliability with them are presented in Table 12.4. Each method gives a measure of consistency, but they are not all the same. Consumers need to be aware of how reliability was established before using a particular instrument. Furthermore, to say that an instrument is reliable has relatively little meaning. Each statement of reliability must specify the type of reliability, strength of the reliability coefficient, and population used.

TABLE 12.4
Summary of Methods Used to Assess Measurement Reliability

Method	Usual statistic
Test-retest reliability. Stability over time with same instrument	Correlation (coefficient of stability)
Parallel forms reliability: Consistency across presumably equivalent versions of instrument	Correlation (coefficient of equivalence)
Internal consistency: Items that are to be combined (summed) are related to each other	Split half correlation K-R 20 Cronbach's alpha
Inter-rater reliability: Different observers or raters give similar scores	Percent agreement Interclass correlation coefficient Kappa

Typically, if one does not create an instrument but uses an already published instrument, then reliability indices should have been established. The most common places to find studies of the reliability of the instrument are in the instrument manual, which is often referred to in the original journal publication that introduced the instrument. The instrumentation section of any research article that used a particular instrument, also should provide information about reliability.

Summary

Measurement reliability and validity are exceptionally important issues for research in applied settings. Many of the issues are beyond the scope of the present text. For those interested in measurement reliability and validity in more depth, especially for constructing an instrument, we recommend the texts of Anastasi (1988), Cronbach (1990), and Ghiselli et al. (1981).

References

Anastasi, A. (1988). *Psychological testing* (6th ed.). New York: Macmillan.

Bartko, J. J., & Carpenter, W. T. (1976). On the methods and theory of reliability. *Journal of Nervous and Mental Disease, 163,* 307-317.

Cohen, J. A. (1988). Statistical power analysis for the behavioral sciences. Hillsdale, NJ: Erlbaum.

Cromack, T. R. (1989). Measurement considerations in clinical research. In C. B. Royeen (Ed.), *Clinical research handbook*. Thorofare, NJ: Slack.

Cronbach, L. J. (1990). *Essentials of psychological testing* (5th ed.). New York: Harper Collins.

Daniel, L. G., & Witta, E. L. (1997, March). *Implications for teaching graduate students correct terminology for discussing validity and reliability on a content analysis of three social science measurement journals*. Paper presented at the annual meeting of the American Education Research Association, Chicago, IL.

Ghiselli, E. E., Campbell, J. P., & Zedeck, S. (1981). *Measurement theory for the behavioral sciences*. San Francisco: W. H. Freeman.

Goleman, D. (1994). *Emotional intelligence: Why it can matter more than IQ*. New York: Bantam.

Gloeckner, G. W. (1983). *An investigation into the effectiveness of a preservice teacher clarity training unit in two different experimental settings*. Unpublished doctoral dissertation, Ohio State University, Columbus.

Mental Measurements Yearbooks. (1938-2000, Vols. 1-14). University of Nebraska–Lincoln, Buros Institute of Mental Measurements.

Morgan, G. A., Maslin-Cole, C. A., Harmon, R. J., Busch-Rossnagel, N. A., Jennings, K. D., Hauser-cram, P., & Brockman, L. (1993). Parent and teacher perceptions of young children's mastery motivation: Assessment and review of research. In D. Messer (Ed.), *Mastery motivation in early childhood: Development, measurement and social processes* (pp. 109-131). London: Routledge.

Ottenbacher, K. (1986). *Evaluating clinical change*. Baltimore, MD: Williams & Wilkins.

Schmitt, N. (1996). Uses and abuses of coefficient alpha. *Psychological Assessment, 8*, 350-353.

Shavelson, R. J. (1988). *Statistical reasoning for the behavioral sciences* (2nd ed.). Boston: Allyn and Bacon.

Suen, H. K. (1990). *Principles of test theories*. Hillsdale, NJ: Erlbaum.

Chapter 13

Determining Appropriate Sample Size

Paul E. Krueger

How many participants should be in your study? When is a sample too small to be representative, or needlessly large to where it is cumbersome, time consuming, and costly? Does sample size suggest how many surveys should be mailed on the first administration? What is the appropriate size for a pilot study? Size matters.

Determining sample size is a key component of research design that is often misunderstood. Ambiguity stems from a lack of universal rules (McClelland, 1995; Soriano, 1995), inconsistencies between disciplines (Kraemer & Thiemann, 1987), debate over the size needed to test statistical significance (Hinkin, 1998), and the popular belief that a census of a large population will produce superior results to that of a sample; for example, the continuing controversy where elected officials and political lobbies battle over substituting a sample for the decennial U.S. census of the population (Wright, 1998).

Too often the rationale for sample size is predicated upon budget and time constraints (Mangione, 1995), what has been customarily acceptable, or an arbitrary number that seems appropriate to the researcher (Fowler, 1993). In the last case a rounded number typically appears in the tens, hundreds or thousands without supporting calculations or citations.

What is needed for education and training researchers is a practical approach for determining sample size that strikes a balance between utility and rigor. Such an approach would suggest appropriate sizes for pilot studies, population samples, and the number of participants needed for the initial administration of a survey.

Pilot Study Size

A pilot study is important to conduct before you run your main study. It represents a dry-run of your data collection methodology. Survey instruments can be administered by mail, web, face-to-face, or telephone to a small number of individuals, followed by an opportunity to ask whether the survey questions were clear, reasonable, and formatted in a manner that would encourage their participation. Pilot data can be validity and reliability tested to reduce the risk of administering a flawed questionnaire to the population (Sapsford, 1999). In multiple regression studies pilot data can be tested to rule out the threats posed by multicollinearity, or where a high degree of correlation between two or more independent variables poses "adverse effects on the standard errors of the regression coefficients" (Walsh, 1990, p. 297). And, equally important, the modes of data analysis that will be used to statistically compute and report the main study results can be tested to ensure that they are adequate for measurement purposes.

How many subjects should be in a pilot study? Babbie (1998), Fink (1995), and Mangione (1995) recommend that 10 or more people, who have similar characteristics to the study population, be pilot tested. If item analysis is being conducted, Patton (1998) advises that at least 25 be included in the pilot in order to have a sufficient number of people to conduct statistical computations. This suggests that a range in pilot size may be necessary given the requirements of the research problem and population. Munsinger (Isaac & Michael, 1997) appears to agree, contending that pilot sample sizes of between 10 and 30 individuals is large enough to conduct statistical calculations and a preliminary test of null hypotheses.

The pilot study size may have to be increased beyond a minimum of 10 to allow for proportional representation of diverse populations (Soriano, 1995). For example, if the population of interest was 50 percent African American, 30 percent Asian American, 15 percent Latin American, and 5 percent Native American, one Native American in a pilot of 10 subjects would be over-represented if included and not represented if excluded (e.g., 5 percent of 10 equals one-half of a participant). Given these demographics, a minimum of 20 people would be needed to proportionately represent the population with one Native American included in the pilot study. In like manner, other forms of population stratification, meaningful to the research problem, may be included in the pilot study provided that the size does not become unrealistic.

Different modes of data analyses may suggest different pilot study sizes. In addition to the 25 person minimum for item analysis mentioned earlier, a minimum of 30 people are recommended for correlational research (McMillan, 1996; Williams & Monge, 2001), more individuals than factors for factor analysis, and enough people to ensure that there are at least 5 cases per cell for chi-square tests (Grady & Wallston, 1988).

Pilot study size may be affected by the method of data collection. Fowler (1993) observes that surveys specifically designed for data collection by face-to-face interview should have from 20 to 50 individuals to pretest the survey instrument. Interviewers assume two roles in this method: collecting the survey data, and observing the survey procedures to recommend process improvements.

In summary, it is important to determine an appropriate pilot study size given the research problem, population, and anticipated modes of analysis. To simply state an arbitrary number of participants for a pilot study without a rationale and supporting citations may reflect on the credibility of the research.

Sample Size Estimation

Size may be estimated for randomly selected samples based upon an associated sampling error formula not reproduced here but available in Isaac and Michael (1997, p. 200). The formula takes a conservative approach to calculating size and assumes a population proportion of .50. In other words, if sample members were asked to give their opinion about something, it is assumed that their answers would be equally distributed across response choices, with 50 percent tending to agree and 50 percent tending to disagree on an issue (Soriano, 1995). This approach leans toward overestimating rather than underestimating sample size, and is intended to lend credibility to these size estimates.

Table 13.1 has been constructed from this formula as a convenient guide to aid researchers in estimating needed sample size. Three key components are necessary to implement this sample size estimation technique: confidence level, confidence interval (Babbie, 1998), and the population size. To further simplify this task the 95 percent confidence level was adopted due to its high degree of acceptance in business (Sekaran, 1992), social (Walsh, 1990), behavioral, and educational research (Isaac & Michael, 1997).

TABLE 13.1

Estimating Sample Size Given a 95% Confidence Level, Confidence Intervals, and Population Sizes for Normal Distributions

Population size	Confidence intervals (%) and sample size				
	1	2	3	4	5
10	10	10	10	10	10
20	20	20	20	19	19
30	30	30	29	29	28
40	40	39	39	38	36
50	50	49	48	46	44
60	60	59	57	55	52
70	70	68	66	63	59
80	79	77	74	71	66
90	89	87	83	78	73
100	99	96	92	86	80
200	196	185	169	150	132
300	291	267	234	200	169
400	384	343	291	240	196
500	475	414	341	273	217
600	565	480	384	300	234
700	653	542	423	323	248
800	739	600	457	343	260
900	823	655	488	360	269
1000	906	706	516	375	278
2000	1655	1091	696	462	322
3000	2286	1334	787	500	341
4000	2824	1501	843	522	351
5000	3288	1622	880	536	357
6000	3693	1715	906	546	361
7000	4049	1788	926	553	364
8000	4365	1847	942	558	367
9000	4646	1896	954	563	368
10000	4899	1936	964	566	370
20000	6489	2144	1013	583	377
30000	7275	2223	1030	588	379
40000	7745	2265	1039	591	381
50000	8057	2291	1045	593	381
75000	8514	2327	1052	595	382
100000	8763	2345	1056	597	383
1000000	9513	2395	1066	600	384

Expressed as a percentage the confidence level is a measure of how much confidence we can place in our sample size determination. This confidence level is, in turn, associated with a measure of accuracy called a confidence interval (Soriano, 1995). If we were to take an infinite number of samples the upper and lower limits of this confidence interval suggest how close the samples would fall together. Table 13.1 shows confidence intervals for 1, 2, 3, 4 and 5 percentage points.

An example of how the confidence interval is reported comes from a January 2001 post-presidential CNN/USA/Gallup election poll. Holland (2001) states,

> Sixty-two percent say Bush will not go too far in delegating authority when he moves into the White House later this month, and only 30 percent say that Cheney will make more important decisions than Bush in the next administration....The poll consists of interviews with 1,018 adult Americans and was conducted January 5-7. The margin of error for all questions is plus or minus 3 percentage points. (p. 1)

The "plus or minus 3 percentage points" is the confidence interval. The 95 percent confidence level is normally assumed by pollsters and left out of media reporting to reduce confusion by the public. What this suggests is that if you had asked the entire U.S. population this question, and not just a sample of 1,018 Americans, you could be 95 percent confident that between 27 and 33 percent of Americans would "say that Cheney will make more important decisions than Bush;" that is, the lower limit is calculated by subtracting 30–3 = 27, and the upper limit by summing 30+3 = 33.

For the next example, refer to Table 13.1 and determine an appropriate sample size. The first column represents the population while the remaining five columns headed by a confidence interval percent form the body of the table representing respective sample size estimates. For practice go down the population column until you find 100 then go right (across the row) to the last column and find 80. This suggests that for a population of 100, you would be 95 percent confident that a randomly drawn sample size of 80 subjects would be within plus or minus 5 percentage points of accurately measuring your phenomenon.

It is important to note that the sample sizes given in the body of the table are *minimums* that must be realized in order to represent their respective populations at 95 percent confidence within the confidence intervals specified. In the example a minimum of 80 people must participate in the research if the population of 100 is to be represented. A researcher may not claim to have reached the 95 percent level of

Research Pathways

confidence with a margin of plus or minus 5 percentage points if less than 80 subjects participate from the population of 100.

Why are some sample size determinations difficult to decide? During spring 2001 a Chamber of Business and Industry for a county in Pennsylvania contacted the Pennsylvania State University's Institute for Research in Training and Development (IRTD) to see if there might be a mutual interest in conducting a training needs assessment mail survey of their 800 member organization. They agreed that a 95 percent level of confidence in the results would be appropriate for this survey. Referring to Table 13.1, what estimated sample size would be required if they wanted to be within plus or minus 2 percentage points in accuracy?

What if for budget reasons they could not afford to obtain a minimum sample size of 600 members which would require multiple survey mailings to get a minimum of 75 percent of their total membership to return a survey questionnaire (600/800 = 75%)? This suggests that there may be other factors affecting the confidence interval decision that must be accounted for in the research design. While these factors may be important to determining the sample size for a study, I recommend here that researchers review statistical concerns first, before introducing non-statistical ones, rather than the other way around.

Up to this point, estimates of sample size have been intended for populations that were absent of strata that may affect the variable being measured. When such strata exist, one solution is to take separate random selections by strata, with separate sample size estimates for each (Sapsford, 1999), that is, a random stratified sample. For example, the Current Population Survey of the U.S. Census Bureau (2000) acknowledges the demographic and labor market differences between states by drawing an independent sample of housing units for each state. When reporting results, the state would be the unit of analysis.

In like manner, organizations can exhibit strata that may affect the variable being measured. To simply draw a random sample from the organization as a whole may result in an overrepresentation of operations, and the under-representation or exclusion of one or more small departments (McClelland, 1995). A solution to this dilemma is to first estimate the sample size for the organization as a whole using Table 13.1, then to draw a stratified random sample that is proportionately representative for each department. For example, an organization that has 400 employees requires a minimum sample size of 240 employees at the 95 percent confidence level with a plus or minus 4 percent margin of error. The sales department has 20 employees or 5 percent of the company workforce (20/400 = 5%). To ensure that sales is proportionately represented in the company sample, 12 employees would be randomly drawn from the 20 in the sales department (12/240 = 5%). Using this sampling frame the organization is the unit of analysis, and the sampling error associated with stratification by department approaches zero (Babbie, 1998). More complex forms of stratified sampling can be accomplished where such factors as gender, age, education, marital status, and political affiliation are accounted for in the sampling frame. As more factors are included, complexity increases.

A word of caution should be made at this point. These approaches to estimating sample size specify the *minimum* sample and not the *optimum* size, assume univariate measurement, and often lend themselves to an overestimation of precision in that they are attempts at reducing sampling error, but not all error (Mangione, 1995).

Sample Size and First Survey Mailing

How many survey questionnaires should be sent in the first mailing? Fink (1995) contends that over-sampling may be necessary to offset low response rates with unsolicited surveys often receiving as low as 20 percent participation after the first mailing. But she and others (Babbie, 1998; Fowler, 1993; Isaac & Michael, 1997; Kraemer & Thiemann, 1987; Mangione, 1995; McMillan, 1996; McNamara, 1994; Miller, 1991; Patton, 1998; Sapsford, 1999; Soriano, 1995) fail to address precisely how many names to randomly draw and mail above the *minimum* needed to be statistically representative of the population.

This problem is further compounded by the lack of a uniformly accepted standard for a minimum survey response rate (Fink, 1995; Fowler, 1993). While there is general agreement that nonresponse error is a serious source of bias there is little agreement on a minimal response rate. Mangione (1995, p. 5) recommends that a response rate of 75% should be a "safeguard standard" for mailed surveys. He further concedes that responses in the 60 to 70 percent range are "acceptable." McMillan (1996, p. 99) suggests that response rates of less than 60 percent should trigger an analysis of "the implications of excluding a significant portion of the population," but does not go so far as to reject surveys with lesser rates. Babbie (1998) feels that "a response rate of 50 percent is adequate for analysis and reporting" (p. 262), but qualifies his position by indicating that it is only a "rough" guide without a statistical basis.

The number of questionnaires mailed in an initial administration also serves as the denominator for computing the survey response rate. The numerator is represented by the sum of all survey questionnaires received (Fowler, 1993), typically after successive mailings of surveys and reminders have been conducted as a strategy to improve the number of returns (Sapsford, 1999).

One solution to this problem takes into account the estimated sample size, in conjunction with adopting Babbie's (1998) adequate response rate threshold of 50 percent, as the basis for calculating how many surveys should be sent in the first mailing. The calculation is simple: [1] estimate the sample size and [2] multiply this estimated size by two. The product of this calculation is the number to be mailed on the first administration.

This method acknowledges that the estimated sample size is the minimum number of responses that must be received in order for the sample to be representative of the population at a specified confidence level and confidence interval. Furthermore, by multiplying this minimum sample size by two the largest number of survey questionnaires can be mailed within the second condition; that is, if only half of them are returned both the minimum sample size and the 50 percent minimum response rate conditions are satisfied.

Krueger (1999) used this method to determine how many ISO 9000 training survey questionnaires to include in a first mailing. The estimated sample size for a population of 8,425 ISO 9000 registered organizations in the United States was 368. Table 13.1 shows that this sample size was for the 95 percent confidence level with a confidence interval of plus or minus 5 percent. The estimated sample size was then multiplied by two, determining that 736 organizations would need to be randomly drawn from the population of 8,425 and mailed a survey.

Primary and follow-up mailings of questionnaires yielded 420 survey responses by the end of the data collection period. This represented a 57 percent response rate (420/736=57%) which exceeded the necessary estimated sample size of 368 and the minimum 50 percent response rate suggested by Babbie (1998, p. 262) to be "adequate for analysis and reporting."

Smaller Sizes for Sequential Sampling

Industrial methods of quality control use sequential sampling of a product as it passes through the manufacturing process. Small samples of the population are taken at various points along an assembly line or batch processing system and compared against a standard to ensure that quality is maintained from start to finish (Sapsford, 1999). Sample sizes randomly taken at each point in a process are typically small ranging from 5 to 10 parts or units. It is assumed that the measurements of the parts or units produced will be normally distributed with most clustering around the mean of the population. Standard deviations are typically used to measure the variation about this mean with about 68 percent of the population falling plus or minus one standard deviation, about 95 percent within plus or minus two standard deviations, and about 99 percent within plus or minus three standard deviations. These percentages are typically rounded for convenient reference and are alternatively called sigma 1, 2 and 3 by quality professionals. They are used to assess if a process is normal, or abnormally distributed and out of control (Berger & Hart, 1986).

Action research studies in education measure new teaching and training practices while they are being implemented in classrooms (McMillan, 1996). Sequential sampling methods borrowed from industry could be employed where small numbers of students (e.g., 5 to 10) were randomly drawn from a classroom or workshop population and measured at stages of the instructional process. Input from these measures could be compared against a standard and serve as feedback to shape and improve teaching and training practices.

Existing teaching and training programs could be evaluated using small random samples to identify their processes, design defects, and procedural barriers, serving to inform decision-making and suggest refinements (Isaac & Michael, 1997). Sequential sampling methods could be combined with a time-series design that functions to measure the processes at different points over time (Babbie, 1998). Measures taken at different points in time that are longitudinal in nature, overcome many of the "one-moment-in-time" limitations of cross-sectional studies, and contribute to the understanding of cause-and-effect relationships (Sekaran, 1992).

Drawing conclusions from industrial, educational, and training studies using small, sequential samples should be exercised with caution. They may be representative of the population from which they were selected (i.e., the specific batch, class, or workshop) but not generalizable to other populations.

Size and Statistical Power Analysis

A statistical power analysis calculation is a method used to estimate the sample sizes necessary to compare two groups, experimental and control, in terms of a hypothesized relationship between two or more variables. Cohen (1988), and Kraemer and Theimann (1987) review and discuss this topic at length in their books on statistical power analysis. Several tables are provided in these works that suggest sample sizes by power, significance, one or two-tailed tests, critical effect sizes, and statistical modes of analysis. Statistical proficiency at an intermediate level or the help of a statistician are recommended for researchers interested in using this complex method to estimate sample size (Soriano, 1995).

Conclusions

1. Pilot studies should not have arbitrary sample sizes, but rather a specific size that takes into account the research problem, population characteristics, methods of data collection, and modes of analysis.
2. Sample sizes may be estimated after three key components are determined: confidence level, confidence interval, and population size.
3. Sample size estimates should be calculated before other non-statistical factors are considered.
4. Population stratification may require multiple sample size estimates.
5. Organization stratification may suggest a proportionate representation by substructure after the sample size has been estimated.
6. The number of surveys sent on the first mailing should not be an arbitrary number drawn by the researcher, but rather one that takes into account the sample size estimate, and an adequate response rate for analysis and reporting.
7. Sequential sampling may permit small sample sizes to be randomly drawn during the implementation of a process to assess if it is normal, or abnormally distributed and out of control.

References

Babbie, E. (1998). *The practice of social research* (8th ed.). Belmont, CA: Wadsworth.

Berger, R. W., & Hart, T. H. (1986). *Statistical process control: A guide for implementation*. New York: Marcel Dekker.

Cohen, J. (1988). *Statistical power analysis for the behavioral sciences* (2nd ed.). Hilsdale, NJ: Erlbaum.

Fink, A. (1995). *The survey handbook*. Thousand Oaks, CA: Sage.

Fowler, F. J. (1993). *Survey research methods* (2nd ed.). Newbury Park, CA: Sage.

Grady, K. E., & Wallston, B. S. (1988). *Research in health care settings.* Newbury Park, CA: Sage.

Hinkin, T. R. (1998). A brief tutorial on the development of measures for use in survey questionnaires. *Organizational Research Methods, 1*(1), 104-121.

Holland, K. (2001). *Poll: Bush enjoying a traditional honeymoon.* Retrieved January 8, 2001 from the World Wide Web: http://europe.cnn.com/2001/allpolitics/stories/01/08/cnn.poll/index.html

Isaac, S., & Michael, W. B. (1997). *Handbook in research and evaluation* (3rd ed.). San Diego, CA: EdITS.

Kraemer, H. C., & Thiemann, S. (1987). *How many subjects? Statistical power analysis in research.* Newbury Park, CA: Sage.

Krueger, P. E. (1999). *Human resource training and ISO 9000 international quality assurance standards.* Unpublished doctoral dissertation, University of Southern California, Los Angeles.

Mangione, T. W. (1995). *Mail surveys: Improving the quality.* Thousand Oaks, CA: Sage.

McClelland, S. (1995). *Organizational needs assessments: Design, facilitation, and analysis.* Westport, CT: Quorum.

McMillan, J. H. (1996). *Educational research: Fundamentals for the consumer* (2nd ed.). New York: Harper Collins.

McNamara, J. F. (1994). *Surveys and experiments in education research.* Lancaster: Technomic.

Miller, D. C. (1991). *Handbook of research design and social measurement* (5th ed.). Newbury Park, CA: Sage.

Patton, M. L. (1998). *Questionnaire research: A practical guide.* Los Angeles: Pyrczak.

Sapsford, R. (1999). *Survey research.* London: Sage.

Sekaran, U. (1992). *Research methods: A skill-building approach* (2nd ed.). New York: Wiley & Sons.

Soriano, F. I. (1995). *Conducting needs assessments: A multi-disciplinary approach.* Thousand Oaks, CA: Sage.

U.S. Census Bureau. (2000). *Current population survey: Design and methodology.* Retrieved January 8, 2001 from the World Wide Web: http://www.bls.census.gov/ cps/tp63/html

Walsh, A. (1990). *Statistics for the social sciences.* London: Harper & Row.

Williams, F., & Monge, P. (2001). *Reasoning with statistics* (5th ed.). Fort Worth, TX: Harcourt.

Wright, T. (1998). Sampling and census 2000: The concepts. *American Scientist, 86*(3), 245-253.

Chapter 14

Research Using Available Data: Secondary Data Analysis[*]

Li-Shyung Hwang, Zhicheng Zhang, and Jeffrey Chen

Everyday we hear or talk about numbers concerning stock indices, mortgage rates, divorce rate, mortality, unemployment rate, rankings of SAT scores, tuition increases, and more. Likely, we do not produce the data and conduct the analysis on our own. Rather, we take those numbers as given. We are, in fact, using the product of available (secondary) data in one form or the other.

It is common for researchers to view original data collection as a *must* component of any research process or, at least, a better practice than using extant data. By virtue of our experiences of working with various types of data we contend that real life speaks otherwise. This chapter introduces the use of *available or secondary data* as an alternative to data analysis with coverage of conceptual and pragmatic considerations for such research designs. Our proposition begins with a definition of

[*]This chapter is a product of collaborative efforts. We highly appreciate the input from many individuals, especially those who reviewed and gave valuable suggestions to the manuscript. Special thanks go to Dr. Meihua Zhai, Director of Research and Planning, West Chester University of Pennsylvania; Dr. Jing Luan, Director of Institutional Research, Cabrillo College, California; and Dr. Randall Hickman, Director of Institutional Research, Macomb Community College, Michigan.

useful terms and a delimitation of the scope of this chapter followed by a discussion of reasons for using available data, classifying and locating sources of secondary data, accessing available data, and data evaluation. An exemplary list of databases and their sources (especially those for post-secondary education) is provided. We present technical issues on how to retrieve data sets, select proper variables, handle missing values, and recode variables. A number of analytical methods demonstrate how statistical analyses may be performed on secondary data. Throughout the discussion of technical issues a few large-scale databases, studies based on these databases, and examples of analyses drawn from these studies are used for illustration. Finally, several caveats for secondary data analyses are addressed.

Definition of Terms

By a*vailable data* we simply mean data already collected and available to any user, independent of the original data collection. Analysis of available data is often referred to as *secondary analysis, secondary research,* or *secondary data analysis.* Given its frequent appearance in the literature the term secondary data is used, along with the terms available data and *extant data,* throughout this chapter. Among these terms, the word *secondary* seems to be a critical one; so much so that a clarification is required before we can use these terms interchangeably. Take the combination "secondary data analysis" for example: It may be subject to varied interpretations that possibly yield, in this case, at least two meanings: analysis of secondary data, and secondary analysis of data. Do they both mean exactly the same thing? Does the word secondary imply a contrast to the word primary? If so, what are primary data and primary analysis?

No attempt is made to explore all these questions in detail. Nevertheless, we define secondary analysis as further analysis of existing data to present interpretations, conclusions, or knowledge that are additional to or different from those presented in the first report on the original inquiry as a whole (Hakim, 1982). What then, is analysis of secondary data? We can distinguish between secondary data and data of secondary source. Stewart and Kamins (1993) viewed secondary data as the raw data gathered by others, while secondary sources are defined as the published summaries of raw data. By such a definition secondary data refers to the raw data existing with an original (primary) purpose and available for further analyses as other (secondary) purposes emerge. Data of secondary sources, on the other hand, refer to the information (not raw data) generated as the results of analysis from primary data sources. Analyses exist that possibly employ data of secondary sources. For example, a meta-analysis uses statistical techniques to quantitatively synthesize research results from several studies; and some qualitative studies are based largely on second-hand information such as historical accounts or literature. While using data of secondary sources is a valid research approach, it is not our focus.

There may be disagreement on the distinction between *secondary data* and *data of secondary sources,* especially when the separation of these two types of information can become fuzzy in practice. We are aware of various conceptions and debates associated with the terminology that we adopted for this chapter. However, our attention is primarily focused on numeric raw data that have already been collected and made available to users. The following illustration will not only shed additional light on definitions, but also help to delineate the scope of this chapter.

A researcher designed a survey questionnaire to gather information on the characteristics and educational activities of the adult population of a small town we'll call *Learningville.* We can consider the information collected by this researcher as the data of primary source if the main purpose of the study was to understand adult education participation in the local community. The researcher may also wish to compare Learningville data with data from a national study such as the Adult Education Component of the National Household Education Survey (NHES) published by the National Center for Education Statistics. In this example, data from the NHES are considered secondary data. We refer to analyses based on the available data from NHES as secondary data analyses.

Reasons to Use Available Data

There are a spectrum of reasons and opportunities for using available data, falling into one of four categories: [1] requirements and demands set forth by authorities, [2] benefits of economy, quality, and knowledge production of extant data, [3] impact of advanced technology on available data, and [4] opportunities for secondary research.

Requirements and Demands

There are situations where researchers need—in fact, are duty bound—to conduct analyses of given databases. In the educational arena, analyzing secondary data as a *must* task may be attributed to the increased demands on performance and accountability measures for programs and organizations, especially those supported by public funding. It is common nowadays for funding agencies to require some type of assessment, evaluation, and/or status report to account for the expenditure of grant funds. Federal and state governments have, historically, been at the forefront in collecting educationally-relevant data due in part to administrative and regulatory functions, as well as in response to increasing public demand for accountability. Public and private educational institutions, agencies, and organizations also gather data as part of normal operations. Further, commercial data services supply syndicated or customized data to meet an organization's special information needs. Consequently, a wealth of information has been generated and is available to educational researchers.

Economy, Quality, and Knowledge

Aside from dutiful acceptance of extant data it may be a matter of personal choice for some researchers to use secondary data. The primary and distinctive advantage of using available data is generally said to be the economy presented in terms of cost, time, and labor as compared to research involving original data collection (Bowering, 1984; Hyman, 1972; Myers & Rockwell, 1984; Stewart & Kamins, 1993). Another possible benefit of using available data is the quality of large-scale secondary data. Since most large studies require considerable resources, procedures for survey response rates, data collection and entry procedures are given special attention. Other practical benefits include the use of secondary data in preliminary analyses to inform the development of primary research studies. The preliminary function can help researchers formulate research problems, hypotheses, and methods.

In addition to practical benefits, Hyman (1972) points out that social benefits also exist. The use of secondary data can provide a logical alternative when faced with severe obstructions that can exist in collecting original data, as well as the restraint of oligarchy in a discipline, by insuring public access to bodies of raw data. A second benefit of secondary research lies in the expansion of theory and substantive knowledge. Secondary data analysis can contribute to an understanding of the past and change through examination of problems comparatively, improvement of general knowledge through replication and enlargement, and the elevation and expansion of theory.

Convenience and Efficiency

The advanced technology of our present time makes the use of available data an attractive alternative to primary data collection and analysis. Information technology has greatly simplified the daunting tasks (by yesterday's standards) involved in the process of using and analyzing secondary data. Those tasks might include library searches to locate data sources, contacting agencies that own the data for acquisition, satisfying technical requirements for retrieving data, and preparing data files for analysis. According to Bowering (1984), a lack of knowledge and skill in dealing with secondary data and uncertainty about data quality of this sort could be reasons that keep some researchers away from using existing data. But, new technologies have minimized or even eliminated these challenges. Since CD-ROM technology became popular, the availability and accessibility of machine-readable data, particularly large-scale data sets, have been considerably pervasive. Internet technology provides researchers with even more powerful access to databases through the World Wide Web (WWW). Moreover, the latest trend of data warehouse, data archiving, and any variation of electronic data services dramatically enhances the instant availability of secondary data.

Opportunities

Infinite opportunities exist to use available data to conduct analyses as long as research questions can be appropriately addressed by the secondary data. Secondary data analysis, as a form of research, can incorporate primary data to conduct trend analyses, in developing contextual designs, cross-national designs, panel designs, or used as a comparative tool for various comparative studies. A review of studies based on secondary data analysis and a discussion of the potential of secondary research suggests an array of opportunities including studies of fundamental phenomena, studies of change, cohort analysis, assessment and evaluation, policy research, peer comparison, trend analysis, and benchmarking (e.g., Hyman, 1972).

Classification of Data

Data, the information organized for analysis, can be either qualitative or quantitative in nature. For the present, we focus on numerical raw data, rather than derived data, that are suitable for computer processing. There is no single comprehensive way to taxonomically categorize extant data. Different dimensions or typologies can be constructed to better understand specific data structures. On one dimension there might be a contrast between data for the entirety of a given population and data for subsets of a given population studied.

Data for a total population—for example, administrative data intended for administrative purposes—are typically collected on a 100 percent basis rather than as a sample (Thomas, 1996). The administrative data of an institution, for instance, may contain student information—including variables for demographics, admission, financial aids, and academic records—of the entire student body of that institution. Understandably, access to administrative data is restricted, limited to authorized users. In contrast to data for an entire population, there may be sample data from which information, as an example, is generated from survey studies. Survey research designs usually involve a scheme of sampling by which a group of respondents is drawn from a population in the assumption that inferences about the population can be made by means of studying this smaller group, namely, the sample (Vogt, 1993). Census may be deemed as a unique survey study that collects data on every member of a given population.

In terms of the units of data organization, a contrast can be made between micro-data and aggregate data. Micro-data (information given on individual records) sometimes refers to unit record data since each record (a unit of input for the computer) in a data file is an individual unit not derived from other data (Myers & Rockwell, 1984; Thomas, 1996). Aggregate data (data derived from unit record data), on the other hand, gathers single units together in a sum based on certain criteria. Macro-data, when summarized from micro-data, are sometimes viewed as aggregate data. It is important to note that data aggregation is a relative process and concept. Depending on the level of analysis a set of aggregated numbers may be treated as a set of single units of analysis. For instance, the Integrated Postsecondary Education Data System (IPEDS)—a well-known database in higher education designed to collect data at the institutional level—gathers information concerning student enrollment and faculty salary, for example, from participating institutions. Information aggregated from single records of students and faculty at individual institutions, i.e., aggregate data, becomes a unit of record for the IPEDS database at an institutional level. The meaningful use of available data depends on the knowledge of the dimensions of data characteristics and conditions, and how the particular data file in question is located on these dimensions.

Sources of Available Data

Many established databases, especially those resulting from publicly funded and large-scale data collection, are publicized to announce their availability. Some authors like Myers and Rockwell (1984) have noted that the academic sector has historically played a more active role in disseminating data than the federal government. It is possible and relatively convenient for researchers to be aware of the availability of such databases as decennial census data and the most popular databases in their professional fields. However, a conventional search for research information still remains the basic way for many researchers to locate appropriate data sources. Traditional ways of locating available data include seeking guidance from experts, authorities, and experienced researchers in the field, and use of library searches and literature reviews. Nowadays, CD-ROM and Internet technologies have made computer-assisted and on-line searches easy ways to identify potential sources of available data. The following two strategies are highlighted as a way to start the search process.

- *Seeking assistance from a reference librarian in the library:* A few tips on search etiquette from experienced librarians often prove to be invaluable, especially from those whose daily duties include assisting researchers to locate the research information.
- *Seeking suggestions from the professional associations:* Various and instant feedback may be efficiently obtained from the "cyber" associations (e.g., listserv groups where communication is mostly through electronic mail, discussion groups, and chat rooms where communication is actually real-time electronic conversations of specific topics and interests).

These steps, generally yielding extensive clues to the information sought in short order, have been proven to be a time saver as well as lead to successful searches.

In general, the federal and state governments are the principal agencies that own a majority of publicly available databases although the actual work of such data collection and production are commonly done by major research organizations through contractual arrangements. Certainly, there are databases available outside of government. Data are collected, produced, and disseminated by non-governmental organizations in both pubic and private sectors. Some commercial information firms provide data services for profit. These types of data production usually focus on market research such as sales and market share information. Since the primary research interests of most education researchers are in education, databases from government agencies and the academic sector appear most appropriate. The Appendix (at the end of this chapter) lists some sources for obtaining secondary data and examples of data sets relevant to education. Given the over-abundance of existing information this list is by no means comprehensive. However, it does illustrate the results we obtained from sampling currently available data sources using an Internet search.

Accessing Available Data

Data accessibility may vary depending on the policy of data sources and the researcher's resources and association. Generally, it is easier to gain access to aggregated or summarized data on a particular topic, while it is harder to access the complete raw data set. Raw data such as survey response sheets or original electronic recordings with identifiable individual information are rarely available without some form of consent. Publicly accessible databases are normally organized in a way that confidentiality and privacy issues are addressed, yet still of research utility.

Do not assume that the information contained in public sources are always readily accessible to the general public. Some information remains restricted mainly due to privacy issues. For instance, some state agencies such as the Departments of Education and Labor have agreed to share data so that issues related to educational attainment and postgraduation employment can be studied. Although the data of both agencies are public in nature, access of such data is very much proprietary because the integration of these data requires merging two sources of public information using sensitive identifying keys such as social security numbers. With some extra steps and special efforts researchers can gain access to restricted data sources. In case that data are only available on a proprietary basis, it is possible to obtain the needed data sets from individual agencies following necessary policy and procedures. Certainly, when handling any sensitive data you should always follow ethical considerations and take precautions against violating information privacy issues.

Additional considerations for data accessibility when determining the appropriateness of data for a proposed research project include:

• *Assessing the level of accessibility of the interested secondary data:* Researchers should know whether or not the intended data are available at the level of accessibility that is needed for the research.

For instance, many large-scale databases may be, typically, expected to exclude distinctive identifying keys. Researchers need to decide if such individual information is critical to the analysis, and if using or giving-up the database is necessary.

• *Assessing the lag-time between the time of data-collecting and that of data becoming available to the public:* Sometimes there is a cost associated with the most up-to-date data or any data that are not in the format of general summary. Most importantly, time should be taken into account. When information becomes obsolete the data are useless even if they are readily accessible.

The days of hand tallying and computing raw data have long passed. Nowadays, researchers have a variety of ways to access data easily and quickly. At the present time common formats on which data are stored include magnetic tapes, cartridges, floppy disks, CD-ROM, and on-line storage. On-line storage is associated with Internet technology that allows instant access to data, namely, downloading (i.e., transferring or file copying) the data files through web servers, if the data sets are published on the Internet or by means of File Transfer Protocol (FTP). Downloading data simply means transmitting a file from one computer to another and it implies sending a file rather than processing interactively with the data.

The Internet is a powerful tool to locate, access, and extract data. Many web sites of electronic data services contain such utilities as Data Access Tools (DAT) and Data Analysis Systems (DAS) to facilitate the instant utilization of data sources. As a tool for accessing data interactively DAS allow users to obtain customized reports (e.g., frequency tables, tables of percentages, means, correlation coefficients) simply by choosing variables and analytical functions. Most web sites are designed to have links to other relevant sites. In many cases users may find the capacity to link (to other related sites) considerably efficient and productive. However, because the purposes and designs of each web site differ, users are challenged to compare and evaluate the vast expanse of research related information provided at web sites.

Data Evaluation

The University of California, Berkeley (Weise, 2000) recently released a major study that attempted to quantify the amount of unique information produced each year. The study estimated that the world's total annual production of data amounts to 1.5 exabytes, which if stored on floppy disks would stack 2 million miles high. We are indeed flooded with a sea of information. The challenge facing us is to learn to swim rather than drowned in that sea. The production of data and information far outgrows any individual human capability to understand. As technology improves it is easier and faster to access available data sets. It is extremely important that researchers take steps to ensure the appropriateness of available data in relation to their research needs prior to committing to use the data.

Authors such as Stewart and Kamins (1993) address relevant issues when evaluating secondary data. Along with their "Why, Who, What, When, and How" questions about the quality of data collection, we suggest the following for consideration.

- *The relevancy of the available data to the research question:* You should ask why the existing data were originally collected to determine how relevant the original purpose is to the purpose of the proposed research.

- *The credibility of the data source:* Knowing who was responsible for data collection may provide some basis to judge the quality and reliability of the data if you has knowledge of the general reputation the data-collecting party has established.

- *The temporal aspect of the available data:* When were the data collected? The time lag between when data were gathered and when they are made available, in some cases, is a crucial issue to the research design. Elapsed time may make information obsolete and meaningless as for the research question.

- *The method of data collection:* How were data collected? The method of collection could greatly affect data validity. Data collection instruments (e.g., questionnaires, interview guides, protocols), the size and nature of samples, response rates, experimental procedures, validation efforts all play a part in the quality of the data sets.

- *The content and organization of the available data files:* What information was actually gathered? What were the organizational units? How were the available data originally coded, including the treatment of missing values? Understanding such details is critical because the original data recording might be quite different from what you intend to study.

- *The consistency of the databases:* A strategy used when evaluating data quality is to check a database against another one of the same or similar nature from multiple sources. If great discrepancies exist among different sources and little basis for evaluating the data collection process is in place, you should be alerted to this inconsistency, and initiate further scrutiny of all data sources.

When possible, always make efforts to contact the individuals involved in the original data sources for their insights and cautions. The information gathered from sources may supplement what is not found in published documentation, including prior uses and errata, as well as other important information pertaining to data quality.

Preparing Data Files for Analysis

Secondary data may be stored on a CD or a floppy disk. It may also be obtained electronically either via FTP or downloaded from the Internet. Depending on the number of items included and the way variables are coded a secondary data file may have a varying degree of complexity and can be hard to access. Often large-scale data files such as those released by the National Center for Education Statistics (NCES)—for example, Integrated Postsecondary Education Data System, National Educational Longitudinal Study of 1988/1994, National Study of Postsecondary Faculty: 88/93, Baccalaureate and Beyond Longitudinal Study: 93/94—have some sort of access tools to facilitate use of the data. Researchers who use data from these national studies should be particularly familiar with two available tools, Data Analysis System (DAS) and Electronic Codebook (ECB).

DAS is a Windows®-based software program that generates tables for variables selected by a database user. Output tables contain the estimates (usually in percentages) and corresponding standard errors that are calculated to account for complex sampling designs. DAS can also create correlation matrices that may be used as input for statistical software programs for multivariate analysis. ECB is a Windows® interface that allows users to browse through variables contained in the data files and extract subsets of data into ASCII text files, data files of data management systems such as dBase and Access, or data sets of software packages for statistical analysis (e.g., SAS, SPSS, Stata, S-Plus). For users who prefer to do statistical analyses using SPSS, ECB is an ideal choice. All users need to do is to tag (select) desired variables in the ECB interface and save results in an SPSS syntax file. Running the syntax file in the SPSS environment will generate an SPSS data file. From that point forward users can enjoy the freedom of performing statistical analyses on the extracted data. DAS and ECB usually come with a CD-ROM that contains the survey data. The information on how to use these tools is normally contained in the readme.txt file. If DAS or ECB are not readily available on CD, users may get a free download of these tools from the web sites where the data sources are located. Learning to use these tools is the first step in accessing data of a national survey.

Secondary data may also come from less formal sources such as organizations or individuals. In these cases it is crucial that users of the data have a good understanding of how the variables are positioned and defined in the data file(s). Obtaining a copy of the coding scheme and matching it with the actual items on a survey is an essential part of the verification process (Fortune & McBee, 1984). This is especially true for ASCII or *flat* files that only contain numerical values. Based on the variable definitions a program file can be developed to convert raw data into SPSS or SAS files to facilitate further analyses. Windows® interfaces can also convert raw data to Access or Excel files.

Selecting Variables to Answer Specific Research Questions

Most secondary data files contain more variables than most researchers would need for a specific study. This is particularly true for national studies where data are collected from multiple sources and over a long period of time. Thus, it is necessary for researchers to narrow down the scope of variable selection to a manageable scale. Strictly speaking, variable selection should be guided by the theoretical framework that underlies your investigation. Variable selection must also tie nicely with the research design and statistical analysis you intend to perform on the data.

Viewed from this perspective variable selection should be integrated into the following process. [1] Start with a general idea about the focus of investigation before approaching the data. In order for the investigation to have a strong theoretical foundation the idea should be based on previous research or existing literature. [2] Browse through the variables in a data file to see how well the existing data fit your research plan. When misfits occur, either due to the unavailability of some items or the restriction of data format, you need to modify the original research plan or, when possible, merge the data with other files to ensure the inclusion of necessary information. [3] Work out the details of the research design, deciding on what variables will be selected, what statistical analyses will be performed, and identifying the dependent and independent variables in the analyses. Also, you will need to determine at this stage if certain variables need to be recoded to answer specific research questions. [4] Extract data for statistical analyses.

Using a theoretical framework to guide variable selection has been reported in well-designed studies. For example, in a study of the role of parental involvement in student success, Yan (1999) used social capital theory as a conceptual framework to guide variable selection. The 11 items selected from the NELS:88 database served to define social capital along four dimensions; parent-teen interaction, parent-school interaction, interactions with other parents, and family norms. Guided by social cognitive theory and the status attainment model Mau and Bikos (2000) selected data from the NELS:88 data set to form four clusters of independent variables (psychological, family, school, gender and race) and two dependent variables (college aspiration and occupational expectations) in their longitudinal study of educational and vocational aspirations of minority and female students. The theory-driven approach was also adopted by Singh (1998), who tested the hypothesis that the intensity of work has a negative effect on academic achievement, a position that supports the zero-sum model. The variables selected from the NELS:88 (hours worked per week, school grades and standardized test scores on English, math, science, and social studies, gender, and social economic status) are all directly related to the focus of the investigation. Lan (1999) proposed a model of relationship between parenting style and students' academic achievement based on Baumrind's theory of parenting styles. The parenting practice variables selected from NELS:88 (expectation, concerns over academics, provision of learning opportunities, involvement at school, after-school supervision) operationalize the socialization mechanism that helps explain how an authoritative parenting style facilitates student educational outcomes. The use of a theoretical framework to guide variable selection and subsequent statistical analysis gives each of these studies a clear sense of direction and helps to place a specific research endeavor within the continuous flow of scientific inquiry.

Handling Missing Values

Missing data is an inevitable problem faced by most researchers. The inclusion of missing values in a statistical analysis may generate misleading results. For data obtained from large-scale studies, such as those released by the NCES, you should be aware of two types of missing values, *coded* and *uncoded* missing values. Coded missing values are those clearly specified as missing by the original researchers who collected the data and built the database. Uncoded missing values refer to cases that contain no values for a given item. In a subset extracted from the NELS:88 data set, for example, variable FIS39A has 235 coded missing values and 8915 uncoded missing values. In addition, there are 10 cases where the response is labeled "refusal" and 320 cases where the response is labeled "multiple responses." Since these responses are assigned non-zero code values (*98* for "missing", *97* for "refusal", and *96* for "multiple responses"), the inclusion of these values may distort analysis results. These values should be excluded from statistical analyses because they do not contribute to the measure of the attribute under investigation. In SPSS this can be done by specifying the values *96, 97,* and *98* as discrete missing values.

Once missing values are clearly specified, the next step is to choose an appropriate method to handle missing values. Several methods are available to handle missing values including listwise deletion, pairwise deletion, regression, and expectation maximization. Listwise deletion discards cases with a missing value on any variable and thus is wasteful of data. Pairwise deletion computes covariances between all pairs of variables eliminating those that have a missing value for one of the two variables (Glasser, 1964). The regression methods provide estimates of missing values based on the information contained in non-missing values of other variables. In the expectation maximization method, missing values are functions based on conditional expectations (Little & Rubin, 1987). These methods of handling missing values are available in most statistical software.

Researchers may be troubled about selecting the appropriate method to handle the missing values in a given situation. Witta's (2000) research on the effectiveness of the four methods sheds some light on this issue. Based on a comparison of the four methods using samples of different sizes and different proportions of missing cases Witta concluded that, when 30% of the cases in a sample are incomplete, all four methods adequately reproduce the target sample covariance matrix and mean vector regardless of sample size. The choice of method could be made based on considerations of data loss or other substantive reasons. When 50% of cases were incomplete, only listwise and pairwise deletion were effective under all conditions. When 70% of cases were incomplete listwise deletion is the only method of choice.

Recoding Variables

Depending on the specific design of an investigation, variables from a secondary database may need to be recoded before statistical analysis. This is necessary because the original designer of a survey may have used use a coding scheme that does not suit your purposes. In the

NELS:88 data, for example, 10th grade students' course grades for mathematics, English, history, and science are coded as follows: 1 = not taking subject, 2 = mostly A, 3 = half A and half B, 4 = mostly B, 5 = half B and half C, 6 = mostly C, 7 = half C and half D, 8 = mostly D, 9 = mostly below D. To be consistent with the convention that a higher value indicates a greater degree of the attribute measured, Singh (1998) reversed the coding scheme so that 8 = mostly A, 7 = half A and half B, 6 = mostly B, 5 = half B and half C, 4 = mostly C, 3 = half C and half D, 2 = mostly D, 1 = mostly below D. Notice the original value of 1 is left out from the recoding because there is no need to include respondents who do not have grades for these school subjects. Singh's also recoded several other variables including hours worked per week and other achievement-related variables.

In a study of the educational and vocational aspirations of minority and female students Mau and Bikos (2000) accessed the NELS:88 datbase and defined two dependent variables, postsecondary education aspiration and occupational expectations. Postsecondary education aspiration was measured by the question, "As things stand now, how far in school do you think you will go?" Responses to this question were originally coded as 1 = won't finish high school, 2 = will finish high school, 3 = vocational training after high school, 4 = will attend college, 5 = will finish college, and 6 = higher schooling after college. In order to satisfy the requirements for a logistic regression model, Mau and Bikos classified the six responses into two dummy categories: non-college aspirations, and college and beyond aspirations. For the question on occupational expectations, "Which occupation do you expect or plan to have when you are 30 years old?" the 11 responses were classified into the three categories of unskilled-semiskilled, technical-semiprofessional, and professional. After recoding these two dependent variables, logistic regression analyses were conducted to identify the psychological, family, school, and gender and race variables that predicted students [1] who aspired to a bachelors degree versus non-bachelors degree and [2] those aspiring to professional versus non-professional occupations. In this example, dichotomizing the two dependent variables is prerequisite for the logistic regression analysis.

Similar techniques for recoding variables have been reported by other researchers. In their study of non-Asian minority under-representation in science and engineering fields, Peng, Huang, and Hill (1998) redefined students' motivation to learn science with 1 for those who were self-motivated ("Because I am interested. . .") and 0 for those with other reasons to study science ("Required by graduation,"

"Advised by teachers," "Advised by school"). They also created a dichotomously-coded variable for advanced science courses with 1 for those taking one or more advanced science courses in 10th and 12th grades, and 0 for those who did not. Again, the recoding of these variables was completed before performing logistic regression analysis on the data.

New researchers may be confused as to the level of freedom they enjoy in variable recoding and data manipulation before performing statistical analyses. Our suggestion is that the decision to recode a variable, to create a new variable based on existing variables, or to form a composite variable should be made based upon a good understanding of the nature of the data, the purpose and design of the research undertaken, the conceptual tie to theory or previous research, and specific statistical methods to be performed. A composite variable may be generated from several survey items based on factor analysis or interrelationships among survey items (Fortune & McBee, 1984). Having a rationale for recoding a variable and being aware of the advantages and potential problems of any data manipulation techniques are two effective ways to prevent careless moves by researchers.

Statistical Analyses

Secondary data from national studies typically contain a huge amount of information and offer a broad spectrum for statistical analyses. Data in the NELS:88 database, for example, have been collected from students, teachers, schools, and parents on four different occasions over a period of seven years. Researchers can perform a variety of statistical analyses on this rich source of data to address pressing issues in education. In this section we introduce a few statistical methods that can be applied to secondary data. Whenever appropriate examples are provided to illustrate the discussion.

Analysis of Variance (ANOVA)

One-way ANOVA involves the analysis of one independent variable with two or more levels (Hinkle, Wiersma, & Jurs, 1988). When the independent variable only has two levels ANOVA produces the same results as a *t*-test. In an ANOVA, changes in the dependent variable are presumed to result from changes in the independent variable. One-way ANOVA was used in Mau and Lynn's (1999) study to examine the differences in school achievement (dependent variable) as a function of racial group (independent variable with four levels: Asian, Black,

Hispanic, and white). Following a significant *F* value for the overall test, Scheffe follow-up tests were used for pairwise comparisons between different racial groups. ANOVA is a simple yet effective technique to detect differences in a variable (e.g., achievement, attitude, self-efficacy, occupational aspiration) as a function of another (e.g., gender, race, education level, academic major, family environment).

Multivariate Analysis of Variance (MANOVA)

One-way MANOVA is applicable when the differences in several dependent variables are presumed to be a function of an independent variable. For example, one-way MANOVA may be used to determine whether teachers' proficiency in using paper-pencil tests (dependent variable 1), performance assessment (dependent variable 2), and interpreting standard test scores (dependent variable 3) vary by their teaching level (independent variable with three levels: elementary, middle school, high school). If we include exposure to measurement training (have had measurement training, have not had measurement training) as another independent variable in this example, the appropriate statistical technique would be a 2-way MANOVA. Specifically, we need to perform a 3 (teaching level) x 2 (measurement training) MANOVA to examine how teachers' proficiency in classroom assessment may be affected by their teaching level and exposure to training in measurement.

One-way MANOVA was applied to a subset of NELS:88 data to determine whether students' academic achievement, time spent on homework, non-school activities, and parental involvement vary by different ethnic groups of Asian immigrants, Asian Americans, and white Americans (Mau, 1997). Since NELS:88 contains a wealth of information collected from different sources including students, teachers, school, and parents, it provides an excellent opportunity to apply multivariate analytical techniques to address pressing concerns in education (e.g., how students' performance, educational aspirations, and career choice may be affected by different factors such as family support, teaching styles, and school environment).

Multiple Regression

Multiple regression analysis involves predicting a criterion variable (Y) based on the information from a number of predictors (X). Suppose previous research suggests that high school GPA, SAT scores, college preparedness variables such as study skills, aspiration for achievement, and aspiration for graduate school have a positive impact on freshman GPA. A regression model could be established where pre-college cognitive variables and variables of college preparedness are used to predict freshman GPA. Notice in this case the criterion (freshman GPA) is a continuous variable. If the criterion was a dichotomously-coded variable as in the case of retention status (leavers vs. stayers) or effects of medical treatment (dead vs. living), the analytic technique to use would be logistic multiple regression. Some researchers choose to redefine a variable dichotomously in order to perform logistic rather than regular multiple regression analysis because the former permits violation of normality and is interpretable in terms of probability (Mau & Bikos, 2000).

In Mau and Bikos' (2000) logistic regression model the predictors were psychological (self-esteem, locus of control, academic self-efficacy), family (parents' education, parent school involvement, parent academic involvement, number of siblings), school (academic proficiency, academic program, school setting, school size, school type), and gender and race variables, whereas the criterion was educational aspiration (bachelor's degree vs. non-bachelor's degree) in one analysis and occupational expectation (professional vs. non professional occupations) in the other. The predictors were entered in blocks using a forward stepwise method and the regression coefficient was used to judge the predictive power of each variable.

Chi-Square Test of Independence

As a nonparametric technique the chi-square test of independence is frequently used to compare two or more groups on a nominal variable with two or more categories (Hinkle et al., 1988). In a chi-square test of independence design observed frequencies are compared with expected frequencies. A statistically significant test statistic indicates that the distribution of a sample on one variable differs across k categories of another variable. Standard residuals are then calculated to determine where the differences lie between k categories. The chi-square statistic is particularly appropriate for explorations intended to detect population differences resulting from nominal factors such as ethnicity, career choice, and parenting styles. Mau, Domnick, and Ellsworth (1995), for example, applied a 2 x 5 chi-square test of independence to a subset of the NELS:88 data to determine whether female students' aspirations for two distinct career paths (science and engineering vs. homemaking) differed across five ethnic groups (African American, Asian, Hispanic, Native American, white). Their study revealed that

Asian American and African American students had higher percentages of science and engineering career aspirations than homemaking aspirations, whereas Hispanic, white, and Native American students had lower percentages of science and engineering aspirations than homemaking career aspirations.

Structural Equation Modeling

Structural equation modeling (SEM) is a comprehensive statistical approach to testing hypotheses about relationships among observed and latent variables (Hoyle, 1995). SEM involves specifying and testing two models, a measurement model and structural model. The measurement model identifies the latent variables measured by a set of observed variables (survey items) based on a confirmatory factor analysis. In the structural model, relationships between latent variables are specified according to previous research or existing theory and evaluated based on a number of fit indices. A confirmed structural model of relationships contributes to the expansion of existing knowledge under investigation. SEM proves to be a useful tool to analyze secondary data from national studies.

Lan's (1999) used SEM to study parenting styles and student achievement. Six latent variables were identified from 22 items in the NELS:88 based on a measurement model including [1] parents' expectation, [2] parents' responsiveness, [3] students' behavioral attributes, [4] students' personal attributes, [5] students' motivational attributes, and [6] students' academic performance. The final structural model indicated that parental expectation and responsiveness are fundamental variables affecting students' personal attributes which, as a mediating variable, affects students' behavioral attributes, motivational attributes, and academic performance.

SEM was also used in Singh's (1998) investigation of the effects of part-time employment on academic achievement. The relationship between part-time employment, gender, socio-economic status, previous academic achievement, and current academic achievement were examined in a structural model. Once again, the specification of parameters between various latent variables were guided by previous research and existing theory. Singh's study confirmed, among other things, that students with higher achievement in the past are less likely to work longer hours and that the number of hours worked per week has a significant negative effect on academic achievement either as measured by school grades or standardized test scores.

The analytical techniques provided are by no means an exhaustive list of statistical methods. You are referred to further reading on other chapters in this text concerning data analysis. However, the exemplified methods do illustrate the variety of analytic tools available for secondary analysis. It should be noted, though, that there are still limitations and ethical concerns that should be taken into account as secondary data analysis is considered.

Caveats

Limitations of secondary research and ethical issues concerning secondary data are noteworthy. No code of ethics has been formulated specifically for research that is based on secondary data. You are referred to the web site http://www.iit.edu/departments/csep for a selection of on-line ethics codes collected by the Center for Study of Ethics in the Professions at Illinois Institute of Technology. The most explicitly relevant codes in dealing with available data are provided by the Association for Institutional Research. In the *Execution* section, the item *Quality of Secondary Data* clearly states that "the institutional researcher shall take reasonable steps to insure the accuracy of data gathered by other individuals, groups, offices, or agencies on which he/she relies, and shall document the sources and quality of such data." Since secondary data do not result from the original data collection component, researchers are, supposedly, less burdened with such concerns as information privacy and other confidentiality issues pertaining to data gathering. Nevertheless, one particular code set forth by the American Statistical Association (ASA) addresses the confidentiality consideration in relation to secondary analysis. According to the ASA code, professionals should "ensure that, whenever data are transferred to other persons or organizations, this transfer conforms with the established confidentiality pledges, and require written assurance from the recipients of the data that the measures employed to protect confidentiality will be at least equal to those originally pledged."

In its broadest definitions secondary data are exist with their original purposes which may differ from that of the current one, or are data that were collected from the processes somewhat or fully beyond the monitoring of the researchers of a given study. While the advantages and demands of using secondary data become attractive and necessary for data analysis, researchers ought to be aware of the disadvantages and trade-off of using available data. Myers and Rockwell (1984) point out that the ideal research design may be compromised by the constraints imposed by using data that were gathered by other people for different purposes. The issues related to the research design of using available data can be just as fundamental as the problems embedded in the data structure. For example, in large-scale secondary data sets identifiable individual information is usually not released in order to protect privacy. Thus, some analyses cannot be performed without a distinctive identifying key. Moreover, secondary data are not always available at the individual level. Instead, data are sometimes aggregated in particular ways and the unit of aggregation may not be appropriate for a particular analysis (Stewart & Kamins, 1993). The units and coding on which available data files were originally organized are closely related to the units of analysis of secondary research. In short, understanding various dimensions of data can impact the issues related to the internal and external validity of secondary analysis. A researcher's sensitivity to the constraints of extant data and incorporation of appropriate changes to the original data (within the scope of maintaining data integrity) are crucial to the successful use of available data.

References

Bowering, D. J. (Ed.). (1984). *Secondary analysis of available data bases* (New directions for program evaluation, No. 22). San Francisco: Jossey-Bass.

Fortune, J. C., & McBee, J. K. (1984). Considerations and methodology for the preparation of data files. In D. J. Bowering (Ed.), *Secondary analysis of available data bases* (New directions for program evaluation, No. 22; pp. 27-49). San Francisco: Jossey-Bass.

Glasser, M. (1964). Linear regression analysis with missing observations among the independent variables. *Journal of the American Statistical Society, 59,* 834-844.

Hakim, C. (1982). *Secondary analysis in social research.* London: Allen & Unwin.

Hinkle, D. E., Wiersma, W., & Jurs, S. G. (1988). *Applied statistics for the behavioral sciences* (2nd ed.). Boston: Houghton Mifflin.

Hoyle, R. H. (1995). The structural equation modeling approach: Basic concepts and fundamental issues. In R. H. Hoyle (Ed.), *Structural equation modeling: Concepts, issues, and applications* (pp. 1-15). Thousand Oaks, CA: Sage.

Hyman, H. H. (1972). *Secondary analysis of sample surveys: Principles, procedures, and potentialities.* New York: Wiley & Sons.

Lan, W. Y. (1998, April). *A model of parenting style and students' academic performance.* Paper presented at the annual meeting of the American Educational Research Association, San Diego.

Little, R. J. A., & Rubin, D. B. (1987). *Statistical analysis with missing data.* New York: Wiley & Sons.

Mau, W. (1997). Parental influences on the high school students' academic achievement: A comparison of Asian immigrants, Asian Americans, and White Americans. *Psychology in the Schools. 34,* 267-277.

Mau, W., & Bikos, L. H. (2000). Educational and vocational aspirations of minority and female students: A longitudinal study. *Journal of Counseling and Development, 78,* 186-194.

Mau, W., Domnick, M., & Ellsworth, R. A. (1995). Characteristics of female students who aspire to science and engineering or homemaking occupations. *Career Development Quarterly, 43,* 323-337.

Mau, W., & Lynn, R. (1999). Racial and ethnic differences in motivation for educational achievement in the United States. *Personality and Individual Differences, 27,* 1091-1096.

Myers, D. E., & Rockwell, R. C. (1984). Large-scale data bases: Who produces them, how to obtain them, what they contain. *Secondary analysis of available data bases* (New directions for program evaluation No. 22, pp. 5-25). San Francisco: Jossey-Bass.

Peng, S., Huang, G., & Hill, S. (1998, April). *Understanding non-Asian minority under-representation in science and engineering fields.* Paper presented at the annual meeting of the American Educational Research Association, San Diego, CA.

Singh, K. (1998). Part-time employment in high school and its effect on academic achievement. *The Journal of Educational Research, 91*(3), 131-139.

Stewart, D. W., & Kamins, M. A. (1993). *Secondary research: Information sources and methods* (2nd ed.). Newbury Park, CA: Sage.

Thomas, R. (1996). Statistical sources and databases. In R. Sapsford & V. Jupp (Eds.), *Data collection and analysis* (pp.121-137). Thousand Oaks, CA: Sage.

Vogt, W. P. (1993). *Dictionary of statistics and methodology: A nontechnical guide for the social sciences.* Newbury Park, CA: Sage.

Weise, E. (2000). *Society grappling with info overload.* Retrieved November 11, 2000 from USA Today on the World Wide Web: http://www.usatoday.com/life/cyber/tech/cti688.htm

Witta, E. L. (2000, April). *Effectiveness of four methods of handling missing data using samples from a national database.* Paper presented at the annual meeting of the American Educational Research Association, New Orleans, LA.

Yan, W. (1999). Successful African American students: The role of parental involvement. *Journal of Negro Education, 68*(1), 5-22.

APPENDIX
Selected Sources of Available Data

Sources of data/sample of databases	Accessing data
Primary sources in postsecondary education	*Direct website, direct data access*
NATIONAL CENTER FOR EDUCATIONAL STATISTICS (NCES) is the primary federal entity for collecting, analyzing, and reporting data related to education in U.S. and other nations. http://nces.edu.gov	Users can use electronic catalogs to find the most recently released data sets and to search for publications and data products. *Data Access Tools* are available to obtain information from data sources.
POSTSECONDARY SURVEYS • Baccalaureate and Beyond • Beginning Postsecondary Student Longitudinal Study • Integrated Postsecondary Education Data System • National Household Education Survey • National Postsecondary Student Aid Study • Postsecondary Education Quick Information System • Recent College Graduates Study	*Survey and Program Areas* have page links to NCES data products and specific home pages of associated surveys and programs. Users also can obtain pre-defined reports such as statistical compendium from *Encyclopedia of Ed Stats* and *Quick Tables and Figures.* Due to confidentiality legislation, some NCES raw data (e.g., student transcripts) are accessible only through restricted data license.
LONGITUDINAL SURVEYS • High School and Beyond • National Educational Longitudinal Study of 1988/1994	*Data Analysis System* is available to generate basic on-line analyses.
EDUCATION ASSESSMENT • National Assessments of Adult Literacy	CD-ROMs and on-line downloading are the modes of obtaining data from NCES. Both modes present micro-data files and related documentation.

Primary sources in postsecondary education	*Direct website, direct data access*
PROGRAM AREAS Data on Vocational Education The *COOPERATIVE INSTITUTIONAL RESEARCH PROGRAM* is a national longitudinal study of American higher education, at the Higher Education Research Institute, UCLA. http://www.gseis.ucla.edu/heri/cirp *FRESHMAN SURVEY* *ENTERING STUDENTS SURVEY (ESS)* *COLLEGE STUDENTS SURVEY (CSS)* *FACULTY SURVEY* *FEDSTATS.* The Federal Interagency Council on Statistical Policy (FICSP) maintains this site to provide access to the full range of statistics and information produced by government agencies for public use. http://www.fedstats.gov *EDUCATION LINKS TO NCES SITE.* *U.S. National Archives and Record Administration (NARA), Center for Electronic Records* provides access to records of the U.S. government that have been accessioned in the National Archives in electronic format. http://merrimack.nara.gov/nara/electronic/	Arranged in a fixed-field format, the data are accessible for analysis by statistical packages such as SPSS, SAS or BMDP; or by database management programs such as dBase or Access. Data files and reports, not available on line, can be ordered with a fee. Text and numeric databases are available from Federal agencies for policy analysis and general research. Web-based tools allow browsers to view predefined reports and generate custom tables with data obtained through searches and queries of summary and micro-data files. Copies of electronic records at NARA are available in a variety of electronic formats. In general, NARA's electronic records cannot be accessed on-line via the Internet
Related data sources in the academic sector	*Comprehensive and easy access*
The *COLUMBIA ELECTRONIC DATA SERVICE* (EDS), a joint operation of AcIS (Academic Information Systems) and Columbia University libraries.. http://www.columbia.edu/acis/eds	Presented in alphabetical order, data sources in academic sector (left-hand column) are selected simply as samples. No attempt is made to promote any particular institutions.

Related data sources in the Academic sector	*Comprehensive and easy access*
INTEGRATED PUBLIC USE MICRODATA SERIES (IPUMS), located at Minnesota Population Center, University of Minnesota, provide census micro-data for social and economic research. http://www.ipums.umn.edu/ The *INTER-UNIVERSITY CONSORTIUM FOR POLITICAL AND SOCIAL RESEARCH* (ICPSR), located in the Institute for Social Research at the University of Michigan, is a membership-based, not-for-profit organization serving member colleges and universities in the United States and abroad. http://www.icpsr.umich.edu/ *INTERNATIONAL ARCHIVE OF EDUCATION DATA* (IAED) include primarily NCES data. *ROPER CENTER*, located at University of Connecticut, is the library of public opinion data. http://www.ropercenter.uconn.edu/ *UNIVERSITY OF CALIFORNIA DATA ARCHIVE AND TECHNICAL ASSISTANCE* (UC DATA), a part of the University's Survey Research Center, is the principal archive of computerized social science and health statistics information at UC–Berkeley. http://ucdata.berkeley.edu/	Common features of these selected data sources in the academic sector include: • Maintain collections of machine readable files and offer numerical data resources and related service. • On-line searching of data resources is available. • Electronic data are available in a variety of formats. • Data are related to social science and humanities in which education data are included. • Data access tools, data analysis systems, and related documentation such as codebook are available for locating data and performing on-line analyses. • Some data are available on-line and ready to be downloaded. • Direct links are available to data libraries and data archives for publicly available data, also to data organizations that sell and distribute data for a fee. • Many publicly available databases are accessible to anonymous users while some are accessible only to authorized users. • Some sources provide statistical tables and printed reports while others focus on providing raw data. • Regardless of various designs and individually specific purposes these electronic data services all contribute to promoting academic research by facilitating the use of secondary analysis materials.

Note. The information for these selected sources of available (secondary) data are mainly derived from the web sites noted in the table.

Chapter 15

Analyzing Categorical Data with Chi-Square and Log-Linear Models[*]

Jay W. Rojewski

The analysis of categorical data has relied heavily on the traditional chi-square test. While useful chi-square is limited to testing single pairs of variables. Over the past several decades a powerful extension to chi-square analysis, able to analyze associations among several variables simultaneously, has been developed. This multivariate extension known as log-linear analysis offers opportunities for investigators to analyze and interpret categorical data with greater precision than previously possible. In this chapter I review the major steps involved in chi-square and log-linear analysis. First, formulas used by chi-square and log-linear analyses are presented. Then, log-linear analysis is explained and demonstrated using data from the National Education Longitudinal Study of 1988 (NELS:88; 1996). Log-linear analysis offers opportunities to investigate and interpret categorical data with greater precision than previously possible, especially as it relates to the examination of interaction effects.

Traditionally, chi-square tests have been recommended as the most appropriate statistical procedure for analyzing categorical variables that are exclusive, independent, and exhaustive, that is, either nominal or

---

[*]A slightly different version of this chapter was originally published as Rojewski, J. W., & Bakeman, R. (1997). Applying log-linear models to the study of career development and transition of individuals with disabilities. *Exceptionality, 7*, 169-186. Adapted with permission of the publisher.

ordinal (Minium, 1978; Wickens, 1988). Nominal data refers to grouping on the basis of observed, qualitative distinctions such as gender, racial/ethnic background, or type of school program. Ordinal data refers to rank-ordered data where the assignment of numbers reflects degree rather than kind, such as incremental categories of income, educational aspirations, or age group.

Chi-square tests provide either a measure of [1] the goodness of fit for the distribution of a single variable when compared to some theoretical distribution, or [2] the association or relationship (i.e., a test of independence) between two variables. This is done by comparing observed frequencies with frequencies that would be expected or theorized on the basis of *a priori* hypotheses (Bakeman & Robinson, 1994; Kennedy, 1992; Minium, 1978). Large discrepancies between observed and expected frequencies result in large chi-square statistic values, which indicate that a poor fit or significant association exists. As a result, the null hypothesis of independence is rejected.

Green (1988) observed that while traditional chi-square tests are extremely useful in analyzing categorical data, they are limited to testing a single pair of variables at a time, regardless of the number of variables involved. Thus, the traditional test is not able to *simultaneously* examine the potential interactions among multiple variables. Analysis of categorical data has been limited to this two-dimensional approach to significance testing (Kennedy, 1992). However, in recent years a powerful extension to traditional chi-square analysis, able to analyze associations among several variables, has been developed. This extension is known as hierarchical log-linear analysis and can be viewed as the multivariate equivalent of the traditional two-dimensional chi-square test. The advantage of log-linear techniques over conducting multiple chi-square tests is that both main and interaction effects of categorical variables can be analyzed simultaneously (Marascuilo & Busk, 1987). Results are structured and interpreted in a hierarchical fashion starting with the highest order effect (saturated model) and then proceeding to lower-order effects.

Fundamentals and Formulas

The logic used in chi-square analysis is fairly straightforward. For two-dimensional models a set of observed frequencies are compared to a corresponding set of expected frequencies that are calculated by estimating cell values under the null hypothesis. If observed values are close to the expected ones then the null hypothesis is deemed true. The fit of observed to expected may be assessed with the Pearson chi-square statistic, which is symbolized by χ^2. Wickens (1988) noted that "in essence, χ^2 is an adjusted sum of the squared differences between observed and expected frequencies. Large values indicate big discrepancies between the two sets of frequencies, and small values indicate a close fit" (p. 19). The formula for calculating the Pearson chi-square statistic for a two-dimensional table is $\chi^2 = E\ (f_{ij} - F_{ij})^2\ /\ F_{ij}$ where i represents the ith row, j represents the jth column, f represents observed (actual) frequencies, and F represented expected frequencies. Expected frequencies are calculated using the formula $F_{11} = n_i n_j\ /\ n$ where i represents the i marginal (row) frequency and j represent the j marginal (column) frequency. Finally, since the value of the χ^2 statistic is tied to the number of discrepancies involved in the calculation, the degrees of freedom (df) associated with a particular χ^2 value must also be considered. In a four-fold (2 x 2) contingency table, df is calculated with the formula $df = (r - 1)(c - 1)$ where r refers to the number of rows (levels of the first variable) and c represents the number of columns (levels of the second variable). Residuals—differences between observed and expected frequencies—are often examined when statistically significant χ^2 values are obtained.

Several points must be made regarding any discussion of chi-square formulas. First, the formula for calculating expected frequencies is correct only for two-dimensional tables and only when structural zeros are not present. Structural as opposed to random zeros occur when "certain cells are excluded from consideration. These vacancies may be intrinsic to the phenomenon being studied or may be part of a hypothesis under test" (Wickens, 1989, p. 12). Second, it is important to remember that for fairly simple models, like a two-dimensional one, expected frequencies and corresponding degrees of freedom can be calculated using the formulas provided. However, complex chi-square and likelihood-ratio chi-square models require *iterative* procedures that rely on the speed and accuracy of computer calculations.

A second statistic used to assess goodness of fit is the likelihood-ratio chi-square, symbolized by G^2. The formula for calculating it is $G^2 = 2\ \Sigma\ [(f_{ij})\ (\log f_{ij}/F_{ij})]$, where log references the natural logarithm (i.e., logs to the base e, where e is approximately 2.718). Both χ^2 and G^2 are distributed approximately as chi-square, but for technical reasons G^2 is usually preferred for log-linear analyses. Technically, analyses of frequency tables, whether two or some higher dimension, could use either χ^2 or G^2. Log-linear analysis typically uses G^2 because it can be used for hierarchical tests. The difference between two estimates of chi-square are distributed as chi-square with degrees of freedom equal to the difference between the degrees of freedom for the two estimates if the two estimates are likelihood-ratio chi-squares but not if they are Pearson chi-square. For small samples Pearson chi-squares are usually better estimates. This is one reason why χ^2 and not G^2 has traditionally been taught to social scientists and appears in most introductory statistics textbooks.

A 2 x 2 x 3 Contingency Table (2 Independent and 1 Response Variable)

For illustrative purposes I take data from one of my studies that examined whether the occupational aspirations of early adolescents differ on the basis of gender and postsecondary transition path (i.e., employment- or college-bound) from school to adult life. While basic answers to questions like this have a number of benefits. First, possible precursors to the discouraging postsecondary attainment experienced by many individuals might be identified in the early stages of preparing for adult life. Second, information could guide counselors and educators in developing and targeting career development and work preparation programs for these segments of the student population. Finally, answers to this general question can provide a better understanding of how youths view, plan for, and begin to execute the transition from school to adult life.

Assuming that a sound theoretical framework exists, three categorical variables are included in this analysis—gender, transition path, and occupational aspirations. The variables of *gender* and *transition path* each possess two possible outcomes: male or female, and employment-bound (entering the workforce immediately upon high school graduation) or college-bound (entering some type of postsecondary education immediately upon high school graduation), respectively. The third variable, occupational *aspirations,* can be categorized in different ways. I have often used three categories that reflect low, moderate, and high levels of prestige.

To determine whether differences exist in occupational aspirations, separate two-dimensional chi-square analyses could be performed to compare the occupational aspirations of adolescents on the basis of gender and transition path. This approach is, in some ways, analogous to using several one-way analysis of variance (ANOVA) procedures for interval-level data rather than employing a factorial design. However, the possible interactive effects of gender and transition path on one another are ignored; each analysis would be interpreted independently of the other. Since past research has indicated a possible interactive effect between these two variables, an analysis that considers this effect would be desirable. For nominal or ordinal data an equivalent of an ANOVA factorial design is log-linear analysis. Data in Table 15.1, taken from the first follow-up phase of the National Education Longitudinal Study of 1988 (NELS:88; 1996), is used to illustrate the major steps in analyzing a 2 (gender) x 2 (transition path) x 3 (occupational aspirations) contingency table using log-linear analysis.[2]

TABLE 15.1
Aspirations of Early Adolescents by Gender and Transition Path

Groups	Occupational aspiration categories[a]						Total
	Low prestige		Moderate prestige		High prestige		
	n	%[b]	*n*	%	*n*	%	
Work-bound							
Male	176	8.7	1,134	56.1	713	35.2	2,023
Female	404	22.9	442	25.0	921	52.1	1,767
College-bound							
Male	86	4.6	663	35.1	1,142	60.4	1,891
Female	259	10.4	435	17.4	1,809	72.3	2,503
Total	925		2,674		4,585		8,184

[a]Occupational aspirations were assessed by asking adolescents to indicate the job or occupation they expected to have at 30 years of age. Questionnaires listed 17 distinct occupational categories. For analysis, occupational categories were collapsed into three groups reflecting high, moderate, and low levels of education, prestige, and status attributed to these occupations. [b]Percentages reflect _row_ totals and may not total 100% due to rounding error.

Model Specification

Since development of log-linear techniques in the 1970s, the primary focus of analysis has been on model building, or *symmetrical* analysis. Symmetrical log-linear analysis is used to study simple and interactive relationships or association between two or more variables. This is accomplished by testing the discrepancy between observed and expected frequencies for a series of models containing various combinations of the variables of interest. Models are constructed in a hierarchical fashion and presented in a forward-addition manner. "Models are hierarchical in the sense that if a higher-order term appears in a model, its corresponding lower-order relatives also appear in the model . . . . each ensuing model contains all terms in prior models plus the addition of a 'new' term" (Kennedy, 1988, pp. 7-8).

Hierarchical log-linear models refer "to a series of nested models in which successively more complex models incorporate all terms included in less complex ones" (Bakeman & Robinson, 1994, p. 28). A number of models are specified from which expected cell frequencies can be calculated. Expected frequencies are used, in turn, to calculate likelihood-ratio chi square (G^2) statistics. Successively complex models take into account additional information, thus imposing additional constraints on the cell frequencies. The model that contains all terms is called the *saturated* model which generates expected frequencies that are identical to the observed frequencies. The goal is to identify "the simplest model (i.e., the model with the fewest terms) that generates expected frequencies not too discrepant from the observed ones" (Bakeman & Robinson, p. 29).

Typically, in symmetrical analysis of a three-way contingency table a series of seven hierarchical models might be considered. The most complex or saturated model contains seven terms, and 3 one-way terms. The series of seven models is formed by removing successive terms, beginning with the most complex. The hierarchical nature of log-linear models and the additive properties of the G^2 statistic allow models to be compared to one another. Comparisons can determine the amount of loss in fitting the observed data; attempts are made to determine which of the competing models produce expected frequencies most consistent with the observed data. The greater the increase in G^2, the poorer the fit (Bakeman & Robinson, 1994; Kennedy, 1988).

The use of log-linear analysis in a hypothesis testing or *asymmetrical* mode has also been advocated. When using a hypothesis testing approach two sets of variables are established—independent and dependent. This approach is quite similar to ANOVA where hypothesis testing is the norm, except that response in log-linear analysis is measured categorically and the absence of an error term requires that log-linear analysis compare differential models to determine statistical significance (Marascuilo & Busk, 1987). Asymmetrical log-linear analysis focuses on independent variables related to the dependent variable, not the interrelationships of independent variables to each other (Kennedy, 1988; Wilson & Moore, 1989). As a result, only four not seven hierarchical models are considered.

The distinction between symmetric and asymmetric analysis is, of course, broader than log-linear analysis and refers to the way investigators think about their variables not to differences in the analyses themselves. This is an important point; conceptual differences between symmetrical and asymmetrical models do not infer different analysis options. In fact, technical aspects of log-linear analysis are the same, regardless of the designated relationship of variables: A hierarchic analysis is conducted that begins with a saturated model and deletes terms until a fitting model is found. An asymmetrical analysis stipulates that all models that include the designated outcome variable need to be analyzed. The interaction between independent variables (e.g., gender and transition path) is not usually of direct interest, but all other effects are conditional on it. Therefore, it is included in all models.

Table 15.2 presents the models generated to examine the effects of gender and transition path on occupational aspirations. Using bracket notation (Fienberg, 1980), let [G] represent gender, [T] represent transition path, and [A] represent occupational aspirations. A three-factor analysis, such as the one depicted here, is analogous to a two-factor ANOVA in that the single and combined effects of two variables are examined on a third, outcome, variable. Each model depicted in Table 15.2 is used to generate different expected cell frequencies and residuals expressed in natural logarithms which are used to calculate corresponding G^2 statistics (Kennedy, 1988). The terms presented in each model impose certain constraints on the expected frequencies. This is critical in that the goal of log-linear analysis is to find "the simplest model that still generates expected frequencies not too discrepant from those observed" (Bakeman & Robinson, 1994, p. 62).

A search for the simplest fitting model, the goal of log-linear analysis, begins with a saturated model and ends with the simplest model that makes sense. Bakeman and Robinson (1994) observed that

in principle, searching for a fitting model is straightforward. We begin with the saturated model. Although it is the most complex model possible, we know it fits the observed data. Next we examine simpler and simpler models until we find one that generates expected frequencies that do not fit those observed, as assessed with a chi-square goodness of fit test. Then we retreat to the previous model. . . because it is the simplest model that nonetheless fits the data. (p. 50)

TABLE 15.2
Asymmetrical Log-linear Models for a Three-way Contingency Table

Model	Observed marginal fitted by model
(5)	[GTA]
(4)	[GT] [GA] [TA]
(3)	[GT] [GA]
(2)	[GT] [TA]
(1)	[A] [GT]

Note. A useful feature of the model building in log-linear analyses is adherence to the hierarchy principle. "Models are hierarchical in the sense that if a higher-order term appears in a model (e.g., AC), its corresponding lower-order relatives also appear in the model (e.g., A and C)" (Kennedy, 1988, p. 7). Here, Models 2 and 3 are not hierarchical, in the sense that one is not a subset of the other. Therefore, two hierarchies of the models are possible: The first hierarchy is (5)-(4)-(3)-(1) and the second is (5)-(4)-(2)-(1). Since two options are available, a decision must be made about the specific hierarchy to be analyzed. The most desirable solution is to declare, *a priori*, interest in one of the hierarchies and conduct the analysis accordingly. This decision should be based on previous research literature and researcher interest (Wilson & Moore, 1989).

The saturated model includes all possible terms: GTA, GT, GA, TA, G, D, A. The [GTA] term represents the saturated model and implies the inclusion of all six other terms. As a result it is the most complete or complex model for a particular table. This particular model contains none of the restrictions imposed by simpler models. The saturated model has expected frequencies that match observed ones perfectly, and produces a likelihood chi square ratio equal to zero with 0 degrees of freedom. In this example, Table 15.1 presents the expected frequencies associated with the saturated model. Working backward from the saturated model each subsequent model becomes less complex in nature and includes one fewer term, accounting for less of the information and allowing for greater degrees of freedom.

Once the saturated model is examined, the next step is to remove the highest order term associated with the model, in this case [GTA]. The resultant model implies a fundamental association between each pair of factors—[GT][GA][TA]. In this case, the model can also be viewed as containing the combined effects of gender and disability status on occupational aspirations. Eliminating the [GTA] term imposes some constraint on how the marginal frequencies can vary and results in expected frequencies that differ from the saturated model. Table 15.3 provides the differences between observed and expected frequencies, also known as raw residuals. A raw residual is calculated using the formula $d = x - m$, where d symbolizes the difference (raw residual), x refers to an observed cell frequency, and m refers to the expected cell frequency. If the model fits the observed data well, residuals are small in value and do not have any discernible pattern (Norusis, 1988).

The next step is to remove one additional term, either transition path by aspirations or gender by aspirations, from the model. Based on theory and researcher interest, a decision was made, *a priori*, to remove the [TA] term (association between transition path and aspirations) from the model first. This would provide information about the direct effect of transition path on occupational aspirations. Model 2, [GT][GA], shows the raw residuals for the model when the [TA] term is removed. If the goodness of fit statistic is significant, the search for the best-fitting models ends. However, nonsignificant, then additional terms are systematically removed until significance is reached.

Since we are concerned about whether the two research variables, gender and transition path, affect occupational aspirations a base model is also defined. Model 1 represents the base model which consists of all observed factors and is the simplest of all models for a particular table. In this case the base model also indicates that the marginal frequencies for the gender-transition path association are fixed to account for the designation of occupational aspirations as the outcome variable. The base model, [A][GT], requires that expected frequencies reflect the cross-classification of gender and transition path. These remain in the base model because this cross-classification is due to the sampling design and so is not of interest—in effect, it is part of the procedure. Notice that the [GT] term is included in all models.

Log-Linear Results

As with two-dimensional chi-square analysis expected frequencies generated by each model in a log-linear analysis are compared, in turn, to the observed frequencies. Differences between observed expected frequencies are assessed with a chi-square statistic known as the likelihood-ratio chi-square (G^2). One reason for preferring the G^2 statistic over χ^2 is that it can be partitioned into unique components that

TABLE 15.3
Raw Residuals of Adolescents' Occupational Aspirations by Gender and Transition Path for Asymmetrical Log-Linear Models

Groups	Occupational aspirations categories		
	Low prestige	Moderate prestige	High prestige
[GT][GA][TA] / Model 3			
Work-bound youth			
Male	− 1.8	+ 29.8	− 28.0
Female	+ 1.8	− 29.8	+ 28.0
College-bound youth			
Male	+ 1.8	− 29.8	+ 28.0
Female	− 1.8	+ 29.8	− 28.0
[GT][GA] / Model 2			
Work-bound youth			
Male	40.6	205.2	− 245.8
Female	129.6	79.1	− 208.7
College-bound youth			
Male	− 40.6	− 205.2	+ 245.8
Female	− 129.6	− 79.1	+ 208.7
[GT][A] / Model 1			
Work-bound youth			
Male	− 52.7	+ 473.0	− 420.4
Female	+ 204.3	− 135.3	− 68.9
College-bound youth			
Male	− 127.7	45.1	+ 82.6
Female	− 23.9	− 382.8	+ 406.7

Note. G = gender; T = transition path; A = occupational aspirations

have additive properties similar to sums of squares in ANOVA (Marascuilo & Busk, 1987; Wilson & Moore, 1989). Another statistic, ΔG^2 (delta G^2), is easily calculated and represents the difference between two G^2 or, more specifically, the importance of the term just deleted from the model.

Results of the log-linear analysis are presented in Table 15.4. The G^2 statistic for the [GTA] model, saturated model, equals 0 and has no degrees of freedom. Removing the [GTA] term from the model results in a small, nonsignificant reduction in fit, $G^2 = 9.3$, indicating that a simpler model is available to explain our data. We can conclude that there is no interaction between gender and transition path on career aspirations. Next, the [TA] term is deleted and results in a very large and statistically significant partial chi-square ($\Delta G^2 = 441.5$, $p < .01$). This significant deterioration in fit results in our accepting the [GT][GA][TA] model as the best fitting model. We can conclude that transition path affects career aspirations independent of gender (the TA term was required for a fitting model), and that gender affects career aspirations independent of transition path (the GA term was also required for a fitting model). If the partial chi-square (ΔG^2) had been nonsignificant when the [TA] term was removed, the [GA] term would be deleted. A significant partial chi-square at this stage would have indicated that the [GT][GA] model was the best fitting model, or that gender affected career aspirations but that transition status did not.

TABLE 15.4
Summary Table for Hierarchical Asymmetrical Log-Linear Analysis of Effects on Occupational Aspirations

Model	Q^2	ΔQ^2	G^2	df	Term deleted	ΔG^2	Δdf
[GTA]	1.00	—	0.0	0	—	—	—
[GT] [GA] [TA]	.99	.01	9.3	2	[TGA]	9.3	2
[GT] [GA]	.59	.40	450.8	4	[TA]	441.5	2
[GT] [A]	.00	.59	1106.2	6	[GA]	655.4	2

Note. To determine statistical significant $G^2_{crit} = 12.60$ at $p = .05^*$ level; 16.81 at $p = .01^{**}$ level for 6 degrees of freedom.

A unique feature of the model building used in log-linear analysis is adherence to the hierarchy principle. "Models are hierarchical in the sense that if a higher-order term appears in a model (e.g., AC), its corresponding lower-order relatives also appear in the model (e.g., A and C)" (Kennedy, 1988, p. 7). The specific order in which terms are deleted is decided, *a priori*, based on previous investigations, theory, and research interest (Wilson & Moore, 1989). In this particular example, I was interested in determining the effect of transition path first and then any additional effect of gender on aspirations.

The Q^2 statistic (Bakeman & Robinson, 1994) is also included in Table 15.4 and provides an assessment of the effect size or magnitude of a particular model. This statistic is an analog to the more familiar R^2 statistic used in multiple regression analysis. The Q^2 for a particular model is easily calculated using likelihood ratio chi-square statistics in the formula: $Q^2_{model} = G^2_{base} - G^2_{model} / G^2_{base}$. Knoke and Burke (1980) suggested that any model with a Q^2 greater than .90 provides an acceptable fit to the data even if the chi-square is significant. This is especially important to consider when extremely large data set are analyzed. In this example, Q^2 for the [GT][GA][TA] model = .99 which indicates that 99.0% of the variance is still explained when the interaction term [GTA] is deleted from the model.

Follow-Up Procedures

Once significant model effects have been identified, the next step is to conduct post hoc analysis to determine where specific differences exist. Post hoc analysis can be completed by comparing observed and expected frequencies and residuals if the independent and dependent variable are dichotomous (Kennedy, 1992). However, when one or more variables is polytomous, other methods are warranted. Several different post hoc analysis methods exist including comparison of two-way tables and residuals; winnowing out anomalous cells with structural zeros; examination of lambda parameter estimates, log odds and log odds ratios; and, forced comparisons that analyze partial chi-squares in a series of single degree of freedom tests (Bakeman & Quera, 1995; Bakeman & Robinson, 1994; Kennedy, 1988; Swafford, 1980; Wickens, 1988).

Residuals. Model complexity—for example, total number of dimensions contained in the contingency table—is one determinant of the appropriate follow-up method. Wickens (1988) suggested that the most direct post hoc analysis is to examine the deviation between observed and expected cell frequencies produced by the selected model to determine where the large discrepancies exist, these discrepancies are known as raw residuals. The raw residual is not by itself a useful measure because it is affected by overall counts and cannot be easily compared across tables. Therefore, raw residuals are transformed into standardized or adjusted residuals to alleviate this problem.

For 2 x 2 tables, standardized residuals are calculated using the formula:

$$s = x - m / \sqrt{m},$$

where s symbolizes the standardized residual, x refers to observed frequencies, and m refers to expected frequencies. Standardized residuals can be viewed as components of Pearson chi-square because the sum of squared standardized residuals equals χ^2. These statistics usually have lower absolute values than corresponding adjusted residuals resulting in a more conservative analysis. The formula for adjusted residuals is more complex than for standardized residuals. For a 2 x 2 table with no structural zeros the formula is:

$$z_{ij} = x_{ij} - m_{ij} / \sqrt{m_{ij}(1 - p_{i+})(1 - p_{+j})} \,,$$

where p_{i+} and p_{+j} are the probabilities of the ith row and jth column (Wickens, 1988). While both transformed residuals are acceptable, Bakeman and Robinson (1994) recommend the use of adjusted residuals because the values are larger than standardized residuals and its distribution is nearly normal (i.e., has a mean of 0, standard deviation of 1.0). Also in the case of a 2 x 2 table, "the absolute values of the four adjusted residuals will be equal, reflecting the equality of the raw residuals" (p. 23).

Claims of statistical significance are not used in post hoc analysis of residuals because log-linear models rarely meet ideal conditions. However, critical values are still established to judge the meaningfulness of transformed residuals. A residual value of absolute 1.96 is typically used to indicate $p < .05$ and an absolute value of 2.58 is used to indicate $p < .01$. These reflect significant z values found at the .05 and .01 levels for a normal distribution under ideal conditions.

Explicating main effects using example. In my example, log-linear analysis revealed significant main effects for transition path and gender. Since each of these main effects can be represented by a two dimensional table, the most straight-forward post hoc analysis is to explicate the main effects by collapsing the 2 x 2 x 3 table into two separate tables, T x A and G x A, each with its own set of observed and expected frequencies and residuals. If the best fitting model had contained interaction effects (a table with three or more dimensions), then a search for anomalous cells or a forced comparisons method might have been a more appropriate post hoc alternative. As a general rule each term in a fitted model suggests a collapsed table worth exploring. When a dimension of the collapsed table is two, a preferable strategy is to examine ways that the two profiles differ guided by the pattern of adjusted residuals.

Table 15.5 presents the adjusted residuals obtained for the transition path (T x A) and gender main effects (G x A), respectively. To analyze the transition path main effect, adjusted residuals are examined to, first, identify all residuals that are larger than the established critical value (i.e., 1.96 or 2.58), and second, to look for patterns in the deviations of the residuals. Based on these criteria, the profiles for work-bound and college-bound adolescents differed. First, the value of all three sets of residuals exceed the established critical values indicating the presence of meaningful differences. Since the T (work-bound–college-bound) and G (male–female) dimensions each have two levels, adjusted residuals will be the mirror image of one another; 1 degree of freedom, one piece of information. The sum of adjusted residuals for a dimension with 3 levels will equal 0 but have 2 degrees of freedom, a dimension with 4 level will have 3 degrees of freedom, and so on.

TABLE 15.5
Post Hoc Analysis: Observed Frequencies, Expected Frequencies, and Adjusted Residuals for Collapsed Two-Way Models

	Occupational aspirations categories		
	Low	Moderate	High
Transition path model (T x A)			
Work-bound group	+ 5.19	+ 13.70	– 15.74
College-bound group	– 5.19	– 13.70	+ 15.74
Gender model (G x A)			
Males	– 12.08	+ 19.34	– 10.47
Females	+ 12.08	– 19.34	+ 10.47

Next, observed frequencies are examined for differences (see Table 15.1). We find that work-bound youth are more likely to aspire to low (15.3% vs. 7.9%) and moderate (41.6% vs. 25.0%) prestige aspirations, while college-bound youths are more likely to aspire to high prestige aspirations than their work-bound learning peers (67.2% vs. 43.1%).

The main gender effect is also meaningful. Profiles for males and females differ at all three levels of aspiration based on adjusted residual values, each exceeding established criteria. Females are twice as likely to aspire to low (15.5% vs. 6.7%) and high prestige (63.9% vs. 47.4%) occupations. Conversely, male adolescents aspire to moderate prestige careers twice as often as females (45.9% vs. 20.5%).

Conclusions

Comparison of Log-Linear Analysis and ANOVA Results

The similarities between log-linear analysis and ANOVA were detailed earlier in this chapter but are worth noting a second time. Using our present example, a 2 (transition path) x 2 (gender) ANOVA model could be used—assuming that the dependant variable, occupational aspirations, was continuous—to examine the interaction effect of transition path and gender on aspirations. Like log-linear analysis, if the interaction effect is not statistically significant, each of the main effects can then be examined for possible difference. Descriptive data and effect size coefficients could be used to determine the practical significant of identified statistical differences.

In contrast, asymmetrical log-linear analysis starts with the specification of hierarchical models that allow for a sequential examination of the interaction effect and, if needed, main effects. Descriptive data—e.g., cell proportions, and adjusted residuals (standardized differences between observed and expected cell frequencies)—can be calculated and interpreted using critical z values.

Thus, despite procedural differences, results obtained from these two analyses are roughly equivalent. Major differences emerge when considering the conceptualization of the dependent, or response, variable, underlying assumptions of the generated statistics, and the interpretation of results. For ANOVA, occupational aspirations would be considered a continuous variable. In several studies, I have used a 4-digit socioeconomic index code (Stevens & Cho, 1985) that quantifies the prestige attributed to various occupations. Sums of squares represent the variability between individual SEI scores and group means. These scores can be used in calculating an F ratio that is compared to a critical value of F distributed according to appropriate degrees of freedom. Conversely, in log-linear analysis, occupational aspirations are arranged in categories based on education levels and occupational prestige. Hierarchical models are systematically examined using G^2 values to represent the goodness of fit of each model. Likelihood-ratio chi-square values were compared to critical values of χ^2 distributed with appropriate degrees of freedom. Residuals are calculated to determine specific differences between observed and expected cell distribution patterns.

Considerations in Selecting Log-Linear Analysis

I have promoted the positive benefits of using log-linear analysis and the accompanying likelihood-ratio chi-square: A unified, flexible technique that can simultaneously analyze multidimensional contingency tables. Although log-linear analysis offers several advantages over traditional chi-square testing, perhaps the most important advantage is the ability to analyze higher order interactions (Bakeman & Robinson, 1994; Baker, 1981; Burnett, 1983; Green, 1988; Marascuilo & Busk, 1987; Wickens, 1989). The inclusion of higher order interactions better reflects the multivariate nature of and complexities inherent in reality. Thompson (1994) suggested that given a complex world with multiple outcome and multiple possible causes of those outcomes, "it is critical that the full network of all possible relationships be considered simultaneously within the analysis" (p. 16).

Although log-linear analysis provides several unique advantages, researchers should also be aware of the potential limitations inherent in this multivariate technique. First, the perceived advantages and disadvantages of using categorical data rather than interval-data must be considered. Statistical texts often discourage the use of categorical data in educational research because of more limited sensitivity and statistical power resulting from less variability found in grouped data. In response, several researchers (Bakeman & Robinson, 1994; Kennedy, 1988) have countered that qualitative, or categorical, data constitute an important part of many educational research settings and should not be ignored. Wickens (1989) explained that it is inappropriate to think of categorical analyses as less powerful alternatives to ANOVA or multiple regression. He claimed that the characteristics of frequency data demand unique sets of hypotheses and procedures.

A related concern when considering log-linear analysis is the predominant focus of most statistical texts on traditional chi-square testing. In fact, relatively limited literature, accessible to average researchers, is available (Bakeman & Robinson, 1994; Kennedy, 1992, and Wickens, 1989, are notable exceptions). Baker (1981) criticized the nature of information available about log-linear analysis, noting that the inherent logic of G^2 has been obscured by the tendency for statisticians to describe the technique using a "bottom-up" formula-driven explanation, resulting in limited knowledge of the availability and potential of log-linear analysis.

Green (1988) asserted that a reason for the limited use of log-linear methods was due to limited understanding of the log-linear paradigm.

This represents a third potential problem for researchers wishing to utilize a log-linear approach.

> Model testing and comparison as a data-analytic strategy is generally less familiar. . . than is hypothesis testing. In hypothesis testing, one searches for a significant result—that is, for a null model that is rejected. In model testing, however, one searches for a model that can be retained as a plausible one for the data at hand and then interprets parameters that make a significant contribution to the model. (p. 20)

Adopting a model testing approach, rather than a traditional hypothesis testing approach, can pose problems. Model building and testing requires that researchers rely on substantive theory and hypotheses, developed *a priori*, to build hierarchical models or in logically connecting independent and response variables. Furthermore, a sound conceptualization of theory is essential for researchers to artfully employ likelihood-ratio model development and to successfully interpret results (Hinkle, McLaughlin, & Austin, 1984; Reshetar & Swaminathan, 1992; Saupe, 1991).

Researchers are faced with a somewhat bewildering array of possible post hoc analyses that can be employed to follow-up significant omnibus results. Until recently, post hoc analyses have relied heavily on model parameter estimates to locate and interpret significant effects. These are fairly cumbersome and difficult to interpret. Fortunately, recent attempts to clarify post hoc options should help to reduce this problem in the near future (see Hinkle et al., 1988; Kennedy, 1992; or Wickens, 1989, for additional information about the options available for post hoc analysis).

Finally, one additional analytical possibility should be mentioned. When a binary response variable and all predictor or independent variables are defined as categorical, then log-linear analysis is the most appropriate alternative. However, if some predictor variables are interval-scaled, then logistic regression should be used. Interested readers may wish to consult Menard (1995) for additional explanation.

References

Bakeman, R., & Quera, V. (1995). Log-linear approaches to lag-sequential analysis when conservative codes may and cannot repeat. *Psychological Bulletin, 118,* 272-284.

Bakeman, R., & Robinson, B. F. (1994). *Understanding log-linear analysis with ILOG: An interactive approach.* Hillsdale, NJ: Erlbaum.

Baker, F. B. (1981). Log-linear, logit-linear models: A didactic. *Journal of Educational Statistics, 6*(1), 75-102.

Burnett, J. D. (1983). Log-linear analysis: A new tool for educational researchers. *Canadian Journal of Education, 8,* 139-154.

Fienberg, S. E. (1980). *The analysis of cross-classified categorical data* (2nd ed.). Cambridge, MA: MIT Press.

Green, J. A. (1988). Log-linear analysis of cross-classified ordinal data: Applications in developmental research. *Child Development, 59,* 1-25.

Hinkle, D. E., McLaughlin, G. W., & Austin, J. T. (1984). Using log-linear models in higher education research. In B. D. Yancey (Ed.), *Applying statistics in institutional research* (New Directions for Institutional Research No. 58, pp. 23-41). San Francisco: Jossey-Bass.

Ingels, S. J., Dowd, K. L., Baldridge. J. D., Stipe, J. L., Bartot, V. H., Frankel, M. R., Owings, J., & Quinn, P. (1994). *National education longitudinal study of 1988: Second follow-up—Student component data file user's manual.* Washington, DC: U.S. Department of Education, National Center for Educational Statistics.

Kennedy, J. J. (1988). Applying log-linear models in educational research. *Australian Journal of Education, 32,* 3-24.

Kennedy, J. J. (1992). *Analyzing qualitative data: Log-linear analysis for behavioral research* (2nd ed.). New York: Praeger.

Knoke, D., & Burke, P. J. (1980). *Log-linear models* (University Paper Series on Quantitative Application in the Social Sciences, Series No. 07-020). Beverly Hills, CA: Sage.

Marascuilo, L. A., & Busk, P. L. (1987). Log-linear models: A way to study main effects and interactions for multidimensional contingency tables with categorical data. *Journal of Counseling Psychology, 34,* 443-455.

Menard, S. (1995). *Applied logistic regression analysis.* Thousand Oaks, CA: Sage.

Minium, E. W. (1978). *Statistical reasoning in psychology and education* (2nd ed.). New York: John Wiley & Sons.

Nichols, R. C. (1992). The national longitudinal studies: A window on the school-to-employment transition. In A. J. Paulter, Jr. (Ed.), *High school to employment transition: Contemporary issues* (pp. 49-60). Ann Arbor, MI: Prakken.

Norusis, M. J. (1988). *SPSS/PC+ advanced statistics v2.0.* Chicago: SPSS International.

Owings, J., McMillan, M., Ahmed, S., West, J., Quinn, P., Hausken, E., Lee, R., Ingels, S., Scott, L., Rock, D., & Pollack, J. (1994). *A guide to using NELS:88 data.* Washington, DC: U.S. Department of Education, National Center for Education Statistics.

Reshetar, R. A., & Swaminathan, H. (1992, April). *A comparison of the log-linear and weighted least squares approaches for the analysis of categorical data.* Paper presented at the annual meeting of the American Educational Research Association, San Francisco. (ERIC Document Reproduction Service No. ED 346 118)

Rojewski, J. W. (2000). Vocational aspirations, work-related experiences, and early career choice patterns of work-bound youth during early adolescence. *Manuscript submitted for publication.*

Saupe, J. L. (1991). *A spreadsheet for a 2 x 3 x 2 log-linear analysis.* Paper presented at the annual meeting of the Association for Institutional Research, San Francisco. (ERIC Document Reproduction Service No. ED 336 047)

Stevens, G., & Cho, J. H. (1985). Socioeconomic indexes and the new 1980 census occupational classification scheme. *Social Science Research, 14,* 142-168.

Swafford, M. (1980). Three parametric techniques for contingency table analysis: A nontechnical commentary. *American Sociological Review, 45,* 664-690.

Thompson, B. (1994). *Common methodology mistakes in dissertations, revisited.* Paper presented at the annual meeting of the American Educational Research Association, New Orleans, LA. (ERIC Document Service Reproduction No. ED 368 771)

Wickens, T. D. (1988). *Multiway contingency tables analysis for the social sciences.* Hillsdale, NJ: Erlbaum.

Wilson, M., & Moore, S. (1989). Desktop loglinear modeling. *Australian Journal of Education, 33,* 197-219.

Notes

1. The NELS:88 database is administered by the National Center for Educational Statistics, U. S. Department of Education, and represents a national probability sample of over 24,000 adolescents who have been followed at 2-year intervals since 1988. Data about selected schools and students has been collected from school administrators, parents, teachers, and students at each collection interval (Nichols, 1992; Owings et al., 1994). Additional details can be found in recent *National Education Longitudinal Study: 1988–94* (National Center for Educational Statistics, 1996) user's manuals and technical reports (e.g., Ingels et al., 1994; Owings et al., 1994).

2. Data for this example is from Rojewski (2000) which examined the early career choice patterns of adolescents based on gender and postsecondary transitional path.

Chapter 16

Top Ten Reasons Why Most Omnibus ANOVA *F*-Tests Should Be Abandoned*[*]

Stephen Olejnik and Brian Hess

This chapter examines the data analytic practices of researchers who published studies comparing population means in the *Journal of Vocational Education Research* from *1990* to 1996 as a way to discuss preferred comparative analysis strategies using analysis of variance (ANOVA). Typically, researcher(s) begin with an omnibus ANOVA F-test, followed with a post-hoc analysis when the initial hypothesis is rejected. The studies reviewed generally involved large sample sizes but do not report effect sizes or the use of confidence intervals in reporting findings; nor do they typically discuss data assumptions such as normality and homogeneity of variance. To improve current data analytic practice, we suggest that most omnibus ANOVA *F*-tests can be abandoned and replaced with contrasts and focused tests of specific hypotheses. Ten reasons are offered to justify this recommendation.

The simultaneous comparison of several population means in a single analysis using the omnibus ANOVA *F*-test is a common practice among researchers in the behavioral sciences (Edgington, 1974; Goodwin & Goodwin 1985). Several reasons for ANOVA's popularity exist including: [1] the ANOVA model can be used to analyze data from a wide variety of designs (e.g., single and multiple factors, randomized and

[*] Portions of this chapter were adapted with permission from Olejnik, S., & Hess, B. (1997). Top ten reasons why most omnibus ANOVA *F*-tests should be abandoned. *Journal of Vocational Education Research, 22,* 219-232.

nonrandomized designs, between-groups and within-group factors), [2] there is no theoretical limit on the number of populations that can be compared, [3] when three or more populations are being compared, the risk of a Type I error (rejection of the null hypothesis when it is true) is controlled, [4] ANOVA *F*-tests have a relatively long history of acceptance in the behavioral sciences, [5] most current researchers have received formal training in using and interpreting the procedure, and [6] computer software is readily available.

Educational researchers publishing in the *Journal of Vocational Education Research* (JVER), like their colleagues in other disciplines, have found the ANOVA model useful in analyzing their data when population means are compared. We reviewed past issues of the JVER, dating from 1990 to 1996, and found 19 articles that reported the ANOVA F-ratio to test one or more hypotheses. In our review, we found that [1] single factor designs were slightly more popular than factorial designs, [2] Fisher's LSD post-hoc test was the most popular follow-up procedure to a significant *F*-test, [3] average sample size was large (mean $N = 531.9$, median $N = 457$), [4] little attention was given to data assumptions; and [5] estimates of effect size and confidence intervals were never reported. Table 16.1 summarizes our analysis.

An alternative to the omnibus ANOVA *F*-test that is generally discussed in most ANOVA textbooks (e.g., Keppel, 1991; Maxwell & Delaney, 1990), but is rarely used in practice, is that of focused tests through contrast analysis. The omnibus ANOVA *F*-test is a diffuse test that compares several population means simultaneously. For the single factor design, the null hypothesis states that the population means from which the samples were selected are identical (H_0: $\mu_1 = \mu_2 = ... \mu_J$, $j = 1, ..., J$). A problem with the simultaneous hypothesis test is that when it is rejected, it is not immediately clear without further investigation what contributes to the rejection of the null hypothesis. A focused test, on the other hand, is one in which a specific research question is addressed by comparing only those populations of specific interest. That is, rather than testing whether several populations have identical means, a focused test determines whether one population mean differs from a second population mean or whether the mean of one set of populations differ from the mean of a different set of populations.

To answer focused questions, contrasts are formed. A sample contrast, $\hat{\psi}$, is a linear combination of sample group means, $\hat{\psi} = \sum c_j \overline{Y}_j$ that reflects the researcher's question. Where $\overline{Y}_j$ is the sample mean of group j, and c_j is the coefficient for sample mean of group j such that $\sum c_j = 0$.

TABLE 16.1
Summary of ANOVA Applications Published in the JVER (1990-1996)

Design		
One-way	8	
Two-way	5	
Three-way or more factorial	2	
Repeated measures	2	
Multivariate with univariate follow-up	2	
Multiple comparisons[a]		
Fisher LSD	5	
Multiple t-test	2	
Tukey HSD	2	
Scheffe	1	
Newman-Keuls	1	
Not appropriate	2	
No test	1	
Not specified	7	
Sample size	Mean N	Median N
One-way	633.2	468.5
Factorial	352.6	353.0
Computer programs		
SPSS	1	
SAS	2	
Unspecified	16	
Data assumptions		
No comment	15	
Variances	2	
Normality	2	
Effect size	0	
Confidence intervals	0	

[a]Some studies used more than one approach.

When group 1 and group 2 are compared, for example, $c_1 = 1$ and $c_2 = -1$ (or equivalently $c_1 = -1$ and $c_2 = 1$). To test the hypothesis that the population means from which the samples were selected are equal ($H_0: \mu_1 = \mu_2$ or $H_0: \mu_1 - \mu_2 = 0$), a test statistic can be computed by taking the ratio of the contrast to its standard error.

$$t = \frac{\hat{\psi}}{S_{\hat{\psi}}} = \frac{\sum c_j \overline{Y}_j}{\sqrt{S^2_{pooled}(\sum(c^2_j/n_j))}} \qquad (1)$$

The standard error of the contrast, $S_{\hat{\psi}}$, is a measure of the variability of a contrast over replications and can be computed as follows:

$$S_{\hat{\psi}} = \sqrt{S^2_{pooled}(\sum(c^2_j/n_j))} \qquad (2)$$

Where S^2_{pooled} is the average variance of observations within the J groups being compared. If sample sizes are equal, then S^2_{pooled} is the sum of the within-group variances divided by the number of groups ($S^2_{pooled} = \sum S^2_j/J$; where S^2_j is the variance of the observations in group j and J is the number of groups). If sample sizes are unequal, then the group variances must be weighted by the number of individuals in each group minus 1, $S^2_{pooled} = \sum(n_j - 1)S^2_j/(N - J)$, (n is the total sample size, $N = \sum n_j$). The interpretation of the computed test statistic, t, is discussed in a subsequent section (see Reason 2).

The primary purpose of this chapter is to discuss the benefits of focused testing over that of the omnibus ANOVA F-test. In our review of the studies published in the JVER over the past eight years, we found that all of the studies that compared group means, began with a general research question about the relationship between an explanatory (grouping) variable and some outcome (e.g., Is there a difference between vocational teachers, students, and administrators with respect to some measure?). None of the studies reviewed used focused tests. Interestingly, however, most of the studies that used the ANOVA also used a post-hoc analysis procedure to determine specific group differences. We believe that many of these studies could have benefited from a focused testing approach rather than the combination of omnibus testing followed by post-hoc testing.

We offer 10 reasons (there may be more) why focused testing should be considered in lieu of the omnibus ANOVA F-test. Although we recognize that there are legitimate situations where the omnibus F-test is justified and even necessary, we believe that those contexts are relatively limited (e.g., higher order interactions, exploratory research). In the tradition of the contemporary late night television talk show host David Letterman and his top ten lists, we begin by delineating these reasons from least important (Reason 10) to most important (Reason 1). Although some may disagree with our ranking, we hope that most will agree with our conclusion that most omnibus ANOVA *F*-tests can and should be abandoned and replaced with focused tests.

Reason 10: Focused Tests via Contrasts are Easy to Compute and Understand

Equation (1) shows that the computation of the test statistic for a focused test only involves basic descriptive statistics: sample means, sample variances, and sample sizes. These statistics are the foundation of quantitative analyses and should be routinely examined and reported by researchers. In our review of the 19 articles in JVER that used the ANOVA *F*-test, 17 (89%) of the studies provided group means, 8 studies (42%) reported group standard deviations, and, in most studies, it was difficult to determine the number of individuals (n) per group. Although many researchers publishing in the JVER have chosen not to report this basic information, the basic descriptive statistics can be easily computed.

Contrasts are easy to understand because they generally require no greater knowledge of statistics than what is typically presented in an introductory statistical methods course. Further, for most problems these calculations can be performed with the aid of an inexpensive handheld calculator. The only difficult aspect of focused testing is the determination of the appropriate coefficients. But even here, the coefficients are a direct result of the researcher's question. If the researcher can clearly state a research question, a contrast can be formed and a focused hypothesis tested.

The omnibus ANOVA *F*-test, on the other hand, is neither intuitively obvious nor easy to compute particularly when sample sizes are unequal. Some researchers find it difficult to understand why variances (mean square between and mean square within groups) are computed when the interest is in comparing the population means. Further, the calculation of the omnibus *F*-test generally requires computer software and in a factorial design when sample sizes differ, several approaches have been suggested for computing the test statistic (see Keppel, 1991, pp. 288-293). Choosing among the alternatives is often confusing even to experienced researchers.

Reason 9: Focused Tests are Very Flexible

Focused tests through the examination of contrasts are very flexible. The simplest and easiest type of contrast is a comparison between two means (pairwise contrast) but the general form described above can incorporate multiple groups in what are called complex contrasts. For example, a researcher might be interested in comparing the mean of first year and second year students with the mean of teachers and administrators on an outcome measure of interest. This could be achieved by assigning the appropriate coefficients to the respective groups. In the present example, the following coefficients might be used: $c_1 = .5, c_2 = .5, c_3 = -.5, c_4 = -.5$. In a factorial design where two or more explanatory variables are being studied, the interaction between factors can be examined with a complex contrast. For example, in a 2 x 3 factorial design where the two level factor is, say, gender (male = 1, female = 2) and the three level factor is an intervention factor (treatment A = 1, treatment B = 2, and control = 3), the question of whether the difference between treatment A and the control is the same for males and females can be answered using the following coefficients: $c_{11} = 1, c_{13} = -1, c_{21} = -1$, and $c_{23} = 1$ ($c_{12} = 0, c_{22} = 0$). Where the first subscript represents the level of the gender factor and the second subscript refers to the level of the intervention factor. For more complex designs, higher order interaction tests can be computed using the appropriate coefficients (see Rosenthal & Rosnow, 1985, pp. 24-39).

Focused testing is not limited to the comparison of independent groups. Contrasts involving repeated measures can also be evaluated. The computation of the contrast is the same as that presented previously but the standard error must take into consideration the lack of independence between levels of the repeated measures. The dependence between the measures is considered when difference scores, based on the contrast, are computed for each individual. In the case of a pretest-posttest design, the pretest score is subtracted from the posttest score for each individual. If the design is a pretest-posttest-delayed posttest and a comparison between the pretest and the average of the posttest measures (posttest and delayed posttest) is of interest, then the pretest score is subtracted from the average of the posttest and delayed posttest scores ($c_1 = -1, c_2 = .5$, and $c_3 = .5$) for each individual. The standard error is computed by taking the square root of the ratio of the variance of the difference scores to the number of individuals in the sample $S_{\hat{\varnothing}} = \sqrt{S_{dif}/N}$. Keselman and Keselman (1993) discuss the procedure where there are grouping variables along with the repeated measures factor (mixed model or split-plot design).

Focused tests can also be used when multiple response variables are viewed as reflecting a single construct. In such cases, a multivariate analysis is appropriate. Multivariate contrasts are computed and tested in a way similar to univariate contrasts when only one response variable is examined. The difference between the two approaches is that the multivariate procedure considers vectors of outcomes and the standard error of the contrast reflects the correlation between the outcome measures. For a discussion of multivariate contrasts see Huberty (1994, pp. 196-200). Two studies that we reviewed in JVER used MANOVA *F*-tests but when the multivariate hypotheses were rejected the authors followed with a series of omnibus univariate *F*-tests, thereby ignoring the interrelationship among the response variables.

Reason 8: Contrasts Can Examine Trends in the Data

The omnibus ANOVA *F*-test for the single factor design tests the hypothesis that the populations from which the samples were selected have identical means. When the explanatory variable is quantitative (e.g., years in a program), then the nature of the relationship between the quantitative explanatory and response variable can be examined in greater detail through a series of focused tests. Specifically, investigators can determine whether the relationship is linear, quadratic, cubic, or perhaps even a more complex relationship. The test for trend can be achieved by selecting the appropriate coefficients for a specific relationship. For example, suppose a researcher is interested in students' level of satisfaction of a vocational program over a span of four years. For a linear trend involving four populations, the coefficients are $c_1 = -3$, $c_2 = -1, c_3 = 1, c_4 = 3$. For a quadratic trend, the coefficients are $c_1 = 1, c_2 = -1, c_3 = -1, c_4 = 1$. The same coefficients would be used whether the four measures are obtained from a longitudinal study of repeated observations from the same sample of individuals or a cross-sectional study of a sample from each of four populations taken at a single point in time. Most textbooks presenting analysis of variance models provide the appropriate coefficients for different relationships (e.g., Keppel, 1991, p. 520; Maxwell & Delaney, 1990, p. 749).

The omnibus ANOVA *F*-test cannot test the hypothesis on trend, but the sums of squares between groups can be divided into independent components to investigate the nature of the relationship between the quantitative explanatory variable and the outcome. The F-tests for the separate components are equivalent to the focused tests that we advocate.

Reason 7: Confidence Intervals Can be Obtained Using Contrasts

While hypothesis tests still dominate the analysis of data reported by behavioral scientists, there is increasing interest in reporting findings using interval estimates or confidence intervals. With a hypothesis test, researchers examine their data to decide whether there is either sufficient or insufficient evidence to reject the null hypothesis. Some (e.g., Cohen, 1990; Schmidt, 1992; Serlin, 1987) have argued that such dichotomous decisions do not advance the knowledge base of a discipline. Rather, they suggest that researchers should focus on reporting the actual magnitude of the differences and to report these differences in terms of intervals to acknowledge sampling errors. From their perspective, it is much more meaningful to report the magnitude of the difference rather than simply stating that there is a difference. A confidence interval is a range of values within which the population parameter being estimated is captured with stated probability (see Kirk, 1984 p. 322 for additional interpretations). The upper limit of this range is obtained by adding to the contrast value the product of the standard error and the appropriate reference distribution for the contrast. Similarly, a lower limit for the interval is obtained by subtracting from the contrast value the product of the standard error and the reference distribution. The upper and lower limits of the interval estimate are provided by the following:

$$\hat{\psi} \pm t_{df} S_{\hat{\psi}}.   \text{(3)}$$

Where t_{df} is the reference distribution for the contrast with df degrees of freedom. For example, a pairwise contrast may use the Student t distribution with $N - J$ degrees of freedom. The choice of reference distribution when the difference in population means is of interest depends on the method of controlling the Type I error rates which is discussed later (see Reason 2). If the hypothesized value for the contrast (H_0: $\psi = 0$) is not captured by the interval, then the null hypothesis can be rejected. In addition, the upper and lower limits of the interval provide useful information of the magnitude of the difference. Furthermore, the width—the difference between the upper and lower limits—of the interval provides some indication of the precision with which the difference in population means is estimated. A wide interval would indicate that the researcher has not estimated the effect very precisely and therefore its meaningfulness may be limited. None of the JVER articles reviewed reported confidence intervals. The omnibus ANOVA F-test cannot be used to provide interval estimation for a parameter and is, therefore, viewed as a serious limitation for this approach to data analysis.

Reason 6: Adjustments for Violations of Data Assumptions Can be Made

For a valid interpretation of the omnibus ANOVA F-test for between–groups research designs it is assumed that [1] individual units are independent of each other, [2] the population distributions of the response variable are normal, and [3] the variance of units within each population are equal. For repeated measures designs an additional assumption of sphericity is made—the variance of difference scores between all measures are equal for all differences. Violating the assumption of independence is very serious in all inferential statistics. When experimental units are not independent of each other two solutions are suggested: [1] aggregate individual units by computing means and use the mean score as the unit of analysis, or [2] use a hierarchical model (Bryk & Raudenbush, 1992) which considers the dependency between units. Nonnormality only becomes important when population distributions are extremely skewed. If the data are extremely nonnormal, a nonparametric procedure would be recommended or a normalizing transformation might be suggested (Kirk, 1995). Variance heterogeneity can be a serious threat to statistical validity even when sample sizes are equal (Wilcox, Carlin, & Thompson, 1986) but is particularly serious when sample sizes differ. When sphericity is violated, the actual risk of a Type I error can be substantially greater than the stated significance level when the unadjusted F-test is used.

Focused tests make the same assumptions as the between–group omnibus ANOVA F-test. However, when variances are heterogeneous, equation (1) can be modified to adjust variance differences. This adjustment, however, is only an approximate solution because the exact sampling distribution of the test statistic under variance heterogeneity is not known exactly. Even so, the approximation is quite good (Hsiung & Olejnik, 1994). The numerator remains the same but the standard error is computed using the separate group variances rather than pooling the group variances (Wilcox, 1987). Specifically, the standard error of the contrast is computed as:

$$S_{\hat{\psi}} = \sqrt{\sum(c^2{}_j S^2{}_j / n_j)}. \qquad (4)$$

The degrees of freedom for the test is computed as:

$$df = \frac{[\sum(c^2{}_j S^2{}_j / n_j)]^2}{\sum[(c^2{}_j S^2{}_j / n_j)^2 / (n_j - 1)]}. \qquad (5)$$

In the case of repeated measures designs, the sphericity assumption is not necessary for focused tests.

The majority of articles published in JVER within the past eight years failed to report information regarding assumptions (i.e., homogeneity of variances, normality, etc.). But 15 (78.9%) of the reviewed studies involved comparisons having unequal sample sizes to estimate the population means. In the worst case, one group involved over six times as many participants as another group with which it was being compared. When sample sizes differ by that much, it is better data analytic practice to use a procedure that does not rely on the assumption that the populations have equal variances. This can be easily done using contrasts and focused tests as described above.

The omnibus ANOVA F-test can also be adjusted for variance heterogeneity but the recommended procedure, the Welch-James approach (Hsiung, Olejnik, & Huberty, 1994; Lix, Keselman, & Keselman, 1996), is computationally intensive and has not been incorporated within major statistical packages. Focused tests provide a relatively easy solution to the problem of heterogeneous variances.

Reason 5: A More Interpretable Measure of Effect Size is Available

In addition to reporting statistical findings, several methodologists (e.g., Cohen, 1990; Schmidt, 1992) have recommended that researchers report some index of effect size. The rationale for this recommendation is that the null hypothesis states that the population means being compared are identical. Some (e.g., Cohen, 1994; Meehl, 1978) have argued that this is never true! The omnibus null hypothesis should always be rejected. The problem is that even trivial differences can be judged to be statistically significant if the sample size is large enough. Consequently, it has been argued (Richardson, 1996) that an index that reflects the meaningfulness of the difference should also be reported. When several populations are being compared simultaneously with the omnibus ANOVA F-test the most common measure of effect size is eta-squared or omega-squared (Stevens, 1990). Both indices can have values ranging between 0 and 1 and both reflect the proportion of variation in the response variable that is explained by the independent variable. While we feel that these measures of effect can be useful, they are generally not very meaningful to the typical researcher or practitioner. We believe the difficulty arises from the metric free status of these indices. That is, they are proportions that are independent of the outcome measures themselves. We prefer an index of effect that reports the findings that can be translated in terms of the measures taken. One such measure is the standardized mean difference. Cohen (1969) introduced this index in his text on power analysis and later was promoted by Glass (1976) in the development of meta-analysis. When two populations are compared, the difference between the sample means is divided by the pooled standard deviation ($([\overline{Y}_1 - \overline{Y}_2]/S_{pooled}$). The observed difference between group means are expressed in standard deviation units. Assuming the variability (standard deviation) of the populations is known, the difference between means can be interpreted in terms of the units on which they are being compared (e.g., items on a test, classroom attendance, number of tasks performed). If a treatment group trained to take the Scholastic Aptitude Test (SAT) outperforms a control group on the verbal portion of the test by a half standard deviation, then we can conclude that intervention increased test performance by 50 points. A 50 point difference is likely to be more meaningful to someone who uses the SAT as a criterion for admission to a college or university than to say that the treatment condition variable explained 6% of the variation in test performance.

Alternatively, Cohen (1988) suggested that the standardized mean difference can also be interpreted in terms of the percent of overlap between two normal distributions. If a treatment group outperforms the control group by a half standard deviation, this difference can be interpreted to mean that 69% of the treatment group outperformed the mean of the control group. (Cohen suggested two other distribution overlap interpretations of the standardized mean difference that may also be useful.) Because focused tests examine population differences in the form of contrasts, the same type of interpretation is possible. Such an interpretation is likely to be more meaningful to applied researchers and practitioners than the proportion of variance explained by the independent variable that is typically reported when the omnibus ANOVA *F*-test is reported.

Reason 4: Accurate Determination of Sample Size

A major concern among methodologists over the years has been that researchers frequently conduct their investigations with far too few participants (Brewer, 1972; Cohen, 1962; Sedlmeier & Gigerenzer, 1989). Procedures for determining the minimum sample size for hypotheses involving several populations are described by Cohen (1988) and Kraemer and Thiemann (1987), as well many ANOVA textbooks (e.g., Keppel, 1991; Maxwell & Delaney, 1990; Stevens, 1990). For focused tests, Wahlsten (1991) suggests that sample sizes be determined as follows:

$$n = \frac{(Z_\alpha - Z_{1-\beta})^2 \sum c^2_j}{\delta^2_k} + 2. \tag{6}$$

Where Z_α and $Z_{1-\beta}$ are the values from the standard normal distribution identifying the percentile points corresponding to the acceptable risk of a Type I error (α), the desired power ($1-\beta$), and δ^2_k is the minimum effect size (standardized contrast difference (ψ/σ)) that is important to detect for contrast k. Wahlsten (1991) demonstrated that the sample size needed for testing the omnibus test may not be sufficient when testing specific contrasts. If specific differences in populations are important to detect, the appropriate sample size must be used or a Type II error may occur.

In our review of JVER articles, sample sizes were quite large but none of the authors provided a rationale for the sample size used. Using a large sample size is generally viewed positively, but too large a sample size may be a waste of limited resources and, more importantly, with large sample sizes it is likely that even trivial differences between populations will be judged to be statistically significant. Determination of appropriate sample size is an important aspect of planning an efficient and meaningful research study.

The sample size needed to test the omnibus hypothesis may not be sufficient to test all follow-up hypotheses of interest. Consequently, some true differences between populations may be missed. Further, the procedure for determining minimum sample size for a hypothesis test can be made easier if specific contrasts are identified. Power curves or sample size charts are needed to determine the sample size for the omnibus F-test, but sample sizes needed for testing specific contrasts can be determined by simply using the standard normal Z distribution. Using focused hypothesis tests makes the task of determining the appropriate sample size easy.

Reason 3: Provides a More Powerful Test

The omnibus ANOVA F-test, by its definition, is a nondirectional testing procedure. While the null hypothesis states that the population means are identical, the alternative hypothesis states that the population means are *not* identical. With a focused test it is possible to predict the direction of the difference. If theory suggests that directionality can be reasonably anticipated, this added knowledge can be used to test a directional hypothesis. The advantage of a directional test is that while the risk of a Type I error is the same as a nondirectional test, the risk of a Type II error (failing to reject the hypothesis when it is false) is reduced. A reduced risk of a Type II error means that statistical power is increased. By taking advantage of all of the information available, sensitivity to population differences can be increased without affecting the Type I error rate or changing the sample size, or population characteristics. Alternatively, for fixed power, the sample size needed for a directional hypothesis test will be smaller than the sample size needed for a nondirectional hypothesis test. For example, comparing two population which differ by at least a half standard deviation with statistical power equaling .80 with $\alpha=.05$ and using equation (6), a sample size of 48 individuals per group are needed. But with a directional test a sample size of 37 per group would be needed, which is a reduction of almost 23% of the nondirectional hypothesis sample size. Omnibus F-tests cannot take advantage of all the information available to the researcher so statistical power is lost.

Reason 2: Type I Errors Can be Controlled

An important advantage of the omnibus ANOVA F-test over repeated applications of t-tests is the control of the risk of making one or more Type I errors. If a t-test is applied with each hypothesis tested for statistical significance at the .05 level (α_H), then the familywise error rate (α_{FW}, the probability of at least one Type I error over the set of tests) is $1 - (1 - \alpha_H)^k$, where k is the number of hypotheses tested. If all pairwise comparisons are made among four populations then $k = 6$. Testing each hypothesis at the .05 level of significance, the familywise error rate, that is the probability of at least one Type I error in the set of six tests, equals: $\alpha_{FW} = 1 - (1 - .05)^6 = .265$. Most researchers are aware of this problem, so following the rejection of the omnibus null hypothesis, a post-hoc procedure is generally selected to control this problem. In our review of

JVER, we found that the Fisher LSD procedure was the most popular follow-up analysis to a significant F-test. This procedure will work if there are only three levels of the grouping variable (Levin, Serlin, & Seaman, 1994), but will not control the familywise error rate when more than three groups are compared (Keselman, Keselman, & Games, 1991). One approach to control this inflated Type I error rate problem is to adjust the criterion used for statistical significance. The Bonferroni method sets the criterion for statistical significance for each hypothesis tested by dividing the desired familywise error rate by the number of tests to be computed, $\alpha'_H = \alpha_{FW}/k$. The use of the Bonferroni method does not require the results of the omnibus ANOVA F-test. The problem with the Bonferroni method, however, is that when there are a substantial number of hypotheses tested the criterion for significance for an individual hypothesis can be very small. With the small significance criterion the statistical power for any individual hypothesis can be very low. Statisticians have been studying this problem for several years and have identified several alternatives to the Bonferroni method that can increase the power for individuals hypothesis tests. One simple alternative to the Bonferroni method was suggested by Holland and Copenhaver (1987). The Holland Copenhaver method requires the researcher to rank order the computed test statistic from largest to smallest ($t_{(1)},...,t_k$) and sets the criterion used to test each hypothesis as: $\alpha'_{H(i)} = 1 - (1 - \alpha_{FW})^{1/(k-i+1)}$, where k is the number of hypotheses to be tested and i is the rank order of the hypothesis. Further details on this and other enhancements to the Bonferroni adjustment are beyond the scope of this paper but Holland and Copenhaver (1988) review several of the improved Bonferroni-type adjustment procedures and Wilcox (1996) provides applications several of these alternatives. A disadvantage of enhancements to the Bonferroni method is that they cannot be used to determine confidence intervals.

Controlling the probability of making a Type I error is often the rationale given for using the omnibus ANOVA F-test. This argument is no longer a sufficient justification for adopting omnibus testing approach because, as discussed above, Type I errors can be controlled by adjusting the criteria used for significance testing.

Reason 1: Focused Tests Answer Research Questions

Last, but not least, the most important reason why we believe most omnibus testing can and should be abandoned is that omnibus tests simply do not address a research question that is of real interest to the researcher. As stated previously, the omnibus hypothesis test examines whether several population means are identical. We believe that most researchers have something more specific in mind when they design their investigations. If the general question was really of interest, then we would expect to find at least some researchers ending their analyses with the omnibus test. No one did. All researchers followed the significant omnibus test with a series of post-hoc tests to further understand what differences contributed to the rejection of the omnibus test. We believe that researchers design their investigations to answer specific questions (e.g., "Is intervention A better then no intervention?" or "Are any of the new methods better than the traditional method?") The analysis procedure used should reflect the true purpose of the investigation. Making all possible pairwise comparison among several populations does not require the omnibus test. An additional bonus to focused tests is that they require investigators to have a deeper understanding of the research literature and populations they are studying. Rather than taking a *shotgun* approach to research and just seeing what we hit, focused tests require the researcher to think, plan, and integrate theories, beliefs, and previous findings before they act. Such purposeful behavior can do nothing but help the discipline.

Conclusion

We believe that research should be theory based. That is, the goal of research is to test the validity of our beliefs and understandings of observed behaviors. A discipline like vocational education can only advance if the theories, on which its behavior is based, are critically examined. To test a theory requires researchers to make specific predictions regarding what is expected to be observed in specific contexts. These specific predictions are the foundations of focused tests. The omnibus test lacks the necessary specificity so it cannot contribute meaningfully to the advancement of a science. The current practice, therefore, of first simultaneously comparing several populations followed by post-hoc comparisons tests should be abandoned for most research. As we have argued in this paper, this strategy does not address a research question of interest to the investigator, statistical power can be lost, and results are not generally reported in a meaningful way. Focused tests, on the other hand, can address each of these concerns plus they are easily understood and can be applied in a wide variety of contexts. We suspect that a primary reason researchers begin by reporting omnibus tests is that all computer programs begin with these results and some packages (i.e., SPSS) do a poor job computing contrasts analyses in factorial designs. SAS, on the other hand, does an excellent job with contrasts analyses in the GLM procedure.

We hope we have provided a strong argument for focused tests and the abandonment of *most*, but not all, omnibus tests. So when might a researcher prefer the omnibus test? We can think of two situations where the omnibus test might be preferred. First, when little is known about the relationship among the variables of interest. That is, theory does not guide the research and few investigations involving the variables have been done in the past. Under these situations the research is primarily exploratory. There are times when this argument is legitimate, but we doubt that all research in JVER comparing population means is exploratory. Perhaps too many researchers may have used this argument in the past to justify their use of the omnibus test.

A second reason for using an omnibus test might be to test higher order interactions in complex factorial designs. Such tests might be used to examine complex relationships with the hope that the model can be simplified. We agree with Cohen (1990), that when it comes to research, simpler is better. A well designed and executed study involving limited variables is likely to make a greater contribution to a discipline than a complex, poorly controlled and designed study. Complex studies involving multiple explanatory and multiple response variables should generally be avoided. The sample size needed to adequately test a four or five factor interaction would likely be prohibitive and even with an adequate sample size a significant four or five factor interaction is likely to be noninterpretable.

To conclude, a word of caution should be given with regard to focused tests. Focused tests are planned at the beginning of the study and are generally limited to a small number of hypothesis tests. Sometimes interesting data patterns emerge as the data are analyzed. Changing the research questions and hypotheses tested to reflect these interesting patterns after examining the data is inappropriate. Such a strategy would likely result in serendipitous findings and an increase in Type I errors. If unanticipated patterns do emerge such results would have to be considered exploratory. Additional research could then be designed to specifically to investigate these patterns and focused tests could be used to test the specific hypotheses.

References

Brewer, J. K. (1972). On the power of statistical tests in the American Educational Research Journal. *American Educational Research Journal, 9,* 381-401.

Bryk, A. S., & Raudenbush, S. (1992). *Hierarchical linear models.* Newbury Park, CA: Sage.

Cohen, J. (1962). The statistical power of abnormal-social psychological research: A review. *Journal of Abnormal and Social Psychology, 65,* 145-153.

Cohen, J. (1969). *Statistical power analysis for the behavioral sciences.* New York: Academic Press.

Cohen, J. (1988). Statistical power analysis for the behavioral sciences (2nd ed.). Mahwah, NJ: Erlbaum.

Cohen, J. (1990). Things I have learned (so far). *American Psychologist, 45,* 1304-1312.

Cohen, J. (1994). The earth is round (p<.05). *American Psychologist, 49,* 997-1003.

Edgington, E. S. (1974). A new tabulation of statistical procedures used in APA journals. *American Psychologist, 29,* 25-26.

Glass, G. V. (1976). Primary, secondary, and meta-analysis of research. *Educational Researcher, 5,* 3-8.

Goodwin, L. D., & Goodwin, W. L. (1985). Statistical techniques in AERJ articles, 1979-1983: The preparation of graduate students to read the educational research literature. *Educational Researcher, 14,* 5-11.

Holland, B. S., & Copenhaver, M. C. (1987). An improved sequentially rejective Bonferroni test procedure. *Biometrics, 43,* 417-423.

Holland, B. S., & Copenhaver, M. D. (1988). Improved Bonferroni-type multiple testing procedures. *Psychological Bulletin, 104,* 145-149.

Hsiung, T. H., & Olejnik, S. (1994). Power of pairwise multiple comparisons in the unequal variance case. *Communications in Statistics–Simulation, 23,* 691-710.

Hsiung, T. H., Olejnik, S., & Huberty, C. J. (1994). Comment on a Wilcox test statistic for comparing means when variances are unequal. *Journal of Educational Statistics, 19,* 111-118.

Huberty, C. J. (1994). *Applied discriminant analysis.* New York: John Wiley & Sons.

Keppel, G. (1991). *Design and analysis: A researcher's handbook* (3rd ed.). Englewood Cliffs, NJ: Prentice Hall.

Keselman, H. J., & Keselman, J. C. (1993). Analysis of repeated measurements. In L. K. Edwards (Ed.), *Applied analysis of variance in behavioral science* (pp. 105-145). New York: Marcel Dekker.

Keselman, H. J., Keselman, J. C., & Games, P. A. (1991). Maximum familywise Type I error rate: The least significant difference, Newman-Keuls, and other multiple comparison procedures. *Psychological Bulletin, 110,* 155-161.

Kirk, R. E. (1984). *Elementary statistics* (2nd ed.). Monterey,CA: Brooks/Cole.

Kirk, R. E. (1995). *Experimental design: Procedures for the behavioral sciences* (3rd ed.). Monterey, CA: Brooks/Cole.

Kraemer, H. C., & Thiemann S. (1987). *How many subjects? Statistical power analysis in research.* Newbury Park, CA: Sage.

Levin, J. R., Serlin, R. C., & Seaman, M. A. (1994). A controlled, powerful multiple-comparison strategy for several situations. *Psychological Bulletin, 115,* 153-159.

Lix, L. M., Keselman, J. C., & Keselman, H. J. (1996). Consequence of assumption violations revisited: A quantitative review of alternatives to the one-way analysis of variance *F* test. *Review of Educational Research, 66,* 579-619.

Maxwell, S. E., & Delaney, H. D. (1990). *Designing experiments and analyzing data.* Belmont, CA: Wadsworth.

Meehl, P. E. (1978). Theoretical risks and tabular asterisks: Sir Karl, Sir Ronald, and the slow progress of soft psychology. *Journal of Consulting and Clinical Psychology, 46,* 806-834.

Richardson, J. T. E. (1996). Measures of effect size. *Behavior Research Methods, Instruments, & Computers, 28,* 12-22.

Rosenthal, R., & Rosnow, R. L. (1985). *Contrast analysis: Focused comparisons in the analysis of variance.* Cambridge, UK: Cambridge University Press.

Schmidt, F. L. (1992). What do data really mean? Research findings, meta-analysis, and cumulative knowledge in psychology. *American Psychologist, 47,* 1173-1181.

Sedlmeier, P., & Gigernzer, G. (1989). Do studies of statistical power have an effect on the power of studies? *Psychological Bulletin, 105,* 309-316.

Serlin, R. C. (1987). Hypothesis testing, theory building and philosophy of science. *Journal of Counseling Psychology, 34,* 365-371.

Stevens, J. (1990). *Intermediate statistics: A modern approach.* Hilsdale, NJ: Erlbaum.

Wahlsten, D. (1991). Sample size to detect a planned contrast and a one degree of freedom interaction effect. *Psychological Bulletin, 110,* 587-595.

Wilcox, R. R. (1987). *New statistical procedures for the social sciences: Modern solutions to basic problems.* Hilsdale, NJ: Erlbaum.

Wilcox, R. R. (1996). *Statistics for the social sciences.* San Diego: Academic Press.

Wilcox, R. R., Carlin, V. L., & Thompson, K. L. (1986). New Monte Carlo results on the robustness of the ANOVA F, W, and F^* statistics. *Communications in Statistics–Simulation and Computation, 15,* 933-943.

Chapter 17

Reporting Information in Multiple
Correlation and Multiple Regression Studies

Carl J Huberty and Mohamed H. Hussein

The reader is well aware of the myriad methods of data analysis—from simple correlation analysis through complex analyses of variance to highly involved multivariable analyses. Many papers, journal articles, book chapters, and entire books have been written in efforts to describe the methods themselves and how to use them in addressing research questions. Currently, it is fairly routine when it comes to quantitative data analysis to use computer statistical packages. There is a growing number of package manuals available to obtain assistance in conducting particular analyses. There are very limited resources, however, for quantitative education researchers to obtain guidance on what quantitative information should be reported and how to report such information. Some of the writings that have appeared deal with general issues on writing manuscripts (Bailer & Mosteller, 1988; Guion, 1983; Maxwell & Cole, 1995; Thompson, 1995). What is and is not reported in some studies that used univariate and multivariate analyses of variance are discussed by Keselman et al. (1998). Some hints regarding reporting are also provided by Wilkinson et al. (1999).

This chapter provides some suggestions for what quantitative information to report and how to report it in the contexts of multiple correlation analysis (MCA) and multiple regression analysis (MRA). A real data set related to vocational education is utilized. The data source is the same as that used by Huberty and Petoskey (1999). Six sections follow: pre-analysis, data inspection, computer programs, multiple correlation analysis, multiple regression analysis, and comments.

Pre-Analysis

Purpose

The purpose of research studies should be stated very explicitly—manuscript titles often do not make the research purpose very clear. For a multiple correlation study a purpose might be, "The purpose of this study was to investigate the relationship between grade point average and a collection of nine student characteristics and behaviors." An example of a purpose statement for a multiple regression study might be, "The purpose of this study was to determine, and assess the quality of a rule for predicting Academic Achievement using a set of 13 predictors that reflected student and parent characteristics."

Sampling

Having made the purpose explicit researchers should clearly describe the method of sampling, analysis units, sample units themselves (e.g., twelfth-grade high school students), and number of units. Huberty and Petoskey (1999, p. 16) give references pertaining to sampling (e.g., Henry, 1999; Jaeger, 1984), discuss the issue of sample representativeness, and suggest an approach to determining a desirable sample size. With regard to the latter, for 10 predictors and an expected ρ^2 value of about .30, a desirable sample size is about 30.

Variables

Initial choice of variables is a very important consideration in both MCA and MRA contexts particularly in the former. If an MCA is the focus it is essential that the collection of the, say, X variables constitute a *system* of variables that are interrelated in that they share some analysis unit attribute(s); they *hang together* in some substantively theoretical manner. This is essential because the purpose of a study for which an MCA is used focuses on the relationship between the Y variable and a linear composite of the X variables. To meaningfully interpret the results of an MCA one needs to make a substantive interpretation of the X composite. Such a substantive interpretation would not be feasible unless the collection of X variables constitute some type of substantive attribute system. On the other hand, the collection of X variables in an MRA context—also called predictor variables—may constitute a hodgepodge of predictors. For either an MCA or an MRA a rationale for the initial choice of X variables should be made clear; the choice could be based on substantive theory, previous research, common sense, or, in the case of an MRA context, societal expectations.

Having defined the variables (i.e., analysis unit attributes), it is necessary to indicate how each variable is measured. It is our opinion that for variables other than, for example, some unit demographics (such as age and ethnicity), a single item response on an instrument should *not* be considered a *variable* measure. Therefore, if a survey instrument is used to measure some unit attributes some type of item composites should be seriously considered. An example of such an item-based instrument is given below in the introduction of the Multiple Correlation Analysis section. However the variables are measured it would be informative if some qualities of the variable measures are reported, particularly reliability and validity.

It may be that the Y variable and some of the X variables are categorically measured. If so, then such variables need to scaled—that is, some method must be used to assign numbers to each category (see Huberty & Petoskey, 1999, p. 29). For three or more ordered categories, a simple integer scaling may be used; whereas for three or more unordered categories, a scaling method described by Huberty (1994, pp. 153-154) may be used. [We do not espouse the popular *dummy coding* method.]

Different overall analysis results may be expected by using different variable scaling methods. Researchers must describe in some detail how categorical variables are scaled, citing references where appropriate.

Issues pertaining to the reporting of purpose, sampling, and variables will be discussed specifically with respect to MCA and to MRA in later sections in the contexts of the examples used.

Data Inspection

There is an adage pertaining to data analysis that has gained considerable attention in recent years: *Look at your data.* Viewing a data set (i.e., data matrix) is greatly facilitated by the use of the statistical computer packages. There are two things to initially look for: [1] aberrant variable measures and [2] missing measures. Measures may be aberrant because of data entry errors or because they are outliers. What is done with the presence of outliers has become a bit controversial (Lovie, 1985; Orr, Sackett, & Dubois, 1991). Whatever is done about outliers should be mentioned; even if there are no outliers, the narrative should mention that an inspection was made. The use of graphical methods may be very helpful in the data inspection process (Bailer & Mosteller, 1988, p. 270; Wilkinson et al., 1999, pp. 601-602).

Having missing data is a whole new issue. The choice of data imputation method to be used is also controversial. Three fairly readable discussions of data imputation are given by Kromrey and Hines (1994), Little and Schenka (1995), and Roth (1994). Even if there are no missing data it should be stated that such a search was made. Having made such a statement and one about the presence or absence of outliers would indicate that the researcher is cognizant of the two potential problems.

In sum, it is suggested that the following information be reported.

• Search for and handling of outliers
• Search for and handling of missing data

Computer Programs

No researcher is going to conduct an MCA or MRA without using some statistical computer package(s) or program(s). If a package is utilized researchers should supply readers with detailed information; name (e.g., SPSS or SAS), version (e.g., 9.0), procedure (e.g., SPSS REGRESSION), and any specific non-routine options that were used (e.g., SPSS CORRELATIONS). There may be occasions when more than one package or more than one procedure is used—this may be for verification purposes. Huberty and Petoskey (1999, p. 18) list five SAS procedures and SPSS commands for use in MCA and MRA studies.

MCA	*MRA*
Regression	Regression
/variables egpa c_1 c_2 ... c_q	/variables egpa c_1 c_2 ... c_q
/descriptive mean stddev	/statistics collin tol
/dependent egpa	/dependent egpa
/method enter.	/method {enter} {stepwise}
	/scatterplot (*resid *pred).

SAS commands for an MCA and for an MRA are as follows:

MCA	*MRA*
Proc reg data = MCA;	prog reg data = MRA;
Model egpa = c_1 c_2 ... c_q;	model egpa = c_1 c_2...c_q/adjrsq maxr;
run;	run;

This information would also be informative when so reported. In sum, computer program information to be reported follows.

- Name of computer package(s)/program(s) used
- Package version
- Specific package procedure(s) used
- Specific package commands used

Multiple Correlation Analysis[1]

Introduction

The data set utilized by Huberty and Petoskey (1999) and herein is from the National Educational Longitudinal Study (NELS) of 1988. The data were obtained via a survey of twelfth-grade high school students in 1992. Because of some data recording problems eight students were deleted, leaving 447 students to be considered. A subset of 26 survey items was considered for the MCA example. The 26 items and how each is scaled are given in Table 17.1.

Because of an *extreme* vector of 26 scores, one student was deleted (see Huberty & Petoskey, 1999, p. 19) leaving an N of 446. A principal components analysis was used to define nine response variables (see Huberty & Petoskey, pp. 19-21), scores that were to be correlated with the response variable, *Academic Performance* (measured by grade point average–GPA). Because the quality (specifically, reliability) of single item scores is usually questionable, we prefer to use scores on item composites. One way to obtain somewhat meaningful composites is to conduct a principal components analysis (PCA—see e.g., Rencher, 1995, Chapter 12). With a PCA linear item composites are determined in such a way as to maximally account for the variability among the X variables. So, we have one response variable on the left-hand side (i.e., Y variable) and nine response variables that represent study habits, future plans, and peer academic orientation (i.e., p X variables) on the right-hand side. The purpose of the analysis, then, is to investigate the relationship between academic performance and the collection of nine student characteristics (as defined by the nine principal components).

A summary of information we suggest should be reported early in a manuscript involving an MCA includes:

- Purpose of the study
- How analysis units were sampled
- Support for representativeness of sample
- Sample size

TABLE 17.1
Survey Items and Scales for Correlation Example

Item	Scale
1 How often you go to class without pencil or paper.	1 = Usually
2 How often do you go to class without books?	2 = Often
3 How often you go to class without homework done.	3 = Seldom
	4 = Never
4 Time on math homework in school?	0 = None
5 Time on math homework out of school?	1 = Less than 1 hr
6 Time on science homework in school?	2 = 1-3 hrs
7 Time on science homework out of school?	3 = 4-6 hrs
8 Time on English homework in school?	4 = 7-9 hrs
9 Time on English homework out of school?	5 = 10-12 hrs
10 Time on history/social studies homework in school?	6 = 13-15 hrs
11 Time on history/social studies homework out of school?	7 = 16-20 hrs
12 Time on all other subjects in school?	8 = Over 20 hrs
13 Time on all other subjects out of school?	
14 Total time spent on homework in school?	
15 Total time spent on homework out of school?	
16 Reading done per week on own outside school?	0 = None
	1 = Less than 1 hr
	2 = 2 hrs
	3 = 3 hrs
	4 = 4-5 hrs
	5 = 6-7 hrs
	6 = 8-9 hrs
	7 = 10 or more hrs
17 How many hours on weekdays do you watch TV?	0 = Don't watch TV
18 How many hours on weekends do you watch TV?	1 = Less than 1 hr
	2 = 1-2 hrs/day
	3=2-3 hrs/day
	4=3-5 hrs/day
	5=Over 5 hrs/day
19 Among friends, how important is it to study?	1=Not important
20 Among friends, importance to get good grades?	2=Some importance
21 Among friends, importance to finish HS?	3=Very important
22 Among friends, importance to continue past HS?	
23 How many friends have no plans for college?	1 = None of them
24 How many friends plan to work full-time after HS?	2 = A few of them
25 How many friends plan to attend 2-yr or tech college?	3 = Some of them
26 How many friends plan to attend a 4-yr school?	4 = Most of them
	5 = All of them

- Rationale for initial choice of all $p + 1$ variables
- All $p + 1$ variables and how each is measured (like Table 17.1)
- If applicable, how variables are scaled
- Information on validity and reliability of variable measures

Data Analysis Preliminaries

Table 17.2 presents some descriptive information on the 10 variables. [Scores on the nine principal components were the X–variable scores.] We favor the *five-point description* of minimum score, three quartiles, and maximum score along with the mean and standard deviation, over simply reporting the latter two numbers. Table 17.3 reports the 10 x 10 Pearson correlation matrix. The correlations among the nine X variables are modest in magnitude; the range is about $r = -22$ to .41 with a median of approximately .03. Correlations between the Y variable and each of the nine X variables range from about $r = -.30$ to .29 with a median of about .05. The information in Tables 17.2 and 17.3 gives a *picture* of the response variable score distributions and variable interrelationships. Such descriptives may be informative for readers and for subsequent related research.

TABLE 17.2
Component Descriptors

	Min	Q_1	Q_2	Q_3	Max	*sd*
1	−2.03	−.52	−.03	.47	2.44	.77
2	−2.50	−.48	−.05	.49	2.31	.79
3	−2.03	−.56	−.00	.61	2.08	.78
4	−1.54	−.44	−.09	.38	2.77	.66
5	−2.63	−.61	−.04	.61	3.26	.87
6	−2.42	−.54	−.05	.48	3.01	.82
7	−3.33	−.64	.03	.63	2.62	.97
8	−5.21	−.62	.16	.81	2.43	1.27
9	−4.21	−.78	.09	.85	3.42	1.25
GPA	.76	2.21	2.89	3.43	4.93	.82

Note. 1 = Total time on homework in and out of school, 2 = Time on work for core courses, 3 = Time watching TV, 4 = Reading done on own, 5 = No educational plans past HS, 6 = Total time on non-core courses, 7 = Time on non-core subjects out of school, 8 = In-class preparedness, 9 = Peer academic orientation. Means on the 9 components are equal to 0.00. Mean GPA = 2.84.

TABLE 17.3
Component Correlation Matrix

	1	2	3	4	5	6	7	8	9
1									
2	.000								
3	.064	-.039							
4	-.156	.035	.099						
5	-.084	-.173	.037	.201					
6	.315	-.125	.031	-.036	.057				
7	.409	.034	.036	-.191	-.063	-.127			
8	.126	.069	-.017	.024	-.050	-.150	.171		
9	.092	.184	.140	-.136	-.222	-.086	.196	-.020	
GPA	.201	.292	-.304	-.200	-.229	-.067	.169	.046	.059

Note. 1 = Total time on homework in and out of school, 2 = Time on work for core courses, 3 = Time watching TV, 4 = Reading done on own, 5 = No educational plans past HS, 6 = Total time on non-core courses, 7 = Time on non-core subjects out of school, 8 = In-class preparedness, 9 = Peer academic orientation.

The universal multiple correlation (and regression) model considered is one that involves a *linear* relationship between the Y variable and X variables. The linearity condition may be assessed via a residual plot or a formal statistical test (see Weisberg, 1985, pp. 89-95). Throughout this chapter we assume that the data fit a linear model. There are data analysis conditions that, technically speaking, need to be met to make a linear multiple correlation analysis *legitimate*. The three initial conditions are independence of student score vectors, Y-variate normality, and homogeneity of Y-variable variance across the X-variable-score possibilities. That it was reasonable to conclude that for the 446-by-10 data matrix these three data conditions are met is discussed by Huberty and Petoskey (1999, p. 24). Briefly, a *probability plot* was used to subjectively assess the normality condition and a *residual plot* was used to assess the homogeneity condition—these assessments indicated both conditions were satisfactorily met. Independence of score vectors is determined by the study design and assessed by researcher judgment.

There is another aspect of the data matrix that should be checked before proceeding with the MCA. This aspect pertains to determining if some students have an extreme influence on the analysis results—it should be noted that a highly influential student vector need *not* be that for an outlying student.

Details about checking for the current data are given by Huberty and Petoskey (1999, pp. 24-25). Briefly, what is assessed is the influence of individual students on the precision of the weights for the X variables (the nine components) that define the composite that is correlated with the Y variable, academic performance. One index useful in assessing this influence is the *covariance ratio* (CVR); students with extremely small or extremely large CVR values would be deleted (which did not result with our data set).

So, with respect to data analysis preliminaries what should be reported? This question may be addressed by a simple list as follows.

- Five-point descriptives (like Table 17.2)
- $(p + 1) - by - (p + 1)$ correlation matrix (like Table 17.3)
- Defense of independence of unit score vectors
- Support for approximate Y-variable normality
- Support for approximate Y-variable variance homogeneity
- Support for no undue influence of unit score vectors on biased or imprecise estimation—or support for deleting units with undue influence

Interpreting the Relationship

Because the purpose of an MCA study is to investigate relationship, a numerical index of the estimated relationship should be reported. The *relationship* to which we refer is that between the Y variable and a linear composite (or combination) of the p X variables. [The weights of the X variables for the composite are derived in such a way that the simple correlation between the Y variable scores and composite scores is maximized. The resulting composite is thus considered the *optimal* composite.] The index we favor is an adjustment of the sample squared multiple correlation coefficient, R^2. The adjustment espoused is

$$R^2_{adj} = R^2 - \frac{p}{N-p-1} (1 - R^2)$$

$$= 1 - \frac{N-1}{N-p-1} (1 - R^2) ,$$

where p denotes the number of X variables and N is the sample size. It is strongly recommended that R^2_{adj} be reported—rather than R^2—to three decimal places. Suppose, that $R^2_{adj} \nabla .253$; then it may be estimated that approximately 25% of the variation in the GPA scores is shared with the obtained linear composite of the nine components.

Inferentially thinking, the following question should be addressed. Is the obtained percent of shared variance greater than what would be expected *by chance*? The details of this statistical test are given by Huberty and Petoskey (1999, pp. 25-26). Briefly, what is being tested is the difference between Δ^2 and the expected value (i.e., the long-run mean) of R^2 which is equal to $p/(N - 1)$. An associated effect size index, $E = R_{adj}^2 - p/(N-1)$, should be calculated and the E value should be reported. It has not been standard practice to report such an effect size index value in the context of multiple correlation. Thus, there are no standard cut-offs to define *low* or *high E* values. Some judgment calls will necessarily have to be made in the interpretation process.

Substantively, there is a more important question to address, "With *what* is student academic performance related?" The *what* pertains to the *construct* defined by the linear composite of the nine components (i.e., the nine X variables) in our example. This question of *structure* may be addressed by examining the nine structure r's, that is, the simple correlations between each of the nine components and the linear composite of the nine components. A squared structure r reflects the variance shared between a component and the linear composite. For our data set, the structure r's are given in Table 17. 4.

From the r values (see Table 17.4) the construct may be considered to be basically defined by components 2 and 3 and supplementally by components 1, 4, 5, and 7. We concluded that *Orientation Toward Academics* was a reasonable label for the construct. That is, the relationship inferred was one between *Academic Performance* and *Orientation Toward Academics*—the estimated correlation was approximately .50 ($R^2 \, \nabla \, .253$).

So, for relationship studies, the following should be reported:

- R_{adj}^2
- $R_{adj}^2 - p/(N-1)$ value—an effect size value
- Results of the statistical test of a better-than-chance relationship—
  F value,
  df values, P value (to three decimal places)
- Structure correlations (like Table 17.4)
- Construct interpretation

TABLE 17.4
Structure Correlations

Component	Structure r
1	.39
2	.56
3	−.59
4	−.39
5	−.44
6	−.13
7	.33
8	.09
9	.11

Note. 1 = Time on homework in / out of school, 2 = Time on work for core courses, 3 = Time watching TV, 4 = Reading done on own, 5 = No education past HS, 6 = Time on non-core courses, 7 = Time on non-core subjects out of school, 8 = In-class preparedness, 9 = Peer academic orientation.

X–Variable Ordering

It is *natural* for both researchers and readers to ask the question, "Which X variable(s) is(are) the most important and which is(are) the least important?" To answer this question another question must first be addressed, "Important with respect to what?" The *what* in an MCA may refer to the relationship between the Y variable and the obtained optimal linear composite of the X variables or it may refer to the definition of the construct defined by the composite. A reasonable approach to determining the relative contribution of the p X variables with respect to the relationship focus is to conduct p MCAs each with p − 1 X variables. That X variable which when deleted decreases the R^2 value the greatest is considered the most important variable. One could equivalently consider decreases in the R^2_{adj} value. For our data set the nine eight-component analyses are given in Table 17.5. Some tied ranks are assigned because it was judged that some values of R^2_{adj} were *close* to each other. From these results we may conclude that components 3 and 2 contribute most to the relationship between academic performance and the nine-component composite while components 6, 7, 8, and 9 contribute the least.

TABLE 17.5

Results of the Eight–Component Analyses

Variable deleted	R^2	R^2_{adj}	Rank
3	.191	.176	1.5
2	.207	.193	1.5
1	.242	.228	3.0
5	.253	.239	4.5
4	.256	.242	4.5
6	.263	.249	7.5
7	.266	.253	7.5
8	.268	.254	7.5
9	.268	.254	7.5

Note. 1 = Total time spent on homework in and out of school, 2 = Time spent on work for core courses, 3 = Time spent watching TV, 4 = Reading done on own, 5 = No educational plans past high school, 6 = Total time spent on non-core courses, 7 = Time spent on non-core subjects out of school, 8 = In-class preparedness, 9 = Peer academic orientation.

A reasonable approach to determining the relative contribution of the p X variables to the definition of the construct defined by the p-variable composite is to simply compare the (absolute values or squares of the) structure r's. For our data set the structure r's in Table 17.4 indicate that components 2 and 3 are most important (in terms of construct definition) while components 6, 8, and 9 are least important.

With respect to X-variable ordering, the following information should be reported:

- $(p-1) - X$-variable analyses (like Table17. 5)
- Structure correlations (like Table 17.4)
- Variable ranks

Multiple Regression Analysis[1]

Introduction

The reader may recall the MCA–MRA distinction briefly mentioned in the Pre-Analysis section; an MCA would be conducted if the research question of interest pertains to *relationship* whereas an MRA would be conducted if the research question pertains to *prediction*.

Just as for the MCA example data from the NELS:1988 database are used for the MRA example. For our example the Y variable is *Academic Achievement* (as measured by a standardized test composite of reading and mathematics skills). The collection of 12 X variables plus the Y variable along with a description of how all 13 variables are measured, are given in Table 17.6. The 12 X variables are considered *predictor* variables in this example.

TABLE 17.6
Variables and Their Measurements for the Regression Example

Variable	Measurement
Self-concept	Z–score composite of all self-concept items
Locus of control	Z–score composite of all locus of control items
Socio-economic status	Quartile coding of SES with 1 = low to 4 = high
Mother education	1 = Some HS; 2 = Graduated HS; 3 = Some college; 4 = Graduated college; 5 = Graduate
Father education	1 = Some HS; 2 = Graduated HS; 3 = Some college; 4 = Graduated college; 5 = Graduate
Gender	0 = Male; 1 = Female
Race	1 = White; 2 = Black; 3 = Other
Enrollment	1 = College prep; 2 = Vocational; 3 = General; 4 = Specialized; 5 = Other; 6 = Don't know
Expected work	1 = Craftsperson; 2 = Farmer/Housewife/Laborer; 3=Military/ Police/Security; 4 = Business/Sales; 5 = Science/ Technical; 6 = Service; 7 = Other; 8 = Don't know/Won't work
Family income	1 = Less then $7,500; 2 = $7,500 to $14,999; 3 = $15,000 to $29,999; 4 = $25,000 to $49,999; 5 = Greater than $50,000
Mother occupation	1 = Housewife; 2 = Clerical/Craftsperson; 3=Administrative/ Operative; 4 = Laborer/Sales/ Technical; 5 = Professional; 6 = Service; 7 = Don't know/Don't work
Father occupation	1 = Clerical/Craftsperson; 2 = Manager/Operative/ Owner; 3 = Laborer/Sales/Technical; 4 = Military/ Protective/Service/ Professional; 5 = Don't know/ Don't work
Academic achievement	Reading plus mathematics scores obtained via standardized instrument

The first two listed variables are considered continuous; measurement on each was a standard score. Scoring for the one dichotomous variable (gender) was simply 0–1. The four categorical variables (socioeconomic status, family income, mother education, father education) with ordered categories were scored using integer scaling; for example, 1, 2, 3, 4 for socio-economic status. The scaling method for the remaining five categorical variables with unordered categories is described by Huberty and Petoskey (1999, p. 29). The scaling method used is accomplished by simply using the mean of the Y scores for the analysis units in each respective category.

Access was acquired to 368 1992 twelfth-grade students on whom measures on all 13 variables were available. Because four students had Y scores and X-vector scores that were judged to be outliers (because they were extensively deviant from the Y mean and X-vector of means), they were deleted. The five unordered-category variables were rescaled for the $N = 364$ students using the method described in the immediately previous paragraph.

The purpose of our MRA, then, was to study the predictability of academic achievement score using scores on 12 predictor variables. [The purpose of a study involving an MRA should be explicitly reported along with other information as listed at the end of the MCA Introduction subsection.]

Data Analysis Preliminaries

Table 17.7 presents some descriptive information on the 13 variables. Table 17.8 gives the 13 x 13 Pearson correlation matrix. The correlations among the 12 predictors range from approximately $r = -.26$ to .60 with a median of approximately .14. Correlations between each predictor and academic achievement are all positive and rather moderate; the range is from about $r = .03$ to .30 with a median of approximately .21.

The data conditions that are assumed to have been met (see Huberty & Petoskey, 1999, pp. 31-32) include independence of student score vectors, linearity, Y-variate normality, variance homogeneity, and lack of extreme influence of student score vectors on the estimates of the 12 regression weights. For statistical assessment of the four latter conditions see Weisberg (1985, Chapters 5 & 6). With respect to MRA data analysis preliminaries, then, we suggest that the list of information given at the end of the MCA subsection, *Data Analysis Preliminaries*, also be reported in a study using MRA.

TABLE 17.7
Predictor Descriptors

	Min	Q_1	Q_2	Q_3	Max	Mean	*sd*
Self-concept	-2.91	-.69	-.24	.23	1.21	-.26	.74
Locus of control	-2.33	-.76	-.29	.22	1.35	-.28	.65
Socio-economic status	1.00	1.00	1.00	2.00	4.00	1.74	.88
Mother education	1.00	1.00	2.00	2.00	5.00	1.93	1.01
Father education	1.00	1.00	2.00	2.00	5.00	1.85	.97
Gender	1.00	1.00	2.00	2.00	2.00	1.59	.49
Race	38.16	40.59	43.23	43.23	43.23	42.06	1.73
Enrollment	39.51	41.02	41.54	42.96	45.20	42.06	1.61
Expected work	39.37	40.56	42.57	43.34	44.95	42.06	1.63
Family income	1.00	2.00	3.00	4.00	5.00	2.86	1.17
Mother occupation	40.05	41.08	41.77	41.77	44.80	42.06	1.49
Father occupation	40.89	41.62	41.63	41.65	45.02	42.06	1.21
Academic achievement	29.25	36.03	40.05	47.23	65.68	42.06	7.66

Note. Predictors *Race* through *Expected Work*, plus *Mother Occupation* and *Father Occupation* were scored using the mean academic achievement score for the categories of each of the five predictors. Other variable scoring is indicated in Table 7 in Huberty and Petoskey (1999, p. 30).

The Prediction Equation

Because for our data set it was judged that the five data conditions were satisfactorily met, we proceeded to determine the regression weights (i.e., *b* values) in the optimal (for our data set) composite of the 12 *X* variables:

$$\hat{Y} = b_0 + \sum_{i=1}^{12} b_i X_i.$$

Now the question is, "How well does the resultant equation *fit* the data for our 364 students?" The fit is numerically assessed by the correlation between the *Y* values and the $\hat{Y}$ values, the predicted *Y* values given in the above equation. This simple Pearson correlation is the so-called multiple correlation denoted by *R*. For our data, we found $R^2 \triangledown .277$. For inferential purposes we want to know if this value is significantly

TABLE 17.8
Predictor Correlation Matrix

	1	2	3	4	5	6	7	8	9	10	11	12
1 Self-concept												
2 Locus of control	.454											
3 Socioeconomic status	.049	.130										
4 Mother education	.001	.101	.454									
5 Father education	.031	.107	.540	.554								
6 Gender	-.257	-.108	-.059	-.029	-.138							
7 Race	-.067	.014	.170	.009	.046	-.033						
8 Enrollment	-.087	.018	.146	.071	.145	-.003	.123					
9 Expected work	.142	.140	.067	.101	.060	-.002	-.080	-.014				
10 Family income	.002	.128	.599	.187	.287	-.026	.235	.146	.148			
11 Mother occupation	.085	.089	.277	.249	.203	-.053	.101	.082	.123	.200		
12 Father occupation	.045	-.011	.117	.140	.258	-.084	.021	.052	.020	.025	.125	
Academic achievement	.035	.282	.259	.113	.235	.026	.226	.210	.213	.298	.195	.158

larger than the value that would result by chance, that is, "Is the R^2 value of .277 significantly greater than the chance value of $p/(N-1) = 12/(364-1) \nabla .033$?" We concluded that the predictions of Y using the 12-predictor composite were significantly better than chance predictions ($P \nabla .000$).

From another inferential perspective, researchers may be interested in knowing how well the derived prediction equation will fit data based on new samples. That is, it would be desirable to estimate the true *squared validity coefficient* (ρ_v^2), which is approximately the mean R^2 over repeated samples for which the regression weights are those derived from the original sample. This estimation is based on a formula that is different from the R_{adj}^2 expression used in an MCA. A fairly simple formula is

$$R^2_{adj\bullet} = R^2 - \frac{2p}{N-p} (1-R^2)$$

$$= 1 - \frac{N+p}{N-p} (1-R^2).$$

For our example, $R^2_{adj\bullet} \nabla .227$. The how-much-better-than-chance question is thus addressed by using $R^2_{adj\bullet} - p/(N-1)$, which for our data was approximately .194. *In general*, it looks as though we have found a prediction rule with some limited utility.

A relatively low $R^2_{adj\bullet}$ value indicates that the predicted criterion scores (i.e., $\hat{Y}$ values) may not be real close to the actual Y scores across *all* predictor score vectors. There may, however, be some particular predictor profiles for which the $Y - \hat{Y}$ values are relatively small. For a situation where it is desirable to apply a derived prediction rule to new analysis units further investigation is needed. One might search for predictor profiles for which the residuals, $Y - \hat{Y}$, are *small* to discover particular units for which prediction is good, or for which residuals are *large* to discover unit types for which prediction can be expected to be poor. As discussed by Huberty and Petoskey (1999, pp. 35-36), for the current data set we considered a residual small if the $\hat{Y}$ value was within 3.0 (i.e., approximately less than one-half of $\sqrt{MSE}$) of the Y value. Another example of such an investigation is given by Huberty and Allen (1999).

Information to be reported regarding the prediction equation should include the following.

- R^2 value
- Better-than-chance prediction test (F value with df values, P value)
- R^2_{adj*} value
- $R^2_{adj*} - p/(N-1)$ value
- If appropriate, prediction information for some predictor profiles

Predictor Deletion

Part of the reporting in an MCA includes a rationale for the initial choice of the X variables; this is also called for in an MRA study. Given a rationale for initially choosing the predictors, why might a researcher want to consider deleting some? A goal in MRA is to develop a rule that yields the best prediction for the available data set. One way to look at this situation is to seek the rule that yields the highest R^2_{adj*} value for the data on hand. As noted at the very end of the immediately preceding subsection the deletion of some predictors may lead to a rule that yields a higher R^2_{adj*} value than that value yielded by the complete set of p predictors.

So, how does one go about deciding which, if any, predictors should be deleted? First of all, the researcher needs to decide if there is a subset of predictors that would be retained in the final subset *no matter what*. Such a decision could be based on previous research, substantive considerations, user expectations, subjective judgment, or some combination of these. Suppose there are three predictors that the researcher deems relevant for inclusion, leaving p-3 to consider. The approach we suggest for deciding which variables to retain is an *all-possible-subset analysis*.

For our data set, three of the 12 predictors were *forced in*. So then it was necessary to determine the best subset of size 4 (in the sense of yielding the largest R^2_{adj*} value), the best subset of size 5, ..., the best subset of size 11. For each subset size (3 to 11), the R^2_{adj*} is the basis for determining the *best* subset (see Huberty & Petoskey, 1999, pp. 34-35). Results of the analyses are given in Table 17.9. From these results it might be judged that a subset of size 8 or 9 would suffice—this judgment is based on the incremental increase in R^2_{adj*}.

TABLE 17.9

All–Possible Subsets Analyses for Regression Example

Subset size	Predictors in best subset	R^2_{adj}
3	X_1, X_2, X_3	.109
4	X_1, X_2, X_3, X_8	.151
5	X_1, X_2, X_3, X_4, X_5	.181
6	$X_1, X_2, X_3, X_4, X_5, X_6$	.201
7	$X_1, X_2, X_3, X_4, X_5, X_6, X_8$	.215
8	$X_1, X_2, X_3, X_4, X_5, X_6, X_7, X_8$	.224
9	$X_1, X_2, X_3, X_4, X_5, X_6, X_7, X_8, X_{11}$	.228
10	$X_1, X_2, X_3, X_4, X_5, X_6, X_7, X_8, X_{10}, X_{11}$	.230
11	$X_1, X_2, X_3, X_4, X_5, X_6, X_7, X_8, X_9, X_{10}, X_{11}$	.231

Note. X_1 = Locus of control, X_2 = Mother education, X_3 = Father education, X_4 = Expected work, X_5 = Race, X_6 = Enrollment, X_7 = Father occupation, X_8 = Family income, X_9 = Self-concept, X_{10} = Mother occupation, X_{11} = Socio-economic status

The predictor-deletion issue may be an important one when it is anticipated that the derived prediction rule might be used with analysis units in the future or at different sites. In light of the practical utility of a prediction equation one might consider retaining the second best subset of a given size. This may be reasonable when the second best subset yields an $R^2_{adj^*}$ value that is close to the value for the best subset. The second best subset may be preferred because collecting data for this subset may be easier and/or less expensive than for the (numerically) best subset. For predictor deletion, the following information should be reported.

• The *forced-in* predictors

• A table of $R^2_{adj^*}$ values for all best subsets

If some predictors are deleted then the complete MRA would be done with the retained predictors.

Predictor Ordering

Having developed a prediction rule with the desired number of predictors it is natural to attempt to determine which of the predictor variables contribute most to the prediction accuracy and which contribute little. To assess predictor relative contribution (i.e., predictor ordering), we suggest doing p MRAs, each with $p - 1$ predictors. That predictor which when deleted is associated with the largest drop in the R^2_{adj*} value is considered the most important predictor. [Note that the p value used in calculating the p R^2_{adj*} values is actually $p - 1$.] Table 17.10 reports the predictor ordering information for our MRA data set. It is very typical to have some predictors judged to be of equal importance because of close R^2_{adj*} values.

TABLE 17.10
Results for Determining Predictor Relative Importance

Predictor deleted	R^2_{adj*}	Rank
None	.227	1
Locus of control	.132	2
Expected work	.172	3
Race	.203	5.5
Enrolled program	.215	5.5
Father occupation	.218	5.5
Family income	.222	5.5
Father education	.222	9.5
Self-concept	.226	9.5
Mother occupation	.226	9.5
Gender	.227	9.5
Mother education	.227	9.5
Socio-economic status	.231	12

For our results we judged that three subsets of predictors could be assigned equal ranks. It should be noted that deleting a variable may result in an *increase* in R^2_{adj*}; note that for our example, deleting SES results in an R^2_{adj*} value (.231) that is higher than the R^2_{adj*} value (.227) with all 12 predictors—this implies that SES as a predictor variable makes a questionable contribution to predictive accuracy.

Information to be reported with regard to predictor ordering should include the following.

- The p all-but-one-predictor R^2_{adj*} values
- Predictor ordering conclusions

Comments

We differentiate multiple correlation analysis (MCA) from multiple regression analysis (MRA) based on the associated study purpose, some numerical information, and interpretation of analysis results. Another point of view regarding differentiation is that MCA is typically applied to more substantive theoretical questions whereas MRA is applied to more substantive practical questions. It may also be argued that the deletion of X variables in an MRA context is an important consideration (because of the potential of determining a *better* prediction rule) whereas the deletion of X variables in an MCA context is a non-issue. [The differentiation between MCA and MRA is somewhat analogous to the differentiation between descriptive discriminant analysis and predictive discriminant analysis (Huberty, 1994) and to the differentiation between canonical correlation analysis and multivariate multiple regression analysis (Stevens, 1996, pp. 130-134).]

In our introduction we mentioned four writings that discuss the general issues of writing manuscripts. One article (Maxwell & Cole, 1995) gives 15 tips for technical writing. A summary of steps that may be considered for MCA and MRA is given in Figure 17.1.

We conclude this chapter with three fairly specific comments. First, the use of subjective judgment on the part of the researcher should not be downplayed. There are at least 11 instances pertaining to MCA and/or MRA in which judgment calls must be made: [1] initial variable choice, [2] representativeness of sample, [3] quality of variable measures, [4] existence of outliers, [5] existence of influential variable measures, [6] support for meeting data conditions, [7] interpretation of statistical test information, [8] better-than-chance magnitude, [9] construct interpretation, [10] relative magnitudes of adjusted R^2 values, and [11] variable rankings.

Second, if references are made to books or book chapters give the specific relevant page numbers pertaining to the concept/table/formula being discussed. Having such page numbers enables the reader to easily locate needed information.

The third specific comment pertains to a stepwise analysis. Our advice is simple: Don't do it! The typical use of a stepwise analysis is to determine which variables are to be deleted or to determine a variable ordering. It has been argued elsewhere (e.g., Huberty, 1989) that a stepwise analyses may not suggest the best (based on the data on hand) variable subset of a given size nor a good ordering of the variables. There are better methods (illustrated herein) to accomplish both purposes.

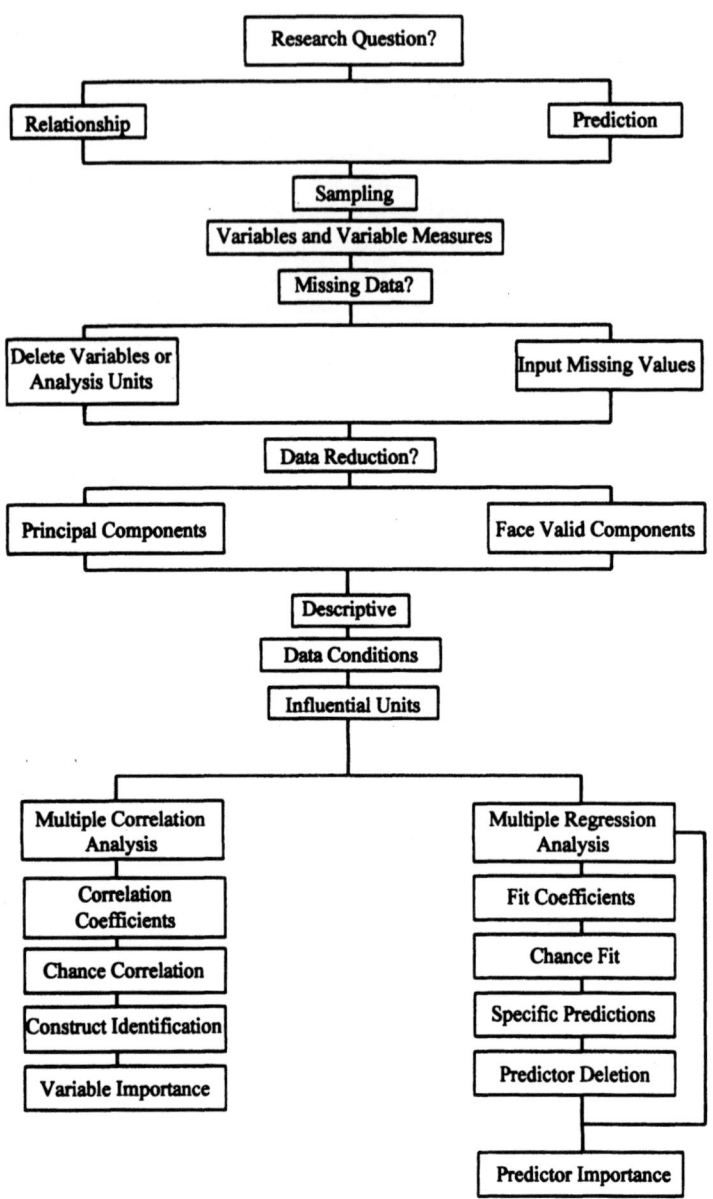

FIGURE 17.1. Summary of reporting information from a multiple correlation analysis and multiple regression analysis.

References

Bailer, J. C., & Mosteller, F. (1988). Guidelines for statistical reporting in articles for medical journals. *Annals of Internal Medicine, 108,* 266-273.

Guion, R. M. (1983). Editorial: Comments from the new editor. *Journal of Applied Psychology, 68,* 547-551.

Henry, G. T. (1990). *Practical sampling.* Newbury Park, CA: Sage.

Huberty, C. J (1989). Problems with stepwise methods—Better alternatives. In B. Thompson (Ed.), *Advances in social science methodology* (Vol. 1, pp. 43-70). Greenwich, CT: JAI Press.

Huberty, C. J (1994). *Applied discriminant analysis.* New York: Wiley.

Huberty, C. J, & Allen, J. B. (1999). Interpreting regression analysis results: An example. *Multiple Linear Regression Viewpoints, 25,* 29-32.

Huberty, C. J, & Petoskey, M. D. (1999). Use of multiple correlation analysis and multiple regression analysis. *Journal of Vocational Education Research, 24,* 15-43.

Jaeger, R. M. (1984). *Sampling in education and the social sciences.* New York: Longman.

Keselman, H. J., Huberty, C. J, Lix, L. M., Olejnik, S., Cribbie, R. A., Donahue, B., Kowalchuk, R. K., Lowman, L. L., Petoskey, M. D., Keselman, J. C., & Levin, J. R. (1998). Statistical practices of educational researchers: An analysis of their ANOVA, MANOVA, and ANCOVA analyses. *Review of Educational Research, 68,* 350-386.

Kromrey, J. D., & Hines, C. V. (1994). Nonrandomly missing data in multiple regression: An empirical comparison of common missing-data treatments. *Educational and Psychological Measurement, 54,* 573-593.

Little, R. J. A., & Schenka, N. (1995). Missing data. In G. Arminger, C. C. Clogg, & M. E. Sobel (Eds.), *Handbook of statistical modeling for the social and behavioral sciences* (pp. 39-75). New York: Plenum Press.

Lovie, P. (1985). Identifying outliers. In A. D. Lovie (Ed.), *New development in statistics for psychology and the social sciences* (pp. 44-69). London: The British Psychological Society.

Maxwell, S. E., & Cole, D. A. (1995). Tips for writing (and reading) methodological articles. *Psychological Bulletin, 118,* 193-198.

Orr, J. M., Sackett, P. R., & Dubois, C. L. Z. (1991). Outlier detection and treatment in I/O psychology: A survey of researcher beliefs and an empirical illustration. *Personnel Psychology, 44,* 473-486.

Rencher, A. C. (1995). *Methods of multivariate analysis*. New York: Wiley.

Roth, P. L. (1994). Missing data: A conceptual review for applied psychologists. *Personnel Psychology, 47,* 537-560.

Stevens, J. (1996). *Applied multivariate statistics for the social science.* Mahwah, NJ: Erlbaum.

Thompson, B. (1995). Publishing your research results: Some suggestions and counsel. *Journal of Counseling and Development, 73,* 342-345.

Weisberg, S. (1985). *Applied linear regression.* New York: Wiley.

Wilkinson, L., & APA Task Force. (1999). Statistical methods in psychology journals. *American Psychologist, 54,* 594-604.

Note

1. All of the details of analysis and of reporting information will not be presented in the MCA example and in the MRA example [see Huberty and Petoskey (1999) for most details]. Lists are given at the end of subsections for the two analysis examples.

Chapter 18

Considerations for Statistical Significance Testing[*]

Jay W. Rojewski

Debate about the inherent worth of quantitative versus qualitative research paradigms and investigations that was all too common in the late 1980s–early 1990s has lessened in recent years, owing perhaps to a more mature understanding of the purposes, advantages, and disadvantages of each approach. The rapid growth of qualitative inquiry—characterized by a belief that phenomena must be experienced and explained in the context where it occurs to be properly understood (Hultgren & Coomer, 1989)—surfaced partly as a result of dissatisfaction with the tendency of quantitative methods to minimize individual description in favor of groups or phenomena. A perception exists that qualitative methods can provide results directly relevant to specific individuals and groups but remain illustrative of larger phenomenon or population and maintain a strong sense of "humanness," that is, people are the focus, not numbers.

One of many possible reasons for the increased attention paid to qualitative methods in recent years might be a growing mistrust or disillusionment with "numbers" and their inherent meaning or value[1]

[*]Earlier versions of this chapter were presented at a doctoral research seminar sponsored by the Department of Workforce Education, Pennsylvania State University (1999, April), and published in the *Journal of Vocational Education Research,* 24(1), 1-18 as an editorial titled "Five Things > Statistics in Quantitative Educational Research." Adapted with permission of the publisher.

and a sense of detachment from quantitative results; rather than talking about people with names and experiences, thoughts and actions, quantitative researchers provide null hypothesis significance tests, rather cold statistical formulas, numeric output, and interpretation that focuses on group or average rather than individual lived experiences.

Both quantitative and qualitative paradigms can provide meaningful and valuable, albeit different, knowledge about the world (Gall, Borg, & Gall, 1996; Little, 1992; Thomas, 1989). My focus in this chapter is on quantitative methods and their value in enhancing and enriching our understanding of phenomena and lived experience. While quantitative inquiry is potentially useful, many novice researchers become beholden to, in awe of, or perhaps even at the mercy of, the statistical methods they select for analysis, for example, picking a statistical technique because of familiarity or ease of use and then designing a study around the method. Invariably, then, the focus of quantitative research gravitates toward results of statistical analysis instead of the important issues; resolution or enhanced understanding of research problems.

Numerous efforts have been made over the past decade to place a caveat on the use (and misuse) of statistical analyses. Some researchers (e.g., Carver, 1993; Schmidt, 1996; Shaver, 1993; Thompson, 1996) have explained how statistical significance testing is nothing more than determining the likelihood of obtaining a given result assuming that the null hypothesis is true. My personal favorite, Rozeboom (1997) declared that "null hypothesis significance testing is surely the most bone-headed, misguided procedure ever institutionalized in the rote training of science students. . . . [It is a] wonderment that this statistical procedure has remained so unresponsive to criticism" (p. 335).

Researchers often place more emphasis or value on statistical results than is actually warranted. Yet, the practice persists. Why? Numerous reasons have been suggested for this problem including the unthinking or pressured adoption of accepted, albeit questionable, practice; the facade of *scientism* provided by statistics, coupled with a belief that mathematics is essential to science and quantitative inquiry; and, a combination of confusion and desperation about the purpose and application of statistical methods (Shaver, 1993; Thompson, 1998).

Quantitative investigation can really only accomplish three things: describe, relate or predict, and compare. Depending on the form(s) of data and number of variables involved, statistical analysis can be fairly straight-forward or quite complex. Regardless, statistics are merely tools that are selected to address a particular research question. Once a question is constructed mechanisms are in place for decisions to be made about the specific type of analysis required (see Table 18.1).

TABLE 18.1
Partial List of Statistical Tests Available to Analyze Quantitative Data

Variables	Describe	Relate		Compare	
		Categorical	Continuous	Categorical	Continuous
One variable	$n, \underline{M}, SD,$ Mdn, Mode, σ^2, %, range				
Two variables (groups)					
Treated separately	Same	ρ, τ^b	r, r^2	χ^2	t-test
Treated together				χ^2	1-way ANOVA
Multiple variables					
Univariate (1DV, 2+IVs)	Same	G^2, PDA^c Logistic regression	R, R^2 Factor analysis	G^2, χ^2	2+way ANOVA
Multivariate (2+DVs, 2+IVs)		R^2_c SEM		DDA^d	MANOVA

[a] Variables are identified as being independent (IV) or dependent (DV).
[b] Spearman's rho and Kendall's tau are examples of several correlational techniques available to researchers depending on form of variables.
[c] PDA refers to predictive discriminant analysis.
[d] DDA refers to descriptive discriminant analysis.

While underlying assumptions, process, and appropriate application of statistical methods are important, I believe that less focus of quantitative study should be on statistics. Rather, there are several issues that are either ignored or given only passing attention in many quantitative studies. Shaver (1993) rather bluntly stated, "The dominance of statistical significance testing is dysfunctional. . . .[and] also diverts attention from more appropriate strategies such as replication and consideration of the practical or theoretical significance of results" (p. 294). Abelson (1995) recently observed that "somewhere along the line in the teaching of statistics in the social sciences, the importance of good judgment got lost amidst the minutiae of null hypothesis testing" (p. 2).

Given this context, several issues have consistently reappeared and frustrated me when conducting or reviewing quantitative research. As a result of these experiences, I believe that, in addition to our traditional focus on statistical output, formulas, numbers, and so on, quantitative researchers (and readers) should address several concerns that hold as much importance as specific statistical issues surrounding an investigation—a basic recognition that all research is subjective; a theoretical framework to establish context, as well as for explaining results; precision in instrumentation development or selection, validity and reliability, and in design; attention to practical significance of results—effect size; and manuscript consistency.

All Research is Subjective

Quantitative and qualitative researchers differ on their assumptions about the nature of reality. A positivistic or quantitative perspective assumes an objective, relatively constant social reality. Alternatively, a phenomenological or qualitative perspective assumes that social reality is continually being constructed by participants. These fundamental beliefs are reflected in how people or situations of interest are investigated: Quantitative studies assume an objective, detached, value-free position; qualitative studies adopt a more subjective, involved, value-dependent stance (Gall et al., 1996; Johnson, 1993; Szymanski, 1993).

Despite firm grounding in basic tenets of objectivity quantitative research still involves a number of subjective elements. Over three decades ago, Hamlin (1966) pointed out,

> Some researchers are obsessed with the need for objectivity. Granting that we want as much objectivity as possible, there is no completely objective research. Subjectivity enters in the choice of a subject, in the selection of data to be gathered, and in the interpretation of data. (p. 2)

Huberty and Morris (1988) noted that "as in all of statistical inference, subjective judgment cannot be avoided. Neither can reasonableness!" (p. 573). Hillison (1990) echoed the notion of common sense and subjective judgment in quantitative study. "The reality is that numbers do not have meaning until they are interpreted, and interpretation is a qualitative dimension" (p. 5). Indeed, the use of statistical methods in data analysis is never "cut and dried."

> The use of quantitative methods implies to some a high level of objectivity. But the experienced empirical researcher is, or should be, well aware of the potential high level of subjectivity that enters into quantitative research. . . .Data analysis and interpretation abound with subjectivity. Subjectivity is necessarily so prevalent because of the many judgments needed in the research process. (Huberty, 1994, pp. 22-23)

Thompson (1993) bluntly observed, "Like it or not, empirical science is inescapably a subjective business" (p. 365). Thus, an acknowledgment of the subjective nature of quantitative study—

selection of research topics, determining data collection methods, interpretation of results, and drawing conclusions—seems important for several reasons. First, the acknowledgment of subjectivity in quantitative studies is not necessarily a bad thing but must be addressed. By doing so researchers may be less likely to be lulled into a false sense of certainty about obtained results. Second, decisions requiring common sense, as well as statistical sense, can be explored and identified as to advantages and limitations they impose. All too often they are simply ignored or treated post hoc as a priori decisions. Third, a responsibility is directed at researchers to replicate and extend findings; to address potential doubts about whether results reflect an objective reality or are more reflective of researcher-based decisions (e.g., sample size, measurement instrument, design validity).

Theoretical or Conceptual Framework

If educational research is to be meaningful and relevant it must be grounded in theory, thoughtful conceptual arguments, and precise descriptions of problems, past inquiry, and constructs found in the research literature. A theoretical or conceptual framework provides a distinct point of view that explains the need and circumstances surrounding problems selected for study, defines relevant variables, aids in selecting appropriate research designs and data analysis, and supports the interpretation of results. Unfortunately, when a need for certainty, exactitude, and statistical calculations are emphasized over the nature and application of results—as is often the case in quantitative research—the role of theory tends to be minimized (Abelson, 1995). The use of theory is further arrested by the generally dynamic state of theory in most of the social sciences, including education. Pedhazur and Schmelkin (1991) blamed the unsatisfactory character of theory on the primitive nature of and deficiencies in quantitative measurement, design, and analysis.

Theory must be integrated with a discussion of specific problems requiring study—a context or rationale. Creswell (1994) explained that "one builds an extensive literature review in the introduction, setting the project firmly within a body of literature" (p. 45). Research contexts or rationales introduce readers to important terms and current level of knowledge, define concepts and terms, and explain the types of knowledge needed and why: Is there a deficiency in the literature? An inconsistency in findings? What are the specific issues or problems addressed by this study? What contribution will this study make to understanding the topic? Independent and dependent variables should be clearly identified: How are variable(s) conceptualized, defined, and measured? How does this conceptualization affect the study? This last question seems especially important given an increased recognition of the multivariate nature of many research interests (Fish, 1988). Maxwell and Cole (1995) recommended that "before proving anything with number and formulas, prove to the reader that what you propose can make a real difference" (p. 194) Why is this study important? Without clear answers to these types of questions, statistics have limited, if any, meaning or application.

Precision in Instrumentation Selection/Development and in Methods

People are sloppy, sometimes. Quantitative researchers are people too. Perhaps no other aspect of an empirical investigation is more important than the precision of the research design and specific instrument(s) used to gather data. Why? Parker (1993) noted that "it is a widely accepted truism that all published research is flawed to some extent" (p. 130). The key, then, is to minimize possible pitfalls to the greatest degree possible, for example, boost confidence in claims that collected data reflects intended constructs (measurement validity and reliability), or eliminate competing explanations for findings (internal and external design validity).

Instrument Validity

Few authors provide sufficient evidence of instrument validity, particularly for self-developed instruments, often limiting their discussion to face validity. However, the precise description of data collection instruments including conceptualization, development, basic structure, validation, reliability, and administrative concerns is a critical issue in quantitative inquiry for several reasons: [1] research is always dependent on measurement, and [2] there are no direct means for measuring educational/ psychological constructs (Ary, Jacobs, & Razavieh, 1990). The old adage "garbage in, garbage out" applies here. A clear understanding and description of the intended construct(s) an instrument or individual scale item is designed to measure is necessary to understand, generalize, and replicate results. Otherwise, the literature reflects nothing more than the cumulative effect of an academic exercise with little, if any, degree of certainty as to the accuracy of reported findings.

Different types of validity are often used to support the inferences made from instrument (test) scores including construct, content, and criterion. However, validity is actually an unitary concept, i.e., a general claim that indicates how precise a score or series of scores from an instrument reflect whatever is purportedly being measured. Claims of instrument validity are often supported by past validation efforts but should also include evidence of validity for the particular group, situation, and/or time of an intended study. There are several reasons for thinking of the validation process as a continual one. First, validity claims are not *all or nothing* declarations but a matter of degree that can change over time. Second, researchers do not validate an instrument, per se, but the interpretation of scores derived from an instrument (Ary et al., 1990; Benson, 1995).

Although establishing validity involves some subjective judgment, various methods can be used to build a body of evidence that supports the validity of scores for a particular instrument including theoretical justification and definition, pooled expertise, exploratory or confirmatory factor analysis, item/subscale intercorrelations, and correlations with other instruments. Information about instruments used in a study can provide consumers with some understanding of the purported intent of the measures and aid in establishing validity. What was the content of instruments and their items? What are a couple of examples of the items used and how were they arranged (number and description of scales/subscales, number of items per scale, etc.)? Scoring? Response time? What method(s) were used to calculate subscale scores?

Instrument Reliability

Reliability refers to the degree of consistency (or stability) in the scores of an instrument and reflects the amount of random or systematic error inherent in the process of measurement, the ratio of true-score variance to observed-score variance (Ary et al., 1990). Evidence of instrument score reliability is more commonly reported in research studies than validity probably because reliability can be more easily calculated and high reliability coefficients are relatively easy to attain. While important, Pedhazur and Schmelkin (1991) caution that "reliability is a necessary but not a sufficient condition for validity. That is, a measure cannot be valid, if it is not reliable, but being reliable it is not necessarily valid for the purpose its author or a user has in mind" (p. 81). Given this caveat, reliability is an important element in establishing precise measures. "The concern for score reliability in substantive inquiry is not just some vague statistician's nit-picking. Score reliability directly (a) affects our ability to achieve statistical significance and (b) attentuates the effect sizes for the studies we conduct" (Thompson & Snyder, 1997, p. 11).

Information about instrument reliability may include results of scores obtained from pilot testing (e.g., obtaining measures of test stability using test-retest methods) or past investigations. However, data about instrument consistency obtained from the actual pool of study participants is also important (e.g., Cronbach alpha reliability coefficient). As with validity, "reliability is a characteristic of scores for the data in hand, and not of a test per se" (Thompson & Snyder, 1997, p. 10).

Three broad categories of methods are available to determine and describe the reliability of scores obtained from a particular instrument including test-retest, equivalent forms, and internal consistency approaches. Test-retest methods represent the simplest and most straight-forward approach to determining score reliability. A group of people is measured twice using the same measure. The resulting scores are then correlated producing an estimate of consistency or repeatability over time. While test-retest methods can provide some estimate of the stability of scores, Pedhazur and Schmelkin (1991) identified serious deficiencies with this approach and argued against its use. Equivalent or alternate forms reliability correlates scores taken from two instruments designed to measure the same phenomenon (Gall et al., 1996). "The usefulness of this approach is limited primarily by difficulties in constructing equivalent forms and in determining whether they are in fact equivalent" (Pedhazur & Schmelkin, p. 89). Measures of internal consistency such as the split-half method or Cronbach's alpha assess the degree that an individual responds to similar items on any given instrument is a consistent fashion (Huck & Cormier, 1996).

Internal and External Validity

Although data collection instruments might be determined valid and reliable flaws in the design of an investigation can still threaten the precision of gathered data and the interpretations drawn from them. Cook, Campbell, and Peracchio (1990) distinguished between several major threats to the integrity of research results including internal and external validity.

Internal validity is, perhaps, the most important type of research design validity and represents the extent that extraneous variables (sources of error variance) have been controlled. Are results due to the variables being investigated or manipulated or can they be attributed to other variables? Can results be attributed solely to the treatment variable(s)? While it is beyond the scope of this chapter to detail specific types of internal validity a number of threats do exist including history, maturation, sample selection, testing, statistical regression, and participant mortality. Several ways to reduce or eliminate threats to internal validity include random assignment, use of control groups, pretesting, either holding extraneous variables constant or including them in the design, and employing methods of statistical control (Gall et al., 1996; Parker, 1993; Pedhazur & Schmelkin, 1991).

External validity refers to the generalizability and representativeness of research results to other individuals and settings beyond those studied. Sample representativeness can often be demonstrated by simply providing a description of the group studied, including key demographic variables deemed most important to the larger population. Another aspect of external validity is the problem of experimental artificiality, study designs that are not representative of real-life environments (Gall et al., 1996; Huck, Cormier, & Bounds, 1974).

While many questions surrounding external validity cannot be answered directly there are indicators for judging the extent of a study's generalizability to other persons, settings, and time; selection bias, experimental arrangements, multiple treatment interference, and interaction effect of testing. Random selection and assignment are often viewed as the most effective technique for controlling threats to external validity, although replication and building new research through completed studies is also an important way to establish the external validity of findings (Gall et al., 1996). O'Reilly (1983) lamented that "it is unfortunate that even the word replication seems to leave a bad taste in many peoples' mouths. Rigorously conducted replication studies cannot only substantiate the validity of research findings, but also can broaden their application" (p. 38).

Thompson (1997) indicated that empirical evidence for the replicability of research results could either be external or internal. He envisioned external replication studies as the approach most typically thought of when conducting replication, invoking a new sample measured at a different time or place. In contrast, internal replication uses "the sample in hand to combine the participants in different ways to try to estimate how much the idiosyncrasies of individuality within the sample have compromised sample results" (p. 19). Major internal replicability analyses include cross-validation, jacknife, and bootstrap methods. Thompson explained,

Internal evidence for replicability is never as good as an actual
replication, but is certainly better than presuming that a statistical
significance test assures result replicability. . . .Because replicability
evidence is critical to the cumulation of knowledge, more authors should
be expected to provide some evidence of result replicability. (pp. 19-20)

Robinson and Levin (1997) enthusiastically supported Thompson's
(1997) recommendation for replication of published results. However,
they were more cautious about the recommendation for increased use
of internal replication analyses. They argued that "most internal
replicability analyses represent a poor, potentially discomforting,
replacement for the real thing. . . .such analyses do not take into
account the potential vagaries and hidden biases associated with a one-
time study based on a single sample of participants" (p. 25). Thus, it
appears that the jury is still out about the most preferred or useful
methods for replicating and reporting published research results.

A close relationship exists between internal validity, external
validity, methodology, and research questions, making it difficult, at
times, to examine any one of these issues in isolation. Ideally, of
course, studies would be designed for perfect internal and external
validity. Realistically, researchers must negotiate a balancing act where
decisions to exert more stringent control (internal validity) may result
in less representativeness or generalizability (external validity).

Practical Significance of Results—Effect Size

The meaning of numbers, particularly the results of statistical tests,
tend to be rather limited without some context for judging their impact
or importance. Too many researchers rely on statistical significance as
the sole indicator of importance, when in fact most statistical results
merely answer the question, "Given that a null hypothesis is true, what
is the probability of obtaining this or more extreme results?" Thompson
(1993) argued that a "superficial understanding of significance testing
has led to serious distortions, such as interpreting a statistically
significant result involving small effect sizes while ignoring
nonsignificant results involving large effect sizes" (p. 365). In fact,
many researchers believe that statistically significant results are, by
default, also important ones—unlikely results are erroneously equated
with inherently interesting ones (Thompson, 1996). Shaver (1993)
mused, "One can only wonder at the number of articles in which results
are either interpreted as important because of statistical significance or
in which the probability level appears to be taken as an indication of
magnitude" (p. 302).

One way to clarify the interpretation of statistically significant results is with measures of effect size. Effect size refers to the magnitude or strength, and subsequently the practical importance, of an observed difference or relationship. Magnitude or strength is important because observed differences that are "highly significant statistically, very unlikely to have occurred by chance, may nevertheless have a very small effect size, i.e., have virtually no practical effect on the outcomes of interest" (Haller & Virkler, 1993, p. 173). Statistical significance is a direct function of sample size, as sample size increases the threshold to obtain statistical significance decreases. Huston (1993) suggested that without some measure of practical significance the implications of results for theory or practice may be obscured or overstated.

A number of effect size estimates are available that can be categorized into two broad classes, *variance-accounted-for* measures or correlation ratios (such as R^2, ω^2, eta^2) that are computed by dividing the sum of squares for an effect by the total sum of squares, and *standardized differences* (such as Cohen's d) which are measures of a difference between two or mean scores expressed in terms of standard deviation units (Thompson, 1989). While effect size coefficients can be quite useful in determining the relative importance or strength of observed differences, Thompson (1997) warned that

> Effect size is no more a panacea than is a statistical significance test, for two reasons. . . .First, because human values are also not part of the calculation of an effect size, any more than values are part of the calculation of p, largeness of effect does not guarantee practical importance any more than statistical significance does. Second, more researchers seem to have adopted Cohen's (1988) definitions of small, medium, and large effects with the same rigidity that α =.05 has been adopted. Such rigidity is inappropriate. (pp. 11-12)

Thus, "statistics can be used to evaluate the probability of an event. But importance is a question of human values, and math cannot be employed as an....escape from responsibility for making value judgments" (Thompson, 1993, p. 365). Interpretation of statistical results is always contextual, somewhat subjective, value-based, and dependent on research goals.

Manuscript Consistency: Preparation and Presentation

Any number of how-to books, pamphlets, and articles have been published that offer advice on how to write successfully for scholarly publication (e.g., see American Psychological Association, 1994; Creswell, 1994, 1998; Moore, Burnett, & Moore, 1986). And, while it may seem perjorative, many problems, both conceptual and technical, associated with rejected manuscripts result from not following sound writing principles such as those outlined in the APA publication guidelines. West (1992) noted that "the consistency that results from observing its [APA Manual] specifications saves the time of the author, the reviewers, the editor, and the printer. Even more important than mechanics is the orderly account that results from following the manual's advice" (p. 132). The 4th edition of the APA Manual (1994) provides excellent guidance in developing research manuscripts and should be referenced frequently during the writing process.

Establishing a Rationale/Context for the Study

Authors frequently encounter criticism for lack of a strong rationale or context for the investigation being reported. First, important variables, concepts, and terms should be introduced and defined. What do select variables mean and how are they used? What do these variables or concepts contribute to the issue at hand? Independent and dependent variables should be clearly identified. How are the dependent variable(s) conceptualized, defined, and measured? Why? How does this conceptualization affect your study? This last question seems especially important given an increased recognition of the multivariate nature of many research interests (Fish, 1988).

Second, specific connections between identified variables or concepts should be established. Eichorn (1985) suggested that "the literature research in a journal article cannot be exhaustive. Rather, it should selectively but systematically inform the reader about the key theoretical and research issues and about previous and current research; it should also provide a context for understanding the present investigation" (p. 1315). The context or introduction should lead readers to a logical end, the purpose, and clearly tie the investigation to a larger body of literature and an established theoretical base.

Results

While quantitative results sections are fairly straight-forward presentations of statistical findings, several problems seem to occur with a fair amount of regularity. First, a clear connection between results and purpose need to be established. Too frequently, stated research objectives do not mesh with data presented. Second, a descriptive foundation should be established before the results of higher-order statistical analysis are presented.

Discussion

Discussion sections provide opportunities for evaluation and interpretation of results. However, many times discussion sections merely reformulate and restate points already made (American Psychological Association, 1994). Another problem frequently encountered is that discussion goes well beyond the established parameters of the study by drawing unwarranted or overly-broad conclusions (Eichorn, 1985). Huck and Cormier (1996) suggest that authors use discussion sections to explain what results mean and why they turned out the way they did.

Discussion sections should be clearly tied to the available literature base. What is the answer to the main questions posed by this investigation? How do these results compare to past studies? What is new here? What is the contribution of this study to our understanding? What is important for an understanding of the field? How are identified inconsistencies resolved? What explanations have been provided by past studies or theorists that could be used to explain these findings?

Summary

Scarr (1983) suggested that excellence in scholarship is determined by examining two complementary aspects of any research manuscript, the quality of the study reported, and the quality of writing. I have attempted to address these two aspects by describing features of scholarly writing that are as important in quantitative study as the appropriate selection and use of statistical procedures. To be sure, specific presentation styles and preferences of authors vary over time. Even so, I believe that the advice offered here should remain fairly constant and applicable to authors into the forseeable future.

References

Abelson, R. P. (1995). *Statistics as principled argument.* Hillsdale, NJ: Erlbaum.

American Psychological Association (APA). (1994). *Publication manual of the American Psychological Association* (4th ed.). Washington, DC: Author.

Ary, D., Jacobs, L. C., & Razavieh, A. (1990). *Introduction to research in education* (4th ed.). Fort Worth, TX.

Benson, J. (1995, July). *Developing a strong program of construct validation: A test anxiety example.* Presidential address to the Society for Stress and Anxiety Research, Prague, Czech Republic.

Carver, R. (1993). The case against statistical significance testing, revisited. *Journal of Experimental Education, 61*(4), 287-292.

Cook, T., Campbell, D., & Peracchio, L. (1990). Quasi-experimentation. In M. Dunnette & L. Hough (Eds.), *Handbook of industrial and organizational psychology* (2nd ed., Vol. 1, pp. 491-576). Palo Alto, CA: Consulting Psychologists Press.

Creswell, J. W. (1994). *Research design: Qualitative and quantitative approaches.* Thousand Oaks, CA: Sage.

Creswell, J. W. (1998). *Qualitative inquiry and research design: Choosing among five traditions.* Thousand Oaks, CA: Sage.

Eichorn, D. H. (1985). Dissemination of scientific and professional knowledge. *American Psychologist, 40,* 1309-1316. 10

Fish, L. J. (1988). Why multivariate methods are usually vital. *Measurement and Evaluation in Counseling and Development, 21,* 130-137.

Gall, M. D., Borg, W.R., & Gall, J. P. (1996). *Educational research: An introduction* (6th ed.). White Plains, NY: Longman.

Haller, E. J., & Virkler, S. J. (1993). Another look at rural-nonrural differences in students's educational aspirations. *Journal of Research in Rural Education, 9,* 170-178.

Hamlin, H. (1966). What is research? *American Vocational Journal, 41*(6), 14-16.

Hillison, J. (1990). Using all the tools available to vocational education researchers. *Journal of Vocational Education Research, 15*(1), 1-8.

Huberty, C. J. (1994). *Applied discriminant analysis.* New York: Wiley & Sons.

Huberty, C. J., & Morris, J. D. (1988). A single contrast test procedure. *Educational and Psychological Measurement, 48,* 567-578.

Huck, S. W., & Cormier, W. H. (1996). *Reading statistics and research* (2nd ed.). New York: HarperCollins.

Huck, S. W., Cormier, W. H., & Bounds, W. G. (1974). *Reading statistics and research.* New York: HarperCollins.

Huff, D. (1982). *How to lie with statistics.* New York: W. W. Norton.

Hultgren, F H., & Coomer, D. L. (Eds.). (1989). *Alternative modes of inquiry.* Peoria, IL: Glencoe.

Huston, H. L. (1993). *Meaningfulness, statistical significance, effect size, and power analysis: A general discussion with implications for MANOVA.* Paper presented at the 22nd annual meeting of the Mid-South Educational Research Association, New Orleans, LA.

Johnson, G. M. (1993). Conceptual resolution of the educational research paradigm dichotmoy: Q-continuum. *Teacher Education Quarterly, 20*(2), 91-103.

Little, D. J. (1992). Criteria for assessing critical adult education research. *Adult Education Quarterly, 42,* 237-249.

Maxwell, S. E., & Cole, D. A. (1995). Tips for writing (and reading) methodological articles. *Psychological Bulletin, 118,* 193-198.

Moore, G. E., Burnett, M. F., & Moore, B. A. (1986). Approved practices in reporting quantitative research. *Journal of Vocational Education Research, 11*(4), 1-24.

O'Reilly, P. A. (1983). Assessment of the external validity of recently published vocational education research. *Journal of Industrial Teacher Education, 20*(3), 25-38.

Pedhazer, E. J., & Schmelkin, L. P. (1991). *Measurement, design, and analysis: An integrated approach.* Hillsdale, NJ: Erlbaum.

Robinson, D. H., & Levin, J. R. (1997). Reflections on statistical and substantive significance, with a slice of replication. *Educational Researcher, 26*(5), 21-27.

Rozeboom, W. W. (1997). Good science is abductive, not hypothetico-deductive. In L. L. Harlow, S. A. Muliak, & J. H. Steiger (Eds.), *What if there were no statistical tests?* (pp. 335-392). Mahwah, NJ: Erlbaum.

Scarr, S. (1983). An editor looks for the perfect manuscript: In American Psychological Association, Committee on Women in Psychology and Women's Program Office, *Understanding the manuscript review process: Increasing the participation of women* (pp. 5-17). Washington, DC: Author.

Schmidt, F. (1996). Statistical significance testing and cumulative knowledge in psychology: Implications for the training of researchers. *Psychological Methods, 1*(2), 115-129.

Shaver, J. P. (1993). What statistical significance testing is, and what it is not. *Journal of Experimental Education, 61*(4), 293-316. 11

Szymanski, E. M. (1993). Research design and statistical design. *Rehabilitation Counseling Bulletin, 36,* 178-182.

Thomas, R. G. (1989). Alternative research paradigms: A contrast set. *Journal of Vocational Home Economics Education, 7*(1), 48-57.

Thompson, B. (1989). Statistical significance, result importance, and result generalizability: Three noteworthy but somewhat different issues. *Measurement and Evaluation in Counseling and Development, 22,* 2-6.

Thompson, B. (1993). The use of statistical significance tests in research: Bootstrap and other alternatives. *Journal of Experimental Education, 61,* 361-377.

Thompson, B. (1996). AERA editorial policies regarding statistical significance testing: Three suggested reforms. *Educational Researcher, 25*(2), 26-30.

Thompson, B. (1997). Editorial policies regarding statistical significance tests: Further comments. *Educational Researcher, 26*(5), 29-32.

Thompson, B. (1998, January). *Why "encouraging" effect size reporting isn't working: The etiology of researcher resistance to changing practices.* Paper presented at the annual meeting of the Southwest Educational Research Association, Houston, TX. (ERIC Document Reproduction Service No. ED 416 214)

Thompson, B., & Snyder, P. A. (1997, March). *Use of statistical significance tests and reliability analyses in published counseling research.* Paper presented at the annual meeting of the American Educational Research Association, Chicago, IL. (ERIC Document Reproduction Service No. ED 408 303)

West, L. J. (1992). How to write a research report for journal publication. *Journal of Education for Business, 67,* 132-136.

Note

1. Remember Huff's (1982) text entitled *How to Lie with Statistics,* or Disraeli's declaration that there are three kinds of lies: lies, damned lies, and statistics?

APPENDIX
Research Critique Form—Beyond Statistical Findings

1. Certain elements of research are inherently subjective, although to varying degrees from one study to another, e.g., selection of research topic, justification for study, specific design, instrument selection, determination of critical alpha level, interpretation of findings, implications of results for theory and practice, etc. What subject elements can you detect in this article, if any? Do the subjective elements influence the study positively or negatively? What indicators alert you to the degree of subjectivity and its influence (potential or real) on results? When it is all said and done, do subjective elements of

the study critically threaten the integrity of the study? What could be changed to increase the integrity or precision of this study.

2. Theory can provide researchers with a foundation for explaining the phenomenon of interest, e.g., establishing context, defining variables and their relationships, predicting outcomes, and interpreting results. What theory(ies) is used to justify this study? Is the theory explained in enough detail to be meaningful to readers? Is a consistent and clear line of logic applied throughout the article? How does the use of theory guide the selection of a population, instrument(s), explanation of findings? How does theory bridge the gap between results of this study and the body of literature on this topic? Theoretically (or practically) what is the contribution of this study? What could be changed to increase the usefulness of theory to understanding this study?

3. The precision of (a) instruments used to collect data and (b) research design are, arguably, the most important elements in a quantitative research study, e.g., instrument score validity and reliability, threats to internal and external design validity. What instruments were selected to collect data of interest? How are constructs conceptualized and measured by instruments, e.g., univariate, multivariate? Does analysis support this conceptualization of variables? Do authors establish prior attempts at validation and determining reliability? What evidence is offered to (re-)establish the validity and reliability of the scores obtained and analyzed in this study? What threats exist to the integrity of these findings? Do authors examine and either minimize or eliminate competing explanations for findings? Can these results be generalized to a larger group/population? If so, describe that group and any delimitations. Have efforts been made to verify or replicate these results through cross-validation, jacknife, or bootstrap methods?

4. Statistics provide an indication of the likelihood of obtaining a given result, assuming that the null hypothesis is true (i.e., no actual difference). Are descriptive data provided for all variables (and levels of variables) included in analyses? Do authors rely solely on statistical significance to determine the importance of relationships or difference? Are p values used as indications of magnitude or practical importance? Are effect size coefficients reported and used to frame the importance of findings? If used, do authors acknowledge the criteria or delimitations used to interpret coefficients? Are adjustments made in alpha levels to maintain a priori significance levels (Type I error rate)

and avoid probability pyramiding? Are reasons offered for selecting family-wise or experiment-wise approaches?

5. Published research articles typically contain a rationale/context, purpose, methods, report of findings, and discussion of findings sections. A clear and consistent description of the background and approach(es) taken to address select issues or problems can provide the structure needed to describe, discuss, and interpret research results. Rationale—Important concepts, and terms should be introduced and defined. Have all variables (both independent and dependent) been adequately described in terms of how they are conceptualized, operationally defined, and measured? Do authors indicate the effect or contribution of their decisions? Specific connections between identified variables or concepts should be established. Is a clear context and direction for the investigation established early and then followed? Does the context or introduction lead to a logical end, i.e., the purpose, and clearly tie the investigation to a larger body of literature and an established conceptual or theoretical base. Results—A clear connection between results and purpose should be established. Do results provide answers to questions originally posed? Are descriptive data provided and described before the results of higher-order statistical analysis are presented? Are data presented in the most parsimonious form? Discussion—Discussion should be clearly tied to the available literature base. What is the answer to the main questions posed by this investigation? How do these results compare to past studies? What is new here? What is the contribution of this study to our understanding of theory and practice in the field? How are identified inconsistencies resolved? What explanations have been provided by past studies or theorists that could be used to explain these findings?

Chapter 19

Preparing a Research Summary,
Conclusions, and Recommendations Section

Curtis R. Finch

So you planned a study, conducted the research, and wrote the results. Finally you can see some light at the end of the research tunnel. You're telling everyone, "The rest of my work on this study will be a breeze." Great! But wait a minute. How do you know you're almost done? Have you talked to any of those experienced, gray haired researchers about your progress? If you asked them, they might say that the most difficult part of your work is just starting. Since a research study's summary, conclusions, and recommendations are usually the final sections to be written, they represent the three last hurdles to finishing your investigation. And they often give researchers some of the greatest writing challenges and thus, the most difficult hurdles to surmount, of the entire research process.

In this chapter I offer suggestions for preparing a summary that actually summarizes, conclusions that really conclude, and recommendations that will recommend. Those looking for specific rules or recipes or "how-to" directions may be disappointed. Most suggestions for creative writing are just not that specific. Instead, I will focus on useful ways that the summary, conclusions, and recommendations can link closely to each other and build upon the research results. Much of the information presented applies directly to both qualitative and quantitative research. Examples from both research areas have been included.

The Summary

The research summary should describe succinctly the main points of the research study. Two types of research summaries, those for journal articles and those for dissertations (or theses), are examined.

Article Summary

The article summary is typically found at the beginning of a research article or paper. It serves as a quick overview of the study and can also be an advance organizer for those who plan to read the entire article. Each journal may have its own specifications for an article summary length. However, the typical length is 100 to 150 words. An example of a summary was prepared by Wulff and Ethington (1999) for their article "A Model Comparison of Career Indecision Among Females Enrolled in Vocational and College Preparatory Tracks" which appeared in the *Journal of Vocational Education Research.*

> A path model was developed to investigate the antecedent variables associated with the career indecision of females enrolled in college preparatory and vocational curriculum tracks. A sample of 300 high school females was studied consisting of 167 enrolled in college preparatory classes and 133 from vocational education programs. Career self-efficacy was the only variable to have a direct effect on career indecision of females enrolled in both programs and also served as the primary mediator for the indirect influences of other variables on career indecision. (p. 227)

A well-prepared article summary may be the most important part of an article since it may eventually be included in electronic abstracting systems. The American Psychological Association (1994) indicates that a good summary should be accurate, self-contained, concise and specific, non-evaluative, and coherent and readable. Summaries reflect the purpose and content of the actual article (study). A self-contained summary includes everything important for the reader to know to understand the scope and results of the investigation. A concise and specific summary is one in which every part is effective as well as brief. All superfluous numbers, words, and phrases have been removed. A non-evaluative summary reports rather than assesses the study. The coherent and readable summary is written clearly such that all content is easily understood. Considering its brevity the preparation of an article summary is not an easy task. Condensing the content of an entire article, thesis, or dissertation into just a few words may require much more time than anticipated.

Thesis and Dissertation Summaries

In contrast to an article summary, a thesis or dissertation summary is quite comprehensive and, thus, more difficult to create. A thesis or dissertation summary should describe clearly and concisely what has been detailed in Chapters 1 through 4 (e.g., problem area, problem, purpose, research questions or hypotheses, related research, design and procedures, data analysis, and results). As with an article summary, a thesis or dissertation summary is of value to persons who want to understand your study but may not want to read the entire thing. However, it may also be of value to persons who have already read the dissertation and want to refresh their thoughts about its content.

Thesis or dissertation summaries are typically located at the beginning of Chapter 5 and precede Conclusions and Recommendations sections that are also contained in that chapter. Although there is no exact length for the summary a useful rule of thumb is from 12 to 18 double–spaced pages. This recommended length is tied to a suggestion. Valuable time can be saved by preparing thesis or dissertation summaries using the format found in most research articles. Why look at journal articles? The answer is simple. It will allow you to make progress toward completing a journal manuscript concurrent with the preparation of the summary section. When the summary has been completed much of the content for a future journal manuscript will be sitting right there in Chapter 5. A second reason for doing this deals with the summary content. Since a research article should be concise and easy to understand, preparing a summary using a research article format should result in a section that is concise and easier to read and understand.

When preparing the summary in a journal format the following or similar, sub-headings may be used, but sub-headings and content may vary depending on the focus, quantitative or qualitative, of the research:

- *Introduction.* Include the need for your research, conceptual or theoretical framework, related research, study purpose, and research questions or purpose.
- *Method.* Briefly describe the participants, instruments or protocols, research procedure, and analysis of the investigation.
- *Findings.* Summarize the results generated from your analysis but don't include tables and figures.

This approach works fairly well with graduate students but a problem may arise. When sub-headings within the summary section are prepared in this way they may not agree with what some universities prescribe in their graduate student handbooks. To resolve this problem it is important to know how your university wants the thesis or dissertation to be formatted. Also, make sure your research advisor will support the "article in Chapter 5" approach.

Conclusions

Conclusions answer the following question, "What specific inferences may be made from the research results?" Conclusions should not regurgitate the results nor should they consist of vague, non-supportable claims. The Conclusions section may begin by focusing on whether or not your findings offer support for the original research questions. It is also useful to point out how your results are similar to or different from the results of related research (American Psychological Association, 1994). Connecting your findings with past investigations provides a link with studies reviewed in Chapter 2 of the thesis or dissertation. A good example of linking results with past studies was provided by Sipon (1996) in his quantitative study.

> Contrary to Herzberg's theory which posits that only motivator factors determine job satisfaction, and only hygiene factors determine job dissatisfaction; both types of factors were sources of job satisfaction/dissatisfaction for Malaysian polytechnic instructors. This result was consistent with the findings of other studies (Al-Mekhlafie, 1991; Atta-Safoh, 1985; Bowen, 1980; Congo, 1986; Davis, 1983; Malone, 1993; Murray, 1983; Nagle, 1987; Openshaw, 1980). (p. 220)

It is acceptable to speculate in the Conclusions section but only if such speculation is closely aligned with either the study results or theoretical/conceptual base. Speculation beyond this point is strongly discouraged. Yaakub (1998) provided the following passage in his quantitiative study that reflects a solid approach to informed speculation.

> Although the mean achievement for supplemental CAI was higher than the mean achievement for replacement CAI, the difference was not significant. This non-significance may be due to the amount or proportion of additional instruction in supplemental CAI in relation to the traditional instruction received by the experimental and control groups. Some supplemental CAI studies provided only five hours of additional computerized instruction. Perhaps a minimum amount of supplemental CAI must be provided before a significant difference may be achieved. (p. 82)

With qualitative studies the author may choose to present research conclusions in a more encompassing manner. In other words, the researcher is not bound by what some people refer to as traditional quantitative research structure and rules. Roe (1993) offers an example from an ethnographic study of a corporation.

> While management was viewed as making innovation efforts possible, it was also perceived as largely responsible for preventing the process from working. Respondents indicated that management was the greatest disadvantage to innovation. In particular, managers were thought to be risk-adverse and over-controlling. The Five Part Management Process, which was developed to manage new venture development and "empower" the Business Concept Teams (BCTs), was thought by those closely involved with it to actually interfere with new venture development. (p. 167)

Recommendations

The Recommendations section focuses directly on how the current investigation links with future activities. Thus, all recommendations must be clear and concise. Clarity can be enhanced by linking each recommendation back to the study's results.

Each recommendation should be presented in paragraph form. Although numerous theses and dissertations may be found that include long lists of recommendations, such lists immediately generate questions such as "Why?" and "So what?" Preparing a small number of the most important recommendations, writing a concise paragraph about each recommendation, and linking study results with future directions can greatly enhance the application of recommendations made by scholars.

Theses and dissertations conducted in applied fields often include recommendations for both future research and practice. Including both types of recommendations can provide valuable information for both researchers and practitioners. A qualitative study by Mooney (1998) that focused on family contributions to the work readiness of youth with learning disabilities includes several useful recommendations for future research. One of these is provided below.

> The theme of independence appeared throughout the text. Perhaps future research could examine this theme more closely. Several points of interest may be investigated, such as the coexistence of independent and compliant behaviors in school and work settings, the identification of appropriate advocacy roles for families in the youths' work settings, and the identification of effective, proactive strategies for youth dealing with difficult work situations. (p. 144)

Another useful set of recommendations for future research was prepared by Daughtry (1995). The following recommendation is from her quantitative study.

> The results of this study have particular relevance to persons at the local, state, and university educational levels who work with leadership development programs. The finding that others do not perceive a difference between male and female effectiveness supports the androgynous nature of the effective leader and the development of a diverse population of leaders. These findings provide a rationale for making decisions relative to program development and program content. (p. 119)

Putting It All Together

It is important to recognize that quality inquiry is grounded in both quality writing and quality research. Even the best research will not be accepted if it has not been communicated properly; and poor research cannot be made better by using even the most convincing writing style. Much of the quality of a research article, thesis, or dissertation may be linked to a statement that is at odds with the laws of physics: The whole equals more than the sum of its parts. Related to writing, this means the various sections and sub-sections of a research document must contribute to the document as a whole and in the process make it more valuable than its parts. To accomplish this researchers must link various parts of the study in subtle ways so they work together to benefit the whole research document.

The preparation of a quality research summary, conclusions, and recommendations is reflected in the following questions:

- Does the summary capture the essence of the research study and, in doing so consume much less space and retain an impact that is similar to the entire study?
- Do the conclusions draw directly from the study results and build specific inferences from them?
- Do the recommendations focus in a clear, concise manner on how the study links with future activities (i.e., practice and research)?
- Collectively, do the summary, conclusions, and recommendations contribute to the research document as a whole and, in the process, make it a more valuable study?

When these four questions have been answered satisfactorily you should be well on your way to completing your research study.

Writing that links parts together in this way can be very challenging. It is the sort of thing that can be felt but at the same time is extremely difficult to describe. However, this is what researchers should seek to accomplish. What benefits can accrue from such an accomplishment? Perhaps the two that are most important include getting published and becoming a graduate student emeritus!

References

American Psychological Association. (1994). *Publication manual of the American Psychological Association* (4th ed.). Washington, DC: Author.

Daughtry, L. (1995). *Vocational administrator leadership effectiveness as a function of gender and leadership style.* Unpublished doctoral dissertation, Virginia Polytechnic Institute and State University, Blacksburg.

Mooney, A. (1998). *Family contributions to the work readiness of youth with learning disabilities.* Unpublished doctoral dissertation, Virginia Polytechnic Institute and State University, Blacksburg.

Roe, A. A. (1993). *Corporate ethnography: An analysis of organizational and technological innovation.* Unpublished doctoral dissertation, Virginia Polytechnic Institute and State University, Blacksburg.

Sipon, A. B. (1996). *The applicability of Herzberg's two-factor theory to the job satisfaction of Malaysian polytechnic instructors.* Unpublished doctoral dissertation, Virginia Polytechnic Institute and State University, Blacksburg.

Wulff, M. B., & Ethington, C. A. (1999). A model comparison of career indecision among females enrolled in vocational and college preparatory tracks. *Journal of Vocational Education Research, 24,* 227-238.

Yaakub, M. N. (1998). *Meta-analysis of the effectiveness of computer-assisted instruction in technical education and training.* Unpublished doctoral dissertation, Virginia Polytechnic Institute and State University, Blacksburg.

Chapter 20

Tips on Proofreading and Editing

Sherilee R. Carpenter

Writing papers, theses, and dissertations can be a daunting task. It is true that writers are more often made than born. Gaining the skill, however, is worth the effort for many reasons. The ability to write well will be valuable after graduation. It is the rare job that does not require some sort of writing. Most job announcements today include the words "excellent written and oral communication skills" for a reason. Those who will enjoy future success know how to write well.

Good writers not only have effective communication skills but can take those important last steps in the writing process, editing and proofreading, that demonstrate commitment to making the best possible written presentation. The first step, though, is learning to write well. It is vital to an effective authorial experience to write to your comfort level in communicating about your topic. Most good writers develop excellence through practice, practice, and more practice, followed by seeking constructive comment and guidance and learning from others' example. One of the first pieces of advice I give students who are developing writing skills after gaining a good grasp of grammar and structure basics, is to pay attention to other authors' styles. As you conduct research and read through gathered materials pay attention not only to the authors' scholarship but to their writing style.

What is style? Style takes two forms: [1] it serves as your distinctive manner of expression in writing, and [2] it is a convention with regard to spelling, punctuation, and capitalization. Two of the most used style guides are the *Publication Manual of the American Psychological*

Association (1994, 4th ed.) and *The Chicago Manual of Style* (14th ed.). Here, we're talking about the first form: the way students express themselves in writing. As you seek examples of good writing, ask the following questions: "How effective is the article in making its argument?" "Is the style worthy of emulation?" "Can readers follow the style comfortably and effectively?" "What is the difference between good, clear writing and less effective communication?" Answering these questions through careful analysis of written material and learning good writing skills and processes from that analysis will go a long way toward becoming a good, effective communicator.

This chapter contains tips and advice writers will find helpful as they advance through the process of preparing a paper, thesis, or other written document. First, I offer a list of three basic rules of thumb when writing; this is followed by lists of grammar and style problems and issues commonly found in papers. Then a checklist for basic organization of a paper is provided. Since headings are an important organizational strategy in writing, one that aids readers in negotiating various sections of a paper and the complexities of a topic, a suggested format is provided that follows the *APA Publication Manual* (1994).

Over the years students have told me that guidance on compiling and formatting references is useful. Readers find reference lists valuable for many reasons not the least of which is their service as sources of information on a topic. I offer some tips about reference lists, and provide the APA style for formatting references. When compiling a reference list or citing references in a text the primary issue is consistency. The APA style is included here so that students have one possible style guide for references. In addition, information is provided on citing electronic and Internet sources in reference lists. Since proofreading is the second main topic of this chapter a list of proofreading tips and techniques is provided. Students have found several of these recommendations especially helpful in turning in the most professional end product. Finally, a short list of proofreading symbols, a sort of editorial shorthand, is provided to familiarize you with the symbols editors and proofreaders use when marking a paper. Tips on resources writers may find useful in gaining and maintaining narrative skills end the chapter.

Three Important Rules of Thumb

Over the years, three issues have appeared consistently in student papers: lack of sources in citations; nonappearance of page numbers on papers; and lack of proofreading. Here are several remedies:

• Always include the **source** for a quote or information not commonly known.

The following style is suggested.

For example, if the reference would appear in the reference list as Nisberg, J. S. (1990). *The Random House handbook of business terms* (3rd ed.). New York: Random House, then the text reference (the reference you would use in your narrative) would be (Nisberg, 1990, p. [insert appropriate page number]). Using this style provides your readers with important information: the author of your quote/source, the year it appeared, and the page number so they can locate the information themselves.

• Always put **page numbers** on your document.

• **Always proofread.** Proofread papers carefully. Presentation of ideas is as important as content. The time you take in both writing and reviewing your paper says a lot about your professionalism. Proofreading tips are offered later in this chapter.

General Issues

There are several issues students commonly encounter in writing. The following list and explanations should help you avoid these problems.

1. **Collective nouns.** Collective nouns such as jury, committee, audience, community, government, etc., name a class or group. They are usually singular because they emphasize a group functioning as a unit. Firms, as corporate entities, are frequently included in this category, for example, "Disney is proud of its employees."

2. **Noun/verb agreement.** Take the extra time to ensure that verbs agree with their subjects in number (singular or plural) and in person (first, second, or third).

3. **Who, Which, That.** Use *who*, not *which*, to refer to persons. Generally, use *that* to refer to things or, occasionally, to a group or class of people.

4. **Its vs. It's.** A common grammar mistake involves it's and its: it's is *shorthand* for it is, while its is a possessive.

5. **Active vs. passive voice.** Keep track of active vs. passive voice. When a verb is in the active voice the subject of the sentence does the action. In the passive voice the subject receives the action.

6. **Affect and effect.** Affect is usually a verb meaning "to influence." Effect is usually a noun meaning "result." Effect can also be a verb meaning "to bring about."

7. **Write effectively.** Effective writing means avoiding redundancies, empty or inflated phrases, and needlessly complex structures, as well as eliminating confusing shifts in point of view. It also means using active verbs whenever possible.

8. **Citation/reference agreement.** It is very important to be sure that the citation of author(s) and year listed in your narrative agrees with the reference list you include at the back of your paper.

9. **Additional style/grammar issues.**

Between/among. Use **between** when the object of the preposition consists of only two items; use **among** when describing three or more items.

Cannot. Preferred form of can not.

Commas around transitional adverbs and similar interpolations. Words like therefore, accordingly, indeed, certainly, of course, perhaps, and however often need to be surrounded by commas because such words frequently break the continuity between verbs and objects, or require commas to prevent misreading.

May possibly, might possibly. Verb constructions including both *may/might* and *possibly* express possibility twice, because each does the same job in this type of construction. Use either may/might, or possibly, but not both.

Serial commas. In a series of coordinate words, phrases, or clauses in which a conjunction precedes only the final item, a comma should follow every item. *For example.* On the New York Stock Exchange yesterday the industrials were up 9.5, the transports were down 4.35, and the utilities were unchanged.

Manuscript Preparation Instructions

Other authors in this volume cover the "how-to's" of organizing a research paper. The checklist provided in Table 20.1 serves to summarize that guidance. An effective paper is not only exhaustively researched but is organized to put the information at its best advantage in arguing a question or explaining a topic. Aside from the commonly acknowledged organization strategy, there are various tips that further enhance effective communication. These are provided as well.

TABLE 20.1
Paper Organization Checklist

TITLE
- Should be informative

INTRODUCTION
- Include your thesis statement
- Include a brief summary of the relevant facts for your topic (in most cases this summary should be about one-two paragraphs)
- Save specific details for illustrating particular points later in the paper
- Include a brief paragraph that outlines the basic format of your discussion, a sort of road map for the reader

BODY
- Should be a complete examination of the topic
- May be divided into two parts
- Background on the topic and literature/citation of authorities
- The body/discussion of the topic as represented in [1] your research and [2] your assessment of the research as it affects the discussion of your topic. This could include identifying key issues or questions and then looking at them one by one according to the information you've collected.
- How are those most involved in the topic reacting to it?
- What are the most pertinent points of the debates?
- Are there solutions to issues raised in the topic?
- Possible policy implications?
- Recommendations? Assertions, claims, or recommendations should be backed up with facts. A thorough job of research will provide you with the material needed to take either side of a topic. Be prepared to discuss pros and cons equally convincingly and intelligently.

CONCLUSIONS
- Should restate the thesis question/topic in light of materials and discussions examined in earlier sections of the paper.
- Offer final observations and reinforce your main points with your research.

Headings

Well-ordered and well-organized papers frequently utilize headings to guide readers, especially if the topic is complex or oft-studied and thus offering many theoretical perspectives and schools of thought. More than the issue of headings as signposts, though, is the need to provide headings in a consistent format. The APA style for headings is offered here as one possible organizational strategy.

Two levels of headings:

Centered, Uppercase and Lowercase Heading

Flush-Left, Underlined, Upper and Lowercase Side Heading

Three levels of headings:

Centered, Uppercase and Lowercase Heading

Flush-Left, Underlined, Upper and Lowercase Side Heading

Indented, underlined, lowercase paragraph heading ending with a period.

Four levels of headings:

Centered, Uppercase and Lowercase Heading

Centered, Underlined, Uppercase and Lowercase Heading

Flush-Left, Underlined, Upper and Lowercase Side Heading

Indented, underlined, lowercase paragraph heading ending with a period.

References

It is vitally important during the writing process to keep track of all references used in constructing a narrative. There is little more annoying than to have to spend hours hunting for lost or incomplete references. As important as it is to ensure that all references cited in the manuscript appear in the reference list, except for personal communications. All entries that appear in the reference list must be cited in the text. Reference list entries normally contain the following elements: author(s), year of publication, title, place of publication, and publisher. The style provided here is from the *APA Publication Manual* (1994).

Some General Rules to Follow

1. Arrange reference entries in alphabetical order by the surname of the first author.

2. Single-author entries precede multiple-author entries beginning with the same surname.

3. References with the same first author and different second and third authors are arranged alphabetically by the surname of the second author, and so on.

4. References with the same authors in the same order are arranged by year of publication, the earliest first.

5. References by the same author (or by the same two or more authors) with the same publication year are arranged alphabetically by title (excluding A or The) by adding a, b, c, etc., to the publication year.

6. References by different authors with the same surname are arranged alphabetically by the first initial.

7. Alphabetize corporate authors by first significant word of name.

8. Only *anonymous* works are alphabetized under Anonymous.

9. Non-authored works are alphabetized by the first significant word of their title, as are legal works.

In text:
(Burton, 1999, p. 1) (Burton & Brannon, 1998; Thompson & Brown, 1997)

In reference list:
Journal article
Bell, A., Harris, H., & Vella, D. (1996). Disturbance in sleep patterns. *Journal of Sleep, 4,* 126-134.

Entire (special) issue of journal
Glaser, R., & Bond, L. (Eds.). (1981). Testing: Concepts, policy, practice, and research [special issue]. *American Psychologist, 36*(10).

Journal supplement
Vella, D., Harris, H., & King, J. K. (1994). Genetic basis of segmentation. *European Journal of Insects, 639*(Suppl. 23), 328-400.

Non-English journal article, title translated into English
Assink, E. M. H., & Verloop, N. (1977). Het aanleren van deel-geheel relaties in her aavankelijk rekeronderwijs [Teaching part-whole relations in elementary mathematics instruction]. *Pedagogische Studien, 54,* 130-142.

Book
   Bell, A., & Harris, C. (1995). *The elements of style* (3rd ed.). New York: Macmillan.

Edited book
   Letheridge, S., & Cannon, C. R. (Eds.). (1980). *Bilingual education: Teaching English as a second language.* New York: Praeger.

Book without authors
   College bound seniors. (1979). Princeton, NJ: College Board Publishers.

Several volumes in a multi-volume book, publication over more than one year
   Wilson, J. G., & Fraser, F. C. (Eds.). (1977-1978). *Handbook of teratology* (Vols. 1-4). New York: Plenum.

English translation of a book
   Luria, A. R. (1969). *The mind of a mnemonist* (L. Solotaroff, Trans.). New York: Avon Books. (Original work published 1965).

Article or chapter in edited book
   Wilson, G., Bell, A., & Head, K. (1990). Onset of senile dementia. In L. M. Poon (Ed.), *Aging* (pp. 2-56). Washington, DC: American Psychological Association.

Article in edited book reprint from another source
   Brown, C., & Smith, J. (1997). Educational paradigms. In J. Rogers (Ed.), *Secondary education* (pp. 7-14). Wantage: Octavo. (Reprinted from *Education Reviews,* 1995, *32,* 211-216)

Proceedings book
   Hypher, J. A. (1987). Second order cognition. In B. Skeif (Ed.), *Proceedings of the First International Symposium on Cognition* (pp. 23-48). Wantage: Octavo.   .

Thesis
   Gartside, S. (1994). *Helplessness and depression.* Unpublished doctoral dissertation, McGill University, Montreal.

Additional Text Reference/Reference List Information: Internet Sources

   Citing Internet documents can be tricky. More often than not they have an author, title, and so on, and can follow the guidelines for citing a regular document. Sometimes the site does not provide an author's name, though. When this is the case, insert the document title where you would normally put the author's name and proceed accordingly. Also provide the Internet address in your reference lists. Doing so is useful to those who may want to consult the document themselves.

The citing of electronic sources of information, that is, information gathered from the Internet, has become a source of concern. Two sites that may be helpful to writers are the APA web site at (http://www.apa.org/journals/webref.html) and a good web site at the University of Vermont, (http://www.uvm.edu/~ncrane/estyles/). Here are some examples:

Citing a web site
Kidpsych is a wonderful interactive Web site for children (http://www.kidpsych.org).

Citing specific documents on a web site
Sleek, S. (1996, January). Psychologists build a culture of peace. *APA Monitor*, pp. 1, 31. Retrieved January 25, 1996 from the World Wide Web: http://www.apa.org/monitor/peacea.html

Citing articles and abstracts from electronic databases
Retrieval statement should include the date of retrieval and source (e.g., DIALOG, WESTLAW, SIRS, Electric Library), followed in parentheses by the name of the specific database used and any additional information needed to retrieve the item.

Examples:

Federal Bureau of Investigation. (1998, March). Encryption: Impact on law enforcement. Location: Publisher. Retrieved from SIRS database (SIRS Government Reporter, CD-ROM, Fall 1998 release).

Kerrigan, D. C., Todd, M. K., & Riley, P. O. (1998). Knee osteoarthritis and high-heeled shoes. *The Lancet, 251*, 1399-1401. Retrieved January 27, 1999 from DIALOG database (#457, The Lancet) on the World Wide Web: http://www.dialogweb.com

Making web citations in text
Follow the author/date format described in the *APA Publication Manual*. To cite specific parts of a Web document indicate the chapter, figure, table, or equation as appropriate. For quotations, give page numbers (or paragraph numbers) if they are available. If page or paragraph numbers are not available (i.e., they are not visible to every reader) they can be omitted from the in-text citation. With most browsers, readers will still be able to search for the quoted material

Proofreading Procedures

Good writing is important but not the end of the writing process. To ensure the best possible product a writer has to be an effective proofreader. A well-written paper connotes respect for the audience/readership, thorough professionalism and scholarship, and a healthy regard for detail.

There are several steps to proofreading that, if followed, break the lock between expectation and perception, enabling you to see what's really in the paper and not what you think is there. Once you've completed these steps, you will have found 99 percent of the errors you are going to find. At this point, give the paper to a friend to read, someone who can provide constructive criticism.

- Don't start proofreading until you are happy with a paper's content; in other words, get your ideas down on paper in some sort of coherent fashion before you worry about subject/verb agreement.
- Once you've finished writing a paper look it over for obvious errors such as spelling errors, typographical errors, punctuation, etc. On this first pass-through the paper read from beginning to end, marking questionable areas. Afterwards, set it aside and do something else. Setting the paper aside is vital; if you don't leave it alone you will be too close to it to catch careless errors.
- After several hours have passed *read through it again*. This time look for grammatical errors, awkward sentence construction, and general things you do not like or want to change. Make your corrections now (or while reading it if you're doing it online).
- *Prune it.* Try to shorten your manuscript by 20 to 30 percent without removing any information. There's always a better way to say the same thing that takes less space.
- *Rebuild.* If you need length and have anything else that needs to be said, add it. Repeat the first three steps as often as you have time for, stopping with the second step. (There's no final answer to "How many times is enough?" Some read a paper as many as fifteen times before handing it in.)
- Do one more quick read for new typographical errors and spelling errors created by your changes.
- *Polish.* Read it aloud slowly and listen to it as though you had an audience listening to you. Make adjustments as you go. Reading seems to be particularly good for catching repetitive word use, faulty parallelisms, and so forth. Check the spelling on anything that

looks weird or odd. Run the spellchecker and look up anything it challenges before you change it.

• If you have a problem seeing errors read your paper word by word from the end to the beginning, backwards. Start at the bottom and look at each sentence in reverse order and fix any problems that appear. Reading backwards forces the writer to slow down and see the words in a new context. It may be tedious but it works.

List of Proofreading/Editing Symbols

Those who provide writing and editorial advice often use a sort of shorthand to communicate changes on a paper. The list below summarizes symbols typically used by editors, proofreaders, and professors.

delete		close up space	
uppercase	caps	period	
lowercase	lc	indent	or
hyphen		italicize	ital
dash		comma	
space		semi-colon	
transpose		colon	

Resources

Web Sites

A good writing-related web site is the Purdue Writing Lab at http://owl.english.purdue.edu. The site contains good advice for writers having specific problems with the writing process (e.g., paper organization, good sentences, etc.), exercises with which to practice grammar and writing, and handouts on writing topics.

Citations are a perennial problem for writers. In education-related areas, the American Psychological Association (APA) Style Guide is more preferred. Comprehensive information on APA style may be found at http://www.apa.org/journals.

How to Determine the Quality of Web Site Information

Apply the common sense filter. Begin by examining the organization's introductory page.

- An organization's first pages should provide clear, concise, objective information about the organization and what it does. There should be contact information and a webmaster and/or other author listed for additional information.
- Examine the URL. A lot can be told about an organization's web address. First, determine whether the address is appropriate to its content. Most use their name or as close as is possible; if the page is stored on GeoCities, for example, it is not likely to be an official web site.
- Bias? Information found on web sites requires critical, careful reading. Bias may not always be readily evident. It's easy to spot when conveyed in a one-sided argument, but more difficult to ascertain when couched in an allegedly objective comparison/pro-con argument. Look for a balance of views and avoid sites that exist primarily to promote specific issues or agendas.

Conclusion

Good writing does not always come easily. It requires skills, patience, and diligence. In following the tips and using the resources described here, good writers will become better, and beginning authors will develop skills and know-how that will serve them well in the course of their professional life. Remember that the guidance offered in books like this one is valuable, but it will have a greater impact combined with working one-on-one with editors and writing specialists when questions arise or feedback is needed.

References

American Psychological Association. (1994). *Publication Manual*, 4th edition. Washington, DC: Author.

Baker, S. (1981). *The Practical Stylist*, 5th edition. New York: Harper and Row.

The Chicago Manual of Style. (1993). 14th edition. Chicago, IL: University of Chicago Press.

Ebbitt, W. A., & Ebbitt, D. R.. (1990). *Index to English*, 8th edition. New York: Oxford University Press.

Hacker, D. (1993). *A Pocket Style Manual*. Boston, MA: Bedford Books, St. Martin's Press.

Hacker, D. (1995). *A Writer's Reference*, 3rd edition. Boston, MA: Bedford Books.

The New York Public Library Writers' Guide to Style and Usage. (1994). New York: Harper Collins.

Schall, J. (1995). *Style for Students: Effective Writing in Science and Engineering.* Edina, MN: Burgess International Group, Inc.

Schwartz, M., & the Task Force on Bias-Free Language of the Association of
American University Presses. (1995). *Guidelines for Bias-Free Writing.* Bloomington, IN: Indiana University Press.
Strunk, W., Jr., & White, E. B. (1979). *The Elements of Style*, 3rd edition. New York: Macmillan.

Subject Index

abstract (*See* Summary)

across–methods triangulation, 117 (*See also* Triangulation)

action research (*See* Applied research)

adjusted R^2 value (*See* Multiple regression analysis)

affiliation variables (*See* Variable)

Alternative research paradigms, 7-13 (*See also* Constructivism, Feminism, Positivism, Postpositivism, Postmodernism, Poststructuralism, Qualitative, Quantitative)

analogical reasoning, 181

analysis of covariance (ANCOVA), 189, 190

analysis of variance (ANOVA), 182, 188-189, 274-275, 289-290, 305-309; focused contrasts, 309-320; post hoc tests, 306-307

APA manual, 368, 375-376, 386

applied research, 110 (*See also* Mixed methods, Mixed models)

archival data, 142

asymmetrical log-linear analysis (*See* Log-linear analysis)

available data (*See* Secondary data)

axiom, 80

basic research, 110

Boolean operators, 46 (*See also* Review of literature, Search strategies)

categorical data, 175-176, 184; coding, 195

case study, 95; analysis, 147-149; case selection, 138-139; data collection, 142-145; definition, 129-131; designs, 134-138, 141-142; examples, 151-153; organizing data, 145-146; reliability, 140-141; reporting, 149-151; single case design, 137-138; types, 132-134; validity of, 139-140

Chapter 1, 57-59; design checklist, 70-71 (*See also* Introduction)

Chapter 2 (*See* Review of literature)

Chapter 5: contents of, 372-373 (*See also* Conclusions, Recommendations, Summary)

chi-square (χ^2) analysis, 196, 276-277, 285-289; formula, 286-288

Cronbach alpha, 240-241 (*See also* Internal consistency reliability)

coding data, 169

The Editors and Contributors

EDITORS

Edgar I. Farmer, EdD

Edgar I. Farmer is Associate Professor of Education, and Director of the Postsecondary Technical and Community College Leadership in Workforce Education and Development program at Pennsylvania State University. He is also Site Director for the National Research and Dissemination Centers on Career and Technical Education. Before assuming current his responsibilities, Dr. Farmer served as the professor-in-charge of the Workforce Education & Development program at the Pennsylvania State University. He served as Director of Graduate Programs in the Department of Adult and Community College Education at North Carolina State University. Dr. Farmer has worked extensively with school districts, government agencies, and other universities as a consultant in vocational education. His research interests focus on postsecondary technical education students and cultural diversity in the workplace He has served as Vice-President for the National Association of Industrial and Technical Teacher Educators, is a past editor of the *Occupational Educational Forum* (a national refereed journal in vocational education), served as Guest Editor for an issue of the *Journal for Vocational Special Needs Education* on international aspects of vocational education for special populations, and is a W. K. Kellogg National Fellow.

Jay W. Rojewski, PhD

Jay W. Rojewski is Professor in the Department of Occupational Studies, University of Georgia. Dr. Rojewski received the PhD from the University of Nebraska-Lincoln in 1990. He has published widely in scholarly journals on the career behavior, career development, and occupational choice of adolescents and young adults with special needs, particularly youth with learning disabilities, economic disadvantage, or from culturally diverse backgrounds. He is a past editor of the *Journal for Vocational Special Needs Education,* and the *Journal of Vocational Education Research.* He was the 1993 AVERA Outstanding Beginning Scholar and 1994 University Council for Vocational Education's Young Scholar. Dr. Rojewski was selected as a University of Georgia Lilly Teaching Fellow for the 1993-94 academic year, has been recognized by the UGA chapter of Kappa Delta Epsilon (student nominations) for excellence in teaching (1994) and as the outstanding faculty member in the UGA College of Education (1996). Dr. Rojewski was also recognized in 1997 with the Richard B. Russell Outstanding Undergraduate Teaching award, one of the university's highest awards for recognition of teaching.

CONTRIBUTORS

Pamela Bettis is affiliated with the University of Idaho. She received her PhD in Educational Theory and Social Foundations of Education at the University of Toledo in 1994 and has taught at Auburn University and the Oklahoma State University. She has published in journals such as *Sociology of Education, Urban Review, Journal of Vocational Education Research,* and *Journal of Negro Education* and has a chapter in Stephen Ball's *Major Writings in the Sociology of Education.* Her research interests include the political and economic contexts of schooling; how race, class and gender operate in schools; postindustrial work; and issues in qualitative inquiry.

James L. Burrow is Coordinator of the graduate Training and Development Program at North Carolina State University. He received his BA and MA degrees in marketing (distributive) education from the University of Northern Iowa and a PhD from the University of Nebraska–Lincoln. He has held faculty appointments at the University of Northern Iowa, the University of Wisconsin-Madison, the University of Nebraska–Lincoln, and North Carolina State University. He has directed or co-directed of 20 research and development projects obtaining funding of over $400,000. He is the author or co-author of three texts in marketing and business, and a professional reference in evaluating adult education and training programs. His research interests include developing models for assessing the transfer of training and the value of performance improvement strategies to the organization.

Ernest W. Brewer is Professor in the Department of Human Resource Development at the University of Tennessee. He is also the Principal Investigator/Director of Federal Programs. He recently completed a two-year appointment as Department Head of the Department of Child and Family Studies. Dr. Brewer has authored or co-authored a variety of books and articles. *Moving to Online: Making the Transition from Traditional Instruction and Communication Strategies* (2001, Corwin Press); *Foundations of Workforce Education: Historical, Philosophical, and Theoretical Applications* (2000, Kendall/Hunt), *Finding Funding: Grantwriting and Project Implementation* (2001, 4th ed., Sage), *Promising Practices* (1999, Holcomb Hathaway), *Characteristics, Skills, and Strategies of the Ideal Educator* (2000, Pearson Education); *and 13 Proven Ways to Get Your Message Across* (1997, Corwin Press) are six of his recent books. He is also Editor of the *Journal of Educational Opportunity* and the *International Journal of Vocational Education and Training*.

Sherilee R. Carpenter is Editor and Research Assistant for the Institute for Policy Research and Evaluation, Pennsylvania State University. She has more than 20 years of experience in the technical editing of peer-reviewed journals, textbook copyediting, and the editing of scholarly work by faculty at universities across the United States. Ms. Carpenter works with students in writing-intensive courses at Penn State and has given several guest lectures on the writing and editorial process.

Jeffrey Chen is Director of Institutional Research and Analysis at Cleveland State University. Prior to joining Cleveland State, he held a similar position at West Virginia University at Parkersburg where he also taught statistics. He received his bachelor's degree from Beijing University of Physical Culture, and both his master's and doctoral degrees from Ohio University. Dr. Chen's research interests include data management, institutional effectiveness and program evaluation, and student outcomes assessment.

Barbara W. Farmer is Principal of Houserville/Lemont Elementary Schools and chairperson of the Professional Development Committee in the State College Area School District, State College, Pennsylvania. She received her Doctor of Education degree from the University of North Carolina, Chapel Hill and master's degree from North Carolina A & T State University, both in Educational Leadership and Policy. Dr. Farmer is a former Business Education teacher in the Hampton City Schools with a BS degree from Hampton University. Her research interests are organizational structures of teachers in traditional and magnet schools, and cultural diversity initiatives in the workplace.

Fadia M. Nasser is Assistant Professor in the School of Education, Tel Aviv University, Israel where she is responsible for teaching research methods and applied statistics. Dr. Nasser received the PhD from the University of Georgia. Her research interests include validity, statistical modeling, and test anxiety.

Curtis R. Finch is Professor of Vocational and Technical Education at Virginia Polytechnic Institute and State University. He has been a senior Fulbright scholar in Cyprus, and visiting Research Fellow at universities in Finland and Australia. From 1988 to 1999 he served as Virginia Tech Site Director for the National Center for Research in Vocational Education. He has been President of three different national associations and has served as Editor of three international professional journals. He has written, presented, and consulted extensively in the areas of technical education curriculum, leadership, and human resource development.

Jeffrey A. Gliner is Professor in the Department of Occupational Therapy and an affiliate faculty member of the School of Education at Colorado State University. His major areas of research emphasis are program evaluation and research methodology. He has evaluated or is currently evaluating projects from the U.S. Department of Education, National Science Foundation, Centers for Disease Control, and Kellogg Foundation. He has over 75 publications, and recently co-authored a textbook on research methods. In 2001, he received the College of Applied Human Sciences Scholarly Excellence Award.

Gene Gloeckner is Associate Professor in Education at Colorado State University. He has taught research methods courses for 20 years. He has published many articles related to quantitative and qualitative research methodology, and has been the evaluator on grants funded by the U.S. Department of Education and National Science Foundation. He recently co-authored a research methods text on the use and interpretation of SPSS.

James Gregson is Director and Professor in the Division of Adult, Counselor, and Technology Education at the University of Idaho. His research and teaching interests focus on the philosophy, sociology, and history of work education. His conceptual and philosophical scholarship, as well as his empirical research, is informed by pragmatism and critical theory. He was awarded a doctorate in vocational education with a minor in sociology at Virginia Tech in 1990 where he was a research associate for the National Center for Research in Vocational Education. He is the author of more than 30 national refereed publications, four of which have won best manuscript awards, and has made over 60 national presentations. He has served as a consultant in such international contexts as Mongolia, Brazil, and Canada.

Edwin L. Herr is Distinguished Professor of Education (Counselor Education and Counseling Psychology), Associate Dean for Graduate Studies, Research, and Faculty Development, and Interim Department Head for Adult Education, Instructional Systems, and Workforce Education and Development, Pennsylvania State University. Until July 1, 1992, Herr served as Head of the Department of Counselor Education, Counseling Psychology, and Rehabilitation Services Education or earlier department iterations for 24 years. During this time, he also served as University Director of Vocational Teacher Education and Director of the Center for Professional Personnel Development in Vocational Education and in 1998-99 as Interim Dean. He received his BS degree in Business Education from Shippensburg State College (1955), an MA in Psychological Foundations, Professional Diploma in Coordination of Guidance Services, and EdD in Counseling and Student Personnel Administration from Teachers College, Columbia University (1959, 1961, and 1963, respectively), where he was an Alumni Fellow.

Brian Hess is Project Director at Psychological Assessment Resources, Inc. in Tampa, Florida. His research interests are applied univariate and multivariate statistics, educational and psychological assessment, and program evaluation.

Roger B. Hill is Associate Professor in the Department of Occupational Studies, University of Georgia. He accepted this position in the fall of 1993 after 18 years of prior teaching experience at the secondary and post-secondary levels. Dr. Hill came to the University of Georgia from Hiwassee College in Madisonville, TN where he was Coordinator of Academic Computing and Professor of Technology Education. He is a graduate of the University of Tennessee, Knoxville in 1992 with a PhD in Education, holds the Master of Science degree in Education from Northern Illinois University, and has a Bachelor of Science degree in Education from North Carolina State University. His research focus is technology education and work ethic.

Carl J Huberty has been Professor in the Department of Educational Psychology, University of Georgia since 1969. He received his PhD from the University of Iowa. Dr. Huberty's teaching and writing interests are focused on multivariate data analysis methods.

Mohamed H. Hussein is a doctoral candidate and graduate research assistant in the Department of Educational Psychology, University of Georgia. He also serves as a consultant in the Academic Computer Center in the College of Education.

Li-Shyung Hwang is Senior Research Analyst of Planning and Research at Central Piedmont Community College in Charlotte, North Carolina. Her principal responsibilities include data management and analysis in support of institution-wide planning, policy development and reporting. She earned a bachelor's degree from National Taiwan Normal University, and received her Master's and Doctorate in Adult and Community College Education from North Carolina State University. Dr. Hwang's research interests also include the area of adult education.

Lee Jones is Associate Dean for Academic Affairs and Instruction and Associate Professor of Educational Leadership in the College of Education at Florida State University. Dr. Jones is the editor of two books: *Brothers of The Academy: Earning Our Way in Higher Education,* and *Retaining African American Administrators in Higher Education: Challenging Paradigms for Retention.* Known as a national speaker, Dr. Jones is in demand to speak at universities and other educational agencies across the country. He has received over 175 awards and citations including the Innis Cosby Scholar Award from Keystone College and the University of Alabama at Birmingham Visiting Scholars award.

Paul E. Krueger, PhD, EdD, is Assistant Professor of Workforce Education, and the Director of the Institute for Research in Training and Development at the Pennsylvania State University. In addition to his two earned doctorates from the South Dakota State University (1988) and University of Southern California (1999), he has extensive human resource managerial experience with multi-national corporations, including Johnson & Johnson and Bio-Rad Laboratories. His research interests include survey research design, ISO 9000 international quality standards, and the relationships between organizational learning, corporate creativity, and organizational performance.

Theodore Lewis is Professor in the Department of Work, Community and Family Education, University of Minnesota. Included in his teaching load is a doctoral-level course on positivistic research. He has published extensively on curriculum issues relating to technology education and education for work. His work appears in journals such as *Curriculum Inquiry, Journal of Curriculum Studies, Philosophy of Education, Oxford Review of Education, and Journal of Vocational Education Research.* Lewis has had visiting appointments at the National Science Foundation, and University of British Columbia. He has been Editor of the Journal of Vocational Education Research, and President of the National Association of Industrial and Technical Teacher Education.

George A. Morgan is Professor of Education and Human Development at Colorado State University. He has developed observational and self-report measures of mastery motivation in children and published extensively on evidence for their reliability and validity. He has also written on research methods and the use and interpretation of SPSS. In 2000, he received the College of Applied Human Sciences Scholarly Excellence Award.

Derek C. Mulenga is Assistant Professor of Adult Education at the Pennsylvania State University. Before coming to Penn State, he served as Coordinator of Adult Education at Buffalo State University. Dr. Mulenga has expertise and experiences in research methods/participatory action research, political economy, and international adult education and policy. His research interests are politics of knowledge production and social transformation, impact on globalization on education and training, and postcolonial theory. His recent publication, *The Impact of Structural Adjustment on Education and Training in Africa: Implications for Adult Education* has been well received by those in adult education.

Stephen Olejnik is Professor of Educational Psychology at the University of Georgia. Dr. Olejnik's research interests include univariate statistical models, research design, and effect size estimation.

Gregory C. Petty is Professor and former head of the Department of Human Resource at the University of Tennessee where he has been on the doctoral faculty since 1982. He has a PhD in Industrial Technology Teaching from the University of Missouri-Columbia, the MS and BSE from the University of Memphis. He has published 22-refereed publications from his original research on the *Occupational Work Ethic*, and has made 80 presentations at national conferences on the topics of work ethic and technical program evaluation. He is currently Executive Secretariat for the International Vocational Education and Training Association (IVETA), has served as Membership Chair, Secretary, Vice President and Trustee for the National Association of Industrial and Technical teacher Educators, and is currently Trustee for the University Council for Workforce and Human Resource Education. He has written and managed federal grants totaling more than $1 million, and consulted with a variety of Fortune 500 companies on organizational development, group facilitation, and team building.

Suzanne M. Tochterman is Assistant Professor of Education at Colorado State University. Her areas of research include teacher training, technology, students with special needs, research methods, school reform, and multicultural issues.

Saundra Wall Williams is Assistant Professor of Training and Development in the Department of Adult and Community College Education at North Carolina State University. She has been involved in the design, development, implementation, evaluation, and management of technical training and instructional technologies, specifically Web-based instruction, since 1990. Dr. Williams teaches instructional design, instructional technologies, training and development research, and training management and has directed research and development projects in the area of adult learning and Web-based training. She has been named a Cyril O. Houle Scholar in Adult Education, and has served as Director of Technical

Training at Syntel, Inc., Senior Training Specialist at Broadband Technologies, and Instructional Designer and Trainer at Nortel.

Carol A. Wright is Education and Behavioral Sciences Librarian at the Pennsylvania State University Libraries, with responsibility for Education Policy Studies, Higher Education, Adult Education, and Instructional Design. Ms. Wright also serves as a Penn State University Schreyer Honors College Fellow and Librarian. She has had a long and continuing commitment to library instruction and information literacy issues, nationally and at Penn State. She was Project Director for the Libraries' information literacy tutorial "Information Literacy and You," and received a grant from Penn State's World Campus/ATT Innovations in Distance Education project to develop library instructional services to distance education students. Her research interests include student use of the Internet.

Zhicheng Zhang is Associate Director of Institutional Research at Virginia Military Institute. Dr. Zhang specializes in applying statistical methods to institutional data. Her previous research has focused on student intellectual and meta-cognitive development, retention, teacher assessment competency, and the impact of faculty evaluation on teaching and teacher efficacy. Her recent experience extends to student assessment in an *e*-learning environment and Web development.

data collection
214

Breinigsville, PA USA
07 February 2011
255004BV00001B/13/P